Bernard Lovell

By the same author

The Bomber's Eye
Bomber Harris

Bernard Lovell

A Biography

DUDLEY SAWARD

ROBERT HALE · LONDON

ISBN 0 7090 1745 6

Robert Hale Limited
Clerkenwell House
Clerkenwell Green
London EC1R 0HT

Photoset in Ehrhardt by
Kelly Typesetting Limited
Bradford-on-Avon, Wiltshire
Printed in Great Britain by
St Edmundsbury Press
Bury St Edmunds, Suffolk
Bound by Hunter & Foulis Limited

Contents

List of Illustrations

Photographs are reproduced by permission of the following: Lady Lovell, 1, 2, 3, 6; Sir Bernard Lovell, 9, 28; Jodrell Bank, 12, 13, 15, 16; *Progress*, the Unilever magazine, 14; the Central Office of Information, 17–19, 21, 22; BBC, 20; Lord Renwick, 23; NASA, 24, 25; the Keystone Press Agency Ltd, 26; Yorkshire Television, 27; AUTHOR, 4, 5, 7, 8, 10, 11

Figures in text

Preface

After completing my biography of Marshal of the Royal Air Force Sir Arthur Harris late in 1975, I was anxious to undertake another biographical task, but I was delayed by two situations. The first was the interminable amount of revision and editing of the Harris book which I found necessary to satisfy my own self-criticism, and which took me well into 1976. The second was the problem of who to ensnare as my subject!

In the autumn of 1976 I found the answer to the second problem. Somewhat unexpectedly, Sir Bernard Lovell asked me if I would co-operate in a television programme about Jodrell Bank which was being planned by Yorkshire Television. He wanted me to join him in the part which was to cover his wartime experiences prior to the Jodrell Bank period. I accepted, and on 30 October of that year I went to RAF Station Coningsby in Lincolnshire to be filmed with him in a Lancaster III bomber discussing his wartime activities for Bomber Command. Travelling back to London on the train that night, it suddenly dawned on me that my very good friend Bernard Lovell was the obvious candidate for the next biography if I could persuade him to entrust such an onerous task to my pen. I had known him since the beginning of 1942 when I was Chief Radar Officer on 'Bomber' Harris's Staff and when Lovell was developing the vital radar equipments that the bomber needed to be able to succeed in its operational function. Harris had been the superb Commander; Lovell had been the superb scientist without whom Harris and his bombers could never have succeeded in contributing decisively to the defeat of Hitler's Germany. Throughout those war years I had worked closely with Lovell and his team, and we had forged an enduring friendship.

After the war Lovell took the lead in the new science of radio astronomy and in this field became an indispensable contributor to the success of the USA and the USSR in their early Space programmes. In the field of astronomical research he gave Britain a remarkable lead which enhanced her prestige in the scientific world. During this post-war period I became involved, if only on the periphery, with some of Lovell's financial problems on the Jodrell Bank radio telescope, and thus our wartime association continued, though to a lesser degree. Because of this, I now knew not only about Lovell's invaluable contribution to the war effort but also about his exciting foray into the new science of radio astronomy and

Space exploration. Between Euston and Waterloo, where I was to catch my train to Winchester for the last leg of my journey home, I made up my mind that Bernard Lovell must be the subject of the next biography.

On 18 November the two of us met in London. I had persuaded Lovell to speak to a group of business men at the monthly dinner of the Solus Club on the subject of radio astronomy and its future. My very dear friend the late Rodney Millard was the club's President that year, and he had asked me to use my influence to persuade Lovell to be the guest speaker at the November meeting. That same night, after the dinner at the Hyde Park Hotel where Lovell and I were also staying, I broached the subject. The following January (1977), Bernard Lovell wrote to tell me that he had discussed the matter with Joyce, his wife, and they both liked the idea. And so, without delay, I began my researches.

First and foremost I must thank both Sir Bernard and Lady Lovell for their tremendous co-operation and for giving me access to an invaluable collection of correspondence, diaries and documents dating back to the early twenties. Also the access I was given to Jodrell Bank files was of inestimable value, as was the help I received from Sir Bernard's staff in my searches into these files. Here I must particularly mention Dr Tom Rackham and Sir Bernard's secretary, Mrs Ella Bradley, who searched for, copied and typed innumerable items of immense importance to the history of Jodrell Bank. Others who helped included Professor J. G. Davies, Fred Smith and Mrs Eaton. Sir Bernard has also kindly allowed me to quote freely from his published books and lectures. Here I must add that I have used occasional passages from my own book *The Bomber's Eye*, verbatim or adapted, in my account of Lovell's wartime work.

For access to certain past files and documents of the University of Manchester concerning the history of the Radio Telescope and the associated financial problems relating to its construction, my especial thanks go to R. A. Rainford, formerly the Bursar of the University. Rainford kindly went through many documents and drew my attention to those that were pertinent, thus saving me much time. Others who contributed invaluable information were Sir Ben Lockspeiser, formerly Chief Scientist to the Ministry of Supply and Secretary of the DSIR, and Colonel Walter G. Hingston, formerly a member of the DSIR. Also I must thank Marguerite Dupree, who was responsible for the editing of Sir Raymond Streat's diary, and Christine Kennedy, Librarian of Nuffield College, Oxford, both of whom enabled me to have a sight of sections of the diary relating to the financial difficulties during the later stages of the construction of the Radio Telescope when Sir Raymond was Chairman of the Council of the University of Manchester.

The 'young' Lovells helped enormously. Susan Driver seemed to take charge and not only provided me with much family information from over the years but also 'organized' Judy Spence, one of her sisters who lived in the Bath area, the homeground of the Lovell and Chesterman families, to act as my guide to the surviving members of these families. Both Susan and Judy were a tremendous help, and I can never thank them enough. Bryan Lovell also contributed greatly, as did my godson Roger Lovell and his twin sister Philippa Holmes. Thanks to Judy, I met Raymond Jones (Jonah), the celebrated organist of Bath Abbey, who provided me with much of the background of Bernard Lovell's musical and social activities as a young undergraduate at the University of Bristol. To Jonah I am very indebted for all his help—also to Marjorie Hall, Lovell's cousin, who took me back to schoolboy days of the twenties. Amongst those to whom Judy introduced me was Joyce Lovell's brother, who was Bernard Lovell's greatest friend over the years. The late Professor Deryck Chesterman was a source of endless information about Lovell's university life as well as his later years. Most importantly, Deryck Chesterman was able to tell me a great deal about Lovell's personal life and beliefs, as well as about his scientific activities. For this I shall always be indebted to him.

Others I must mention and to whom I must proffer my sincere gratitude for their help are Professor Fred Whipple of Harvard University, USA, who kindly spared me much of his valuable time when I interviewed him at Cambridge, Massachusetts; Herr Albert Speer, the German Minister for Armaments Production from 1942 to 1945, who gave me much valuable information on the effects of the RAF bombing of Germany on the occasions that I visited him at his home in Heidelberg; Wing Commander F. S. Lambert, until recently of the Public Record Office, who helped me with my researches into relevant documents held by the Record Office; Lord Renwick, who provided me with a number of his late father's documents relating to Jodrell Bank's financial difficulties, and papers on the activities of the British Space Development Company; and G. K. C. Pardoe, who also helped me to collect together other documents and technical reports and proposals relating to the Space activities of the British Space Development Company.

Lastly, I must thank Gerald Pollinger, my agent and my very good friend, who has advised me and guided me during the writing of this book, and Jan, my wife, who has given me so much help in my researches and has kept me protected from outside interferences and distractions during my work on this exacting task.

Curriculum Vitae

Bernard Lovell entered the University of Bristol as a student in the autumn of 1931, and in 1934 he gained a BSc in physics with First Class Honours. At the end of 1936 he received his PhD at Bristol for researches on thin metallic films deposited in high vacua. In September 1936 he was appointed assistant lecturer in physics at the University of Manchester, where he carried out research on large cosmic ray showers with the late Professor P. M. S. Blackett. On the outbreak of the war in September 1939, he joined the Air Ministry Research Establishment (later the Telecommunications Research Establishment), where he developed centimetric airborne radar and was head of the H2S blind bombing and the ASV anti-submarine groups. In January 1946 he was awarded the OBE for his wartime work.

At the end of the World War II, in 1945, Lovell returned to the University of Manchester as lecturer in physics and immediately started the development of the experimental station at Jodrell Bank, twenty miles south of Manchester. He was appointed senior lecturer in 1947 and a reader in 1949. In 1951 the University created a special chair of radio astronomy, and he became the first professor to hold that chair. At the same time he was appointed to the newly created post of Director of Jodrell Bank.

In 1955 he was elected a Fellow of the Royal Society (FRS), and in the New Year's Honours List of 1961 he was knighted.

Lovell has assisted the Government in the UK by serving on a number of committees. He was a member of the Aeronautical Research Council 1955–8. In 1965 he was one of the original members of the newly formed Science Research Council for the administration of Government funds for research, and until 1970 he was the Chairman of the Astronomy Space and Radio Board of that Council. He was President of the Royal Astronomical Society 1969–71. He was elected an Honorary Fellow of the IEE in 1967, and an Honorary Fellow of the Institute of Physics in 1976, and is an Honorary Member of the New York Academy, the American Academy of Arts and Sciences and the Royal Swedish Academy. He holds honorary doctorates in science at London, Bath, Bristol, Edinburgh and Leicester Universities, and in Law at Edinburgh and Calgary. He was appointed Vice-President of the International Astronomical Union in 1970 and was President of the British Association

1974–5. In 1977 he was made an honorary Freeman of the City of Manchester.

He received the Physical Society's Duddell Medal in 1954, the Royal Society's Royal Medal in 1960, the Daniel and Florence Guggenheim International Astronautics Award in 1961, the Ordre de Mérite pour la Recherche et l'Invention in 1962, the Society of Engineers Churchill Gold Medal in 1964, the Institute of Structural Engineers Maitland Silver Medal in 1964, and the Commander's Order of Merit of the State Republic of Poland in 1977. In 1980 he was awarded the Royal Society of Arts Benjamin Franklin Medal for that year.

Sir Bernard Lovell has written a number of books, including *Radio Astronomy* (1952), *Meteor Astronomy* (1954), *The Exploration of Space by Radio* (1957), *The Individual and the Universe* (1959), *The Exploration of Outer Space* (1961), *Our Present Knowledge of the Universe* (1967), *The Story of Jodrell Bank* (1968), *Out of the Zenith* (1973), *The Origins and International Economics of Space Exploration* (1973), *Man's Relation to the Universe* (1975), *P. M. S. Blackett—a Biographical Memoir* (1976), *In the Centre of Immensities* (1978), *Emerging Cosmology* (1981) and *The Jodrell Bank Telescopes* (1984).

1

Schooldays

In 1739 John Wesley wrote in his journal that he found the colliers of Kingswood, Bristol, to be a tough community: '. . . a people famous, from the beginning hitherto, for neither fearing God nor regarding man: so ignorant of the things of God, that they seemed but one remove from the beasts that perish: and therefore utterly without desire of instruction, as well as without the means of it'. On the paternal side, at least, the boy who was born to Gilbert and Laura Lovell on 31 August 1913 was descended in part from this community. He inherited the rebellious streak in those natives, although the drunkenness which was said to have killed many of his forbears seems to have been excised in the age of his grandparents. Indeed, the first two of the three Christian names with which the boy was endowed, Alfred Charles, were amongst those of the large family to whom his grandfather belonged; one of whom, in reaction against *his* antecedents, founded the village Sunday School. The third name, Bernard, by which the boy was to be known, epitomized the God-fearing nature of Gilbert and Laura—the name being chosen some weeks before the birth during the singing of the hymn 'Jesus, Thou joy of loving hearts' composed by Bernard of Clairvaux.

The village of Oldland Common in which the boy was born, although only a few miles distant from the Kingswood suburb of Bristol, was, in those days, completely isolated. The age of the motor car, radio and television had not yet arrived. The villagers who desired more than the village community offered walked either two miles to the nearest electric tram terminus at Kingswood or a similar distance to the railway station at Bitton—equidistant between Bath and Bristol. Not surprisingly, as in most similar village communities of that age, the inhabitants created their own entertainment, and the chapels and churches were the nuclei of these activities. Thus the boy Lovell lived his first years amongst the peaceful green fields of Gloucestershire. His father, although earning his living as a local tradesman, was far more interested in his activities as a lay preacher. He was an authority on the Bible, had studied English literature and grammar and over forty years later was still bombarding his son with complaints on points of grammar, punctuation and method of speaking. Indeed, no man could preach three or four times every Sunday of the year in the crowded chapels of those times without achieving some skill in oratory, and the efforts to correct his son in the proper use of the English language were pursued relentlessly. The first of his son's Reith Lectures, delivered many years later, he found 'interesting' but condemned because of the poor delivery—especially the failure to use the dramatic impact of the 'pause' and the pronunciation of words like 'just'.

If that typified the paternal influence on the young boy, the maternal influence was altogether more practical and material. Emily Laura Adams came of a family who dominated those aspects of the village far more than the Lovells. The photographs reveal her as a handsome and imposing figure who, as befitted the Adams' prowess at sport, played in one of the earliest women's cricket teams. The Adams of Oldland Common could field their own cricket team, and the annual challenge match of the Adams against the rest was a memorable event—particularly for the young Lovell on the occasion when the Adams suddenly faced the game with one of their members missing and he was summoned to fill the gap on the grounds that, although his name was Lovell, his mother was an Adams.

The parish registers of the village of Bitton record the births, marriages and deaths of the Lovells and Adams since 1596. The unification of the two families by the marriage of Gilbert Lovell and Emily Laura Adams in 1910 brought together these disparate interests and also a common ability in music.

The Lovells were ardent musicians and had been for many generations, as were the Adams, and the two families had their own operatic society and their own 'military' bands, as well as the 'Lovell Band', all of which were renowned locally. Every year at Christmas, almost as a ritual, the village of Oldland Common would perform the *Messiah*, a production which was largely cast around the Lovells and Adams.

Surrounded by these influences, the boy Lovell led the life of an ordinary village child—rolling a hoop or playing hop-scotch, playing marbles or five-stones on the dusty road in the summer, or picking cowslips in the fields.

As a child he attended the local village school. He exhibited no particular signs of brilliance; indeed, he was no more than average and displayed little zest for his school work. But at play, cricket was already becoming an absorbing passion, even by the age of eight. With constant encouragement from his father, who bowled to him regularly at the nets in the garden behind their house, he was soon showing signs of developing into a promising batsman. His other major interest was music, and apart from playing the piano at home for the Sunday evening hymn-singing, he also played for the morning assembly at school. But, strangely, he abandoned his piano playing when he was about ten years of age as a kind of protest against the 'standard' way in which he was taught, playing scales and compositions designed to develop technique rather than a basic love of the sound of music. However, his self-exile from music was not to last for long, and by the time he was twelve some inherent passion turned his attention to the organ, which delighted his uncle, Alfred Adams, who played the organ at the Methodist chapel in Oldland Common and who became his first tutor. In point of fact, Bernard Lovell's aptitude for the organ had him deputizing for his uncle at Sunday services by the time he was only thirteen years old.

Whilst the normal academic pursuits, modest as they were at the village school, barely held the young Lovell's interest, one incident did impinge dramatically upon his mind. It was the occasion when one of his teachers described how she had listened to the new invention called 'wireless'. Shortly after this revelation, at the age of 10½ years, he was transferred from the village school to the newly opened Kingswood Secondary School, which was about two miles from his home and, in the absence of public transport in those days, to which he had to cycle daily in all weathers. With his new obsession, wireless, added to his passions for playing cricket and the organ, he continued to have little time for school work. But with a kind of inborn skill for delicate engineering, he built endless radio receivers and transmitters, starting with crystal sets and quickly moving to valve sets as components became available. His irrepressible enthusiasm for this new pursuit encouraged his father to extend the family business beyond petrol pumps and the sale of bicycles, which had been added at the end of World War I, into radio, a business which was quickly to flourish and to become known as 'The Oldland Cycle and Radio Company'. None of this, however, produced much in the way of good school reports. Indeed, at the end of Bernard Lovell's first term at Kingswood, the spring term of 1924, Major M. J. Eaton, the headmaster, was constrained to say: 'A fair start', whilst his arithmetic master could muster nothing more than: 'Weak. Needs to try harder.' Algebra and geometry earned no better comment, but scripture, understandably, raised a 'Good'. His terminal position in form was 32, and the only worthy observation that could be expressed on such a performance was that, at any rate, he was two from the bottom. He continued in this vein for several years, generally achieving a 'Good' for conduct to counterbalance his lack of academic attainment; but even this was marred on the odd occasion by a comment such as: 'He must control a tendency to be noisy in form.'

Bernard Lovell's lack of success at school was not regarded as any great setback at home. His religious education was sound, and he attended chapel without any show of the reluctance that might have been expected from a young boy in his early teens. Therefore, from his parents' point of view, the progress he was making in the course of growing up was entirely satisfactory. Whether his attitude to religion was stimulated by his

immense respect for his parents or by his love of music and the chance of
playing the organ on occasions at chapel, or both, is a matter for
conjecture. But he certainly co-operated in this part of his up-bringing,
even attending Sunday School until quite a late age. His cousin Marjorie
Hall, née Jefferies, a product of the second Lovell-Adams union, her
mother being Gilbert Lovell's sister and her father a cousin of Emily
Laura, recalls how she was first taken to Sunday School at the age of five
by the young Lovell, nine years her senior. 'He used to take me to Sunday
School every Sunday,' she says, 'and I was very proud of being with him
because it was quite something for a little girl to be escorted by a boy of his
age.' She says he was considerate and kind, and very serious.

Marjorie Hall also recalls to mind her family's first wireless set:
'Bernard made it for my father. It was just a little cabinet with a black face
and black knobs which you twisted around to tune into a station. It was
very good.' Her memory of the young Lovell's prowess in the field of radio
extends to what she clearly regarded as the acme of her cousin's skill in
this new field of scientific invention. This was a two-way communication
system he designed to connect his father with his father's brother, Albert
Lovell, who lived not far away across the road. He built and installed the
two radio transmitter-receivers himself so that his father and uncle could
talk with each other from their homes. 'It was such a clever thing to do
and, in those days, it seemed something of a miracle.'

By the time Bernard Lovell reached the age of fourteen, his progress at
school had improved considerably. In the autumn term of 1927 he duly
moved up into the Lower Fifth Form where his performance was again
quite good. But his heart was not in his school work, nor had he any
ambition to achieve scholastic honours. Instead, his passion for cricket
and music, together with his consuming interest in radio, made him wish
to leave school as soon as possible in order to become a cricketer and to
help his father expand the new radio and electrical side of the family
business. Whilst his father certainly had ambitions for his only son, they
were of the kind that wished to encourage the boy to excel in those
activities in which he showed real promise, and so Gilbert Lovell,
supported by his wife, agreed that Bernard should leave school at the age
of fifteen after sitting for his School Certificate. The decision was taken in
the face of the pleadings of Major M. J. Eaton, the headmaster, who was
now convinced that the young Lovell, although not brilliant, displayed
sufficient academic promise to make his continued education well worthwhile. Certainly he should do two years in the Sixth Form and ultimately
try for his Higher Schools Certificate—Eaton had no doubts that he
would easily pass his School Certificate. In the summer of 1928, at the
end of Lovell's year in the Lower Fifth, Eaton wrote on his report: 'Good.

Has distinct ability in mathematics and science.' It was a kind of last plea in an endeavour to persuade Gilbert Lovell to insist on the continued education of his son.

In the autumn of 1928 Bernard Lovell cheerfully moved into the Upper Fifth. It was, he believed, his last year at school. Then three unexpected incidents occurred. A religious contact of Gilbert Lovell by the name of Champion visited the home, and it so happened that he was a very good mathematician. His visit coincided with a moment when Bernard Lovell was struggling with an intractable piece of mathematics which had been set for homework. Champion's assistance was offered, and his elegant instruction on how to deal with the complex problem made a great impact on Bernard Lovell; it appealed to his perfectionism which had already been evident in his cricket, his playing of the organ and his design and construction of radio equipment.

At about the same time, the minister in charge of the Methodist Circuit referred to Einstein's theory of relativity in one of his sermons, an occurrence which stimulated the young Lovell's interest in the sciences.

The third incident was perhaps an even more subtle manœuvre on the part of Fate. Charles Howard, the physics master at Kingswood School, now upgraded from a Secondary School to Kingswood Grammar School, announced one day during Bernard Lovell's first term in the Upper Fifth that he would be taking a party of boys to Bristol University to hear a series of lectures by Professor A. M. Tyndall* on 'The Electric Spark', a repetition of the 'Children's Christmas Lectures' which he had previously delivered at the Royal Institution. Lovell decided to join the party purely for the outing and with no idea of improving his academic knowledge. This decision was his undoing. The lectures were held in the lecture theatre of the H. H. Wills Physics Laboratory, which was a recent acquisition of the University and which Tyndall had managed to persuade H. H. Wills of the Wills tobacco family to finance. It was greatly in advance of the times. The environment, the apparatus, the demonstrations and A. M. Tyndall himself took Lovell completely by surprise. He was filled with awe. He had had no idea that this kind of world existed, where people studied in a magnificent building, experimented with marvellous equipment and were instructed by such a dynamic personality as Tyndall. It was an absolute revelation to him.

Now, nearly half a century later [he recalls], I still remember vividly the great sparks ripping across the lecture hall, infra-red rays being focussed by a mirror, the effect of ultra-violet light on natural and false teeth, and the

* Denotes biographical details listed in *Who's Who of Persons Mentioned*, page 308.

laboratory steward, Venn, operating a massive slide projector and epidiascope with a hissing carbon arc as the light source. At the age of fifteen I was immensely impressed. I was fascinated by the fact that you could focus heat as well as light, and I was intrigued when Tyndall showed his teeth in an ultra-violet beam. In white light they looked perfectly normal, but in the ultra-violet beam you could see that he had two or three false teeth. It was so exciting and dramatic that in a few minutes Tyndall and the lecture hall had changed my life. The way home was by electric tram to Kingswood, and then a three-mile walk. I must have done the journey many times, but that first night of Tyndall's lectures is the one that is indelibly imprinted on my memory. For the first time I looked up at the stars and wondered what they were.

No longer did Bernard Lovell wish to leave school. From that moment nothing else mattered but to become a student at Bristol University and to study under Tyndall. His father and mother, always ready to encourage their only son in any activity which aroused his interest, accepted the alteration in plans with equanimity and fully encouraged the young Lovell in his change of direction.

At school there was now a spectacular improvement in his progress. In all subjects there was a marked advance in his performance, the most remarkable being in mathematics and science, where he earned comments of 'very good' or 'excellent' against previous 'fairs' and 'could try harders'. Moreover, he shot up from low down in class to the top few. To realize his desire to study under Tyndall, he well knew that he had to achieve high pass marks in his School Certificate results and, later, in those for his Higher School Certificate, and so he worked with dedicated application to the subjects which he knew were essential to attaining his goal. In fact, he now applied the same passion to his academic career as he had done to cricket, music and radio construction, a passion which could take him to any heights whenever and wherever he chose to exercise it—a fact which was to become startlingly evident in his later life.

In the summer of 1929, before his sixteenth birthday, he passed his School Certificate in six subjects: English, modern history, Latin, chemistry, physics and mathematics, all passes being with credits. More-over, his results were marked 'A—qualified for Matriculation'. In the autumn of 1929, he entered the Sixth Form at the age of sixteen and continued successfully to beat a path to university, ably assisted by E. R. Brown, his new mathematics master, for whom he had an immense respect. Brown was a splendid teacher but somewhat unorthodox in his private life for that period. He was a free-living individual, already divorced, rather left in his politics and somewhat of an agnostic. This aspect of Brown intrigued the young Lovell, who had been brought up in a fundamentalist atmosphere, and a friendship which was to last for many years sprang up between them despite the considerable gulf which separated them in age and background. There is little doubt that this friendship broadened Lovell's intellectual outlook. Also, to his surprise, Lovell's father, who might well have been disposed to forbid Brown to cross the threshold of the family home, formed a great impression of the man, and they, too, became friends. Their exchanges on the Bible and Karl Marx impressed Lovell enormously and encouraged him to read more widely than hitherto. Indeed, it was from this time that he began to read about relativity and astronomy as well as the Gifford Lectures (1927–9), which had been given by E. W. Barnes, the Bishop of Birmingham, entitled 'Scientific Theory and Religion'.

Despite all his dedication to his studies in the Sixth Form, the young Lovell had his lapses. Towards the end of his first year E. R. Brown had to write on his report against mathematical subjects: 'This is good; but a light-hearted approach to work must be replaced next year by more serious and strenuous efforts.' Then again, at the end of the spring term of 1931, a few months before he was due to sit for the Higher School Certificate, Brown was constrained to report: 'Should do well, but must definitely decide not to think of cricket when he is doing mathematics or science.' However, at the end of the summer term of 1931 it was known that Lovell had gained his Higher School Certificate with passes in chemistry, mathematics and physics, and it was then that E. R. Brown could safely make the comment on his last school report: 'Has made an enthusiastic cricket captain and has built up a successful team.' No longer was it necessary to cool the boy's ardour for cricket!

Lovell was granted a Major Scholarship of £60 per annum to Bristol University, with a vacancy in October 1931, in the Faculty of Science to follow a three years Honours Physics Course.

2

Bristol University

When Bernard Lovell entered Bristol University in the autumn of 1931, the H. H. Wills Physics Laboratory was comparatively new, having been officially opened in 1927. It was built around Royal Fort House in the Royal Fort Gardens which had been purchased in 1917 by H. H. Wills of the Wills tobacco family and presented to the University. Following on this generous gift, A. M. Tyndall, who became Professor of Physics in 1919 after joining the staff of the University College of Bristol in 1907, persuaded H. H. Wills to dig deep again into his multi-millionaire pocket to finance the project of the construction of a major and highly modern physics laboratory on this site.

Lovell followed the normal three years physics course, which consisted of pure and applied mathematics as well as physics in the first two years, followed by physics only in the third year. He was extremely fortunate to be an undergraduate at that time and to savour the splendid environment of the new H. H. Wills Physics Laboratory; favoured also by the fact that there were only six students on that Honours Course, with the result that each student received much individual attention from the staff who, even by modern standards, were occupied with an astonishing diversity of researches. Apart from research activities into ionic mobility by A. M. Tyndall and C. F. Powell* (Nobel Prize-winner for his discovery of the pi-meson), crystallography under S. H. Piper, X-ray spectra by H. W. B. Skinner, gyromagnetism by W. Sucksmith and H. H. Potter, and low temperature studies being undertaken by L. C. Jackson, there were a number of distinguished Research Fellows also doing work in the laboratories at that time. These included R. W. Gurney, W. Heitler* (originator of the quantum theory of the chemical bond), C. Zener of later zener diode fame and Lennard-Jones, who was Professor of Theoretical Physics and who was later succeeded by N. F. Mott,* another future Nobel Prize-winner. Lovell was greatly influenced by these individuals both at work and in his extra-curricular associations with the staff, who invited him, together with his fellow students, to their homes and for walks on Sundays. But, unquestionably, the greatest influence over Lovell was that of Tyndall, who detected from the outset the latent promise in this young man, a promise which was combined with a kind of ruthless determination.

During his undergraduate days Lovell lived at home. Every morning he walked the two miles to the railway station at Bitton to catch the 8 a.m. train which ran on the old Midland Line to St Philip's Station at the end of Old Market Street in Bristol. From there, he walked through the back streets to the Royal Fort to arrive in time for the 9 a.m. lecture. The day usually began with lectures in mathematics, followed by physics lectures later in the morning and practical laboratory classes in the afternoon. He would then return home by the same route to work deep into the night. Likewise at weekends he would not spare himself, and his cousin Marjorie Hall remembers that, when she called in at the bungalow in the hopes of seeing him, he was, as often as not, shut away in his room immersed in his studies.

He took this dedication to his work even further. He found the atmosphere of the laboratory so dramatic and stimulating that he dreaded the vacations and eventually arranged with S. H. Piper and H. H. Potter to work during these periods on some minor items of their research on crystallography and gyromagnetism which they willingly entrusted to him. Perhaps more surprising was his celibate attitude towards his great passion, cricket. His attachment to his studies was so demanding that he actually turned down the pleas of the captain of the University Cricket XI to play at Coombe Dingle, the University ground, and thus make himself available for selection to the University team. The excuse he gave himself, as well as the captain, was that cricket would become too much of a distraction. No doubt Lovell was bearing in mind the comments of his erstwhile mathematics master at Kingswood, Eddie (E. R.) Brown.

But if cricket was to suffer the fate of a separation, music was at least allowed a modest continuation of attention. Probably this was due to a friendship which sprang up between Deryck Chesterman,* another first year student who was reading physics (he was later to become Professor of Physics in the University of Bath) and Bernard Lovell. They met early in their days at Bristol University in the gardens of the Royal Fort building. Deryck Chesterman recalls that Lovell shared his sandwich lunch with him, including half an apple which served as dessert, and from that moment they became firm friends. But it was more than the sandwiches and half an apple that cemented this early regard for each other: Deryck Chesterman, like Bernard Lovell, was passionately interested in classical music, and the two of them would occasionally go to concerts in Bristol after the day's lectures. Sometimes it was to the Colston Hall to hear a piano recital. Lovell still treasures the score of the Beethoven Opus 109 Sonata with which he followed Schnabel from the gallery in company with Deryck Chesterman, and he remembers vividly Horowitz, as a young man, playing Liszt's *Les Funérailles*. Together they attended concerts of the Bristol Choral Society and the Bristol Philharmonic Society on a fairly regular basis. For some reason music did not seem to disturb Lovell's work in the least. Deryck Chesterman comments: 'He would just go back home after a concert and work, whilst I used to go home and straight to bed!' At other times, the two of them would go to Lovell's home at Oldland Common and listen to concerts on a very early hi-fi set which Lovell had designed and built himself. There, Chesterman recalls that he was always made very welcome by the Lovell family. 'I got on very well with Gilbert Lovell,' he says. 'He was very much of a philosopher, and I think Bernard acquired his deep interest in religious and moral questions from his father. He exerted a great influence on Bernard, an influence which has lasted throughout his life. His mother, too, was an open friendly person, and generally amongst the Lovells and Adams one sensed a powerful unity.'

It was, perhaps, at the Lovell home that the long-standing friendship of these two first-year undergraduates really began, and it proved to be a very important friendship for Bernard Lovell because Deryck Chesterman was unwittingly to have an unexpected influence on his later life in two ways.

The Chestermans lived in Bath, and amongst Deryck Chesterman's friends was Raymond Jones,* later to become organist at Bath Abbey. At the beginning of the thirties, Raymond Jones was the organist at St Paul's Church, Bath, and it was Deryck Chesterman's interest in music that had brought them together. What more natural, therefore, than that Deryck Chesterman should introduce his new university friend to Raymond Jones, particularly as he was aware that Bernard Lovell played the organ in the chapel at Oldland Common. The result of this introduction was to have far reaching effects upon Lovell's musical talent as an organist, but this was not immediate and was to be delayed until nearly three years later. In the meantime, however, a lifelong friendship was forged. At the time of Lovell's first meeting with Raymond Jones, affectionately known as Jonah, St Paul's Church possessed a very fine three-manual organ which greatly attracted Lovell, and he was excited about being allowed to play on it. 'He was very keen and had a good knowledge of music,' Jonah recounts, 'and so I helped him at that stage to develop his skill at playing the organ—but it was later in his university life that he devoted more time to learning the organ and to visiting me at St Paul's for regular teaching.'

The second influence which Deryck Chesterman brought to bear upon Lovell was when he took him home to lunch one day. There he met Deryck's sister Joyce, then aged fifteen, wearing a gym tunic, black stockings and a row of netball and house badges. At the time, neither was conscious of the other, except perhaps that the mature eighteen-year-old looked down at the leggy fifteen-year-old with at most a disdainful glance, whilst the fifteen-year-old looked up at the eighteen-year-old and wondered who on earth he thought he was! However, time was to change all that.

In 1934 Bernard Lovell sat for his finals and at the Degree of Congregation of 30 June 1934, at the University of Bristol, he was to hear the Dean of the University announce those who had gained the Degree of Bachelor of Science with First Class Honours. The name of Alfred Charles Bernard Lovell was amongst them.

On 4 July Lovell received a letter of congratulation from the County Education Office of Gloucester, but the joy and pride expressed by his family and the Adams far exceeded any felicitations that came from elsewhere, however official. As cousin Marjorie declared: 'Well, to go and win a place at University in those days was really quite something. To gain a First Class Honours Degree was out of this world and, naturally, we were all very thrilled.'

In fact, Lovell's 'First' was not awarded without some argument. During his third year, which was spent exclusively on physics, he had become obsessed with an experiment on the 'Zeeman Effect'. Pieter Zeeman was a Dutch physicist who in 1896 had experimented with a sodium flame placed between the poles of a powerful magnet and observed the yellow D lines with a spectroscope. He noted that the spectral lines were split up into components when the source was in a strong magnetic field; also that the components were polarized. From these observations, a theory known as the 'Zeeman Effect' was propounded by Hendrick Antoon Lorentz, another Dutch physicist who was Professor of Mathematical Physics at Leyden University from 1878. The theory was based on the electron theory of matter, giving undeniable evidence of the electro-magnetic origin of light which has since been applied to the study of sunspots. The 'Zeeman Effect', the splitting of the lines of atomic or molecular spectra by the action of a magnetic field, was of great importance in the development of atomic theory and led to a realization that the emission of light from an atom is related to the motion of its electrons. Later it led to a detailed and sensitive test of the correctness of the branch of modern atomic theory known as quantum mechanics. Lovell spent so much time with the experiment on the 'Zeeman Effect' that he neglected and forgot much elementary optics, a weakness which the external examiner was quick to note as a point against him. Also, knowing far more about radio than any of his lecturers at that time, he foolishly flaunted his knowledge in one of his finals papers at the expense of answering some of the questions which he found dull. However, Tyndall was convinced of Lovell's potential, and it seems certain that his influence finally weighed in Lovell's favour.

During all his undergraduate days there was never any doubt in Lovell's mind that he wanted to remain at Bristol and undertake post-graduate research. It is more than probable that Tyndall, by the time Lovell had reached his third year, was equally anxious that he should continue an academic career. Indeed, Tyndall obtained a grant for him from the Department of Scientific and Industrial Research (DSIR), and a letter from the DSIR, to Lovell, dated 7 July 1934, announced that: 'On the recommendation of the Advisory Council for Scientific and Industrial Research it has been decided to make you the maintenance allowance of which particulars are stated below, to enable you to receive training in scientific research under the direction of the Supervisor.' The Supervisor was named as Professor A. M. Tyndall, the period of the allowance was for two years from September 1934 to September 1936, and the rate of payment was the magnificent sum of '£105 p.a. to supplement demon-strating fees of £21'. £126 was quite something, particularly when he was still able to live with his generous and doting parents, who also purchased for him a two-seater Morris 8 open coupé, which in those days cost under £120 brand new! Lovell was now mobile, which helped him enormously in his daily journeys to Bristol, as well as with his other journeys of a more personal nature.

In December 1934, by a letter from the University of Bristol dated the 7th, he learnt that the Senate had that week adopted the recommendation of the Board of the Faculty of Science that he be declared fitted to pursue research for the degree of PhD, his period of research to cover two years, and that he should present his dissertation for his doctorate on or after 1 October 1936. In the autumn of 1934 he had already settled down to research under the guidance of Dr E. T. S. Appleyard,* who, under Tyndall, was his immediate supervisor. Appleyard had drawn his atten-tion at the outset to a paper by Herbert Eugene Ives of the Bell Telephone Laboratories on the electrical conductivity of thin layers of alkali metals. Experimenting with rubidium, the problem was to find out why thin metallic films deposited on glass had a resistivity so much greater than that of the metal in bulk. Fortunately, the laboratory possessed the highly skilled glassblower, J. H. Burrow,* essential for any successful research in this area. Despite the unremitting demands Lovell put upon Burrow for his services when he was already over-burdened with the exacting requirements of almost everybody else in the laboratories, they never came to blows, a situation which might have been expected. In fact, Lovell seemed to win preferential treatment because of his enthusiasm. He also won a valued friend who was to help him with his work long after he left Bristol; such was the persuasive charm of this man which cloaked an almost ruthless resolve in tackling any task he undertook.

To assist Lovell in his experiments, Burrow produced equipment in pyrex which enabled him to deposit layers of only atomic thickness from a molecular gun onto clean glass surfaces in very high vacua—conditions of high vacua which would be considered good even by today's standards. Indeed, Burrow was one of the earliest, if not the first person, in Europe to glassblow with the medium of pyrex. Previous work on the conductivity of thin metallic films over some forty years had produced no consistency in results, the values being widely divergent from those appropriate to the bulk metal. Lovell discovered that this anomalous behaviour was due largely to the effect of impurities contaminating the surface of thin layers, and with Burrow's equipment, built to his specification, he was able to deposit his layers of only atomic thickness from a molecular gun onto clean glass in conditions of high vacua which precluded the intrusion of impurities. Then, with typical Lovell thoroughness, he proceeded to include in his experiments controlled contamination of the surfaces *in situ* of some of his successful deposits in order to reproduce the 'failures' of his predecessors for the purpose of providing a probable explanation for the mass of past anomalies. His perfectionism, as ever, led him to conduct his experiments under the most stringent conditions of purity and cleanliness.

Deryck Chesterman who, with Jonah (Raymond Jones), had become such close friends with Bernard Lovell that the three were as indivisible as the Three Musketeers, says that Lovell was very hard working as an undergraduate, but as a postgraduate he was even more so because he was so determined that his experimental work for his PhD should succeed. 'He was relentless in his demands upon poor Johnny Burrow. Every time his apparatus blew up, whatever the time of day or night, he would get hold of Burrow and have him rebuild it as a priority!' Chesterman, in referring to those days, admits that he had never before met anyone who took his work so seriously and approached his research with such dedicated purpose. 'And,' he says, 'he did this in great depth—I mean, not just working but thinking profoundly about what he was doing when he worked. This was his gift; whether it was physics, playing the organ or anything else.'

The postgraduate days were not all work. For a change, Lovell settled down to enjoy life in tandem with his research and his studies. On Monday evenings he would journey to St Paul's Church in Bath and study the organ under the tutelage of Jonah. During most lunch breaks, he would cross the Clifton Suspension Bridge, which spanned the Avon Gorge, to the church at Leigh Woods on the far side, where he would eat his sandwiches and where he had obtained permission to practise on the organ. Then he would return to the university in time to carry on with his

research work. Such was his love of music that he would spend many
Saturday mornings, as well, playing the organ at Leigh Woods Church,
his newly acquired Morris 8 having given him the mobility he needed.
One Saturday morning when he was playing at Leigh Woods, a wedding
assembly suddenly arrived, whereupon Lovell began to beat a hasty
retreat. Having no organist for the wedding, the party prevailed upon him
· to stay and to play for the ceremony. He delightedly obliged. It was, after
all, his first chance to perform professionally, so to speak. In fact, his
ability as an organist was most promising. Jonah says that he was 'very,
very attracted to the music of Bach—indeed, he was fanatically fond of
Bach'. He also said of this time that Bernard Lovell became 'a pretty good
player' and that had he decided to follow a musical career as an organist he
could certainly have been great.

Music was not the only passion to which he returned wholeheartedly.
During the summer of 1934 he played cricket again and was soon in the
University team. In the summer vacation periods he also played for the
Bristol Optimists and the nearby village of Wick.

More light-hearted activities claimed him too. The University Union
sometimes held dances in the Victoria Rooms. They were very elegant
occasions. Lovell describes them thus: 'Full dress, of course. White tie
and tails and white gloves. I do not remember seeing many men wearing
dinner jackets at these Union dances—that would have been very bad
form—and you always wore your gloves when you were dancing. The girls
wore long evening dresses without exception—and long gloves, often
matching their dresses. Really they were very colourful, romantic and
graceful affairs.' Even so, Lovell's partners, whom he seemed to change
not infrequently, had to suffer from the effects of his postgraduate
experiments. His apparatus demanded replacement of liquid nitrogen
every twelve hours if success was to be achieved, and so the current girl
friend at any dance had to endure a journey to the Royal Fort in the middle
of the night for this ritual!

In 1935 Bernard Lovell's female attachments remained numerous. He
even turned to Deryck Chesterman's sister, now a maturing eighteen-
year-old girl, for introductions to her girl friends. One notable occasion,
in the summer of 1935, was when he asked her if she could introduce him
to a girl who was a good dancer and to another who was keen on classical
music and who would be interested in being taken to concerts. She
obliged, but Lovell inadvertently mixed up the names and assets of the two
girls in question and arranged his dates with the wrong girl on each
occasion. As a result, both evenings were a disaster. The girl he took
dancing could not dance to save her life, and the one he took to a
Beethoven concert was bored stiff. He was furious and vented his intense

annoyance upon the innocent Joyce Chesterman, who was highly amused by the incident. Lovell's usage of Joyce to enlarge his circle of girl friends was, however, limited at this time. She had left school in the summer of 1934 and embarked on a three-year teaching course at the Bedford Training College to prepare herself for a teaching career. Consequently she was only at Bath for vacation periods. At eighteen, she was transformed from the leggy, black-stockinged schoolgirl into a tall, slim and lovely person. By the autumn of 1935 these two were beginning to take slightly more than a passing interest in each other, and during vacations they sought each other's company. The association was not, however, encouraged by the Chestermans, with the exception of Deryck, as Joyce's mother was anxious for her daughter to qualify as a teacher and to take up such a career for at least a few years before contemplating marriage. Indeed, Joyce herself says of this period that at least fifty per cent of her wanted to get a good job and start teaching: 'I was an earnest sort of student and pegged away at my work in spite of distractions from Lovell!' These distractions were soon to be decisive.

At this time Raymond Jones had the use of about forty acres of woodland at Midford, close to Bath. There, in Cleeve Wood, he had built a small timber bungalow which he had christened 'Rookery Nook'. It was here that he held what can best be described as barbecue parties. In 1935 and 1936 Bernard Lovell became his associate in giving these light-hearted functions. 'We used to have the most lovely woodland parties out there,' Jonah recalls, 'and Bernard and I always sent out printed invitation cards. We would hang Chinese Lanterns in the trees all around the bungalow—it was beautiful with the very dense hazelnut bushes and all kinds of trees that surrounded the place. I remember one invitation at the beginning of 1936. It was for 6.30 p.m., Saturday, 4 January. It announced that R. E Jones (Jonah) and A. C. B. Lovell (Bill)—Bernard was always known as Bill in those days—request the pleasure of the company of . . . at Christmas revels. Dress was stated as "No glad rags".' On this occasion Joyce Chesterman was Lovell's partner.

Four days later Lovell had to attend an official ball, but without Joyce. Just prior to leaving home for this function, he wrote in his diary: 'Dressed, not feeling at all like a Ball. I was dressing for x . . ., when, to tell the truth, my heart was with Joyce.' Then, on 14 January, Bernard and Joyce contrived, with the help of Johnnie, Joyce's younger brother, to meet in Bristol. The day began with a note left by Joyce in Bernard Lovell's car which was parked outside the surgery of his dentist where he was having a check-up. The note proclaimed the rendezvous. That evening Bernard and Joyce walked on the Clifton Downs overlooking the Avon Gorge near the Clifton Suspension Bridge and declared their love for each other. It was then, as Bernard Lovell says, 'that it became clear that we wanted to live together forever'. He adds: 'It was very romantic, and it was not spoilt one jot by the fact that Joyce had to be home by 10 p.m.!'

These halcyon days were untroubled by the events in Europe, the rumblings of which seemed far away. The 'Great Depression', which had originated in the USA in October 1929, and which had rapidly spread to Europe gathering a trail of unemployment in its wake, had resulted by 1931 in unemployment in Germany rising to more than six millions. Feeding on this catastrophe, and on the indignity suffered by the German nation arising from the harsh terms of the Versailles Peace Treaty, Hitler and his Nazis had on 24 April 1932, in the Landtag elections, won nearly forty per cent of the votes of the electorate. Then, on 30 January 1933, Hitler was sworn in as Chancellor of Germany and promptly started a programme of massive rearmament contrary to the clauses of the Peace Treaty. In 1934 Dr Dollfuss Chancellor of Austria, was assassinated at the instigation of the Nazis in an effort to take over Austria. It was an attempt which failed, although failure proved in the end to be only a postponement. In August of that year Hindenburg, the President of Germany, died, and Hitler seized total power, establishing himself as Führer of the Third Reich. In 1935 Mussolini launched his campaign against Abyssinia, and in March of 1936 Hitler's forces marched into the demilitarized zone of the Rhineland without any sign of opposition from the British, despite the great outcry in France for the former Allies to mobilize and drive Hitler out. Nothing, in fact, was done to stop the growth of the belligerent powers of either Hitler or Mussolini. In the middle of 1936 the Spanish Civil War broke out, with Franco's right-wing forces being actively supported by Germany and Italy, and the Communist forces being openly backed by Soviet Russia. All of this was news to be read in the papers, but it did not affect the life of the University, or indeed of the population at large. Little did anyone realize that their entire future was to be shattered within a few years by the dramatic events which were then taking place abroad. Certainly Bernard Lovell had no idea of the influence that Hitler was unwittingly to bring to bear upon his future scientific activities—activities which Hitler and his Nazis were bitterly to regret.

By the summer of 1936 Lovell's work on the electrical conductivity of thin metallic films had progressed so well that he was able to write his thesis for the degree of PhD and to submit this in October. But he was to be 'dismayed beyond consolation' as he put it, when Tyndall, despite awarding him a Colston Research Fellowship, advised him that he ought to leave Bristol in order to broaden his scientific outlook and to face greater competition than existed in the laboratories at Bristol. To be torn away from his friends, his organ activities and playing cricket for the University and the Bristol Optimists, seemed a disaster. Nonetheless, Tyndall's will prevailed and Lovell followed up two of his recommendations. On 23 July 1936 he wrote to the Registrar of Manchester University and applied for the three-year post of Assistant Lecturer in Physics, naming his sponsors as Professor A. M. Tyndall, Professor N. F. Mott and Dr E. T. S. Appleyard. The second recommendation of Tyndall's was that he should apply for a job with Professor P. M. S. Blackett* of Birkbeck College in London, who was looking for a young man to assist with the cosmic ray research which he was conducting at Birkbeck. Blackett,* who had served in the Navy during World War I after completing his education at Osborne and Dartmouth, went up to Cambridge at the beginning of 1919 for a six months course by courtesy of the Admiralty. His early visits to the Cavendish Laboratory and the influence of Rutherford* soon determined his future career, and he resigned from the Navy to become an undergraduate. Studying for Part I of the Mathematics Tripos, he gained a Second Class. He was then accepted as a student of physics and in 1921 obtained a First in Part II. He now came under Rutherford at the Cavendish and there worked with C. T. R. Wilson,* the Scottish physicist who introduced the cloud-chamber method of studying ionized particles which proved essential in atomic studies. Blackett, developing C. T. R. Wilson's cloud-chamber technique in 1925, was the first to succeed in taking photographs of nuclear collisions involving transmutation when he photographed an alpha particle splitting a nitrogen nucleus into an oxygen isotope nucleus and a high-energy proton. In 1932, independently of the American physicist Anderson, he discovered the positive electron, or positron as it came to be known. He was, later, the first scientist to observe nuclear disintegration by cosmic rays. Now Blackett was already a 'hero' figure with Lovell, who had read many of his published papers, studied his background and marvelled at his elegant approach to his researches. Therefore, to further Blackett's work on cosmic rays was an immense attraction, and the kind of solace he needed to make up for having to leave his beloved Bristol.

Tyndall himself contacted Blackett and advised Lovell that the great man was prepared to see him. On 1 August, just one week after he had written to Manchester, Lovell despatched a letter to Blackett asking when he should attend for interview. To his embarrassment, he received telegrams from both Professor W. L. Bragg,* Professor of Physics at Manchester (he later succeeded Rutherford at Cambridge), and from Blackett, asking him to attend for interview on the same day—4 p.m. Thursday 6 August at Birkbeck, and the afternoon of Thursday 6 August at Manchester. Lovell, without a moment's hesitation, accepted the

4 p.m. date with Blackett and regretted that he could not manage the afternoon of the 6th in Manchester but could be there on the following morning. In fact, he was convinced he would be offered the job with Blackett on the spot and would, therefore, be able to cancel his appointment with Bragg.

> I optimistically set off for the Blackett interview on a glorious day [he recalls]. I remember Joyce seeing me off at Bath Station. We were madly in love by this time, but not yet engaged—Joyce's parents were still strongly opposed to any thoughts of marriage because they considered she was too young—she was only just twenty and I was only twenty-three! I was fully expecting to return to Bath that night, but Joyce made sure I had everything I needed, just in case. I still have this picture in my mind. Just before the train drew out, Joyce said: 'Now are you sure you've got everything all right?' And I said: 'Yes. I've even got a book on Dostoevsky by Berdiaev which I'll read up on the train.' You see, I knew Blackett was rather Left Wing and interested in Russian and Marxist philosophy, so I thought it would help my chances if I appeared to be not only interested in cosmic rays, but in Russia and Marxism as well.

At the end of the interview at Birkbeck, Blackett told Lovell that he could not offer him the post that night because he had promised to see another young man from Cambridge. Lovell says: 'I was dismayed and inconsolable. Such is the bumptiousness of youth that I thought it incredible that this fellow wouldn't offer me the job there and then. And now there was an additional problem. Obviously I would have to go up to Manchester after all, when I really wanted to get back to Bath to be with Joyce.'

And so Lovell trudged off to Euston and caught the six o'clock train to Manchester. There, on Friday morning, he was interviewed by Bragg and some of his staff and offered the post of Assistant Lecturer in Physics on the spot! To his everlasting shame, Lovell responded by saying: 'Well, I'm afraid I don't know if I wish to accept because I want to work with Blackett in London.' He admits that this was dynamite, as there was a degree of rivalry between Blackett and Bragg. 'Even now I can feel the awful silence that descended over the room, and how R. W. James, [a crystallographer and formerly a member of Shackleton's expedition to the South Pole] one of the interviewers, drummed the table with his fingers and then commented totally irrelevantly: "What a remarkably clear day it is. Why, I can see the time on the Town Hall clock!" Now, forty years later, I'm appalled by my impertinence.' Despite his attitude, Bragg gave him time to make up his mind, but Lovell went off on a cricket tour in Devon and kept him waiting. Then, on 11 August, Blackett sent a telegram to advise him that J. G. Wilson, the man from Cambridge, had got the job because he already had experience of the equipment being used at Birkbeck. Blackett also wrote a charming letter explaining that the reason for his choice was that J. G. Wilson had been working under C. T. R. Wilson with the cloud-chamber technique which he, Blackett, was using at Birkbeck. He also told Lovell that he had advised Bragg of his decision. And so a disconsolate Bernard Lovell finally accepted the Manchester appointment on the same day that he received Blackett's telegram. Bragg acknowledged his letter in a reply dated 12 August, in which he expressed his pleasure at Lovell's decision. With a sense of great understanding, he added: 'Please do not apologise for your inability to decide sooner, which I fully understand. I always feel sympathy towards anyone who has to make a decision about an appointment; it is always an anxious and troublesome business.'

In a letter dated 13 August, Tyndall wrote from his 'Houseboat Merlin', where he was on vacation, congratulating Lovell on his appointment. With blunt wisdom, he went on to say: 'There is one thing about the Manchester job that makes it preferable from one point of view, namely that you finish the 3 years [the period of the appointment as Assistant Lecturer in Physics was for three years] with a dual qualification—teaching and research. I personally was in favour of Blackett's job because I am not at all sure how much patience you will shew in dealings with masses of medicals and engineers with no interest in Physics. But a little schooling in that respect won't hurt you!'

And so Alfred Charles Bernard Lovell BSc (Bristol) was appointed Assistant Lecturer in Physics at Manchester University for a period of three years from 29 September 1936, at the stipend of £300 per annum.

3

Manchester 1936–9

.Lovell would dearly have liked to have had the company of Joyce during those days after hearing that Blackett had decided to appoint J. G. Wilson from Cambridge to the Birkbeck job, leaving him with no alternative to accepting the Manchester appointment, but when he had arrived back from the Manchester interview on 7 August, it was only just in time to say good-bye to Joyce, who was about to depart the next day for a long holiday in Switzerland with her parents and brothers. 'It was on that evening,' Lovell recalls, 'at the moment of parting, that Joyce tossed a book into the back of my car—"to cheer me up"—a book on *The History of Anthropology*! Naturally, I was distraught at not knowing whether I was going to Birkbeck, or whether I would have to go to Manchester—the last place on Earth I wanted to go to. And here was Joyce going abroad for weeks.' Therefore, the bitterness of the final rejection by Blackett had to be borne alone.

After accepting the Manchester appointment, Lovell spent August and September playing cricket for the Bristol Optimists and the nearby village of Wick, and plotting the ways in which he could undertake his duties at Manchester and, at the same time, continue with his Bristol work on thin film techniques. He had firmly made up his mind that he would have nothing to do with Bragg's crystallographic research which dominated the Manchester University Physics Department at that time. He just was not interested in crystallography. The fact that this was the era when Lord Rutherford's Cavendish (Cambridge) and Bragg's Manchester were the only Physics Centres in Great Britain with an international reputation at the time when the splitting of the atom, Heisenberg's uncertainty principle and Einstein's theory of relativity were bringing physics to the fore, left Lovell unmoved. He still resented having to go to Manchester; but even though his perversity was short-lived, he indulged his misery into 1937.

By the autumn of 1936 the Chestermans had begun to accept their daughter's wish to marry Bernard Lovell, but they were still opposed to the announcement of a formal engagement until Joyce had completed her teacher training course in 1937. This was in spite of Joyce's assurance in March 1936 that she would not marry before she had finished her college training. The crisis over an engagement, however, soon came to a head. At the end of October Joyce went home for the half-term holiday from

Bedford College, fully determined to argue with her parents over permission to become officially engaged without further delay. Bernard Lovell arranged to drive down from Manchester on Saturday 31 October, the day after Joyce had arrived in Bath. To keep him advised on the situation, Joyce was to send him a telegram which he was to pick up at Lichfield Post Office on the way down. 'I still remember the agony of that journey,' Lovell says. 'But the relief when I read in that telegram that her parents had agreed that we could become formally engaged at Christmas was tremendous. Always, now, when we go through Lichfield we salute the Post Office!'

In the meantime, the Chestermans had tried to help Lovell to secure suitable accommodation in Manchester when he took up his new appointment in October. Unfortunately, their efforts were less effective than their undoubted good intentions, but in a round-about way they were to be of some assistance in softening Lovell's immediate Manchester miseries. Through their good offices, the minister of the Baptist church near the University of Manchester, whom they had contacted via the Baptist hierarchy in Bath, found Lovell accommodation in a cul-de-sac by the name of Roberts Avenue. Lovell describes these first living-quarters as 'appalling digs' where he was 'so intensely miserable' that he quickly decided he must find some alternative. Fortunately, he became friendly with Arthur Porter, a Research Fellow who was working with Professor D. R. Hartree,* the Professor of Mathematics, on computers. Porter took pity on him and helped him to obtain quarters in Hulme Hall, a student residence, where he was given what he describes as 'a huge and relatively luxurious room'. Through Porter he met Hartree and, to his great delight, discovered that he was deeply interested in music, which was soon to be the cause of a new friendship that began to change his attitude towards his Manchester environment. Hartree had developed remarkable methods of numerical mathematical analysis which made it possible for him to apply the so-called self-consistent field method to the calculation of atomic wave functions of polyelectronic atoms—that is, those which in the neutral condition have more than one electron surrounding the nucleus. He and his collaborators evaluated wave functions for more than twenty-five different atomic species in various states of ionization. Early in his work at Manchester he had become interested in machine calculation and had recently built in the basement of the physics laboratory the first computing machine in Britain—the differential analyser—for the graphical solution of differential equations. This work, added to Hartree's musical ability, appealed greatly to Lovell, and both his friendship and his admiration for Hartree increased. Then, early in May 1937, it became known that Bragg was soon to take up the appointment of

Director of the National Physical Laboratory at Teddington in London. His replacement was as yet unannounced, and Lovell, who was still working unofficially on thin film techniques for Professor Mott and Dr Appleyard at Bristol, contacted Tyndall to seek his advice about the future. In a letter dated 27 May 1937, Tyndall advised Lovell 'to mark time until you learn who is appointed in the place of Professor Bragg'. He wisely added: 'In the meantime, both Professor Mott and I agree it might be quite useful for you to help Professor Hartree. It would also have the political advantage of shewing that you are willing to help the Department in what must be rather an emergency.' This was entirely to Lovell's liking, and he willingly offered Hartree his assistance and was soon working with him on the differential analyser. But he continued with his thin film work.

Prior to working for Hartree on computing machines, Lovell had continued his work on the electrical conductivity of thin metallic films, strongly encouraged by both Mott and Appleyard. The results of his researches at Bristol had been of prime importance, and Mott and Appleyard had been loathe to let the momentum of his work run down. His dissertation on his work had earned him his PhD, a fact which he learnt from Winifred Shapland, the Secretary and Registrar of the University of Bristol, by her letter of 11 December 1936.

The Degree Congregation of 22 December 1936, when he was formally admitted to the degree of Doctor of Philosophy, was only one part of a memorable occasion back at Bristol. After the degree ceremony at the University, Lovell drove Joyce Chesterman to the Mendips where, after parking the car, they walked up to the top of Crooke's Peak. There he planned to place an engagement ring upon Joyce's finger and so confirm their betrothal. 'I do not think,' he says, 'that Joyce knew that this was to be the moment and the place for the formal giving of the engagement ring, but no doubt she sensed that something important was going to happen!' And so Christmas 1936 was a particularly happy one for the young lovers, although it was over all too swiftly.

No sooner was Lovell back at Manchester than he was being pressed for help on thin film work. Klaus Fuchs, under Mott and Appleyard, had continued the work on resistivity of thin films after Lovell's departure from Bristol University. Fuchs was a political refugee from Nazi Germany, though not a Jew, who had found asylum in England. He was then a young man, brilliant and very far to the left in his politics. (He was later, after the Second World War, to be imprisoned for communicating atomic bomb secrets to the Russians to whom he finally defected after completing his prison sentence.) It was in reference to Fuchs' work that Appleyard and Mott wanted assistance—which Lovell willingly gave. With the help of Johnny Burrow, the remarkable glassblower at Bristol,

Lovell was able to continue his work on thin films right through until the end of 1937. From October 1936 there was a stream of letters between Lovell and Burrow, Lovell's containing instructions for the preparation of pieces of equipment he required, and Burrow's containing progress reports on the outcome of the demands, together with amusing local news and gardening advice—both Lovell and Burrow were keen gardeners. These letters were supplemented by two-way visits on rare occasions. Interspersed were notes from Mott and Appleyard asking for figures and references relating to past and present thin film work. Often they requested Lovell's opinion on results being achieved at Bristol. Burrow's equipment was usually transported by Lovell in his Morris 8, although some was entrusted to the London, Midland and Scottish Railway, and Burrow himself made the odd visit to Manchester.

As 1937 progressed, it became a year filled with incidents of great importance. Lovell had already had one paper published on thin films. In 1936, 1937 and 1938 a second paper in three parts was published in the *Proceedings of the Royal Society*. A further paper was published in 1937 in the *Proceedings of the Physical Society*.[1] But by far the most momentous occasion of 1937 was Tuesday 14 September. On that day Bernard Lovell and Joyce Chesterman were married at Manvers Street Baptist Church in Bath. The first hymn was Bernard of Clairvaux's 'Jesus, Thou Joy of loving hearts', a choice which was particularly appropriate because Bernard Lovell was named after the writer. The organist at the wedding ceremony was Raymond Jones. At last a remarkable and powerful union was forged, one which was to have a profound effect upon Lovell's future, because Joyce Chesterman was not only to support him unreservedly throughout his career but also to bring to bear upon him an influence which helped and encouraged him to pursue those activities which he believed to be of scientific significance despite all the disappointments, setbacks and opposition that so frequently impeded his progress on the way to success. This influence, too, was of prime importance in keeping Lovell's feet on the ground and in giving him a close-knit family life to which he could escape from his working life in order to replenish his vigour and his sense of humour.

[1] Electrical Conductivity of Thin Films of Rubidium on Glass Surfaces, *Nature*, Vol. 137, 1936; 'The Electrical Conductivity of thin Metallic Films:- Part I: The Rubidium on Pyrex Glass Surfaces', *Proceedings Roy. Soc. A.*, Vol. 157, 1936; 'Part II: Ceasium and Potassium on Pyrex Glass Surfaces', published jointly with E. T. S. Appleyard, *Proceedings Roy. Soc. A.*, Vol. 158, 1937; 'Part III: Alkali films with the properties of the normal metal', published in *Proceedings Roy. Soc. A.*, Vol. 166, 1938; 'The Electrical Conductivity of Thin Films of the Alkali Metals spontaneously deposited on Glass Surfaces', *Proceedings of the Physical Soc.*, Vol. 49, 1937.

Immediately after their wedding, Bernard and Joyce Lovell returned to Manchester, to a new small house at Northenden on the boundary of Wythenshawe Park. They had bought it for £500, with the aid of a mortgage. There they lived in what Joyce Lovell described as 'a lovely little house' for two years.

On 29 September Lovell received a surprise letter from P. M. S. Blackett, dated 28 September, in which he wrote that 'Hartree tells me that you may like to start on a cosmic ray experiment. . . .' He went on to say that he was sending him some reprints of write-ups of the work done at Birkbeck College, and advised him to obtain a copy of four lectures he had given on the subject of cosmic rays which had been published in 1935 by Hermann & Cie in Paris under the title '*La Radiation Cosmique*'. He also commended to his attention his 1936 Halley Lecture which had been published in Oxford by the Clarendon Press. Rumour had already linked Blackett's name with the new appointment of Langworthy Professor of Physics at Manchester in replacement for Bragg. Even if this was still rumour, a second letter from Blackett dated 9 October finally removed all doubts from Lovell's mind. In this letter he wrote: 'I have been thinking about possible research for you, and have come to the conclusion that possibly the most suitable scheme would be for you to take over the completely automatic counter-controlled cloud chamber which I am bringing with me.' He went on to suggest that it would be best if Lovell could manage to visit Birkbeck for a few days to see the apparatus before it was stripped down and packed up for transportation to Manchester, and then actually supervise the dismantling and packing so that it would be easier for him to re-erect the equipment in the laboratories at Manchester. At last Lovell knew that he was to realize his long-held desire to work on cosmic rays for Blackett. Oddly, Fate had had two hands in this, for Blackett's unexpected appointment to replace Bragg was only part of the reason why Lovell got the job. At Birkbeck, Blackett had a young Chinese, Hu Chien Shan, working for him, and it was Hu who had built the small automatic cloud chamber. But now, with the continuing war in China following the invasion of Manchuria by the Japanese in September 1931, Hu Chien Shan had decided to return to his homeland to help in the fight against Japan. This left a vital gap in Blackett's team. Blackett finished this second letter by saying: 'There is no real reason why you should not collect the apparatus at once—in fact the sooner the better. Let me know what you think of the scheme. If you approve, I can write to Professor Bragg and ask if you could come down for a day or two.'

Lovell's response was prompt. He was delighted and excited. No longer was he disconsolate. But since he still planned to continue his work on thin films in order to complete this work to a specific stage, he remained in correspondence with Bristol, particularly with Johnny Burrow whose glassblowing assistance was as essential as ever. Almost immediately after Blackett's letter of 9 October he wrote to Burrow with some requests. This drew an amusing reply which clearly indicated that Burrow had detected a change in Lovell's mood. 'I was extremely pleased on opening your letter,' he wrote, 'to find that it was written in such a cheerful tone, when I expected little more than another cry for more work. Can it be that marriage has already mellowed that tempestuous character?'

It was finally arranged that Lovell should visit Birkbeck on 22 October. A letter from Blackett confirmed this, but owing to Lord Rutherford's death at Cambridge on the 19th and his funeral on the morning of the 22nd, he excused himself from meeting Lovell for lunch on that day and asked him to arrive at Birkbeck at 2.30 p.m. All went well with the dismantling and packing of the apparatus, and on 2 November, after Lovell had returned to Manchester, he received a telegram from Birkbeck advising him that the van with the packing cases had 'left at 2 p.m. Monday arriving University 9 a.m. Tuesday'. It duly arrived with the equipment in safe and sound condition, somewhat in contrast to another transportation effort in connection with equipment from Bristol for Lovell's continuing work on thin films.

On 6 November Appleyard wrote to Lovell advising him that Johnny Burrow had prepared a large store of rubidium for him—the metallic element with which he was working—but that he had not yet completed the special glass tube he was preparing. After giving the up-to-date situation on the work at Bristol on thin films, and telling him of the problems he still required to be resolved, hoping that Lovell would be able to help, he went on to hazard a guess as to who would replace Bragg at Manchester. The remarkable fact was that it was far from generally known that Blackett was to be the replacement—even at this late stage. Appleyard wrote: 'I suppose you must be a bit bothered about Blackett. My favourites for the seat are: Chadwick, Blackett, Cockcroft, Oliphant, Appleton—in order of precedence. But God knows who they will appoint. These speculations are strictly confidential and my name must not be attached to them.'

Johnny Burrow followed up this letter by advising Lovell that he had prepared two batches of rubidium and that the special tube was ready. 'I have left the bottom open,' he said 'this for easy assembly. Oh, and did you want a new ionisation gauge stuck on? I cannot get off this month. I am broke and in rags etc., so shall I send it on? Waiting instructions.' Lovell replied, yes, and disaster struck. On the 23rd he wrote to Burrow: 'It is with deepest sorrow if not with such agony as a year ago, that I have to place on record that our beautiful apparatus arrived most thoroughly smashed. In fact it could hardly be more complete. I am afraid it is quite irreparable. I am writing to the railway company to see if I can get anything from them, and when they have done their worst I will return the pieces. But what of the future? I can honestly say that the only apparatus which has travelled intact is when I have transported it myself.' He went on to say he was writing to Tyndall to ask him if he could visit Bristol in the Christmas vacation and complete the experiments in the H. H. Wills Physical Laboratories.

In a letter dated the 29th, Burrow replied that he had only just about recovered from the bad news. He went on to report that Tyndall and Mott had discussed the matter with him and agreed to his re-building the equipment and to Lovell's completing the work at Bristol during the coming Christmas vacation. 'If you can get away from your racket early, so as to do the calibration before Christmas,' he wrote, 'we may get the job finished before you go back.'

Most of Lovell's last contribution to research on the electrical con-ductivity of thin metallic films was completed in Bristol during that 1937 Christmas break, although some drifted over into the early part of 1938. However, his full-time occupation with the automatic cloud chamber was rapidly to take precedence over all other activities. When Blackett arrived at Manchester University at the end of 1937, he quickly made sweeping changes. Following such distinguished predecessors as Rutherford and Bragg, he inherited a far stronger and better-equipped department than he had enjoyed at Birkbeck; but this did not stop him from revolutionizing the Physics Department. Under Bragg, the research in the department had been largely concentrated on X-ray crystallography. Within a few months of Blackett's arrival all the crystallography personnel had dis-appeared, the dreary dark brown walls had been painted out with lighter and more cheerful colours, a departmental library had been started, and extra space had been pirated. Soon the entire area was being dominated by personnel and equipment for cosmic ray research. J. G. Wilson, whom Blackett had engaged a year earlier from Cambridge because of his experience of cloud chamber work under E. T. S. Wilson, and the Hungarian L. Jánossy* came up from Birkbeck with others of Blackett's team. At Manchester, both Lovell and George Rochester, another assistant lecturer, survived and joined Blackett. The other major survivor was D. R. Hartree, the Professor of Applied Mathematics, who was re-appointed to a Chair of Theoretical Physics which Blackett persuaded the University to create. And so for the next two years Lovell was to devote his entire time to cosmic ray research. Driven relentlessly by Blackett, he designed a magnet for the cloud chamber, which he had made at

Metropolitan Vickers. With this he measured the energy spectrum of the newly discovered mesons and, in conjunction with Jánossy and J. G. Wilson, he published important papers on extensive cosmic ray air showers.[1]

Blackett was hard-working, brilliant and ruthless. His drive was indefatigable and his energy inexhaustible when applied to those tasks in which he was interested and which he wished to undertake; none of his effort was ever wasted because his organizing and administrative skill was so great that he adroitly and effectively controlled and directed both those who worked in his team and himself. In the earliest lectures which Blackett gave on cosmic rays at the time of his move from working with Rutherford at Cambridge to Birkbeck in 1933, he displayed his fascination with the problem of their origin in the universe, and how this was awakening his interest in astronomy and astrophysics. His scientific outlook made him entirely materialistic, and he was unable to accept anything unless it was scientifically proven. His influence upon Lovell was considerable. Lovell was brilliant too, although as yet immature, and he had the same dedicated application to work. Indisputably, however, he learnt from Blackett the skill of combining application with good organization and administration, and he recognized the advantages of expertly exercising a degree of ruthlessness to get things done efficiently and with expedition. His ruthlessness was already there to be drawn upon; from Blackett he learnt how to apply it.

Work under Blackett at this stage of Lovell's life was to be short-lived. In the international field, 1938 started ominously. In Britain, Anthony Eden finally clashed with Neville Chamberlain, the Prime Minister, over the latter's determination to seek *rapprochement* with Mussolini by recognition of Italy's conquest of Abyssinia and by his further intention to improve Anglo-German relations by almost any concessions demanded by Hitler. Finding his position undermined by Chamberlain's policy of appeasement of Europe's dictators, Eden resigned as Foreign Secretary on 20 February. On 11 March 1938 Germany marched into Austria and occupied that nation by force of arms. Eden's resignation disturbed the academics all over the country, and many universities protested. Manchester circulated a letter to the members of the teaching staff which it was proposed to send to the Prime Minister, with a copy to Eden, setting out their dismay at Britain's foreign policy. A covering letter, dated 3

[1] 'Nature of Extensive Cosmic Ray Showers', published with L. Jánossy in *Nature*, Vol, 142, 1938; 'Investigation of Cosmic Ray Showers of Atmospheric Origin using Two Cloud Chambers', with J. G. Wilson, published in *Nature*, Vol. 144, 1939; 'Shower Production by Penetrating Cosmic Rays' (Lovell sole author), published in *Proceedings of the Roy. Soc. A*, Vol. 172, 1939.

March, inviting members to sign this protest, stated: 'A number of members of the University Teaching Staff wish to express their apprehension at the trend in the foreign policy of H. M. Government which has led to the resignation of Mr Eden from the Foreign Office. They suggest that the enclosed letter should be sent to the Prime Minister, and copies of it to Mr. Eden and to the Press. If you are in sympathy with this course, would you without delay sign the copy of the letter enclosed. . . .' Amongst those instigating this protest was Blackett. The letter was signed by almost everyone including Lovell and Blackett. In fact, it had no effect. Only Churchill, Eden, Brendan Bracken, Robert Boothby and a few other supporters of Churchill and Eden did their best to encourage the British Government to say to Hitler and Mussolini: 'Stop! No further!'

Then, in September of 1938, Chamberlain compromised with Hitler over Czechoslovakia in an act of dismal betrayal, with the result that Czechoslovakia was occupied by the Germans in October and November. War was rapidly approaching.

At the beginning of 1935, a committee of scientists had been formed under Sir Henry Tizard,* Rector of the Imperial College of Science and Technology, to study the application of science to the defence of Britain, in particular against air attack. Amongst its members were Blackett, H. E. Wimperis, Director of Scientific Research at the Air Ministry, Professor A. V. Hill and A. P. Rowe* (assistant to Wimperis and later head of the Telecommunications Research Establishment) as Secretary. By the end of 1938, with the European situation looking distinctly disastrous, the work of this committee, known as the Tizard Committee, became very onerous, resulting in Blackett's being away from Manchester a great deal in late 1938 and throughout 1939. But he was still to point the direction of Lovell's immediate future, even if war was temporarily to interrupt their more permanent working relationship.

If 1938 was gloomy from the international point of view, there was one joyful incident in the Lovell household in October. On the 19th, Joyce presented Bernard with their firstborn, a daughter whom they named Susan. She was born at Bath, Joyce having returned home for the confinement. Then came Christmas for the family in their own home in Northenden, which was somehow a much more meaningful event now that they had their own child. It was to be their first and last Christmas there. Lovell's appointment as assistant lecturer was due to terminate on 30 September 1939, but before then he was awarded a Senior DSIR Fellowship to enable him to take a vanload of cosmic ray equipment across to France and up to the Pic du Midi in the Pyrenees, where there was an important observatory for high-altitude investigations. With all the equipment purchased and prepared, and on a day at the beginning of

August 1939, when the van was parked in Coupland Street outside the Physics Department of Manchester University ready for loading, Lovell's efforts were rudely interrupted by a telephone call from London. It was Blackett, advising him to abandon his plans in view of the European situation. Instead, Lovell was within days to be starting his wartime career. For him it was the end of an era.

4

And So to War

Robert Watson Watt,* when Superintendent of the Radio Department of the National Physical Laboratory, conducted some successful research as early as the beginning of the twenties into methods of locating thunderstorms by the transmission and reflection of radio waves. He then perfected his system for the purpose of measuring movements of the ionized layer around the Earth with the object of determining related weather patterns and the effect of the movements of the layer on wireless reception and put forward the opinion that aircraft could be detected in a similar manner. His theory depended upon the principle of radio waves being transmitted and reflected back by objects such as aircraft and ships in a similar manner to those from the ionized layer, the echoes being received at the source of the transmission. Since the speed of travel of radio waves is the same as that of light, the distance of an aircraft or ship could, he postulated, be measured by timing the period between the moment of despatch of the outgoing transmission and its return to source after striking the aeroplane or ship and being 'bounced' back. In addition, since radio waves, like light, travel in straight lines, the direction of the ship or aeroplane from the source of transmission could be calculated and, therefore, its position, direction of movement, and speed could be constantly monitored. This, clearly, was an important discovery if the theory could be proved in practice, because it meant, in particular, that an enemy air attack could be detected ahead of its arrival, and defending fighters could be despatched directly from their bases to a point of interception before the enemy bombers reached the shores of Britain.

The Committee of Imperial Defence was convinced that, in the event of war with a European country—and even by 1935 the Chiefs of Staff seriously regarded Germany as the potential enemy—the main attack would initially be by bombing aircraft. They were also concerned by the fact that Britain, from having the most powerful Air Force at the end of World War I, had sunk to seventh place in the air stakes. Even worse, her present Air Force was equipped with obsolete wooden biplanes, and the re-equipment of the fighter defence with the recently designed and tested all-metal monoplanes, the Hurricanes and Spitfires, was a long way off. Consequently, a system which would detect an impending air attack well away from the shores of Britain and enable fighters to be conserved on the ground and then despatched to interception, was of paramount importance. Therefore the Air Ministry had given what financial backing it could afford. On 25 February 1935, at 11.58 a.m., Watson Watt detected his first aircraft with his crude experimental equipment, thus establishing that an aeroplane could definitely be located by radio reflection-direction-finding. RDF, later to be known as Radar, was born. On the recommendation of the Tizard Committee, the Air Ministry gave instant support to a requirement for increased expenditure and effort on Watson Watt's experiments. On 25 July 1935 Tizard reported that Watson Watt's experiments had reached a successful stage and were producing results that warranted the construction of a chain of stations. As a result his Committee recommended such a course of action. In addition, it advocated the acquisition of Bawdsey Manor on the Suffolk coast near Felixstowe, where the experiments had been undertaken, as the centre for research work on RDF. In December of the same year, the Treasury granted authority for the building of four RDF stations for the defence of Britain, and for the purchase of Bawdsey Manor. By March 1936 the first chain of RDF stations was being erected along the south coast, and in July 1937 there was a complete review by the Air Ministry of the requirements for the new RDF defence system against enemy air attack, which resulted in approval being given to construct and install by 1939 a chain of twenty stations providing coverage from west of the Isle of Wight to north of the Tees.

The installation of the chain formed only a part of what needed to be done to provide an early warning system. It was also necessary to be able to identify friend from foe, and Tizard and his committee turned their attention to this problem. Soon an equipment was developed which, when carried in a friendly aircraft, would identify it as such to the RDF station. Moreover, there were the problems of the tactics needed for the most effective methods of intercepting the enemy. In conjunction with the Air Staff, a comprehensive system of communications terminating in a central operations room, linking it to the RDF stations and to the bases of the fighter squadrons and the intercepting squadrons in the air was developed. Because the Air Staff believed that, in the event of daylight attacks being beaten off, the enemy would turn to night bombing as in the war of 1914–18, the Tizard Committee had to consider the possibilities of airborne forms of RDF to enable the night fighter to 'see' his target in the dark. At the same time, with fear that the second or concurrent enemy attack would take the form of an assault upon shipping so vital to the supplies of an island race such as Britain, Tizard and his colleagues were given the additional task of studying the possibilities of airborne RDF for spotting and attacking enemy naval units, in particular submarines at night when they surfaced to re-charge their batteries.

Basic to all the brilliant developments of the scientists, however, was a force of aircraft which could utilize these new and highly advanced systems and ideas; and here was the rub. By the beginning of 1939, the Royal Air Force possessed less than a hundred Hurricanes and only six Spitfires, and weekly production rates were so low that they would nowhere nearly have replaced war wastage had Britain been attacked at that time. Night fighters, in the form of the twin-engined Blenheims, were in not much better supply. The same applied to the modern bombers, the production rates of the bomber version of the Blenheim, Whitleys, Hampdens and Wellingtons being quite inadequate. On the other hand, it was known that the German Air Force was between two and three times larger than the Royal Air Force, in terms of first-line aircraft. In addition, their intervention in the Spanish Civil War had revealed the quality of Germany's modern bombers and fighters. The urgency was, therefore, to put first priority on Britain's Fighter Command, which included a speed-up of the supply of Hurricanes and Spitfires, improved gunpower of these fighters to eight guns, the completion of Watson Watt's chain of RDF stations, and the urgent development of airborne RDF for night fighters and for Coastal Command aircraft for defence against the U-boat.

This, then, was the situation into which a number of young British scientists were suddenly plunged in August 1939, when war was imminent.

In July it had been decided by the Air Ministry, largely at the instigation of Tizard's Air Defence Sub-Committee, to run a five-week training scheme on RDF for selected university scientific personnel during the vacation period. Amongst those selected were four from Manchester who were nominated by Blackett: Lovell, J. G. Wilson, Ingleby and Beattie. On 10 August Lovell received a letter from Rutherford's Cambridge colleague Dr J. D. Cockcroft,* who was co-ordinating the training scheme, requesting him to report to the Air Ministry Research Station, Bawdsey, on Monday, 14 August. This visit was for the purpose of introducing the university recruits to RDF and briefing them on the form the course would take. The Superintendent at Bawdsey was A. P. Rowe, and Lovell recalls that the first item that caught his attention when entering Bawdsey Manor was a cricket bag in the hall which he quickly discovered belonged to Rowe. 'It gave me a completely misleading impression of what I was in for!' he comments. In fact, the common love of Rowe and Lovell for cricket was to have quite a bearing on their later relationship—a working relationship which was to last throughout the war. The visitors from the universities were at Bawdsey for only a few days and, as Lovell puts it, 'we were initiated into the mysteries of RDF—or Radar as it was later called—by Rowe who was constantly sucking his pipe. What was extraordinary was that we had no idea—absolutely no idea—that all this development in radio techniques had been going on. This secret really had been well kept.'

From Bawdsey, Lovell returned to Manchester, but only for just over a week. He wrote to Blackett and told him how impressed he had been. On 24 August he received a swift reply from Blackett, thanking him for his letter and telling him that he was to take over the leadership of the Manchester contingent which would shortly be going to Scarborough, and that Watson Watt had confirmed this. It was the same day that mobilization letters were dispatched to all reservists of the three Services and to members of the Naval Volunteer Reserve, the Territorial Army, the Auxiliary Air Force and the Royal Air Force Volunteer Reserve. On the 25th Lovell received an official notification from the Air Ministry posting him for a period of six weeks from Monday 28 August to the Air Ministry Station, Staxton Wold, near Scarborough, Yorkshire.

Staxton Wold was one of the RDF chain stations which had been completed for the detection of enemy aircraft approaching Britain's shores. It was there, in the operations room, that Lovell heard Chamberlain's speech to the Nation at 11.15 a.m. on Sunday 3 September 1939, following Germany's invasion of Poland on 1 September, in which he sombrely announced: 'This morning the British Ambassador in Berlin handed the German Government a final note stating that, unless we heard from them by eleven o'clock that they were prepared at once to withdraw their troops from Poland, a state of war would exist between us. I have to tell you now that no such undertaking has been received, and that consequently this country is at war with Germany. . . .' It was expected in Britain that, immediately following the existence of a state of war between Germany on the one side and Britain and France on the other, hordes of enemy bombers would begin their onslaught. Lovell, who was working on the RDF equipment, was no exception to the others who watched the cathode ray tubes, upon which the attack would be revealed, expecting to see the echoes of enemy aircraft at any moment. In fact, none appeared on the screens; there was only evidence of transient echoes which the Royal Air Force operators referred to as 'coming from the ionosphere'. Lovell's fertile mind put another interpretation upon these occasional sporadic and short-lived echoes. It instantly occurred to him that some of them might arise from ionization caused by extremely energetic cosmic ray showers, and he began to wonder if RDF techniques could be used for detecting the ionization caused by large cosmic ray showers in the atmosphere. War was now upon Lovell, but his mind was, as yet, still on peacetime research.

Directly following the outbreak of war, with visions of the south and south-east of England becoming a target for intense bombing, the Air Ministry Research Establishment under A. P. Rowe was evacuated from Bawdsey up to Dundee. It was from Dundee that Lovell received at Staxton Wold a letter from Dr W. B. Lewis,* Rowe's deputy, dated 9 September, asking him if he would undertake certain investigations into interference with reception of echoes on the RDF equipment, particularly that caused by rain. Lewis wanted reliable information and, knowing he had access to competent young scientists who were attached to the RDF stations, was anxious to use them to the full. Lovell co-operated so effectively that, shortly after his departure from Staxton Wold to visit Joyce and the family, who were in Bath, he received a letter dated 25 September from J. M. Nuttall, Blackett's deputy at Manchester University, saying: 'Blackett has had word from Lewis that you are to report to him at Dundee as soon as possible. . . . Ingleby and Beattie are going also.' Lovell proceeded there immediately and was soon a member of Dr E. G. Bowen's* airborne research division which was occupied with two major tasks: the development of the Air Interception RDF for night fighters known as AI, and the airborne RDF for submarine location, known as ASV. Both of these equipments were in a crude state operating on a wavelength of 1½ metres. In addition Bowen was considering the possible uses of airborne RDF for other forms of operations, including terrain-identification, which he considered to be a likely requirement for the navigation of bomber aircraft and for target-location. But priority demanded that all effort should be concentrated on AI and ASV.

By a letter dated 19 October, Lovell learnt that he was offered the temporary appointment of Junior Scientific Officer at the Air Ministry Research Department, Dundee, at a salary of £330 per annum, which was somewhat less than he had been earning in his last year at Manchester. Moreover, the terms were rough. The appointment was non-pensionable, no additional allowances would be forthcoming in the event of his being required to fly in the course of his duties, and he was expected to be ready to work all hours of the day and night, including Sundays. The whole of his time was to be at the disposal of the Department down to the last split second. On 24 October Lovell wrote back to the Air Ministry accepting the appointment.

In the meantime, Lovell had pitched into his new tasks with his habitual dedication, but he was appalled at the lack of facilities for research and development at Perth Airport and by the poor standard of organization. On 14 October he wrote to Blackett to report on what was going on at Perth. It was a forthright letter of criticism. 'As friend to friend I thought that you might find some unbiased views on the AM useful. They spring from two weeks' acquaintance with the group, which I am told, has defence priority at the moment. . . . To begin with,' he continued, 'the general organisation and method of work used by the AM makes my head swim. It leads to persistent and inevitable bungling. I find it illogical and without the elementals of commonsense. . . . At the beginning of this Summer the group was told to get on with AI and to design it for the Battle!' This was the Fairey Battle, an obsolete single-engined light bomber which was still in service due to lack of adequate numbers of the more modern bombers just coming into service at the outbreak of war. 'They did so and demonstrated in that machine. In June or July they were told to fit 22 *short* nosed Blenheims. They designed all the fittings, brackets etc. *Long* nosed Blenheims arrived.' The Bristol Blenheim was one of the modern all metal twin-engined medium bombers just coming into service in 1939, which had also been designed to perform the duties of a long range fighter and a night fighter. Lovell went on:

They redesigned their fittings, and placed the apparatus near the pilot as per instructions. The first four arrived at Northolt a short time ago. The C-in-C presumably swore and said (a) he had ordered *short* nosed Blenheims (b) the apparatus was not a bit of good in the front, it must be in the back for the gunner. Result, general chaos and further redesigning. This sounds stupid, but it becomes pitiful when you talk to the fitters and testers concerned. They endeavoured to point out that the pilot could never operate the apparatus. They were told not to be obstructionists. Even worse is the story of the apparatus. In 6 tests out of about 12 it has caught fire in the air, due to extremely bad design. The power packs flash over, thin flex leads break off etc. The tester knows exactly how to put this right in future designs; he is *never* consulted, and has given up trying to be helpful in sheer despair.

He went on to express his opinion that equipments were being designed by men sitting in secluded offices who never looked outside to discover the practical problems of installing their designs in aircraft or of using them under operational conditions. Moreover, they had no organizing ability: 'By the peculiar AM system they have attained positions for which they are in no way suited.' Because there was an urgent demand for hundreds of aircraft to be fitted with AI and ASV, the fitters, he reported, were being worked seven days a week and fifteen hours a day, and the depressing thought from their point of view was that they knew 'the apparatus is tripe.' Lovell continued: 'And recently we have reached the . climax of fantasy, in which only 4 planes have been fitted because NO MORE APPARATUS HAS COME FROM THE MAKERS!! This is due to contradictory orders being issued and generally messed up by men of the above group in their offices.' The tirade finished by asking to be forgiven if he had exceeded his privileges, emphasizing that his criticism arose only from a desire to be helpful and to aid Blackett to use his influence to eradicate this kind of muddle in these times of national emergency.

Lovell was probably as concerned as most people at the thought that the enemy would strike swiftly and, if he was not fully aware of the deplorable state of Britain's readiness in the air to meet the onslaught, he was rapidly learning about the deficiencies in the development and production of some of the vital equipment needed to enable pilots and their crews to undertake their defence tasks effectively. Certainly no one knew at the opening stages of hostilities that Hitler would refrain from an immediate attack upon Britain and that there would be a period of nine months of what came to be known as the 'Phoney War', a period that was to be the breathing-space desperately needed to bring Britain's defences up to some semblance of credibility. Indeed, had Hitler attacked at the outset, it is more than probable that Britain would have been defeated within months for she was totally unprepared and denuded of the capability of self-defence by years of policies of irresponsible pacifism and disarmament. Not knowing Hitler's mind, Lovell took the view that enough time must already have been lost in preparing for war and, therefore, not another second must go by in procrastination and 'pottering and doing nothing significant', as he put it to Blackett.

Blackett's reaction to Lovell's complaints was a dampener. In a letter dated 23 October from the Royal Aircraft Establishment, Farnborough, where he had only just been sent to take over the appointment of Principal Scientific Officer, he said he was sorry 'to hear that everything in the garden isn't quite as beautiful as you expected' and advised him not to take minor troubles too seriously. 'You underestimate,' he wrote, 'the difficulties of getting dispersal organisation going properly and of competing with the general expansion. You must be more tolerant too, especially at first till you have really achieved something in these technical fields—then you can criticise safely.' He went on to say that one of the great things to remember was that all defence work is like all Service work, very much a matter of dealing with people—'the qualities of the personnel are part of the experimental facts and it is no use getting too upset about them.' It was good advice and Lovell was young enough to heed it with good grace. Anyhow, it was not long before he was achieving some of the most remarkable results in research and development that were to have a profound effect upon the conduct of the war and which were to make a decisive contribution to the Allied victory over Germany five years later. Oddly enough, too, it was his disenchantment in 1939 and 1940 with the lack of co-operation between the Air Ministry scientists and technicians on the one hand, and the staffs, air crews and servicing personnel of the operating commands of the Royal Air Force on the other, that made him determined to establish a close-knit liaison between them one day in the future. And by 1942 that day had arrived. It was then that a partnership of endeavour and close friendship was forged between members of the Royal Air Force, Bomber Command and Lovell and other members of the Telecommunications Research Establishment (TRE), which formed the ultimate research organization for RDF (radar) for the Royal Air Force. This partnership between TRE and Bomber Command was so powerful that it was to bring disaster to Germany.

At the beginning of December 1939, Bowen's group at Perth was moved to the Royal Air Force Station at St Athan near Barry in Wales. For Lovell it was a good move. At Perth Joyce, who was then living at her parents' home in Bath, had been able to visit him only on an occasional weekend. Now they were lucky enough to find some 'digs' in a very pleasant house in Barry, and so Joyce was able to join Lovell once again. But, sadly, they had to plan to sell their first home near Northenden.

The winter of 1939–40 was a bitterly cold one, with heavy snows and freezing temperatures, and St Athan was not exempted from the arctic conditions. Both Bernard and Joyce Lovell remember well that winter when water-pipes froze up, snow made even the shortest travelling hazardous, conditions at work on the aerodrome made effective progress well-nigh impossible, and fuel rationing left everyone shivering more than usual. Lovell recalls Joyce saying, one day, to the one year and three month old Susan: 'Oh darling, if only you would learn to walk, you would be much warmer!' However, despite the cold, there was the comfort that the anticipated holocaust of massive bombing had not materialized. The British Expeditionary Force with its Advanced Air Striking Force and its Air Component had safely established itself in France and, with the French Army manning the Maginot Line, had taken up positions along the Belgian frontier to link with the French Forces on its right flank. The Allies were ready to face any German moves into Belgium and Luxembourg and to throw back any attempt to invade France itself. And Germany had made no moves.

Shortly after Lovell's arrival at St Athan, he became engaged on another research task in addition to his work on AI and ASV. This was the development of an idea, arising from the work on AI, to produce a system which would make it possible for an aircraft to bomb a target at night, or through cloud without seeing it. Experiments were being carried out in an Anson aircraft using modified AI equipment, operating on 5/10 metres, in an attempt to detect the presence of towns. 'BD' was the codename given to this experimental system. Following a visit to St Athan by Blackett in the first half of December, Lovell wrote to him on the 17th enclosing 'two notes, one on BD and another on what I believe ought to be done with us'. He finished by saying, 'It was super seeing you again, the people here are absolutely dead. Do come as often as you can.' The BD was a complicated system which included using the principles of AI for locating the target on the ground and, in addition, radio-controlling the bomb onto the target. In his note on the idea, Lovell reported that the apparatus had been constructed and partially fitted in a plane, but 'we have been able to do nothing further for the past two months.'

This comment led him to write his second note, which he entitled 'How to resuscitate a research group'. It was to the point, and displayed his habitual impatience and sarcasm in the face of inefficiency. The essence of it was that he wanted to put a stop to research personnel being used for fitting programmes when they should be working on research projects with priority. '6 testers from E. K. Cole and 6 from Pye would perform several hundred % more efficiently on what 80% of our group are trying to do now. That is, the acceptance of apparatus from these firms. The liaison would then be complete and the junk apparatus which Pyes are sending us would soon cease.' The actual fitting of equipment into aircraft could, he wrote, be done by Service fitters working from a prototype installation, and testing in the air could be undertaken by Service wireless personnel, all of whom could be trained in a very short space of time. This, he avowed, would release research personnel to get on with meeting other urgent war requirements and improving those systems already in or going into service. Lovell then advocated the removal of the research personnel to another, smaller aerodrome where 'we are not badgered and hindered by uninterested Group Captains and Wing Commanders. We should be given enough room, electric light, power and heat, and allowed to develop our ideas with close liaison with the Services to be sure we are approximately on the track of what they want.'

It was not to be long before Lovell and his fellow scientists got more or less what they needed, and it is clear that Blackett played an important part behind the scenes in pushing for the establishment of a major research group with its own flying-facilities for testing new ideas and for preparing prototype installations for successful inventions. But it was some time before Lovell achieved that close liaison between scientist and Royal Air Force operating commands which he was convinced was essential to solving the problems that faced aircrews in their efforts to win the war. In between times he was to suffer many disappointments, shocks and elations. The first of the shocks was a disaster which brought the war close to him for the first time, because it involved a personal loss. A Hudson aircraft, which was testing ASV equipment, crashed and killed Peter Ingleby and Beattie, the two young men he had brought with him from Manchester. Lovell was distraught. Death in this fashion was, until that moment, unknown to him. He had lost two friends and colleagues and, as he put it, 'it was tragic for two young men with such good brains, and with so much to live for, to be killed like this. It was such a waste.' Blackett was quick to write to Lovell a letter of sympathy, dated 11 January 1940. 'This is a terrible business,' he wrote, 'I do want to say how I feel for you in the awful shock it must have been for you. I only heard details today from Bowen. Don't let it get you down. It seems so much worse, just because, luckily, the war hasn't started, and it is not happening to hundreds of others. It is enormously important work that you are doing—even though so much is a muddle. I really think that conditions will improve soon. I have been doing all I possibly can to help push in the right direction. Write to me soon and tell me how you are and how things are going.' For the first time Blackett signed himself, 'Yours, Patrick Blackett.' He knew how emotional Lovell was, and he adopted the right note, so great was his sense of human understanding.

As the snow began to vanish, things improved, especially with the arrival of new research recruits to reinforce the team at St Athan. Amongst them were A. L. Hodgkin* and J. W. S. Pringle* from Cambridge; the former was to become President of the Royal Society, the latter Linacre Professor of Zoology, at Oxford. Then there was another visit by Blackett, this time accompanied by Tizard, the purpose of which was to emphasize the urgency of discovering means of eliminating the ground returns on the AI system which limited the range of detection of an enemy aircraft to the height of the fighter above the ground. The echoes from the ground were so numerous that if the fighter was flying at, say, 10,000 feet, it would be unable to detect the enemy at a distance of 10,000 feet or more away, because at that distance, and at greater distances, the echo of the enemy would be lost in the ground echoes. This was a serious limitation. A side line during the visit was Blackett's interest in Lovell's suggestions that when peace returned RDF should be used to detect the ionization from very large cosmic ray showers. Lovell had already suspected that these showers could be detected by using RDF techniques when he had observed unexplained sporadic and short-lived echoes on the RDF screens at Staxton Wold and other stations of the RDF chain. Now he had seen them frequently on the airborne RDF with which he was working at St Athan. For his pains, Blackett demanded of Lovell that he should undertake a serious study, with proper calculations, and submit a paper to him on the subject as soon as possible; this despite the fact that both he and Lovell were deeply immersed in wartime priorities at the time. Lovell did as he was bid and in 1941 a paper was published in the *Proceedings of the Royal Society* (Vol 177) entitled 'Radio Echoes and Cosmic Ray Showers' under the joint names of Blackett and

Lovell. It had far-reaching results, but the ideas deriving from these studies had to be shelved until the war was over. The immediate problem was that of improving the performance of AI, and it fell to Lovell and Alan Hodgkin to find the answer.

Work on eliminating, or at least substantially reducing, the effect of ground returns on the performance of AI began at St Athan, but the real effort took place at Worth Matravers near Swanage in Dorset. Early in 1940, in the absence of enemy bombing and, perhaps, in the vain hope that there would be none, the Air Ministry Research Establishment under A. P. Rowe was moved from Dundee to Worth Matravers where at the end of 1940 it was re-christened the Telecommunications Research Establishment, or TRE for short. In May the team which had been detached to St Athan also moved to Worth Matravers. Flying-facilities were available, according to the Director of Communications Development (DCD) at the Ministry of Aircraft Production, at an aerodrome at Christchurch in Hampshire. To Lovell's dismay, this 'aerodrome', when he eventually found it, turned out to be a small grass field with a few sheds containing one or two Tiger Moths. It was, in fact, a private flying-field, but Lovell and his team managed to fly their twin-engined Blenheims in and out during their experiments with AI. Proper flying-facilities were, however, soon to be provided at RAF Station Hurn, which was near Christchurch, and this became the first aerodrome to be devoted almost solely to experimental flying of RDF airborne inventions and to the prototype installations of those new systems which had been accepted by the RAF for future operational use. This unit was named the Telecommunications Flying Unit, or TFU.

The problems on AI led Lovell and Hodgkin to examine the possibilities of using centimetre wavelengths which could provide a means of transmitting a very narrow beam, thus largely reducing the interference from ground returns experienced on the wavelength of 1½ metres then being used for AI. Experimenting with 10 centimetres, first with a pumped klystron as a transmitter which they set up on the cliff site at Worth, and then with a prototype magnetron which was brought to them from Birmingham University, they achieved promising results. At this stage they came under Dr P. I. Dee* who had joined TRE direct from Cambridge, where he had been working with Rutherford on nuclear physics. At Worth Matravers, Dee was put in charge of a group to whom was delegated the task of producing an operational centimetric AI system and making fundamental investigations into the possible applications of centimetre wavelengths to other airborne RDF systems.

Throughout the remainder of 1940, and into 1941, Lovell concentrated on the centimetre AI development in conjunction with Hodgkin.

Lovell concerned himself particularly with the idea of using a paraboloid as the aerial, and this included a study of various materials for the construction of the aircraft nose, which was where the AI equipment had to be housed to meet operational requirements. At the same time Hodgkin hit upon the idea of using a spiral scanner as a means of overcoming the problem of achieving adequate sky coverage with a narrow beam. The first centimetre AI was airborne in a Blenheim early in 1941, and by the latter part of the year this equipment was in limited production and being introduced into operational night fighters as AI Mk VII. During this period, Lovell constantly obtained assistance from his former colleagues at both Bristol and Manchester with his researches into centimetre techniques, aerial arrays using parabolic mirrors—para-boloids—and the construction of complex pieces of equipment for his experiments specially designed to his specifications. He even obtained from Manchester a watchmaker's lathe and a small 1/8th h.p. single-phase motor which he required for his workshop. His 'scrounging' was endless, and always successful. When he arrived from St Athan at Worth Matravers, he came with a convoy of lorries loaded with equipment which he had obtained from the RAF stores at St Athan and which caused the envious eyes of those who had moved down from Dundee with very inferior equipment to boggle!

Almost immediately after Lovell's transfer from St Athan to Worth Matravers, Joyce followed him with Susan, now 2½ years old. They had quickly found a house to rent at 38 Rabling Road, Swanage. Then, on 6 June, Lovell received notification that he had been promoted to the rank of Scientific Officer with effect from 1 April, at a salary of £400 per annum. Finding a house was not difficult because in late May 1940 the south of England was rapidly becoming a restricted area due to the dramatic and alarming events on the continent of Europe. At dawn on 10 May the German assault on the West was launched. Within days the German armies had overrun Belgium, Holland and northern France. Within less than a month the British Expeditionary Force had been driven out of France at Dunkirk, Calais and Boulogne, and a few days later the British units in south-western France had also been withdrawn back to England. With the final collapse of France on 17 June, when the French asked the Germans for an armistice, the south of England had suddenly become the first line of defence, and there was extensive evacuation of civilian populations from these coastal areas.

Centimetre AI was not to occupy Lovell's talents for much longer, although he did develop a 'lock-follow' centimetre equipment which searched for and then locked onto an aircraft, the device being intended to produce a 'blind-firing' system. Strangely, this idea was to be adopted years later at the end of the war for the rear turrets of the heavy night bombers. However, by the spring of 1941, with the Battle of Britain over and won by the Royal Air Force fighter pilots and the RDF chain, and the German night bombing successfully stemmed by a combination of ground RDF and night fighters equipped with AI, the attention of the Government and the Chiefs of Staff was turned towards the battle against the German U-boats, cruisers and pocket battleships which were causing serious losses to convoys bringing essential supplies to Britain from the USA and other friendly countries, and to the transports conveying troops and materials to Gibraltar, Malta and North Africa. The second demand by the Government was for retaliatory offensive action against Germany, and RAF Bomber Command was the only possible instrument of war that could put this requirement into effect at this stage. Therefore the priorities for the scientists began to switch to offensive airborne RDF.

5

Research for Bomber Command

Winston Churchill's directive of 6 March 1941, which gave absolute priority to the Battle of the Atlantic, remained in force until July of that year, and during that period more than half the total bombing effort was directed against naval targets in support of Coastal Command's direct offensive against U-boats at sea using ASV.[1] Even before the Prime Minister's March directive, the effort against naval targets was considerable, with increased demands upon Bomber Command by the Admiralty for aerial mine-laying, the bombing of the German cruiser *Hipper* at Brest and the bombing of the Focke-Wulf bases at Bordeaux and Stavanger. On top of this came the requirement to delay the completion of the *Tirpitz*, under construction at Wilhelmshaven, which resulted in more than four hundred sorties being dispatched against this target in January and February 1941. This was a relatively small effort compared to the size of bomber raids that were to be mounted from the middle of 1942 onwards, but taken in conjunction with other Admiralty demands, and the small size of the total bomber force at that time, it represented a considerable proportion of the available effort. Finally, it was decided to divert the Blenheim squadrons of Bomber Command to coastal duties in the North Sea so that Coastal Command could be reinforced in the North-West Approaches.

Some of the weight of the attack under this new priority did, however, fall upon Germany itself, but instead of the Ruhr, Berlin or the various oil targets which had theoretically taken precedence, the weight of the offensive was directed against Hamburg, Bremen, Kiel and Wilhelmshaven, which were major ports with dockyards and naval construction facilities. At the same time, the Channel ports on the enemy-occupied coast were constantly attacked, with Brest receiving the giant share after *Hipper* was joined there by *Scharnhorst* and *Gneisenau*, two more of Germany's fast, modern battle-cruisers that were posing a serious threat to Britain's convoy routes. The bombing of the north German ports had some success and was certainly far more effective than the raids deep into Germany. Indeed, evidence was already accumulating to indicate that inland targets were not being found, and bombs were being dropped in

---

[1] RDF system for the detection of ships and submarines on the surface—Air to Surface Vessel.

the open countryside or, at best, in a very scattered pattern on the built-up areas of the towns where the main target was located. In fact, it was evident by the middle of 1941 that the policy of night bombing, which had by *force majeure* to be adopted because of the strength of the German defences, was successful only in moonlight and against targets which were easily identifiable by the presence of large stretches of water or relatively adjacent coastline. The truth was that the existing methods of navigation and navigational equipment were totally inadequate for operating over blacked-out territory in adverse weather conditions when the ground was obscured by cloud, or even in clear conditions when there was no moon to illuminate identifiable landmarks. This ineffectiveness of the bomber was not fully recognized, however, until late in 1941.

It was on 9 July that a new directive was sent to Sir Richard Peirse, the then C-in-C of Bomber Command, by the Air Staff, advising him that a comprehensive review had been made of Germany's political, economic and military situation. This had revealed that the weakest points in the enemy's armour lay in the morale of the civilian population and in his inland transportation system, the latter weakness arising from the very considerable extension of military activities due to Hitler's invasion of his erstwhile ally, Russia, on 22 June 1941. The directive then stated: 'I am to request that you will direct the main effort of the bomber force, until further instructions, towards dislocating the German transportation system and to destroying the morale of the Civil population as a whole, and of the industrial workers in particular.'

It was this directive, which turned Bomber Command onto targets deep in Germany, that began to reveal the inability of the bomber to find a town, let alone a precision target. In fact, it soon became apparent that Bomber Command was incapable of area bombing with any degree of success and had little chance of demolishing a specific target within a town area. Inaccurate navigation was the primary cause, followed by inaccurate bombing when, on rare occasions, the target was correctly located.

Recognition of Bomber Command's problems was essential if any successful offensive against Germany were to be mounted. By the middle of 1941 Wellington bombers were coming off production at a fast rate, and the new highly modern four-engined bombers, the Stirling, Halifax and Lancaster, were due to come into service at the beginning of 1942. In fact, the bomb-carrying capacity was rapidly becoming adequate for effective bombing, whilst the ability to deliver the bombs to the right place was still hopelessly inadequate. In some quarters, however, the process of recognition of the bombing problem had begun. At TRE a revolutionary navigational device known as GEE, which would enable the navigator of an aircraft to determine his exact position with a high degree of accuracy easily and quickly, had reached a stage of development when it was ready for operational trials. It had the major advantage that it required no transmission from the aircraft which would give away its position to the enemy. The system, which was developed by R. J. Dippy, consisted of three transmitters situated as widely apart as possible and transmitting pulse signals simultaneously. The centre station acted as a 'master', the other two being 'slaves', and the pulse signals from the 'slaves' were synchronized to those from the 'master'. The GEE apparatus in the aircraft received these signals, measured the difference in time of receipt between each 'slave' and the 'master' and thereby determined its distance from the 'master' and one 'slave' and from the 'master' and the other 'slave'. This in effect meant that the aircraft lay on a line of constant path difference between the 'master' and one 'slave' and on another between the 'master' and the other 'slave', and the point of intersection of these two lines indicated its exact position. Special maps were designed with many lines of constant path difference drawn upon them so that they looked as if they were covered with a lattice network. Upon these maps the readings from the instrument could be readily plotted. The system could be used in reverse by setting up the readings on the aircraft instrument of the point to

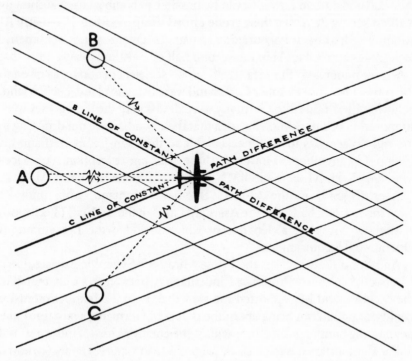

Fig. 1　The Gee fix

which the aircraft wished to fly and then 'homing' to that point by following the guiding indications on the cathode ray tube of the instrument. The system, although going a long way towards solving Bomber Command's navigational problems, had two major drawbacks. Its range from the ground stations, and therefore the shores of Britain, was limited to approximately 350 miles. This brought the Ruhr and parts of western Germany within range but left important more distant targets beyond its range. Moreover, it was recognized that signals from the system over Germany could be jammed, thereby reducing its effective range, and it was estimated that this could happen within six months of an aircraft carrying the apparatus being shot down over enemy territory.

GEE was not the only revolutionary device under development, or consideration, at TRE, but it was the most advanced, and by April 1941 it was ready for installation into Wellington aircraft of Bomber Command to be planned. By August sufficient aircraft of No. 115 Squadron had been equipped to undertake operational trials.

At TRE, as has been mentioned, Bowen and Lovell had, as early as 1940, the ambition to enable an aircraft to be navigated by a self-contained RDF device relying on information from terrain and town reflections as distinct from information from ground stations. Indeed, they had considered how it would be possible to bomb a target accurately without seeing it. Whilst their crude efforts using modified 1½-metre AI equipment had been encouraging, it was the emergence of centimetric techniques applied to AI in the second half of 1940 and during 1941 that gave real impetus to the idea. Even so, no serious attention was given to the subject because Bomber Command were living in cloud-cuckoo land, believing their raids into Germany were devastating the targets they were supposed to be attacking. The idea that their bombs were not dropping in the right place was totally unacceptable to the C-in-C, his staff and his Group Commanders. However, there was one exception, Air Vice-Marshal R. H. M. S. Saundby,* the newly appointed Senior Air Staff Officer (SASO) to the C-in-C Bomber Command, who, until 21 November 1940, had been the Assistant Chief of the Air Staff (Technical) at the Air Ministry, a department which included the Directorate of Operational Requirements.

Another disbeliever was the Prime Minister's Scientific Adviser, Lord Cherwell,* formerly Professor Lindemann. Cherwell was a champion of the bomber, and he supported the view that, even if a bomber offensive could not on its own bring about the defeat of Germany, a sustained and devastating bombing campaign against the enemy's cities of industrial and political importance was an essential prelude to victory. He also believed that the means of production could be destroyed not only by destroying factories but also by intimidating the workers and shattering their morale; and he regarded the installations for production of military requirements, and their associated workers and their homes, as legitimate targets in war. However, by the middle of 1941 he was convinced that the Bomber Force was not sufficiently large to destroy Germany quickly enough and, in addition, he was suspicious that, if it were, it would prove to be incapable of delivering its bomb loads with the required accuracy. He therefore decided that he must have evidence of the true accuracy of bombing before he could know how to help Bomber Command to become a highly effective weapon of offensive warfare.

With all the facilities available to Cherwell, and with his influence with Churchill, he was able to set in motion a most searching enquiry into the performance of the bombers. In the first half of August Mr Butt, a member of the War Cabinet secretariat, examined 650 photographs taken by night bombers during June and July on their bombing approach runs to their targets, fifty per cent purporting to be taken at the time of bomb release on the aiming-point, and fifty per cent being taken independently of bombing but naming the position that was believed to have been photographed in the target area. In addition, Butt studied summaries of operations, plotting reports and various other pertinent operational documents. His statistical conclusions were disquieting to say the least. They were as follows:

1. Of those aircraft recorded as attacking their target, only one in three got within five miles.
2. Over the French ports, the proportion was two in three; over Germany as a whole, the proportion was one in four; over the Ruhr, it was only one in ten.
3. In the Full Moon, the proportion was two in five; in the New Moon it was only one in fifteen.
4. In the absence of haze, the proportion is over one half, whereas over thick haze it is only one in fifteen.
5. An increase in the intensity of AA fire reduces the number of aircraft getting within 5 miles of their target in the ratio three to two.
6. All these figures relate only to aircraft recorded as *attacking* the target; the proportion of the *total sorties* which reached within five miles is less by one third. Thus, for example of the total sorties only one in five get within five miles of the target, i.e. within the 75 square miles surrounding the target.

The 650 photographs which Butt analysed related to 28 targets, 48 nights and 100 separate raids. In short, many of the aircraft then credited with attacking a target successfully had, in fact, dropped their bombs in open country. Indeed, Bomber Command was living in a fool's paradise.

Cherwell used the Butt report to convince Churchill of the supreme importance of improving the Command's navigational and target-finding facilities and, at last, a real priority was given to the development of RDF aids to meet Bomber Command's urgent requirements. He went further. Knowing that GEE was not the only RDF aid that TRE had considered, even if it was the only one that had been developed to a state of readiness for production and installation into aircraft, he recognized the necessity for a co-ordinating authority at the Air Ministry and in Bomber Command to direct the efforts of TRE in liaison with the Command. The fact was that some brilliant ideas were languishing in retarded development due to lack of interest by Bomber Command, and therefore lack of priority. When Churchill backed priority development of these RDF aids, Cherwell again moved behind the scenes and engineered the appointment of Sir Robert Renwick Bt* to co-ordinate the research, development and production of all RDF aids for aircraft on behalf of the Air Ministry and the Ministry of Aircraft Production (MAP). (He was brought into the Air Ministry and Ministry of Aircraft Production by Lord Beaverbrook, the then Minister of Aircraft Production.) This responsibility, as Cherwell realized, would tie in well with Renwick's other major task of progressing the production of the four-engined bomber aircraft—the Stirlings, Halifaxes and Lancasters.

Renwick assumed his new duties in October 1941. He recognized immediately, as had Cherwell, that he would need in the Command Headquarters an organization to plan and to co-ordinate the training of servicing personnel for these new systems, together with the training of navigators to operate the airborne equipments. Moreover, again like Cherwell, he was convinced that the successful development of aids to navigation and bombing would require a close liaison between the Command and TRE to ensure that operational requirements were properly understood by the scientists whose designs should be feasible for efficient production and within the capabilities of RAF technical personnel to maintain in serviceable order under operational conditions. He discussed these matters with Air Vice-Marshal R. H. M. S. Saundby, the new SASO, with whom he had had close contact previously when Saundby was at the Air Ministry as Assistant Chief of the Air Staff (Technical). Saundby was, above all others in the Command, the one man who was intent upon improving the capabilities of the bomber by modern techniques, because he had recognized that it could never fulfil its true role in war until it had at its disposal aids to night navigation and blind bombing far in advance of those available to it at the outset of war. As a result of these discussions it was decided to form an RDF Department at Bomber Command Headquarters at High Wycombe under the command of a Wing Commander who would report directly to the SASO.

I, was the officer selected for this new appointment of Wing Commander. I had previously served in France with an Army Co-operation Squadron in 1939 and 1940, then with a specialist night bomber unit which had been charged with the task of investigating from the air the German blind bombing beam system, and later bombing the enemy transmitters blind, using the Germans' own beams; finally I had been appointed early in 1941 to the Directorate of Operational Requirements at the Air Ministry to progress the development, production and introduction of all RDF aids to the Commands. In this last appointment, I had already been involved with the initial introduction of GEE to Bomber Command for operational trials. I was therefore known to Saundby and to Renwick and already had experience of TRE and its activities. In December 1941 I moved to High Wycombe to take up this new post.

Despite the apathy of Bomber Command, TRE had not been idle. But when the results of the Butt report were known to the scientists, revealing the critical situation of the night bombing efforts, it became a hive of activity in the interests of Bomber Command. On the last Sunday in October 1941, Dee, who with Lovell had been looking at a centimetre AI equipment which was set up on the ground above Swanage at Leeson Girls' School, where TRE was now established after moving from their cliff site at Worth Matravers, suddenly realized that the downward angle at which they were seeing echoes in the direction of the Isle of Wight on the cathode ray tube was not appreciably different from the downward angle from an aircraft when viewing towns or coastline at long range. Lovell had already examined the possibilities of terrain identification, when he was in Bowen's group at Perth and St Athan, using 5/10-metres equipment in an Anson aircraft as well as modified 1½-metre AI equipment. But now, with 10-centimetre equipment, the possibilities of seeing towns and coastlines on a cathode ray tube in the aircraft were immeasurably improved. Dee moved quickly. He immediately arranged for Dr Bernard O'Kane and Hensby, two of his assistants, to fly Blenheim V6000 with a helical scanning 10-centimetre AI, the scanner adjusted to give a depressed forward angle of view. On 1 November, the initial flight took place. The results caused considerable excitement; the photographs of the cathode ray tube demonstrated that a centimetre airborne RDF equipment could give discrete returns from certain areas of ground, such as towns, rivers, coastline and lakes, as distinct from the general ground returns. However, responses on the tube were comparatively numerous, and it was evident that many objects other than towns were giving responses. For example, a landing-screen near Salisbury gave a particularly strong response, as did the aerodrome and camp at Boscombe Down and other military camps on Salisbury Plain. But one photograph of Bournemouth was impressive. Dee placed it on the desk of A. P. Rowe, the Chief Superintendent of TRE, on the Sunday following this flight. It was still wet from the fixing-bath. And thus, a device which was to have a dramatic effect on the course of the war was born.

Rowe agreed immediately to Dee's suggestion that a special group within Dee's division should be set up under Lovell to concentrate on centimetre RDF for offensive purposes in Bomber Command. Events now moved swiftly. Without awaiting the issue of an official operational requirement from the Air Ministry, Lovell and his team began work on designing a system which would assist the bomber. Early in December I visited TRE to meet Dr Dee, and it was then that I first learnt about the new development. The system, which was then known as BN (Blind Navigation) but was later to be called H2S because Cherwell had nick-named it Home Sweet Home, was explained to me. It was as yet a crude system based on the same fundamental principle as radio-location in that it depended upon the fact that very high frequency radio waves travel in straight lines and, in the same manner as light, are reflected back from suitable surfaces in varying degree. With H2S, the reflections, commonly called 'echoes', could be picked up by a receiver and relayed to a cathode ray tube so that they showed as spots of light. The transmissions and echoes being extremely rapid, the picture presented to the operator would constantly record the features of the ground over which he was flying. By using a rotating aerial array or scanner, and by directing the beam of transmission downwards and rotating it through 360 degrees, the features recorded would be those all round and underneath the aircraft. More-over, by using a plan position indicator, where the time-base is like a clock hand rotating round and round, the aircraft's position would be at the centre of the cathode ray tube, and the features below the aircraft would be displayed around that centre. This concept of the system was Lovell's, arising from his imaginative approach to the problem which confronted a navigator at night. The picture, however, was not expected to be a replica of a map or of the detailed landscape which the eye normally sees. Rather would it be a series of spots of light of varying degrees of brightness which had to be understood, but which would be comparable to the map picture and could be correctly interpreted. There would be three distinct types of response, Dee explained, those produced by ordinary land, by water and by built-up areas such as towns. Water would be represented by a dark, shadowy effect, ordinary land by a slightly lighter response, and a town by a bright spot or area depending upon its actual size. The representation would correspond to the general shape of the objects seen. In particular, the contrast between land and water would be sharp, because land gave an appreciable echo whereas water reflected back very little signal. Therefore coastlines and inland waterways were expected to show up with a clear definition. With H2S, it was hoped that the navigator could have a continuously moving picture of the country over which he was flying up to any range because the system would be self-contained.

I asked about the bombing aspects and was told that facilities could easily be incorporated. For example, a line of light along the radius of the screen which would continuously indicate the aircraft heading, could be incorporated. Also, there could be facilities to make it easy to read the ranges of towns and landmarks from the aircraft. To meet all contingencies it would be possible to alter the area of the picture by a switch so that, if the requirement was for navigation, the operator could have a thirty-mile view all round; then by flicking a switch he could enlarge the picture scale for bombing and have a more detailed view of the country within, say, a radius of ten miles. The system could also include a radio altimeter for accurate measurement of the aircraft's height above ground. Whilst this appeared to be the ideal solution to Bomber Command's atrocious record of poor navigation and inaccurate bombing, it was clear that the system was still in a very crude state of development. Moreover, it was obvious that TRE needed close liaison with the Command to ensure the right direction of final development. On this score, Dee made a plea to me for early co-operation, and I assured him that this would be given.

One of the major problems facing Lovell and his team, Dee emphasized, was having to work with a transmitting valve known as the klystron, whereas they wished to use the magnetron, which would provide much more power and therefore ensure a better performance of the system. But the magnetron, a highly secret development, was the reason for the success of the new Mk V11 centimetric AI, and there was great reluctance to agree to its being used over enemy territory for fear that it should fall into enemy hands and be used in equipment against our own bombers. The use of the magnetron was, in fact, the subject of discussion at a meeting of the Secretary of State for Air held in the Air Council Room of the Air Ministry on 23 December, at which Dee and Lord Cherwell were present. Opinion was heavily against its use. This meeting took place a few days after I had visited Dee. It resulted in great despondency in Lovell's group. However, when Flight Lieutenant E. J. Dickie, a navigator with considerable operational experience who was on my staff, arrived at TFU Hurn on 5 January 1942 to fly in Blenheim V6000 in order to assess the equipment from an operational point of view, hopes were revived. Then, when after two flights of two hours each, accompanied by

O'Kane and Hensby, and piloted by Wing Commander Horner, he
compiled an enthusiastic report on the potential of H2S and offered
invaluable suggestions on the form of presentation and bombing-facilities
required, Lovell began to feel even better.

December 1941 had been a disastrous month in general. On Sunday
the 7th, Japan, without any declaration of war, attacked and destroyed the
greater part of the US Pacific Fleet in Pearl Harbor in an unprecedented
air raid. On the same day the Japanese bombed Hong Kong and
Singapore. Then on the 10th they successfully attacked and sank two of
Britain's major warships off Malaya, *Prince of Wales* and *Repulse*. On the
8th Britain formally declared war on Japan, and on the same date
Germany and Italy declared war on the USA. The effect upon Bomber
Command and indirectly upon those concerned with developing bomber
aids was curious. Both Air Chief Marshal Sir Charles Portal, the Chief of
the Air Staff, and Lord Cherwell, had persuaded Churchill that a more
aggressive C-in-C was required for Bomber Command. The man they
had set their eyes on was Air Marshal Harris,* formerly the Air Officer
Commanding No. 5 Bomber Group, later the Deputy Chief of the Air
Staff and now on a buying mission in the USA. During Churchill's visit to
the USA on 22 December to 14 January 1942, together with the Chiefs of
Staff, to set up with Roosevelt a Combined Chiefs of Staff Board, the
Prime Minister took the decision to have Harris sent home to take up the
appointment of C-in-C Bomber Command. On 22 February 1942 Air
Marshal A. T. Harris assumed command. A dramatic change in priorities
for TRE's bomber work was soon to follow.

On 13 February Dickie paid another visit to TRE and discussed with
Lovell a number of points on operational requirements for finalizing the
design of H2S from the point of view of the navigator, but much of what
was needed would be drastically limited, according to Lovell, if they were
denied the use of the magnetron. Prior to this, however, Lovell had been
proceeding apace with plans for installing an experimental equipment in a
Handley Page Halifax four-engined bomber, a type which was just going
into service along with Avro Lancasters and Short Stirlings. The Halifax
was chosen because, after a visit to the Aircraft and Armament Experimental Establishment, Boscombe Down, by Dee, Lovell, O'Kane and
Hensby, it was decided that it offered more alternative positions for the
scanner than the Lancaster or Stirling. The idea of a rotating scanner on
the underside of an aircraft, giving an all-round picture of the ground
below, had taken root. The interest in a forward-looking system in the
nose of an aircraft was on the wane. But tests of both were necessary, and
plans were afoot in January 1942 to have a Halifax aircraft modified to
take the scanner in a perspex cupola fitted to the underside, in place of the

gunner's under-turret, for the purpose of experiments. In his diary of events, Lovell says that, when the Handley Page Aircraft Company first heard of this proposal early in January, 'Mr Handley Page was given his first chance to wave his arms and declare that the performance of his aeroplane would be ruined beyond recognition! It was very difficult since we were not allowed to give one hint of what it was all about. However, as no one else knew a thing about it we had our way and persuaded them to put the scanner in place of the under-turret.' Two such modified aircraft were ordered for delivery to TFU Hurn, and astonishingly this was before an actual operational requirement for H2S had been submitted!

On 10 February 1942, Lovell telephoned his wife's home in Bath to which Joyce Lovell had retired for her second confinement. He was anxious to check up on how everything was going. To his great joy he learnt that he was the father of a son and that the mother was doing well. Bryan Lovell had joined the family.

Following on Dickie's conversations with Lovell on 13 February, I made an urgent trip to Swanage to see Dr Dee. I had been disturbed by Dickie's report that the H2S team were depressed over the official opposition to the use of the magnetron, because they were convinced that the system could never perform adequately with the klystron. On arrival at Leeson School, I was escorted straight to Dee's office where I was welcomed with a cup of tea and the warmth of the small stove in the corner of the office. It was a bitterly cold day. Never one to waste time, Dee asked his secretary to send for Lovell and then immediately embarked upon his problems. He was, as I already knew from Dickie, having the utmost difficulty in persuading the MAP and the Air Ministry that the magnetron was essential to H2S, and he emphasized the need for support from the highest levels in Bomber Command to obtain permission to use it. With H2S a beam of radio waves was directed downwards from the aircraft which, when striking water, was reflected away at an angle of 90 degrees to the line of strike; when impinging on dry land, was scattered in all directions, some reflections coming back towards the source of trans-mission; and when hitting vertical surfaces, such as built-up areas, was largely reflected back to the source of transmission. The problem was to get the reflections from distant objects, such as towns, back as far as the transmitter, and that problem resolved itself into one of power output. For a reasonable range and a strong H2S picture, it was necessary to have the power of the magnetron which was pre-eminently superior to that of the klystron. But the magnetron was the key to the success of the latest AI equipment, gun-laying devices and searchlight control and was likely to provide greatly improved submarine and ship detection equipment for Coastal Command. Because of all this, Dee explained, no one wanted to

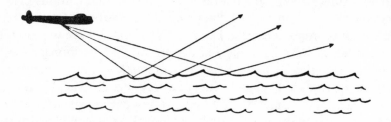

H2S beam strikes water. Energy is reflected away from aircraft

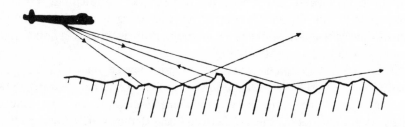

H2S beam strikes land. Some energy is reflected back to aircraft

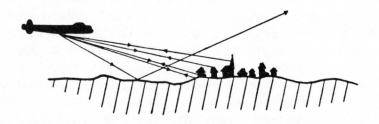

H2S beam strikes built-up area. Much energy is reflected back to aircraft

Fig. 2   Effects of different types of Earth surface on H2S beam

use the magnetron in any equipment which was to be flown over enemy territory for fear of giving the secret to the Germans.

Lovell arrived during my initiation into the birth-pangs of H2S, but I had my back to the door when he came into Dee's office and was not aware of his presence until I heard a strident voice express in no uncertain terms exactly what it thought of the MAP, the Air Ministry and anybody else who opposed the magnetron in H2S. It was apparent that H2S must have the power of the magnetron to be any good. It was also obvious that the voice was of the opinion that the Germans were probably trying to develop the magnetron themselves and, given time, might use it before we did. But if we used H2S with the magnetron in bombers, there would be no productive capacity left standing in Germany to make the things. If I remember rightly, the exact words were, 'the bloody things'. I turned to see the owner of these forthright opinions and beheld a man of medium height and slight build, with thinning hair. He had a sensitive face, keen eyes and a high forehead. I guessed him to be in his thirties but, in fact, he was in his late twenties. It was a dramatic figure. It was a dynamic personality!

At this meeting between Lovell, Dee and myself, I expressed the Command's views on the required performance of H2S to meet the bomber's needs. These included a range of 30 miles at 18,000 feet for really efficient navigation and target approach, with a very clearly defined picture at short ranges for bombing. Lovell was emphatic that such requirements could be met only by using the magnetron. The outcome of this unofficial conversation was that Bomber Command should accept two Halifax bomber aircraft, one equipped with klystron H2S and one with magnetron H2S, for comparative trials. These, when equipped and tested by TRE, should go to No. 1418 Flight, later to become the Bomber Development Unit, or BDU, which had been formed in Bomber Command at my instigation as an experimental unit for developing the methods of use of GEE and any other RDF airborne system to come the way of Bomber Command. It was an entirely new unit, having been officially established on 5 January 1942. The idea of two H2S Halifax going to 1418 Flight for Service trials, and for comparisons between the magnetron and the klystron, was immediately supported by Air Vice-Marshal Saundby, the SASO of Bomber Command, who despatched an official request to the Air Ministry, dated 16 March 1942, for two Halifax aircraft to be allotted to 1418 Flight for this purpose. At the Air Ministry this was supported by Sir Robert Renwick, and approval was given in a letter dated 26 March. But events were to overtake these plans, and the decision on the use of the magnetron was to be taken before the comparative trials in No. 1418 Flight could take place. Nonetheless, No. 1418 Flight did eventually undertake trials to develop techniques in the use of H2S.

One other product of our meeting was the liaison that was instantly created between the scientists and the Command, cemented by the beginnings of a friendship between Lovell and myself that was to endure throughout the years ahead. Indeed, during a subsequent visit to Swanage, I was to be invited to 38 Rabling Road, where I met Joyce Lovell and their two children, Susan, then aged 3½, and Bryan, who was but a few months old. This invitation perhaps implied that Lovell had at last conceded that not all Group Captains and Wing Commanders were uninterested persons specially designed to badger and hinder the scientists!

At twelve o'clock on a sunny Friday morning, 27 March, as Lovell noted in his diary: 'Halifax V9977 circled Hurn—the first of the H2Ss.' By the middle of April Lovell and his team had installed an experimental H2S using a magnetron transmitter/receiver box of the Mk V11 AI design into the aircraft, together with a Nash & Thomson hydraulic scanner in the cupola on the underside of the aircraft. On the evening of 16 April Halifax V9977 'took off for its first flight', Lovell wrote in his diary. 'Nothing worked because the 80 volt supply wasn't switched on. The equipment worked the next morning but only gave returns out to 4 or 5 miles at 8000 feet. Thus we became aware of our polar diagram problems.' Halifax R9490, the second to be allocated for these trials, had arrived on 12 April and was fitted with an electric scanner and EMI designed apparatus, but it was not until 2 June that it made its first flight and, as Lovell wrote in his diary, 'gave the same old succession of aerial troubles'. Many technical problems were expected, but what was not expected was that those who believed in the system would be out-numbered by those who thought it could never work and was therefore a waste of development effort. Dickie and I were amongst those who believed. Flights undertaken on 28 April in Blenheim V6385 with experimental H2S fitted with PPI presentation impressed us immensely. The picture showing an all-round view of the terrain below the aircraft was remarkable, although it was not clear enough for use by operational crews. In fact, it needed not only scientific interpretation but a good deal of imagination as well. Nonetheless, we could see the possibilities, and I kept up the pressure on the SASO, the new C-in-C, Air Marshal Harris, Sir Robert Renwick and Lord Cherwell to demand priority for its development and early production, and to press for permission to employ the magnetron.

In the meantime work on the design of an H2S equipment for factory production had proceeded with vigour under Lovell's tireless direction. Moreover, with the threat of a ban on the use of the magnetron, urgent development was undertaken to make a klystron which was suitable for use as a transmitter giving a peak output of five to ten kilowatts. In fact, many of the difficulties associated with the use of this valve were over-come, but to be able to have the best of all worlds, should the choice be left to him, Lovell produced an H2S which had interchangeable magnetron and klystron transmitter/receiver heads. It was typical of his ingenuity, perfectionism and technical cunning to have two strings to his bow. By the beginning of July such a prototype was ready. However, the battle of the magnetron was perhaps a small worry compared to a setback which was totally unforeseen.

In the latter half of May TRE moved from Worth Matravers to Great Malvern, where they took over Malvern College as their headquarters and for their research laboratories. The facilities and surroundings were infinitely more secure for their activities, being further away from enemy action, including the threat of infiltration by parachute troops and consequent sabotage. At the same time the Telecommunications Flying Unit moved from Hurn to Defford, a newly prepared aerodrome which lay within ten miles of Malvern. These moves occurred at the time when the first Halifax V9977 had had a number of alterations made to its magnetron H2S apparatus, following initial flights in April and May, and was ready for continuing trials. The move, however, put everything in a turmoil, but the eagerness of Lovell to get on with the job enabled time to be regained, and Halifax V9977 was ready for fresh H2S tests from Defford by the first week in June. Undoubtedly the whole of TRE had been stimulated during this period by a procession of Bomber Command successes which could be attributed to two factors, one being the new RDF navigation device, GEE, which by April/May was installed in nearly fifty per cent of the Bomber Force, and the other being the effect of the new C-in-C, Air Marshal A. T. Harris, who, with his SASO, Air Vice-Marshal Saundby, had applied new techniques of target-marking and bombing, made possible by GEE, on the nearer German cities. For the first time in the war, Ruhr towns had taken a battering, a fact proven by aerial photography. Then, on the night of 30–31 May, a bombing raid of unprecedented magnitude was mounted against Cologne when 1,046 bombers dropped 1,455 tons of high explosive and incendiary bombs within ninety minutes with devastating results. On Monday 1 June the newspapers headlined the news and there were hints of Britain's secret weapon. The release of news had been withheld until photographic reconnaissance had confirmed success, reporting a pall of smoke rising to 15,000 feet over the city which was obscuring detailed assessment of damage. Confirmation also came from Germany, whence intercepted messages indicated the initial incredulity that such a disaster could befall a German city from the air. Lastly, there was Churchill's message to the C-in-C Bomber Command which was prominently published in every newspaper: 'I congratulate you and the whole of Bomber Command upon the remarkable feat of organisation which enabled you to despatch over 1,000 bombers to the Cologne area in a single night, and without confusion to concentrate their action over the target into so short a time as one hour and a half. This

proof of the growing power of the British bomber force is also the herald
of what Germany will receive, city by city, from now on.'

The outstanding effect of these results at TRE was that upon those
groups engaged in the research and development of navigational and
bombing devices. In this '1,000 Raid' they saw the future of Bomber
Command crystallize into a solid fact, for they logically argued that no
other military force could possibly have brought about such a defeat upon
one of the enemy's largest and most important industrial centres so
swiftly, convincingly and economically. With their help, people like Lovell
and Dee recognized that Bomber Command could become the one
military formation capable of carrying the offensive into the heart of
Germany until such time as the continent of Europe could be invaded by
an Allied army and the Germans driven out of the occupied territories. It
was this knowledge, and the fact that Bomber Command was now recognizing the importance of TRE's contribution to its growing success, that
partly helped Lovell to face the disaster that was so suddenly to overtake
his latest efforts; partly, because, unquestionably, his tremendous courage
and determination in the face of adversity were of paramount importance.

On Saturday evening, 6 June, Lovell made his first flying-tests of the
modified one and only 10-centimetre magnetron H2S apparatus in
Halifax V9977, which, despite the disruption of the moves from Swanage
to Malvern and Hurn to Defford, he and his group had completed ready
for demonstration to Bomber Command within a few days of the originally scheduled date. All went well. Then on Sunday morning, 7 June,
three leading engineers from EMI, who were working on the production
of H2S and who were visiting TRE and TFU to see and discuss the
magnetron version, undertook a flight in the same aircraft in order to see
the prototype magnetron equipment in operation. They were Blumlein,
Browne and Blythen. With them, to demonstrate the apparatus, went
Hensby and Vincent of Lovell's group, and Squadron Leader Sansom,
who was my liaison officer on loan to Lovell. The aircraft was flown by
Squadron Leader Berrington with a crew of four. At 4.20 p.m., when
returning to Defford, Halifax V9977 crashed six miles south-west of
Ross-on-Wye and burst into flames. Every single person in the aircraft
was killed. Six men with all the detailed knowledge of H2S; six men with
the one and only magnetron equipment; six men with an accumulated
scientific knowledge of inestimable value; one moment they were there
and then, in a flash, there were only the charred remains of six men and
their crew of five.

It was an appalling moment for Lovell, for not only had the sweat and
the labour of the last weary months gone up in a puff of smoke, together
with irreplaceable brains, but colleagues who had become friends in the

unified work for the defeat of Nazism had met an untimely end. On the same Sunday evening, Lovell had to drive to the scene of the crash to recover as much as possible of the secret apparatus. 'It was a searing experience as a young man,' Lovell recalls. Once more he had experienced death at his elbow.

The only part of the H2S that was still recognizable was the magnetron. But throughout the remainder of June Lovell worked, almost single-handed, with a will and a determination that was truly miraculous. By the end of the month he was holding out hopes of having two more magnetron H2S sets ready for installation and flight trials, one with the interchangeable magnetron and klystron transmitter/receiver head for Halifax R9490 and one for Halifax W7711 which had arrived at Defford on 26 June to replace the crashed V9977. Sir Robert Renwick, the now powerful figure at the Air Ministry and Ministry of Aircraft Production, gave Lovell and his sadly depleted team every encouragement and ensured that they were able to obtain everything they required as a matter of priority, and Bomber Command loaned some personnel to assist in the recovery.

If the accident was not enough to disorganize and depress Lovell, another disruptive incident occurred just following the accident. The Americans, who had been examining the system in the USA, decided that it could never work and was doomed to ultimate failure. One of their scientists, the distinguished atomic physicist Dr Rabi,* who was on a visit from the USA to TRE, actually accused Dee and Lovell of personal responsibility for a mad enterprise which was unscientific, unworkable, and which could only result in the Germans being given the secret of the magnetron with no return for the Allies. The American recommendation was that all work on H2S should cease as it was wasting development effort that could better be concentrated on more fruitful schemes. The effect of this attack was most serious, because it gathered adherents from amongst some prominent British scientists and certain highly placed RAF officers at the Air Ministry. The effect upon Lovell was potent, and after urgent conversations with me, requested by Dee in order to report on these events, I returned to Bomber Command and in a minute in my D/O (demi-official) file I wrote: 'Lovell blew his top. He was like a wild beast. I told Dee and Lovell that proof of the practicability of H2S must be given by flight demonstration and therefore a prototype magnetron set must be completed with all possible speed. With Lovell in his present mood we will get one quickly—out of sheer bloody-mindedness!'

On 19 June the Air Ministry proposal for the formation of a 'Pathfinder Force' in Bomber Command was accepted by the C-in-C Bomber Command, and its newly selected Commander, Group Captain D. C. T.

Bennett,* was appointed. On Sunday 4 July I drove Bennett down to Defford to take part in the flying-tests of H2S which were to be on a comparative basis between the klystron equipment and the magnetron equipment. In his diary, Lovell states: 'Bennett stood by at Defford most of July and caused considerable turmoil. He seemed to be happy only when flying at 5.30 a.m. or midnight!' The first few flights with the klystron were a great failure, the range being severely limited and, at best, not more than twelve miles. Moreover, the signals were too weak to permit accurate interpretation of the picture on the cathode ray screen. But the first flights with the magnetron were as promising as the klystron was disappointing. Gloucester was seen at twenty-two miles range, and Birmingham was identified at nearly thirty miles, but interpretation still needed skill. However, the sharp contrast between land and water, as I reported after a flight which I undertook, resulted in coastlines being displayed with clear definition: '. . . the River Severn was discernible almost as far as Gloucester with the Severn Bridge plainly visible'. Perfectionist Lovell was, by contrast, highly critical of his baby. In his diary he wrote: 'It amazes us that so much of the country's effort is being taken up to make these equipments when the only ones flying are terribly bad. . . .' This self-criticism was not a feeling of failure but rather an inspiration to improve H2S in order to produce a near map-like picture, an ultimate conclusion to the development of the system which he had absolute confidence in achieving, provided that the decision of the 'powers that be' was for the klystron equipment to be dropped and for the magnetron equipment to be proceeded with for use in bombers.

   The battle over the magnetron was now rapidly coming to an end. The Secretary of State for Air called a meeting for 15 July at which a decision on the use of the magnetron was to be taken. Just prior to this meeting, Sir Robert Renwick and Air Vice-Marshal Saundby arranged for me to meet Lord Cherwell at Chequers, the Prime Minister's official country residence which was a few miles from Headquarters, Bomber Command, on 9 July. The purpose was to put the case of the magnetron equipment to Cherwell and therefore to Churchill. It was of importance to securing a favourable decision that Cherwell should be on the side of Air Marshal Sir Arthur Harris, the C-in-C (who had received the KCB in recognition of his success at Bomber Command immediately following the outcome of the '1,000 Raid' on Cologne). On 10 July Lord Cherwell, on a visit to Defford, indicated to Dee and Lovell that he was in favour of the magnetron. On the 14th, I submitted the report of the RDF Branch on the magnetron to the C-in-C, and on the 15th Bennett's preliminary report was also available in time for Harris to use at the Secretary of State's meeting. With the backing from Cherwell, Watson Watt and Renwick,

Harris won a decision for the magnetron H2S to be completed in development for use on operations in Bomber Command at the earliest possible moment. The further decision was taken that all work on the klystron version should cease.

The dangers of giving away the secret of the magnetron were accepted because it was felt that the effectiveness of bombing which Bomber Command would gain, would far outweigh the disadvantages of Germany's possibly acquiring the magnetron. In support of this there were also Cherwell's and Watson Watt's views that Germany might well be advanced in the development of the magnetron themselves, an opinion which Lovell had already expressed on several occasions. Strangely, all three were to be proved correct many years later. In April 1977, during a visit by Lovell to the radio telescope at Bonn in West Germany, he had dinner with the director, Professor Hachenberg. The conversation turned to the war years, and Lovell was astonished to discover that as a young research worker at Telefunken, Hachenberg had been the man who had scooped up the bits and pieces of the first H2S equipment to fall into German hands. Asked by Lovell if he had been amazed at the magnetron, he replied that he had not, because they had already developed the device themselves! What had baffled them, however, was the function of what seemed to be an empty glass tube. This was a simple gas-filled spark tube which enabled the same RDF (Radar) scanner to be used for transmitting and receiving!

6

Centimetres and Centimetres

The decision to concentrate on the magnetron H2S and Joyce's arrival
with Susan and Bryan from Swanage to Malvern to occupy their new
home, the ground-floor flat of a shabby Victorian house hastily converted
for the use of three TRE families, conspired to speed progress in finalizing the first version of H2S for Bomber Command. But despite
Churchill's demand at a meeting he had summoned on 3 July 1942, some
ten days before the decision had been taken on the magnetron, that two
squadrons of four-engined 'heavies' were to be ready by the autumn, it
was the beginning of 1943 before H2S was first used on operations. In the
interim a great deal of work was done to improve the system, to develop
techniques in its use, to train navigators in its operation and to train RDF
mechanics to service the equipment.

On 10 August the Germans began to jam GEE successfully. Whilst it
was still usable over Britain and over the Channel and North Sea, its use
over enemy-occupied territory and Germany was gravely impaired. By 16
August the Bomber Command RDF Branch, in conjunction with TRE,
had developed an anti-jamming device which greatly reduced the effectiveness of the German countermeasures and restored the use of GEE as
far as 08.00 degrees East. By the morning of 21 August, after a remarkable emergency plan for the Bomber Command RDF organization to
modify the bombers with the anti-jamming device, six hundred sets had
been modified. But it was quickly evident that the provision of a navigational and bombing system independent of ground stations was a matter of
top priority. Whilst the use of GEE had been partially restored, the major
part of enemy territory which had previously come within its range was
now beyond its effective coverage.

Progressing of H2S immediately became a major concern of Sir Robert
Renwick, who held regular meetings to co-ordinate the needs of Dee and
Lovell and to hasten modification on the production line of the Halifax,
Stirling and Lancaster four-engined heavy bombers to take the equipment. These were the aircraft which had just come into service at the
beginning of the year. I attached a few NCOs and men to the H2S group
at Defford, not only to assist Dee and Lovell in completing development
of the first mark of this equipment but also to take part in installing the
device into the first aircraft for the newly formed Pathfinder Force, a task
which, for the sake of speed, had been accepted by TRE. These Bomber

Command men were then to proceed to the H2S squadrons and there organize the maintenance at their operational stations. At the same time as this was happening, trials on the use of H2S were being conducted at the Bombing Development Unit (BDU), formerly No. 1418 Flight, the first H2S Halifax having arrived at Gransden Lodge aerodrome, the BDU base, on 30 September. The decision had been taken to equip No. 7 Stirling Squadron and No. 35 Halifax Squadron in the first instance, and fitting and training had proceeded as fast as availability of apparatus permitted—without awaiting the results of the BDU trials. Quite apart from continued development work, Lovell and Dee took responsibility for, and organized, the 'crash' fitting programme. By the end of 1942 only fifty H2S sets out of the target number of two hundred had been produced, and therefore Lovell's fitting programme was delayed, but even so, by the end of December 1942 twelve H2S Halifax aircraft had been delivered to No. 35 Squadron, and twelve H2S Stirling aircraft to No. 7 Squadron. The fifty sets came from EMI, the number being in accordance with their promise. The outstanding 150 sets were due from the MAP Radio Production Unit, which failed to deliver even one by the scheduled date!

By the end of November the BDU trials had been completed and their report had been submitted to Headquarters Bomber Command for the attention of the Air Staff. It indicated that H2S showed great promise. As a result, Air Vice-Marshal Saundby despatched a copy to the Air Ministry with a covering letter requesting permission to operate with the H2S magnetron over Germany as soon as the Pathfinder Force had one squadron equipped and trained. I promptly visited Dee and Lovell at TRE to discuss Saundby's letter. Dee had just received a letter from a member of the British Air Commission in America, describing a flight he had made in the USA with H2S in which he had carefully manipulated the gain but had failed to detect any distinction between town and ground. When I arrived, Bernard Lovell was indulging in some pretty scathing remarks about the person in question.

My news on Bomber Command's attitude towards H2S as a result of the trials quickly dispelled the clouds. When they reached that part of the letter which stated that it was considered that H2S fitted with the magnetron valve would be invaluable for the location and effective bombing of targets under all conditions of visibility, Bernard Lovell began to look like a cat with a bowl full of cream! In this letter, which I had prepared for Saundby myself, we went even further. We said that the accuracy of this equipment had proved to be so great that consideration should be given to its use in its present form, as soon as one squadron of the Pathfinder Force could be equipped, for the purpose of marking particular targets for the Main Force to attack. It was emphasized that the use of H2S in small numbers at an early date would increase immediately the ability of our bombers to attack, effectively, important targets at long range during the period of the year when the night hours were long enough to permit the bombing of the more distant objectives. The letter finished with a plea for an improved version of H2S, modified to give a more permanent picture and more simplified operation, for use in all aircraft. It was the Command's view, in fact, that the trials completed to date indicated that, if all aircraft were equipped, any target within flying-range could be located and successfully attacked irrespective of visibility conditions over enemy territory. Lovell fully accepted the implied criticism of the existing system; it coincided with his own opinion. The fact that Bomber Command accepted this 'poor performance', as he described it, and were anxious to use the equipment immediately, pending improvements being made at a later date, inspired him to even greater efforts to give the Command what it needed.

On 8 December, following Saundby's letter, the Secretary of State for Air, Sir Archibald Sinclair, held a meeting to discuss Bomber Command's request to begin operations over Germany with the magnetron H2S forthwith. At this meeting it was agreed by the Combined Chiefs of Staff that authority should be given for such operations at any date after 1 January 1943. The reluctance to use the magnetron over enemy territory had weakened considerably with the change in the war situation. With the dawn of 1943 Germany's position had altered decidedly for the worse. Serious reverses were being suffered by the German forces in North Africa and the Western Desert following the Allied invasion of North Africa on 8 November 1942, and Montgomery's drive across the desert from El Alamein. Also in November, the German defeat at Stalingrad brought their advance into Russia to an abrupt end, and this was followed by a successful counter-offensive launched by the Soviet forces in the Caucasus which, in late December, resulted in considerable advances between the Don and the Donetz. Now, therefore, was the time to strike hard at Germany, and the view was taken that Bomber Command should have everything it needed to enable it to strike successfully.

But the Secretary of State for Air made one proviso: the fitting-programme for 10-centimetre ASV for Coastal Command was not to be disturbed. This equipment, which Lovell had also developed, was an adaptation of H2S used for hunting down enemy ships and U-boats when surfaced at night for re-charging their batteries. It was a vast improvement on the 1½-metre ASV, which was still in use, in that it gave a better performance and was less easy to detect—the Germans had already developed 'listening' devices which could detect the 1½-metre equipment and therefore give crews adequate warning of the approach of the attacking aircraft. This decision meant that it would be doubtful whether No. 35 Squadron could be equipped in January with sufficient H2S Halifax aircraft to provide adequate backing for the initial twelve already delivered. This difficulty was, in fact, resolved by Bomber Command being provided with sufficient sets to install, themselves, using their own special fitting-parties. But the real sting in the tail was the C-in-C's extraordinary and sudden decision to express his view at the meeting that he was doubtful if it would be necessary, or possible, to equip all aircraft, and that if the Pathfinder Force only was equipped, the Command's objective would be largely achieved. It was an unfortunate judgement because, although Air Marshal Sir Arthur Harris was soon to change his mind, due to the influence of Saundby, his SASO, who had in turn been influenced by the RDF Branch, the priority for H2S in Bomber Command slipped in favour of 10-centimetre ASV for Coastal Command. In addition, a smaller production of sets was planned and, temporarily, TRE lost interest. This situation was not easily reversed and Bomber Command had to wait longer for its entire force to be equipped, and to receive a greatly improved system, than would otherwise have been the case.

On the night of 30–31 January H2S was put to the test on operations. The target was Hamburg, and six Pathfinder Halifax aircraft from No. 35 Squadron and seven Pathfinder Stirlings from No. 7 Squadron, all equipped with H2S, were given the task of marking the target for the Main Force of bombers. There was no moon, and visibility conditions over the target, as expected, were such that visual identification was almost impossible. The actual report on weather by crews was summed up in my note on the first operational use of H2S: 'Heavy static was reported and over the Dutch coast much cloud was encountered up to 20,000 feet with severe icing. In the target area itself there was little cloud, but ground haze and the absence of any moon made visual identification almost impossible.' Lovell, determined to be present at the take-off, return and interrogation of crews on this epic night, arrived at No. 35 Squadron's base at Graveley in time to attend 'briefing' before take-off. Dickie and I went to No. 7 Squadron at Oakington for the same purpose. At Defford, J. A. Richards, Robinson, Bert Hinckley, Ramsay and Hillman, all members of Lovell's team, huddled round an old oil-stove in their laboratory waiting all night for news of the raid. Dee, too, waited impatiently at his home in Malvern. There was tension. Many reputations were at stake. In his diary Lovell describes that occasion:

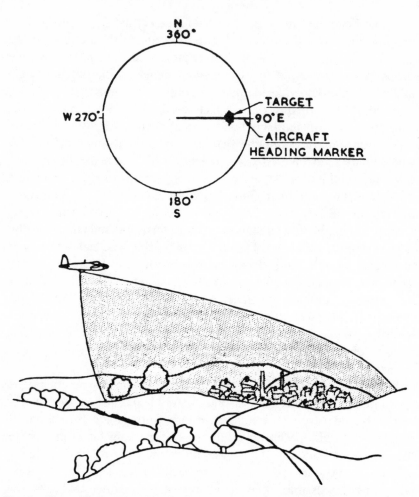

Fig. 3 Type of response from built-up areas seen on cathode ray tube of early
Mks of H2S

Shortly before midnight on January 30th, 1943, seven Stirlings took off from
Oakington and six Halifaxes from Graveley to mark Hamburg. The weather
conditions were appalling and at 6 a.m. the next morning the whole affair
seemed to be a shambles—83 Squadron had never taken off due to a
Mosquito pranged on the runway, 35 Squadron were landing away from base,
a large number of the Main Force returned early and 3 Stirlings (H2S) and 4
Halifaxes (H2S) were already back due to weather or breakdowns (H2S
equipment). It was all terribly depressing but at last one fellow came back in a
Halifax in a fairly high degree of excitement saying he had got it bang on, he'd
been able to see the docks and so on (on H2S). Finally it wasn't too bad and
when day dawned 4 Stirlings and 2 Halifaxes were back having done their job
well.

At Oakington, Dickie and I were more sanguine about the results. When the first H2S aircraft returned, the crews were enthusiastic. They reported that they had had no difficulty in identifying Heligoland, Zwolle, Bremen, Zuider Zee, Den Helder, East and North Frisians, Cuxhaven and Hamburg itself. The average range at which towns were identified was about twenty-three miles, the maximum being thirty-three miles and the minimum 11½ miles. Coastlines, estuaries and rivers were described as appearing on the cathode ray screen 'like a well-defined picture of a map', and the six navigators who reached the target claimed positive identification of the docks, stating that they appeared as 'fingers of bright light sticking out into the darkness of the Elbe'. There was an amusing coincidence on that very morning of 31 January which delighted Lovell. Dee received a letter from America deploring the continued support being given to H2S and suggesting that the time was 'now ripe for settling the controversy as to whether this device will or will not work by doing some scientific measurements'.

Three more raids led by H2S followed hot on the heels of the first. On 2-3 February the target was Cologne, and the number of H2S aircraft marking for the Main Force was ten; on 3-4 February Hamburg was again attacked, led by eleven H2S aircraft; on 4-5 February the raid was against Turin in northern Italy, and the marking was undertaken by eight H2S aircraft. The success of the system was amply proved on each occasion, and it was apparent that a revolutionary device had made its début in the air. Certainly a secret weapon of enormous potential had been introduced into Bomber Command and had shown immediate promise of making the power of the bomber a decisive factor in the war. But its true success still lay in the hands of Lovell, for he did not sit back in satisfaction. Instead, he strove to make H2S display to the navigator as near as possible a perfect replica of the terrain over which the aircraft was flying.

On 9 February 1943 a 'Memorandum on Operational Use of H2S' was prepared by myself and my staff and issued on that date with the approval of Air Vice-Marshal Saundby. It summarized the four operations, covering weather, technical efficiency with an analysis of failures of the equipment in flight, operational effectiveness, bombing effectiveness and conclusions on reliability and recommendations on some features of the installation. For instance, re-design of the scanner system was required to prevent gaps in the picture appearing at heights of 20,000 feet and above, the scanner having been designed originally for a maximum operational height of 15,000 feet. The Halifax aircraft had flown at 18,000 feet and above, and with H2S soon going into the Pathfinder Lancasters, whose operational height was as much as 22,000 feet, it was essential to design for much greater heights than had been required for the initial production. The conclusions at the end of the memorandum were, however, that part of the report which brought the greatest satisfaction to Lovell:

12. *Operational*

(a) H2S in its present form fully meets Air Staff requirements and has exceeded expectations in that towns have proved easy to identify both by shape and relative positions. In addition to the exceptional value of H2S for identification and bombing of the target, its great navigational value has been proved beyond all doubt. The recognition of islands, coast lines, estuaries and lakes has been particularly easy. In fact the problem of accurate navigation under almost any weather conditions is solved by H2S when operated by a trained navigator.

(b) The ease with which targets have been identified and attacked proves that if this device were introduced into as many heavy bombers as possible it would greatly increase the destructive power of the bomber force and considerably reduce the restriction imposed on operations by adverse weather conditions.

On 16 February Air Vice-Marshal Saundby held a meeting at Headquarters Bomber Command to review the RDF requirements for bombers. It was agreed that there were considerable advantages in equipping the Main Force aircraft with H2S, whilst retaining the system of marking targets by the Pathfinder Force. Amongst those that Saundby enumerated was the reduction of the risk of the Main Force being led astray by pyrotechnics fired by the enemy, by decoy fires or by false markers. His most important point, however, was that, with H2S, the Main Force would have a navigational aid which would enable aircraft to reach their target area accurately and at the correct time, and so benefit fully from the Pathfinders' markers. Then, on 21 February, Saundby having prevailed upon Air Marshal Sir Arthur Harris, the C-in-C, to change his mind, a letter was despatched to the Air Ministry stating the Command's requirement for the introduction of H2S into all Lancaster and Halifax aircraft as standard equipment at the earliest possible date. Stirlings were left out of the requirement because they were being phased out of production due to their great inferiority to the Avro Lancaster and the Handley Page Halifax.

Although H2S had started its career so successfully, its full value was yet to be realized. Operational experience had long since proved to be the only sound method for evaluating a new system, and for initiating and inspiring the efficient and rapid further development of such a system to meet comprehensively the stringent requirements of the Bomber Force. In fact, no sooner had H2S embarked upon a life in the squadrons under rigorous conditions than its shortcomings became instantly apparent. No

1   Emily Laura Lovell (née Adams), Bernard Lovell's mother, shown centre as Captain of Kingswood Ladies' Cricket Team prior to World War I

2   Bernard Lovell 1919/20

3   The wedding of Joyce Chesterman and Bernard Lovell, 14 September 1937

4 An Avro Lancaster, showing cupola on the underside housing the H2S scanner—at Defford, 1943

5 Close-up of the cupola housing H2S scanner on the Avro Lancaster

sooner had its immaturity, both technical and operational, revealed itself than Lovell and his team, in co-operation with the RDF team at Bomber Command, were renewing their efforts to make H2S the complete answer to a bomber's prayer. Indeed, a new development was swiftly started to answer the Command's request for a clearer picture and a more exact replica of the topographical features below the aircraft. At the beginning of 1943 Lovell took the initial steps towards developing a 3-centimetre H2S, to be known as X-band H2S.

Bomber Command requirements were not Lovell's only responsibility. ASV on 1½ metres had been effective in hunting down the German U-boats when they surfaced at night to re-charge their batteries. In conjunction with a powerful searchlight with a flat-topped beam and an azimuth spread of about 11 degrees which was mounted in a retractable cupola on the underside of the fuselage, the 1½-metre ASV had proved to be a grave shock for the enemy. The ASV and this light—known as the Leigh Light after its inventor—were fitted in Vickers Wellington aircraft. Previously, the aircraft homed onto the U-boat and then searched for it in the dark, and since it was no easy matter to spot such a relatively small object on the water at night, a successful attack was rarely made. With the Leigh Light, however, when the aircraft had homed onto the enemy, the searchlight was switched on at about a mile distant from the target. With the operator controlling the azimuth and elevation of the searchlight beam, the U-boat could be quickly illuminated and the dropping of depth charges carried out under conditions almost as good as in daylight. However, by late 1942 the Germans had developed a listening-device which could detect the 1½-metre ASV transmissions and therefore give the U-boat crews ample warning of the approach of an aircraft and plenty of time to dive. The result was that the effectiveness of ASV was rapidly diminished, whether used by day or by night, and there was an urgent demand to find a way of circumventing the enemy's newly found counter-measure to ASV attacks. The one obvious technical solution was to change the wavelength of the transmissions, but for this to be more than just a temporary measure demanded a major change. Lovell had the answer—a 10-centimetre ASV. In fact a 10-centimetre version of ASV had been under development in TRE before H2S, having arisen from the work on a 10-centimetre AI in 1940 and 1941 for Fighter Command, but due to the greater priority given to H2S during 1942, centimetre ASV had slipped backwards. Moreover, its progress was not helped by a curious lack of co-operation with TRE on the part of Coastal Command. Never-theless, the ingenious Lovell had designed a 10-centimetre H2S so that it could be used as ASV with certain modifications, and in the summer of 1942 the project of what was known in TRE as H2S/ASVS was begun. At

the same time another centimetre ASV development, known simply as
ASVS, was in progress by another group in TRE, but it was obvious that
with the pressure on the development and production of H2S in 1942,
H2S equipments for conversion to H2S/ASVS were certain to be available long before the alternative version, particularly as EMI had largely
mastered the initial production problems by the autumn of 1942, whereas
Ferranti's, who were to make ASVS, had not started on a centimetre
equipment. The main difference between the H2S as fitted in Lancasters
and Halifax aircraft was in the scanner. In the Leigh Light Wellingtons,
the only possible position for the scanner was in a 'chin' under the nose of
the aircraft, which entailed a re-design to an aperture of 28 inches instead
of 36 inches, together with certain other adjustments necessitated by the
operational height for chasing U-boats being 2,000 instead of 20,000 feet
as required by Bomber Command.

Because of the loss of certain refinements in the H2S/ASVS development which had been promised with ASVS, Coastal Command were
highly critical. But the main issue at stake was that of defeating the
German capability of being able to listen to the approach of existing
1½-metre ASV, and it was obvious that H2S/ASVS could be in operation
months before ASVS. Despite criticism from the C-in-C Coastal, Air
Chief Marshal Sir Philip Joubert de la Ferté, and his Chief RDF Officer,
Sir Robert Renwick took the bull by the horns and, at the end of
September 1942, enforced a decision to drop ASVS in favour of H2S/
ASVS, later designated ASV Mk III. By 30 January 1943 there was one
Wellington with a prototype installation of a 10-centimetre ASV at the
RAF Coastal Command Station at Chivenor in Devon and two further
Wellingtons awaiting fitting. By 15 February there were seven
Wellingtons there, and Lovell sent two of his team, Hinckley and Mould,
to assist with the installation of ASV Mk III into these aircraft and into the
further five Wellingtons, making twelve in all, which had arrived at
Chivenor by 27 February. Hinckley and Mould also had the task of
instructing the RDF mechanics of the RAF on how to maintain the
equipment. On 1 March, thanks to Lovell's efforts on development and to
his remarkable organization of the initial fitting programme, the first two
ASV Mk III Wellingtons were able to take off from Chivenor for the first
Bay of Biscay patrol with 10-centimetre ASV. On the same night, 302
heavy bombers of Bomber Command bombed Berlin, the target being
marked for the first time by H2S aircraft of the Pathfinder Force. It was a
kind of 'Spring Double' for Lovell. Although the Bay patrol produced no
'sightings', the bomber raid on Berlin was highly successful, as evidenced
by photographic reconnaissance on 3 March and subsequent photographic coverage taken later in the month. But it was also apparent that

once over a vast built-up area of the size of Berlin, the H2S was incapable of locating particular areas within the city. Even the large lakes and other waterways were indiscernible due to saturation from echoes of the built-up area. For Berlin to be a good H2S target, a greatly improved degree of resolution was required. Even so, the system emphatically proved itself as an excellent navigational device. By contrast, the ASV Mk III produced exceptional results. On 17 March the first U-boat was sighted at a range of nine miles, but since there was a failure of the Leigh Light, no attack was made. The following night a second sighting was made at seven miles, and this time the Wellington made the approach onto the surfaced U-boat, which made no attempt to submerge until suddenly illuminated by the Leigh Light. Six depth-charges were dropped and a kill was claimed. During March a total of thirteen sightings and attacks were made, followed by twenty-four in April. The successful night attacks by the ASV Mk III/Leigh Light aircraft so unnerved the U-boats that they began surfacing in daylight to re-charge their batteries during the Bay transit. By May, every U-boat crossing the Bay was attacked, and the rapid decline in British shipping losses between the United Kingdom and the Mediterranean was dramatic. Indeed, by the middle of 1943 Hitler was constrained to announce: '. . . the temporary setback to our U-boats is due to one single technical invention of our enemies.'

Lovell's development of a basic centimetre apparatus which could be readily completed as an H2S set for Bomber Command or an ASV set for Coastal Command, proved to be an exceptionally shrewd decision. Certainly it made production much more efficient, but it had another asset. There were many estimates, mostly pessimistic, about the length of time it would take the Germans to develop a listening device to detect 10-centimetre transmissions, and there was some justification for Coastal Command's fears because of the use of H2S over enemy territory and the known losses of some bombers equipped with the system. It was perfectly reasonable, in fact, to assume that the Germans had or would soon discover the wavelength upon which H2S was operating and would therefore develop 10-centimetre listening-devices which they might well try out in U-boats. The idea of a listening- or homing-device to enable the night fighter to locate and track down the bomber was also recognized but was regarded as likely to be less effective than the German night fighters' equivalent of AI which was known to be in service. Bomber Command's urgent requirement as regards H2S was therefore confined to improved definition of picture, whereas Coastal's was for yet another change of wavelength the moment there was evidence of 10-centimetre listening. Lovell had the answer to both causes with 3-centimetre transmissions. For the bomber, 3 centimetres would provide a much narrower beam width rotating round and round and would thereby provide a more detailed picture, because where the beam width of the 10-centimetre H2S illuminated two objects on the ground together and therefore displayed the two separate responses as one echo on the cathode ray tube, the narrow beam width of the 3-centimetre H2S would illuminate the two objects on the ground separately and therefore display the two separate responses as two separate echoes on the tube (see Figure 4). Development of the 3-centimetre H2S and ASV, which had been under way with much enthusiasm by Lovell and his team, backed by Bomber Command, suddenly got an extra boost from Coastal Command, and the priority increased. But in between times much was done to improve the performance of the 10-centimetre H2S. In particular, the improvement in performance due to a change in the aerial system from dipole to waveguide feed, resulting from work done on the aerial system by Ramsay and Hillman, two of Lovell's team, was outstanding. It not only gave better coverage at 20,000 feet, eliminating gaps in the picture, but the reduction

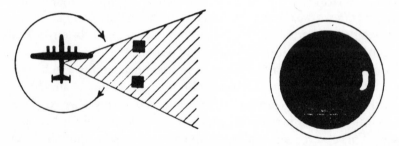

Wide beam of 10 centimetres. H2S displays two separate responses as one echo on the cathode ray tube

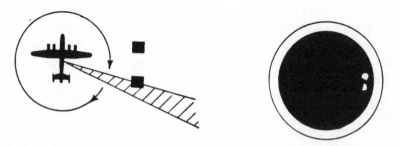

Narrow beam of 3 centimetres. H2S displays two separate responses as two separate echoes on the cathode ray tube

Fig. 4 Differing beam widths with H2S

in the beam width, though not as great as with 3-centimetre H2S, improved definition considerably. Bomber Command was impressed and immediately following demonstrations wrote to the Air Ministry requesting that these changes to design be incorporated on the production line as a matter of urgency. On 29 May Renwick held a meeting at which the modification was approved.

In March, April and May, H2S had been taking second place to another device known as OBOE. This was a system whereby the aircraft could be guided over a target by ground stations in this country and be instructed when to release its bombs. Its accuracy was of a very high order, and tests proved that two OBOE ground RDF stations could control an aircraft flying at 30,000 feet and 250 miles away so that it would release its bombs to fall within 120 yards of a selected spot. But it had its limitations. A pair of ground stations could operate only one aircraft at a time, and range was restricted to a maximum distance of about 300 miles (see Fig 5). Even so, used for marking-purposes on Ruhr targets, it was a formidable weapon, and in the spring months of 1943, with the nights shortening, Bomber Command turned its attention to the short-range Ruhr towns. This Ruhr campaign was highly successful and brought near-disaster to Germany, but for Bomber Command it had its attendant losses; and these were rising to figures which gave cause for concern. In the four months from 1 January to 30 April the losses were 584 aircraft, which included 92 lost on mining operations. This level of just over 4 per cent of sorties flown was disturbing, bearing in mind that the lighter summer nights and the better weather, which favoured the enemy night fighter, were fast approaching. Moreover, it was known that the Germans had put a top priority on night defence and had increased their fighter force and greatly improved their night fighter equipment. Also, it was known that they were beginning to use large numbers of single-seater day fighters for flying into the bomber stream under their own RDF control and relying on the fighter's ability to make a visual attack under the lighter night conditions. Examination of damaged bombers indicated that these attacks were generally being made from astern and from underneath, taking advantage of the better chance of seeing the bomber silhouetted against the night sky.

An equipment had been designed to give the bomber warning of the approach of an aircraft on its tail by employing the technique used in the original AI system. It consisted of a simple pulse transmitter sending out pulse signals in a cone from the tail of the bomber so that the echo of another aircraft coming within the range and coverage of the transmission would be received back in the bomber on a special receiver which converted the echoes into warning 'pips' that could be heard on the bomber's inter-communication system. It was a nice idea, but it had

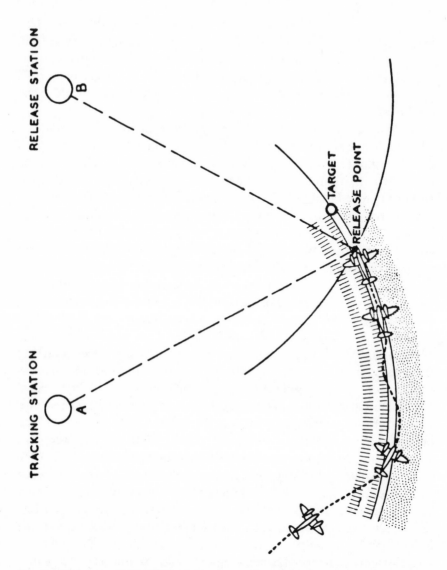

Fig. 5 Diagram of OBOE bombing approach to the target

fundamental disadvantages. When the bomber was flying in the bomber stream, the device 'pipped' incessantly, since so many friendly aircraft were inevitably cruising along in the cone of search of Monica, as the device was named. Moreover, it was impossible to calculate from which angle the unknown aircraft was approaching and to gauge its range or closing-speed. As a result, bomber crews were finding the device more of an embarrassment than a help, and many were therefore leaving it switched off when on operations.

Defence of the bomber was of the utmost importance. Aircraft could be replaced reasonably easily, but crews were indispensable. Survival through a large number of sorties was the means of gaining experience and improving the standard of accurate bombing. If Bomber Command was unable to maintain a large proportion of experienced crews, then the bombing efficiency was bound to drop below that high standard required to annihilate Germany in the shortest possible time. Germany knew this well and was determined to destroy both the quality and the quantity of Britain's only offensive weapon.

On Sunday 18 April, I visited Lovell at TRE to discuss the progress being made with the development of the new 3-centimetre version of H2S for Bomber Command. The first experimental flight had taken place on 11 March in Stirling N3724 and the results, as reported by I. J. Beeching and Rix, the two observers, had been most encouraging. But on this occasion my mind was more on the problem of the defence of the bomber than upon the subject which was the official purpose of my visit. It was a beautiful day, and at the end of the afternoon Lovell drove me up to the Westminster Inn, where he parked the car, and we then walked up to the Beacon high above Great Malvern. We spoke very little until we reached the top, where we stood and gazed eastwards. It was then that I told Lovell of the Command's worries about its losses. Lovell asked about Monica, and I told him that it was useless because it 'pipped' all the time in the bomber stream and gave insufficient information to the crew to be of any value. I added that the Command had asked for urgent development of a suitable defence device and had been told by the Air Ministry that the RDF-controlled gun-turrets with automatic aiming and firing at an unseen enemy would solve all Bomber Command's problems. This was the device known as AGLT (Air Gun Layer Turret), which was under development at TRE in Dee's Division by Hodgkin. Lovell observed that that was unlikely to be ready for at least a year. 'I know,' I said. 'That's what's worrying me. What on earth are we going to do for a stop-gap?' Then I added that H2S gave us a good picture of the ground below us, and it was a pity it couldn't give us a good picture of the aeroplanes around us. Bernard Lovell turned and looked at me, he seemed about to make some comment but looked eastwards again. 'Do you know,' he said, 'there's no ground higher than this until you come to the Urals?' I smiled and thought, 'What an irrelevant remark.' Back at Clydesdale, Lovell's flat in Malvern, we joined Joyce for a drink and listened to the six o'clock news. Another Bomber Command raid was reported. The Skoda armaments factory at Pilsen in occupied Czechoslovakia had received the brunt of a violent onslaught on the night of the 16th–17th. Mannheim had also been attacked and mines had been laid in enemy waters. From all of these operations thirty-nine of our aircraft had failed to return. Lovell looked at me as if to ask if all of the thirty-nine were from Bomber Command. They were. Thirty-seven out of 327 attacking the Skoda works had failed to return to base—a loss of 11.3 per cent. The other two were lost on Mannheim.

Bryan, only just over a year old, was already in his cot, but we spent a short while with Susan, who, nearly five, was lovable and companionable and ready to talk away about anything. At supper the conversation was full of delightful variations. It touched on the upbringing of children, the potentialities of a 3-centimetre magnetron, cooking, Charles Morgan, the resonance of raindrops to extremely low centimetre wavelengths and Bach and Brahms. As I was staying the night with the Lovells, I was spared the long drive back to High Wycombe, and so after the meal I was able to settle into an armchair with the pleasant thought that I could relax. After Joyce had cleared the table, Bernard went across to his piano and played. He was an accomplished performer on the piano as well as on the organ, and I always found it pleasing and satisfying to hear him play. But on this occasion the entertainment was not for long. Within a short while he suddenly stopped playing and turned to look at me. 'Dudley,' he exclaimed. 'H2S—what you said on the Beacon about a picture of the aircraft around you.' I remembered my comment about H2S giving a good picture of the ground below the aircraft and what a pity it was that it could not give a view of other aircraft in the vicinity. 'Of course you can have that picture,' Lovell said, almost exploding with excitement. 'We should have thought of it before!'

H2S scanned through 360 degrees around the aircraft and below it, but the coverage did not extend above the horizontal. In other words, H2S covered the whole area below the aircraft from the horizontal downwards and to the extent of the range of the system in all directions. Therefore any other aircraft coming into the coverage of the system would produce an echo and could be detected, but due to the fact that the navigator was interested only in the echoes from the ground, his indicator in the aircraft was so designed to receive such echoes, and this meant that any echo emanating from an object between the ground and the aircraft was swamped by the ground returns. A picture of the terrain immediately below the aircraft and out to a distance of thirty miles was what was required for navigation, target approach and bombing. To this end the H2S receiver with its cathode ray tube was calibrated to display the echoes from the nearest point on the ground at the centre of the tube, this distance being the height of the aircraft above the ground which was immediately below it. Therefore the centre of the tube was a zero point. Then, echoes arriving from lateral distances out from the centre were calibrated in miles from the centre, or in any other convenient measure-ment. Lovell now explained that what he planned to do was to use a second receiver-indicator in the aircraft which would be calibrated to use that portion of the time-base from the beginning of the transmitter pulse to just before the first ground return. In short, he was considering using that part of the time-base which would receive any echo earlier than the first ground return; that is to say, he visualized an adjustment to a second H2S indicator in the aircraft so that if the aircraft was flying at, say 18,000 feet, then the maximum distance measurable from the aircraft would be 18,000 feet. Thus the first ground return would now appear not at the centre of the tube but on its periphery, leaving the tube clear to display the echoes of any object in the air that passed between the aircraft and the ground. Using Plan Position Indication with the radial time-base rotating round and round like the hand of a clock, as with H2S, the operator would now have a picture of the aircraft around and below him. If an aircraft came into the coverage, it would appear as a moving spot of light, and its movement would always be relative to the operator's aircraft in bearing, distance and speed. For example, the position of the operator's aircraft would be the centre of the cathode ray tube, or Plan Position Indicator as it was technically known in H2S, and, so, if any other aircraft entered the coverage from dead astern and at an overtaking speed, the operator would see a spot of light in a position behind the aircraft and gradually closing into the centre. Apart from showing a suspect enemy aircraft, the system would also show all aircraft within range and therefore echoes from friendly bombers in the bomber stream which came within the coverage would also appear on the indicator, but since their positions would change very little, because cruising speeds would be similar, any echo steadily closing from astern would be even more obvious as a potential danger. In fact, there were two added advantages to the idea. Such an equipment would act as a good collision warning-device and would be useful in indicating to the crew whether or not their aircraft was in the bomber stream.

It was incredibly ingenious. A walk up to the Beacon above Malvern, a conversation, an uninterrupted view from the Beacon to the Urals with no interfering ground returns, so to speak, and then lost in playing Brahms on the piano in the peace of his home. The way Lovell's mind worked was always a source of amazement to me.

We discussed a programme, and Lovell gave it as his view that develop-ment could be achieved in a very short space of time and that production could start within a month or two of design information being finalized, provided I could get Sir Robert Renwick behind the idea. We also discussed the likely reaction of the Ministry of Aircraft Production but decided that the line of official approach would delay the project by months, so I finally promised to speak to Renwick the next day and to tell Harris and Saundby that we were planning a private venture development and might therefore need their protection from the wrath of officialdom. Moreover, as Lovell was short of mechanics, I promised him the loan of Sergeant Walker and two trouble-shooters[1] from my technical department. In return Lovell promised to have a first model available for trials within a month.

Before I left for Bomber Command on the following day, Lovell called a meeting of his team and expounded his ideas. That same evening Sergeant Walker and two trouble-shooters arrived at TRE to assist. I informed Sir Robert Renwick of our plans on Tuesday and received his unqualified support. I also advised Harris and Saundby of our plans. Within two weeks, by dint of ceaseless work, Lovell had a model working on the bench. Shortly after, a second model was ready for installation in an aircraft for flight trials. This was duly installed in Halifax BB360, and after the first flights, which were successful, Lovell telephoned to invite me down for a demonstration. On 27 May I flew with the device from Defford and, with the co-operation of a Mosquito night fighter, was able to evaluate the effectiveness of Lovell's brainwave. It was completely successful, the 'attacking' Mosquito being readily detected from all angles as a small spot of light in the pool of blackness on the tube. It was immediately agreed that two more models should be constructed for urgent trials by the Bombing Development Unit. By the end of the first week in June, trials had proved that Fishpond, as the system was finally christened, was the most successful proximity warning-device yet developed and was likely to assist materially in reducing losses. As a result Saundby wrote to the Air Ministry demanding installation in all H2S aircraft as a matter of high priority and urging the speedier introduction of H2S into all bomber aircraft so that they could have the advantage not just of the facilities H2S provided for navigation and bombing but, now, the added protection from the enemy fighter provided by Indicator Unit 182, as Fishpond was officially designated.

By the beginning of July Fishpond was on the line in the factory. Lovell's diary describes the whole episode succinctly and amusingly:

Another major item started as a strictly private show between *SAWARD* and ourselves in April. We promised Saward to build him a unit to show the potentialities of warning of fighters' approach on H2S if he could produce a

---

[1] A trouble-shooter was a highly experienced RDF mechanic. A pool of these was held in Bomber Command under the direct control of the RDF Department for use where urgently needed.

man to do the construction. The whole affair was to be kept quiet to avoid difficulties at Defford on the trials and elsewhere. Sgt. Walker appeared and commenced to build an indicator unit; meanwhile *SUMMERHAYES* did some clandestine flights in an ordinary H2S Mk II with the centre-zero expanded and produced this exciting picture of a fighter approaching. [See Plate 9.]

We called this *MOUSETRAP*, and so did everyone else until finally an urgent signal forbade us to use this term as it would interfere with the security of impending operations! Finally the gadget was christened *FISHPOND*, by which name it was known thereafter.

The storm soon broke and on May 29th CCE (Renwick) held a meeting to lay on thousands of this Indicator Unit 182.

Fishpond was being used on a small scale in October and November 1943 (there were 553 sorties with it in November compared with 1030 total H2S sorties). . . . As a tail warning device, Fishpond saved many, many aircraft and human lives.

7

The Craziest Plan Possible

Although Lovell was unable to enjoy his growing family as much as he would have liked, home was a much-needed refuge in these difficult times. There he could sometimes indulge his passion for music and occasionally relax with some gardening when time permitted. It fell to Joyce Lovell to preserve him from domestic problems and to provide him with the moral support he needed so badly under the stress of his wartime pressures. Lovell took everything very seriously, and his tremendous sense of duty made him shoulder more than his fair share of tasks. Susan, who was 3½ years old when they moved from Swanage to Malvern, recalls some of her subsequent childhood life at that time.

> Our life was kept going very much by Mummy, who always did and always has continued to protect Daddy against domestic worries. But once Daddy was presented with a problem, he would deal with it right there, very fairly and with no trouble. He was always very approachable and warm, but he was a different sort of father. Our friends had fathers who crawled about on the floor and played bears. He was different. But I particularly remember how both Mummy and Daddy shielded Bryan and me against the worries of the times, and in turn, how Mummy protected Daddy from the domestic worries because he had enough on his plate with his own wartime work. Even at that age I knew by the expression on their faces when all was not well, and some days, when the news was black, Daddy would stand in front of the wireless full of anxiety and often a look of despair.

Then there were the visitors to the flat whose presence seemed to indicate situations of concern and urgency which, however hard Joyce and Bernard Lovell tried to shield their children, transmitted themselves in some degree to Susan. She remembers visitors like Sir Henry Tizard and P. M. S. Blackett: 'Blackett was always hungry and always eating very fast—and very unapproachable to us children. Somebody set apart.' She recalls an awful air disaster when 'some scientists were killed and Daddy was in a dreadful state—terribly depressed.' That was the crash of the Halifax with the first H2S set. But she also remembers times when he was highly elated, or when he was calm and played the piano or pottered around in the garden. The amusing things she recalls too: 'Daddy's preoccupation with details was so funny, even in the midst of all his important work. Clydesdale was divided into three flats, and we had the ground-floor one, and the flats shared three dustbins in the back garden.

Now Daddy was keen on having the dustbins used for different forms of salvage—one for paper, one for tins and one for ashes. And he labelled them accordingly with black paint. And if anyone put things into the wrong bin, he would get furious!'

As has already been mentioned, Dee and Lovell took the initial steps towards developing a 3-centimetre H2S as early as January 1943, by arranging to convert a 10-centimetre H2S to X band (3-centimetre). The first experimental equipment was ready by March, and Lovell and his team managed to complete its installation in Stirling N3724 ready for take-off from Defford at 16.45 hours on 11 March for the first test flight of X band H2S, now christened H2X. The aircraft flew at 5,000 feet across South Wales to Newport, Newport to Nash Point, and Nash Point to Foreland Point. Between Foreland Point and Bath it climbed to 10,000 feet and then flew from Bath to Staverton, Staverton to Worcester and back to Defford, landing at 18.45 hours. Considering the very experimental nature of the equipment, the results were stimulating. At 5,000 feet the River Severn was seen on the tube at 10 miles, Cardiff at 22 miles, Weston-super-Mare at 35 miles, and the north coast of Devon was clearly identifiable at 22 miles. However the results at 10,000 feet were rather poor. Worcester was picked up at 22 miles, followed in to 16 miles and then disappeared from the tube and was not seen again. The evidence pointed to insufficient coverage at 10,000 feet. Lovell's assessment was that, overall, the results were disappointing. But a start had been made, and despite the initial results the system showed promise. Then, at the end of May, a strong contingent arrived from the USA to pour cold water on Lovell's efforts. The Americans, who at the beginning of the year had decried H2S and dubbed it a useless system, had since then developed an H2X apparatus copying Lovell's basic design. Now, they had the effrontery to present cut-and-dried plans for completing their development of this 3-centimetre H2S and fitting it into the Pathfinder Force of RAF Bomber Command! Never had I witnessed such an indignant Dee, and rarely had I seen such an infuriated Lovell.

Lovell had immediately contacted me when he and Dee were confronted with the proposal, for it was obvious that in some quarters of the Air Ministry and the Ministry of Aircraft Production the idea found favour. I agreed to go into battle against this scheme. I was bitterly opposed to this suggestion, because I had little faith in the American ability to develop an equipment that would meet our operational requirements. Their whole conception of bombing was entirely different from ours. I knew that a really worthwhile equipment could be developed only as a result of the most intimate liaison between the operators and the

Boffins.[1] If the equipment was to be developed in the USA, this liaison would be impossible. I consulted with Saundby and received his permission to tell Renwick, Watson Watt and Cherwell that Bomber Command would view such a step with much disfavour and would do all in its power to oppose the transfer of the future development of H2S for Bomber Command to the Americans.

On 7 June Watson Watt, now Scientific Adviser Telecommunications (SAT) to the Air Staff, held a meeting at 14.00 hours at the Air Ministry. Dee and Lovell were present, together with the Americans. At this meeting it was reluctantly agreed by the USA contingent that the TRE proposal to convert two hundred H2S sets to X band working should be adopted and that the Americans should be permitted to concentrate on X band for ASV. It was a proposal which Lovell admitted that he and Dee had thought up almost on the spot! At 16.30 hours on the same afternoon a full-scale meeting was held in Sir Robert Renwick's office, with Renwick in the chair. Those from the Watson Watt meeting were in attendance. In addition, Lord Cherwell, the Director General of Signals and other Air Ministry and MAP representatives were present. In his diary Lovell wrote: '. . . everything was batted through once more, but after much breath-taking suspense it was agreed that the British proposal should be accepted and that the target should be—3 Squadrons by Christmas 1943!' Indeed, the decision was a foregone conclusion for Bomber Command had made it absolutely clear that they would back TRE to the hilt, and both Cherwell and Renwick had already agreed to support TRE and Bomber Command. In fact, thanks to Lovell and Dee, TRE and Bomber Command were becoming a powerful 'political' combination on the subject of offensive RDF.

On 24 June I visited Lovell to discuss a programme of H2X, or H2S Mk III as it was finally designated. That same day I flew in Lancaster ED350 to see a demonstration of Lovell's latest version. Certainly it displayed a picture that was easier to interpret than that received on 10-centimetre H2S. I was impressed by the detail in the picture on the cathode ray tube and realized what a revolutionary effect it could have on bombing operations, particularly against large targets such as Berlin where identification of particular parts of this vast built-up area had proved to be impossible with 10-centimetre H2S. But Lovell knew that much more work would have to be done before the equipment could perform to its maximum potential and before it was in a fit state to be used under operational conditions and to be serviced by squadron RDF mechanics.

Now, however, 10-centimetre H2S was to come into its own. In July

[1] The name given by the Armed Services to the scientists.

1943 Hamburg became a top priority target to attack, with much pressure from the Admiralty for its 'elimination' because it was a major German naval centre with the most extensive shipyards in Europe housing many ships and U-boats under construction and in varying stages of completion. The greater part of its shipbuilding yards, including the famous Blohm & Voss yards, had been given over to the building and assembly of U-boats, and they were responsible for some forty-five per cent of the total output of these German submarines. Hamburg was also the largest and most important port in Germany. It contained 3,000 industrial establishments and 5,000 commercial companies, most of which were engaged in the transport and shipping industries. In addition there were major oil and petrol refineries, the second largest manufacturers of ships' screws, the largest wool-combing plant in Germany and various manufacturers of precision instruments, electrical instruments, machinery and aircraft components. It was the second largest city in Germany and, next to Berlin, the most heavily defended, such was its importance.

Many attacks had already been made against Hamburg in varying degrees of strength, but none in the strength required to make any great impact. The attacks made at the end of January, when Pathfinder Force aircraft had marked the target with H2S, had been on too small a scale to be really effective. Now, however, the situation was greatly changed. Air Chief Marshal Sir Arthur Harris had at his disposal a far greater force of four-engined heavy bombers, and the Pathfinders were all equipped with H2S. In addition, a considerable portion of the Main Force aircraft were now also equipped with H2S. The operation, which went by the ominous name of 'Gomorrah', was planned in detail by Air Vice-Marshal Saundby, the brilliant SASO upon whom so much of the success of bomber operations depended. It was more of a campaign than a bombing raid. As Harris told his crews in his good-luck message: 'The Battle of Hamburg cannot be won in a single night.' Indeed, the operation was spread over four nights. On the night of 24–25 July 740 out of 791 aircraft despatched rained down 2,396 tons of bombs, 980 tons being incendiary. On the 27-28th, 739 bombers dropped 2,417 tons, of which 50 per cent were incendiaries. On the 29–30th, 726 aircraft dropped 2,832 tons of bombs on the city and, finally, on the night of 2–3 August, 462 aircraft out of 740 despatched dropped a further 1,462 tons into what was now a blazing inferno.

The result for Germany was catastrophic, and Albert Speer, the Armaments Minister, warned Hitler that a series of attacks of this ferocity and accuracy extended to six more major cities would bring Germany's armaments production to a total halt. Seventy-five per cent of Hamburg had been razed to the ground; it was as if it had been hit by an unprecedented earthquake. Crew reports from all four raids indicated clearly that success had been primarily attributable to H2S. But then, Hamburg as a coastal port was an ideal target for H2S. What was required now, with the longer nights soon approaching, making deeper penetration raids under cover of darkness possible, was the improved H2S Mk 111, operating on 3 centimetres, which would help Bomber Command to achieve similar successes inland, particularly against Berlin, major centres of oil-production, aircraft and tank manufacture, and other large centres of military production.

By late August, in fact, Bomber Command was ready to turn its attention to the more distant targets such as Mannheim, Nuremberg, Munich, Hanover, Kassel, Stuttgart, Frankfurt and others which were beyond OBOE range and which required the assistance of H2S.

But before this, one other target of vital importance, and which was ideal for H2S, was thrust upon the Command's list with a demand for destruction as a matter of top priority. As early as April 1943 there was suspicion that the Germans were actively engaged in developing rocket bombs carrying warheads of several tons of explosives and capable of travelling considerable distances. Photographic reconnaissance revealed that the chief centre of development was Peenemünde on the Baltic coast. Specific photographs taken from the air showed what appeared to be two very large rockets of at least forty feet in length and six or seven feet in diameter, indicating the possibility of a warhead of a ton or more. Shortly afterwards, Intelligence sources reported the development of a pilotless aircraft which was, in effect, an air mine with wings. This, too, was confirmed by photograhic reconnaissance which exposed at Peenemünde what was evidently a pilotless aircraft launcher with the aircraft mounted on it ready for catapulting into the air. Bomber Command were soon requested to attack this target as a matter of urgency, and on the night of 17–18 August 571 four-engined heavy bombers out of 597 despatched dropped 1,937 tons of bombs. Complete destruction was requested. Complete destruction was achieved. The bombing was so accurate that when the raid was over the Experimental Station looked like a giant solitaire board. Over six hundred persons working there were killed, including Dr Spiel, who was in charge of development. Unquestionably the effectiveness of this raid greatly delayed the German use of the V1 and V2 weapons against England until a time when, however unpleasant, they were of little military significance. The invasion of continental Europe had begun before the Germans were ready, and their launching-sites were overrun before they could put this weapon into full use. Moreover, their production was so set back that the flying bombs and rockets were never in supply at an adequate level to provide anything more than a

6 Professor P. M. S. Blackett (later Lord Blackett), 1939

7 Bernard Lovell photographed by the author in 1943

8 Dr P. I. Dee, photographed by the author in 1943

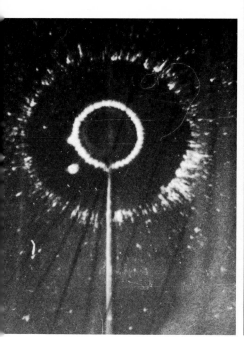

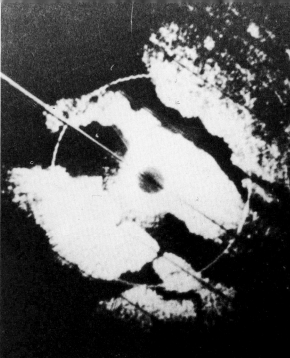

9, 10, 11 *Above left*: 'Fishpond's' first flight trial, 27 May 1943. The centre of the inner ring on the cathode ray tube represents the aircraft; the straight line from the centre to the outside ring represents the aircraft's heading; the spot of light to the left is the echo of the 'alien' aircraft. *Above right*: Over Flakkee and Rotterdam on Mk III H2S from 16,000 feet on the night of 20–1 December 1943. *Below*: H2S Mk VI (K-band 1¼ centimetres)—a picture of the tube taken flying over Milford Haven, 10 September 1944

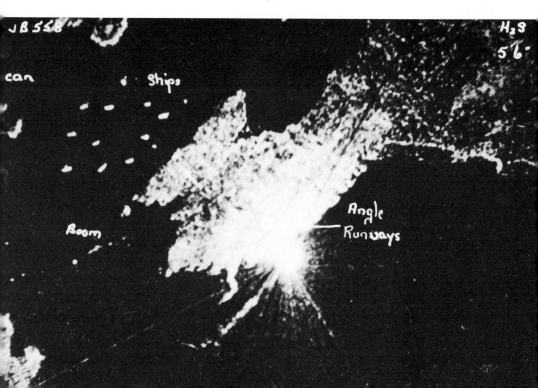

nuisance factor. The real success of this raid was again attributable to H2S. It was at very long range, being on the coast between Rostock and Stettin, and navigation and target location had to depend upon H2S, but once more it was the coastal areas that gave crews a map-like picture of their route which was largely over coastline and waterways, and the island of Rugen, close to Peenemünde, was readily identified, making location of the target itself relatively easy despite the fact that the actual target, due to its smallness, had little to offer in the way of a major H2S response. Once more a triumph for Lovell, and his team under Dee, had been chalked up. But within ten days, disappointment was to follow.

At the end of August and the beginning of September three attacks were delivered against Berlin. On the night of 23–24 August 617 out of 727 aircraft despatched dropped 1,762 tons of bombs on Germany's capital; on the night of 31 August–1 September, 507 out of 621 aircraft despatched attacked and dropped 1,463 tons; and on the night of 3–4 September 298 out of 320 aircraft dropped 980 tons. Although these attacks were not entirely unsuccessful, they were far from spectacular. What emerged from these Berlin raids was what had been expected: H2S operating on 10 centimetres provided insufficient clarity of picture to distinguish aiming-points in such a vast built-up area as Berlin. What was required was the much higher resolution of an H2S operating on 3 centimetres. One other point of interest also emerged: of the Main Force aircraft which failed to reach and find the target area on each occasion, only a statistically insignificant number were fitted with H2S. In fact, virtually all the Main Force H2S aircraft were able to navigate to the target and take full advantage of the Pathfinder Force marker bombs. Arising from these results there came increased pressure from Harris and Saundby for the earliest possible delivery of 3-centimetre H2S. With his eye on a major Berlin campaign in the winter months, Harris demanded that 3-centimetre H2S be made available to the Pathfinder Force by November, if only in small numbers.

The Air Ministry departments concerned and the Ministry of Aircraft Production noted Bomber Command's request, but with the exception of Renwick they regarded the timing as preposterous. The decision taken at the June Renwick meeting for three squadrons to be equipped with Mk 111 H2S by Christmas was already causing hidden smiles behind hands at both Ministries, and, to be fair, not entirely without reason. Mk 111 H2S was far from being fully developed even by August, let alone September. Flight Lieutenant Len Killip, an ex-operational navigator who was working at the Bombing Development Unit, was loaned by the Bomber Command RDF Department to TRE in August as their navigational liaison officer. On his initial flights from Defford with the Mk 111

H2S he was appalled at both the performance and the poor serviceability of the system. Indeed, it was so bad that Lovell admitted he hardly dared to show it to anyone except his own and my people. Flight Lieutenant John Day,* the one-legged navigator in charge of my Operational Research and Development Section, was, however, enthusiastic over the possibilities of the 3-centimetre equipment, and Flight Lieutenant Pete Musselman, the Canadian in charge of my technical training school and technical research section, was confident that the technical reliability would soon improve. But whatever the opinions were at this stage, Lovell was determined to give Harris something towards his needs by the end of November, and with support from D. C. T. Bennett, now an Air Vice-Marshal and Air Officer Commanding the Pathfinder Force, and from myself, Lovell started another of his clandestine plans to equip a small number of aircraft with experimental 3-centimetre H2S as a private venture. The three of us were well aware that such an action would be bitterly opposed by those many official sources who always insisted on more routine channels of approach, and therefore the plan was initially kept a closely guarded secret. The only Air Ministry and MAP person who was 'in the know' was Sir Robert Renwick, whose unofficial support I had sought and obtained. Lovell records the episode in his diary of events:

Backed by the enthusiasm of Bennett, Saward and their cronies, we hatched a desperate plan to equip 6 of the Pathfinder Force Lancasters by the end of October with an experimental X band (3 cms H2S) equipment. Arrangements were made to 'fix' the opposition, and the plan was not announced until it was already started. The progress chart started on September 14th and had jobs for nearly all the H2S people ranging from responsibilities for mounts of the h.f. [high frequency] units to passing out of the Lancasters. On reflection, this appears as one of the craziest plans possible. The performance of the one X band system flying in a heavy was so bad that we daren't show it to anyone, and Killip was so shocked with the performance that he had little interest in flying it. Perhaps the boldness of the plan saved it. We now accumulated a reasonable amount of X band equipment and soon had more than one aircraft to fly it in. The extra interest and intense hard work all helped and on November 13th the first three Lancasters JB352, JB355 and JB365 were delivered to the Pathfinder Force. Towards the end, a converted Killip was flying night and day and the delivery of the 6 was completed by November 17th.

In truth the plan succeeded as a result of Lovell's ingenuity and intense hard work. The boldness of his plan inspired and stimulated everyone to work themselves to the bone and to achieve results that normally they would never have believed possible.

Early in October, Renwick called a meeting at the Air Ministry which had its element of humour. Its purpose was to advise those concerned at the Air Ministry and the MAP that the C-in-C, Bomber Command, had made a demand for a few of the Lancasters of the Pathfinder Force to be equipped with 3-centimetre H2S before the end of the year for certain special operations. The meeting was attended by Dee and Lovell for TRE, myself for Headquarters Bomber Command, Bennett for the Pathfinder Force, and various members of the Air Ministry and the MAP. But only Renwick, Dee, Lovell, Bennett and I were aware that a programme to provide the Pathfinder Force with six equipped Lancasters by the middle of November was in full swing—regardless of the outcome of the meeting!

On 18 November 1943 Air Chief Marshal Sir Arthur Harris, C-in-C Bomber Command, was in the Operations Room by 09.15 hours. Saundby had arrived a few minutes before him. Saundby motioned me towards him with his finger.

'The six special Lancasters are ready?'

'Yes, sir.'

'Are they available for operations tonight?'

'Yes, sir,' I whispered.

'Good!' he muttered.

Then, when the meteorological forecast was over, the C-in-C rose from his chair and turned to Saundby.

'Berlin Plan, Sandy—and we'll keep it going as long as we can.'

He put on his cap and stalked out of the room, his face expressionless.

On the night of 18–19 November, the first attack in the series of the Berlin Campaign was made by 402 heavies out of 444 despatched, dropping 1,590.7 tons of bombs on the city. It was followed on the night of the 23rd–24th, when 382 aircraft dropped 1,326.3 tons of bombs, and it continued with ever increasing ferocity through to 24–25 March 1944. In sixteen major raids on Berlin, 9,112 sorties were despatched, all four-engined heavy bombers except for 162 Pathfinder Mosquitoes, and they dropped 29,341.5 tons of high explosives and incendiaries. The last but one raid was on the night of 15–16 February 1944, when 806 aircraft out of 891 despatched dropped 2,610.1 tons of bombs on the already reeling city in thirty-nine minutes. It was made through thick cloud, and the attack was remarkable for its accuracy, considering that no glimpse of the city was possible. That this campaign was immensely successful was to a major degree attributable to both 3-centimetre H2S, which was used by the Pathfinders for marking aiming-points, and 10-centimetre H2S, which enabled the Main Force aircraft to take full advantage of the Pathfinders' tactics. Another benefit derived from H2S was the use of Fishpond, which was now in virtually all H2S fitted bombers. The total losses of aircraft were 492, which represented 5.4 per cent of those despatched, but an analysis of losses by the RDF Operational Research and Development Section revealed that the percentage losses of those aircraft fitted with H2S and Fishpond were significantly lower than those without these facilities by nearly three per cent. The reports on the performance of the 3-centimetre H2S were extremely satisfying, and the details and definition were far beyond expectations. The inland lakes and waterways amidst the heavily built-up area were clearly seen on the cathode ray tube and were easily identifiable. Even the Tempelhof Aerodrome was readily discerned. Photographs taken of the cathode ray tube at the moment of release of target-markers confirmed the claims of those Pathfinder crews using the 3-centimetre H2S. The effects of the raid were staggering and brought howls of anguish from Dr Joseph Goebbels, the Nazi Minister of Propaganda, and from Albert Speer, the Minister of Armaments Production.

In this series of raids some 5,427 acres of built-up area in Berlin and its suburbs were devastated. The Reich Chancellery was severely damaged and the destruction in the Government administrative area was considerable. Goebbels referred to the desolation in the Wilhelmsplatz and the Potsdamer Platz during the raids, adding: 'Devastation is again appalling in the Government section as well as in the western and northern suburbs. . . . The State Playhouse and the Reichstag are ablaze. . . . Hell itself seems to have broken loose over us. . . .' The Ministry of Armaments Production was totally destroyed; the Alkett Works, a major producer of guns and tanks, was almost completely destroyed; Borsig, another large armaments factory employing 18,000 on the production of guns, suffered tremendous destruction; the Erkner ball-bearing plant was severely damaged; the Siemens electrical combine, the biggest in Germany which manufactured cables, aircraft instruments, electrodes and carbons for searchlights, and various military electronic components and equipments, was devastated. Goebbels wrote: 'The English aimed so accurately that one might think spies had pointed their way.' Speer admitted the terrible blow to the armaments industry. In addition there was complete disruption to normal services and approximately one and a half million people were rendered homeless.

Berlin was not the only distant target attacked during this period. Other vitally important centres of military production were raided, including Stettin on the Baltic coast, Brunswick, Magdeburg, Leipzig, Stuttgart, Schweinfurt, Frankfurt, Essen and Nuremberg. All attacks were immensely successful, and in every case the effectiveness of both 3- and 10-centimetre H2S proved them to be weapons of the utmost importance to Bomber Command. Indeed, perhaps overshadowing the success of the attacks on Berlin was the half-hour raid on Leipzig on the night of 3–4

December, when 449 heavy bombers out of 527 despatched dropped 713 tons of high explosives and 733 tons of incendiaries. There was thick cloud over the target, but two Lancasters of the Pathfinder Force, fitted with 3-centimetre H2S, marked the aiming-points with sky-markers with such precision that the Main Force was able to bomb with devastating results. Damage to industrial property was particularly severe. Plants engaged on the repair of Junkers aero-engines and the sub-assembly of Junkers aircraft fuselages were destroyed; further extensive damage included two gasworks and the virtual destruction of a power station; and four hundred acres of densely built-up area of the main town were razed to the ground. Never before had a bombing attack been executed with such precision against an unseen target. But by the end of March 1944 Bomber Command's role was to change for a period of time from that of a strategic bombing force to that of a support force to the Allied Armies just prior to, during and immediately after the invasion of France on 6 June. Whilst this resulted in a pause in the use of H2S for deep penetration targets, it became a period of fertile development of even more remarkable H2S performance by improving the existing systems.

On 27 December 1943 Lovell was promoted to the rank of Principal Scientific Officer with effect from 1 December, at a salary of £850 + £25 Civil Service Bonus per annum. It was a richly deserved promotion, for already his contribution to the war effort was beginning to exceed that of many officers of the Royal Air Force of Air rank. Not only had he provided the vital assistance that Bomber Command required to do its job, but he had at the same time been responsible for the ASV systems in Coastal Command which had largely negated the efforts of the German U-boats to strangle these islands. Then, he had found the means of giving the bomber aircraft an excellent protection against the night fighter with Fishpond. Finally, rarely appreciated, he had enabled the bomber with its H2S to sow mines in enemy waters near and far with great accuracy due to the detailed definition of coastline visible on the H2S cathode ray tube. This in itself was beginning to strike a blow at enemy shipping and U-boats which was reaching disastrous proportions for Germany.

Despite his wartime work, however, his eyes were always set upon the future and upon peacetime work, and whenever the opportunity occurred, he would devote some time to consideration of post-war scientific research. In this 'day-dreaming' he was often encouraged by Patrick Blackett, who, although separated from him by virtue of their differing wartime responsibilities, maintained the old links by occasional communications or when he was on a visit to TRE. On 28 January 1944 Blackett, who was now Chief Adviser on Operational Research to the Admiralty, wrote to Lovell about future work at Manchester when the war was over. Assuming that Lovell would be returning to Manchester on the cessation of hostilities, Blackett wrote that much was now going on to obtain greatly increased resources for physics in general and for Manchester in particular. 'I am out to treble, at least, the amount of money available for research and am envisaging a quite big expansion.' He enclosed a copy of a draft report on the needs for cosmic ray research which he had produced for the Royal Society Physics Reconstruction Committee. 'Please treat this as confidential. The Vice Chancellor (Manchester) has agreed that it is an entirely sensible plan. If you have any detailed comments on it I would be very glad to hear them.' The proposals included plans for new workshop facilities for the Physics Department, but effectively no extra space. If all went well, Blackett asked Lovell if he would be willing to take on the job of organizing and producing the new workshop including 'collecting machine tools and staff—could you collect staff from the TRE who may be paid off?'

Lovell's reply to Blackett was carefully considered. Generally, he felt that Blackett's draft report on the post-war needs for the Manchester University Physics Department struck the right line as between what was desirable and what was attainable in the immediate post-war years. However, there were a few things that alarmed him. He drew Blackett's attention to the fact that his report scarcely mentioned students. 'The details,' he wrote, 'of their teaching, improvement in teaching facilities, and recruitment of great numbers, is surely of the utmost importance, not only from general social necessities, but because they will be the sink from which the urgently needed new research will come.' He went on to say that he had seen Dee's equivalent report, which he had been asked to write on the needs of Glasgow University's Physics Department, and how impressed he was by the amount of attention Dee had given to the student aspect. 'His plans involve handling four to five times the numbers of physics students compared with pre-war Manchester. The cumulative effect of this in ten years' time should be enormous.' With regard to salaries, he felt that Blackett had dismissed the problems too lightly. Whilst accepting the premise that people might be thankful for what they could get in the post-war years, he thought it most unwise to plan on that assumption. He suggested that since increases in salaries in one depart-ment would automatically mean increases in all other faculties, the proper line of action might be to leave the scientists with certain responsibilities for Government work in order to achieve a balance.

On the subject of the plans for accommodation, he was highly critical. The suggestion that present accommodation would be sufficient 'makes me groan'. Even before the war, he reminded Blackett, they were trying to steal a room from the Electrotechnics Department. 'My opinion is the same as my first reactions to Manchester Physics, namely that the accommodation could scarcely be worse. Neither is this a matter of square feet of floor space only. It is a matter of hopelessly inconvenient distribution. A minor but vital matter—how can one possibly run such an increased establishment without office facilities for workers? This generation suffers a crippling legacy from the great men of the past—the sanctity of their work rooms. "If it was good enough for X it's good enough for you" is unfortunately a sentence still full of meaning.' He went on to say that it might well be impossible to build for years, but that was no reason for not putting the architects to work. 'The Dental Faculty turned a slum into a modern lab. in Coupland Street. Can't Physics transform some of the bomb damage in the same street.'

Lovell finished his letter of comments by referring to the letter Blackett had sent him in the first month of the war, 'a letter so full of wisdom that I shall never forget it'. Blackett had told him to stop complaining about the lack of organization at the airborne research division at Perth and the ineffectiveness of the senior personnel. 'Briefly you told me that I would soon realise that 75% of the new work consisted of dealing with people. For the past two years I have spent 95% of my time dealing with people and I am filled with dismay at the thought of having to teach myself to deal with apparatus again.' Finally, he said that he would certainly see to the workshops and drawing office if he returned to Manchester, and he added that he was confident that he could collect materials and staff from TRE.

Lovell's 'dismay' at the thought of having to learn how to deal with apparatus again was exaggeration. The truth was that he was dealing with apparatus in the most brilliant fashion, due to the fact that he had developed into a combination of a great scientist, a practical engineer and an inspiring leader. In addition, he knew how to co-operate with, and understand, the problems of the Royal Air Force personnel he was trying to assist. Lovell had grown up into a man of stature, and Blackett knew it. He took note of Lovell's comments, and they influenced his later approach to the question of the expansion of Manchester Physics. But that is a matter which chronologically falls into a later part of this story. The war was still on, and Lovell's part in it was far from over.

8

H2S Under Attack

Despite the undoubted success of H2S, it was already evident at the end of 1943 that by and large, it was too difficult to use when related to the amount of training that could be given under wartime conditions. Lovell wrote in his diary that: 'the defences of Germany had attained new degrees of effectiveness as the 1943/44 winter opened, and the altitude of operation and the amount of evasive action increased to an extent which spoiled the H2S picture so much that only skilled people could be expected to use it effectively under the stress of battle. Moreover, the results which people expected from H2S had completely changed since its initiation. It was no longer a question of finding a built-up area, but more of dropping markers and bombs around a precise aiming point in a given town—and a 50% zone of more than 2 miles was now considered hopeless.' The altitude of operation was occasioned by the increasing numbers of Lancasters in service, which operated at heights of between 22,000 feet and 27,000 feet at a cruising speed of 240 miles per hour and carried 8,000 pounds of bombs to Berlin or any other distant German target. Moreover, it was capable of carrying 12,000 pounds well beyond the Ruhr and was also able to carry the enormous 22,000-pound 'Grand Slam' bomb which became available later and which no other aircraft in the world, American, Russian or German, was capable of carrying. Evasive action, the other effect which was detrimental to the H2S picture, was on the increase for two reasons: growing enemy night fighter activity and, ironically, the excellent warning of night fighter approach being given on the Fishpond indicator. The violent banking and twisting from evasive action meant that the H2S scanner was pointing in all directions during such tactics and not just at the ground beneath the aircraft.

Lovell records that: 'We therefore struck hard in the Autumn of 1943 for the rapid introduction of roll stabilisation; the scan corrected Indicator (Type 184); drift line; and in the case of S band (10cms), for the Barrel Scanner Type 63, all of which were being worked on during the summer (1943) and which were now either flying or about to fly experimentally.' The roll-stabilized scanner was so designed that it pointed downwards whatever the attitude of the aircraft; it was a clever piece of engineering. The scan-corrected indicator was a design feature to correct the slant-range distortion which occurred when viewing responses at close range. The Barrel Scanner, which was also to be roll stabilized, was an improvement designed specifically for the 10-centimetre H2S which, with the scan-corrected Indicator Type 184, was confidently expected to give a picture which was clear of ground-return clutter at the centre and which would improve the depth and shape of the responses received, thus making town identification easier.

On 5 November 1943 Renwick held a meeting at Air Ministry to approve a programme for these modifications and to plan the production of the new types that would result from the modifications proposed by Lovell and backed by Bomber Command. It was finally agreed that the 300 3-centimetre H2S Mk 111, already planned for completion by May 1944, should be converted to use the Indicator Type 184 and be called H2S Mk 111B; aircraft equipped with H2S Mk 111B should finally have their scanners changed over to roll-stabilized scanners beginning in March 1944 with completion by July 1944, this version to be called H2S Mk 111A. This part of the programme was for the Pathfinder Force. The Main Force was to continue to be equipped with 10-centimetre H2S, but modified as soon as possible to have the scan-corrected Indicator Type 184 and the roll-stabilized Barrel Scanner, the system to be known as H2S Mk 11C. The change-over on production line to this version was scheduled for August 1944, but an interim crash programme for 10-centimetre H2S Mk 11 fitted with the Indicator Type 184 only was also approved, this version to be called H2S Mk 11D. The dates set for these programmes were much farther ahead than TRE or Bomber Command had optimistically expected. 'We were aghast at these delayed dates,' Lovell wrote, 'but worse was to follow in the months ahead—we had overloaded the firms, people's brains, and probably ourselves. The delays were appalling—it seemed that the whole country had stopped working. . . .' The situation became steadily worse by the spring of 1944. The expectation of an early invasion of the Continent of Europe—D Day—turned everyone's mind to the end of the war, and interest in the needs of the strategic bomber began to wane as the importance of bombing in support of the Allied Armies and attacking short-range targets, such as the rail transport centres essential to the German Army, steadily took precedence over distant targets. This was to prove a mistake, for distant targets were to become of vital importance to the British and American Armies, and to the Russian Army, as the Allied advances began in earnest in the second half of 1944. These targets were associated with oil supplies and with communication centres supporting Germany's eastern front against the advances of the Russians, as well as industrial centres manufacturing armaments for the German forces.

Perhaps one of the causes of delay was that too many versions of H2S were being developed in an effort to produce the finest and most efficient

navigation and accurate bombing device, capable of operating at all
ranges. The best was, in fact, becoming the evil of the good. During 1943,
for example, development work had begun on K band, a 1¼-centimetre
H2S, the project being known as Lion Tamer. It was to include all the
most refined bombing aids possible and, because of its exceptionally
narrow beam width resulting from its short wavelength, it was expected to
provide a picture with superb definition. Indeed, it was believed that not
only rivers and lakes but also railway lines and wide streets in large towns
would be discernible. Lion Tamer was a development in Dee's division,
but in a group which was separate from Lovell's group. Lovell, however,
had convinced Bomber Command, in particular Bennett and myself, that
3-centimetre H2S using a 6-foot scanner could provide as good a picture
as the proposed Lion Tamer and would have the added advantage of
being a system which was already coming into service and therefore
suffering less from the unknown problems of new designs; only the
scanner would be modified, demanding, admittedly, a larger cupola on
the underside of the aircraft. Moreover, another unknown factor was that
of the absorption by water with 1¼ centimetres which might cause poor
performance above clouds. At the beginning of 1944 efforts were made
from some quarters to obtain priority for Lion Tamer, but Bomber
Command felt that all efforts should be concentrated on the roll-stabilized, scan-corrected H2S Mk IIIA for the Pathfinders and the roll-
stabilized, scan-corrected H2S Mk IIC for the Main Force, plus any
improvements to the performance of these 3- and 10-centimetre versions
that could be achieved by fitting a 6-foot scanner. On Friday 4 February
Sir Robert Renwick held a meeting on the subject of Lion Tamer versus
H2S Mk IIIA with a 6-foot scanner, now named 'Whirligig'. Lovell and
Dee, amongst others from TRE, were present; Bomber Command was
represented by Bennett and myself, and the Air Ministry by Watson Watt,
Air Vice-Marshal Victor Tait, the Director General of Signals, and Air
Commodore C. P. Brown, Director of Radar.[1] There were also members
of the MAP in attendance. Bennett and I pressed for H2S Mk IIIA with
the 6-foot scanner in preference to Lion Tamer, thereby backing Lovell,
but I felt that Lion Tamer should continue in development without
priority. This course of action was agreed. A third proposal from Dee,
which came up at the meeting, was for the development of a really
well-engineered and comprehensive 3-centimetre H2S to be known as
Mk IV H2S which would give much-improved definition over 10-centi-
metre H2S, an urgent requirement for Bomber Command—a kind of

[1] The term Radar replaced RDF in 1943. It stood for Radio Direction and Ranging.
'Radar' will be used in the text from now onwards.

H2S to end all H2Ss. Somewhat unreasonably, this was virtually dismissed at this stage, much to the chagrin of Dee, who virtually accused Lovell of fixing the meeting with Bennett and myself beforehand.

On 6 February, at the regular Sunday TRE meeting held in A. P. Rowe's office at Malvern and known as the 'Sunday Soviet', Dee presented a paper which was a counterblast to the decisions taken at Renwick's meeting two days earlier.

The paper did not seem to make a great impression on Renwick and Watson Watt, who were present. Renwick, however, did agree to hold a further meeting to discuss the matter all over again. This meeting took place on Tuesday 22 February, with almost the same people clustering around the long table in Renwick's conference room. The two differences were Dr D. M. Robinson, who had temporarily replaced Dee at TRE whilst Dee was on three months sick leave, and the addition of Lord Cherwell. 'TRE presented four points for discussion,' Lovell recorded, 'Mk IV H2S in all Mk IV Lancasters [this was the latest planned version of the Lancaster, later to be known as the Lincoln]; '6 ft Whirligig on X band (Mk IIIA H2S), versus straight forward K band (1¼ cms), crash programme before the end of the year, and general K band programme. This time, as distinct from the previous meeting, we had a cast-iron possibility for a K band crash programme and after much talk it was almost fixed for TRE to do only the K programme. . . .' But Bomber Command stood firm on its first opinion, as the minutes of this meeting revealed: 'Air Vice-Marshal Bennett thought that it should be possible to produce the Whirligig earlier than K band equipment. Group Captain Saward suggested that the follow-up of Whirligig might be more certain than that of K band equipment.' The final result of this meeting was that work should proceed on both projects, Whirligig and Lion Tamer, the 1¼-centimetre K band equipment now to be officially known as Mk VI H2S. In fact TRE was committed unexpectedly to a double programme which it had hitherto been loath to entertain. The policy of Mk IV H2S was again left undecided, and it was reluctantly accepted by Bomber Command that the Main Force aircraft would have to continue with a programme of roll-stabilized, scan-corrected Mk IIC H2S—that is to say, a 10-centimetre system, instead of the desired 3-centimetre system.

Following this meeting Lovell was requested by A. P. Rowe, the Chief Superintendent of TRE, to write a memorandum on the problems arising from the new programmes with their diversity of systems, covering the shortages of components and parts that were likely to cause delays. This Lovell completed in a document dated 28 February. It was a very distressing report. Not only were dates for the various H2S systems totally unrealistic when considered in relation to supplies of components and sub-assemblies, including those systems which had been designed and approved months earlier, but the ASV programme for Coastal Command was running months behind schedule. 'No one but TRE seems to be worrying as to whether all the bits and pieces for programmes are on order,' he wrote, after listing the shortages in detail and after checking with the Ministry of Aircraft Production departments concerned what was the state of the supply position. 'In the case of the H2S Mk IIIA programme the original target was 300 by March 31st, 1944. The delayed target was 25 in March, 50 in April etc. plus 35 a month for wastage (aircraft losses over enemy territory). The following horrors have surfaced recently, however,' he continued, and then went on to state that production for the wastage rate was not yet covered on a single item and that Bomber Command's requirement for extension of production beyond the Pathfinder Force requirements had received absolutely no attention. Nor had anyone placed extension contracts for H2S beyond those contracts which were due to run out in the course of 1944. On the subject of aircraft fittings to take the installations, a task which belonged to the aircraft manufacturers, Lovell reported on a visit to A. V. Roe, the producers of the Lancaster bomber, an action which he described as 'an extremely great crime from the point of view of the trilogy'. The 'trilogy' comprised the three MAP departments responsible for dealing with the aircraft manufacturers for special installations, and which assiduously resented any direct liaison between the TRE design authority and the aircraft manufacturers. They were so named by Lovell. Referring to the conversations he had with the aircraft manufacturers at A. V. Roe, he wrote: 'Their ignorance of what Radar did was shocking. They thought that we were spoiling their aircraft without any results whatsoever and were quite unaware of the enormous influence of GEE and H2S on navigating and bombing capability. They had no idea of the various Marks of H2S and had received no instructions about changing over the production lines of Lancaster IIIs in July to coincide with the H2S production (new Marks), although arrangements for changing the production line had been in force for at least six months.'

On the subject of the two versions of 3-centimetre ASV, officially designated ASV Mk VI and ASV Mk VIA, Lovell reported that the target for the Mk VI version was one hundred by the end of 1943. 'To-day only 7 are fitted and this only by the personal efforts of TRE.' The date for the Mk VIA version, which had certain refinements added to Mk VI in accordance with operational requirements, was two hundred by 31 March 1944. 'There is not a dog's chance of having 2 dozen by that date,' he wrote, and he listed the reasons which added up to lack of appropriate and prompt action by the MAP departments concerned.

He summed up the whole sorry state of affairs as something which 'might well come from "Alice in Wonderland" '.

His recommendation was that, with the present rate of radar development, the Design Group, that is to say the groups in TRE concerned with each specific radar development, should have a major responsibility in conjunction with the MAP for aircraft installation at the aircraft manufacturing firms, because the Design Group was the only body of people who knew all the facts and who could play 'with changes and substitutes in order to meet production shortages. The trilogy must therefore be dismembered and a new organisation evolved.' In listing his recommendations for urgent action, Lovell, in his usual fiery style, led off with: '(a) Shoot DRP.' DRP stood for Director of Radio Production at the MAP. In his diary he recorded: 'The urgent action to "shoot DRP" unfortunately reached DRP through some unknown channel and this did not improve our relations!'

In the end, very little came of Lovell's efforts to get a more efficient and speedy method of introduction of new or modified systems onto the production line, and instead it fell to Bomber Command in conjunction with Lovell's group to do their own modification and installations. In the case of the Whirligig 6-foot scanner, for example, Lovell decided to place no reliance on the MAP and A. V. Roe to design the cupola to house this new scanner. Instead, he arranged for his Defford group, which was responsible for prototype installations and flight testing, to design and produce a suitable cupola. The Pathfinder Force aircraft which were to take Whirligig were then modified by Bomber Command personnel in conjunction with Lovell's group. Lovell's long-held policy of a close relationship between designer and operator was once again to pay off.

For a while now, attention focused on matters connected with the impending invasion of France, and the shorter-range radar devices of OBOE and G-H came to the fore. G-H was a kind of reverse of OBOE, in that the aircraft transmitted pulses to two fixed ground stations and measured the time taken for them to reach the ground stations, be responded back and received in the aircraft. In this manner the aircraft could be tracked along a path which passed over the target it wished to attack, having measured the distance of the target from the ground station it was using to track itself. Then, with the measurement taken between the target and the second ground station, the navigator could determine the bomb-release point with very great accuracy. Like OBOE, it was limited in range to about 300 miles at normal operational heights, but it had the advantage over OBOE of permitting up to eighty aircraft to operate on the system simultaneously. This meant that effective bombing of small targets within the range of the system could be achieved with great precision absolutely blind and without resort to marking-techniques.

But if the operational heat was off H2S during the run-up to 'D Day', 6 June 1944, when the invasion of France was launched, and for the following few months whilst Bomber Command was placed under General Eisenhower, the Supreme Commander-in-Chief of the Allied Forces in Europe, the heat was not off Lovell and his group at TRE.

On 25 June 'Lancaster ND823 fitted with prototype H2S Mark VI K band ($1\frac{1}{4}$ cms.) equipment had its first flight. The Severn could be seen for 2-3 miles from 5,000 ft,' Lovell wrote in his diary. Then, 'Late in the evening of Wednesday July 4th the 6 feet scanner and blister in Lancaster JB558 became airborne,' was another entry. On Thursday 6 July, '. . . Most of the day at Defford where Bennett had four flights, first of all in JB558 with the 6 ft Scanner, magnetic indicator, but mainly Mark III [the magnetic indicator was yet another of Lovell's improvements to secure a better picture for the operator]. He appeared to be quite impressed. Secondly with Mark IV H2S, after which he wanted Whirligig and Mark IV together. By working over lunch Thompson and company managed to change JB558 into a IIIF (Whirligig) system and Bennett flew with this. Unfortunately the apparatus broke down. The day ended with a short flight in the K band Lancaster at low altitude.' The Thompson referred to was Dr F. C. Thompson, Lovell's deputy. Then on 8 July: '. . . Demonstrations to Saward, Donaldson and Thompson from Head-quarters, Bomber Command, of the 6 ft X band array (Mark IIIF), and Mark IV.' Group Captain O. R. Donaldson was Chief Navigation Officer at HQ Bomber Command; formerly Commanding Officer of No. 7 Pathfinder Squadron. Thompson was Squadron Leader W. H. Thompson DFC, another young scientist turned navigator who had come off operations with a Lancaster Squadron to take over my research section from Squadron Leader J. H. Day, whom I had released to go to the USA to teach the Americans something about the operational use of H2S. He had then returned to England to do a tour of operations on the H2S-equipped Mosquitoes of No. 139 Squadron, despite having only one leg. Lovell's diary continues: '. . . they did not seem particularly impressed with the picture given by the 6 ft Scanner. They agreed that the definition of water against land was by far the best they had ever seen and that contrast was superior, but the towns broke up so much on the 10 mile range as to be almost unusable. . . . They landed full of enthusiasm for Mark IV H2S, but mostly because they had been lucky in seeing an extremely good picture.'

On the following day, 9 July, Renwick held an H2S Policy Meeting at TRE. The Air Ministry were heavily represented by top brass from the

Signals and Radar Directorates, and the MAP by the Directorate of Communications Development. TRE was there in force, from the Chief Superintendent downwards. Bomber Command was represented by myself, Donaldson and Thompson, and by Bennett from the Pathfinder Force. The Chairman, Sir Robert Renwick, opened the meeting by asking HQ Bomber Command for comments on the flights made with Whirligig, now designated Mk IIIF H2S, and with Mk IV H2S. The minutes record that:

> Group Captain Saward stated that the Mark IIIF system which he had seen had not contained certain items which it is recognised should be in this Mark ... the line of flight marker had been non-available, the height marker was unserviceable, the pulse width was 1 microsecond and not ½ microsecond. The centre of the picture wandered and the elevation coverage was not good; an estimated range of 30-35 miles had been obtained. Compared with Mark IIIA the contrast was greater on Mark IIIF.... Mark IIIA gave a better evenness of picture. The land-water discrimination on Mk IIIF was the best he had ever seen on H2S and the resolution was about ¼ mile from a height of 15,000 feet; on the other hand Mark IIIA was preferable for land-town discrimination, especially between 10 miles range and the bombing point. ...

Bennett agreed with these views.

On the subject of Mark IV H2S the minutes record that:

> '... Group Captain Saward stated that the improvement in evenness of picture was better than in Mark IIIA or Mark IIIF and it was certainly the best picture he had ever seen. It was the first time that coastlines and towns had really been seen well, both together, in a British H2S system. ... G/C Saward continued by commenting that the facility of wind finding was excellent. ... The freezing of the picture made bombing a simple and easy process and although he had approached the conception of a stationary picture with a critical mind he had been more than pleased with the presentation. ... In summary, he would not hesitate in saying that Mark IV is a definite requirement for Bomber Command.'

Bennett again agreed.

The fact was that Lovell, by keeping closely in touch with Bomber Command and making a point of understanding their problems, had produced the near-perfect blind navigation and bombing system. The decision was finally taken to proceed with Mk IV H2S as the ultimate system for Bomber Command, although there was last-minute pressure from both Air Vice-Marshal Victor Tait, the Director General of Signals at the Air Ministry, and Dee of TRE, who was now back from his extended leave, that Bomber Command should go for the 1¼-centimetre Mk VI H2S, better known as Lion Tamer or K Band. The minutes record that: 'G/C Saward wanted Mark IV as it was an equipment which existed and was effectively type approved, while Liontamer was only a concept at present. The development of Liontamer was months behind Mark IV and so it could not possibly be introduced for a long time after Mark IV could be introduced. . . .' The interim requirement for Whirligig for both the Pathfinder Force and the Main Force was also agreed. My insistence on Mk IV H2S was heavily influenced by Lovell's advice. He was never in favour of going from 3 to 1¼ centimetres, for he distrusted the perform-ance of the 1¼-centimetre wavelength in cloud conditions. In the event, he was proved right, for 1¼ centimetres was ultimately found to be incapable of providing echoes at the required ranges when flying at normal operational heights and was proved unreliable when used above cloud, mist or fog due to absorption problems at this very low wavelength. Once again Bomber Command benefited by putting its trust in Lovell.

However, Mk VI H2S was not entirely abandoned. At low level, and in the absence of cloud, it could detect remarkably small objectives, and such a performance could be of value to the Allied Armies in France. For example, it was evident that it could detect concentrations of tanks or whether a viaduct had been successfully breached. Indeed its tactical applications were most promising, particularly when 1¼ centimetres were combined with a 6-foot scanner. In the end, it was agreed with Bomber Command that they would set up a special Flight of six Lancasters fitted with Mk VI H2S with the 6-foot scanner under the command of Squadron Leader J. H. Day to undertake special tactical work for the Army. In fact, the war was almost over by the time this Flight was ready to operate.

If the way was now clear towards a rational programme for H2S for the Bomber Force, the efforts to discredit the system, Lovell and all those who had supported H2S suddenly grew to dangerous proportions, and they were helped by an Intelligence rumour. By May 1944 the 10-centi-metre H2S, with its warning device, Fishpond, which indicated the approach of an enemy fighter, was now in almost every heavy bomber of the Main Force, and the Pathfinding forces were similarly equipped but with the 3-centimetre version. The only exception were the Lancasters of No. 3 Group which carried the radar device known as G-H. In April and May Intelligence sources began to report that it was believed that the Germans had developed a listening-device with which they could home into the bomber stream by utilizing the transmissions of the 10-centi-metre H2S equipment. Moreover, once in the stream, it was hinted that the German night fighter could then home onto an individual aircraft. This device they called Naxos. There was, however, no evidence to date that losses were greater amongst H2S aircraft than amongst aircraft not equipped with H2S. Moreover, Fishpond itself was not providing any signs of stealthily stalking enemy fighters. Even so, because of internal jealousies inside TRE aimed more particularly against Dee and Lovell, and similar jealousies aimed against myself and my radar department, Naxos created a real crisis for H2S. Lovell wrote in his diary that this

crisis in H2S probably has the record of being the most violent and emotional of all, and undoubtedly brought the H2S haters to their nearest point of success. . . . On July 21st [Air Commodore] Dalton-Morris, the Chief Signals Officer of Bomber Command, visited Lewis [Dr W. B. Lewis] and complained about the heavy Ruhr losses. They suspected the Germans could now listen to H2S and get into the bomber stream, and he said that a German fighter pilot had already claimed to have shot down a bomber by using Naxos. Now Dalton-Morris was a well known H2S antagonist and an opponent of Saward. Dalton-Morris lined up with Dickens [head of Bomber Command ORS] and with amazing rapidity the situation became acute . . . improbable stories received wide circulation in Bomber Command amongst the crews regarding the danger of radiating H2S and the ease with which a Naxos fighter could home on to and shoot down a bomber. . . . Then on September 1st, Cockburn [Dr R. Cockburn], who had been spending several weeks at Bomber Command, showed his hand at a Divisional Leader's meeting in TRE, maligned H2S from all aspects, said it was "inaccurate" and so "dangerous" re Naxos that it would have to come out of the Command . . . the situation became so bad with so many accusations being made on all sides that at a meeting in TRE on October 22nd Dee was persuaded to spend three weeks investigating the position at first hand. . . .

In Bomber Command, I was not idle. Squadron Leader W. H. Thompson of my staff was a fluent German linguist, and I arranged for him to interrogate the German pilot who had recently been shot down and made a prisoner of war and who was alleged to have made statements about the use of Naxos. Oddly, the Naxos equipment had not been installed in his aircraft, which was reasonably intact in its crashed condition. This interrogation took place at Trent Park, near Cockfosters in Hertfordshire, on 14 October. The prisoner of war explained to Thompson what he knew of the system and how it was used, describing in some detail the method of presentation of the information it received. He also stated, most emphatically, that the device was designed to be used only to locate the bomber stream, the instrument being crude to the extreme, providing no measurement of range or accurate bearing of detected H2S transmissions. This German went on to say that for attack the fighter relied on instructions from his Ground Night Fighter Control and the use of his radar interception equipment known as SN2, which was comparable to Britain's AI.

Then, in the third week of October, an Intelligence report on the subject of the use of Naxos in the German JU 88G night-fighter variant was issued to Bomber Command Groups. This report discussed the function of Naxos and stated that it made use of the H2S transmissions for homing into the bomber stream and finally onto individual aircraft. The statement was entirely based on hearsay. No Naxos equipment had been captured, and the report was at variance with the interrogation of the German pilot by Squadron Leader Thompson. I immediately spoke to Air Marshal Sir Robert Saundby, the Deputy C-in-C who was unaware that the report had been circulated to Groups. He immediately tried to stop circulation below Air Officers Commanding Groups and their Senior Air Staff Officers. But it was already too late. Within a short time the word was around that H2S was unsafe.

Saundby then instructed me to draw up a report on the operational use of H2S for September, analysing losses of aircraft and attaching Thompson's report of his interrogation of the captured German pilot. This document was completed by me under the heading 'Operational Use of H2S—September 1944' dated 23 October 1944. Its circulation was wide, including all Groups, Bases and Squadrons, the Air Ministry, Renwick, TRE, MAP and others. It covered numbers of aircraft equipped, state of training, serviceability, details of bomber raids during the period and use made of H2S on each target, and an assessment of aircraft losses. Out of a total of 3,521 sorties flown during the period by Lancasters and Halifax aircraft, 61 had been lost on operations, just 1.73 per cent, a percentage far lower than the average in 1943. Indeed, from 1 April 1944 to 31 December 1944 Bomber Command despatched 145,190 sorties against all enemy targets for the loss of 1,945 aircraft, just 1.34 per cent. From November 1943 to March 1944 the loss rate had been running at 4.2 per cent, and throughout 1943 it had been averaging just over 4 per cent. The significant change had come, tellingly, with the increase in fitting of H2S together with Lovell's other brainchild, Fishpond. The final paragraphs of my report were devoted to Naxos:

The following are the facts. Nearly all information available on Naxos has emanated from Prisoners of War. No Naxos equipment has as yet fallen into our hands. . . . The attached report is one compiled by Squadron Leader Thompson, DFC, of this Headquarters, who interrogated Prisoners of War with a view to assessing the value of Naxos as a homing aid . . . it will be seen that Naxos may be useful for homing into the stream, but has serious limitations as a 'homer' on to individual aircraft. It may therefore provide early warning of the approach of the Bomber Force, but since the plotting of the Force over enemy territory is already accomplished by other means, i.e. sound location, ground Radar plotting, etc., crews need not be unduly intimidated by the German's use of Naxos. . . . The chief value of Naxos to the Germans may be as a propaganda weapon in an endeavour to stop, or at least limit, our use of H2S. . . . In conclusion, the old maxim has it that "the proof of the pudding is in the eating"—and until H2S losses are significantly higher than non-H2S losses, the effectiveness of Naxos will remain in considerable and justified doubt. Since the loss rate for September is lower than ever recorded in these reports, the success of Naxos is absolutely inconclusive.

A short while after this a complete German night fighter fell into Allied hands. It was equipped with a device named 'Flensberg' which was designed to home onto the British tail warning device known as 'Monica', which had been replaced by 'Fishpond' in all H2S aircraft. However, Monica was still carried in the non-H2S Lancasters of No. 3 Group which were equipped with the blind bombing device known as G-H. It was also carried in those few heavy bombers which were still without H2S. Flight trials with this German equipment were carried out by Wing Commander Derek Jackson,* a scientist from Oxford University and a very experienced operator of the British night fighter AI system. His findings were that Flensberg was a highly efficient device. As a result, Monica was ejected from all aircraft, and the stock of H2S and its Fishpond immediately went up again.

Lovell and his group, now refreshed by the changes in attitude towards H2S and by the series of successes on the important longer-range targets which became a priority in the closing days of 1944 and the beginning of 1945, pressed on even more vigorously to give Bomber Command better and better service. But the end was near. VE Day was rapidly approaching. In February Lovell collapsed from overwork. The last but one entry in his record of the times reads: 'The opponents of H2S were at least tenacious! Having failed on all technical and tactical counts to eject H2S, early in 1945 they commenced a great agitation that the manpower situation was too poor to handle it. . . . Friday February 9th 1945 . . . 14.45 . . . meeting at Headquarters, Bomber Command, to discuss H2S policy with particular reference to the manpower situation. Dee and Cockburn also attended. Saundby in the chair. Renwick and Watson Watt present also. . . .' The decision was quite firmly that H2S was an essential equipment for every bomber and that Mk IV H2S, the version to end all versions, should be introduced as swiftly as possible. Naxos was dismissed as of no consequence, even if it truly existed, because 'our losses for the past few months have been the lowest recorded in the history of the Bomber Force.' In fact, it is interesting to note that between 1 October 1944 and 31 December 1944, when 42,955 sorties were flown against German industrial targets, many at long range, only 372 aircraft were lost, or 0.86 per cent. For the rest of the war, from 1 January 1945 to the end of May 1945, when hostilities with Germany ceased, 57,583 sorties were flown against Germany for the loss of 608 aircraft, or just over one per cent.

On 15 February 1945 A. P. Rowe wrote a letter to Lovell, who had collapsed but was anxious to be available to do some limited work again as soon as possible. It was typical of Lovell's deep sense of duty. In his letter, Rowe said: 'I will not dwell in this letter on my personal sorrow that you are temporarily unfit, but I am sure you know that I sympathise and hope for your speedy recovery. I do not like the details of your proposal at all.' This was a reference to Lovell's suggestion that he would come in to work part time as soon as he was a bit more rested. 'The trouble with us all when we get overtired is that we hang on. You need have nothing whatever on your conscience; if you never did a stroke of work for the rest of your life you would have justified your existence. . . .' Then again, on 22 March, Rowe wrote to Lovell at the home of Joyce's parents, where he was convalescing. 'I wish I had you beside me on the top of the roof of the Preston Lab., because I would push you off. [The Preston Lab was at Malvern College where Lovell's group worked.] There is absolutely no need for you to worry about anything here and you have nothing at all on your conscience. If you had fallen off a mast and had injured your spine, you would not find any psychological difficulty about staying in Plaster of Paris for a few months, however restless you might be. Instead of falling off a mast you have overstrained yourself in another way; incidentally, a way which reflects the greatest credit on you. . . .'

A little after half-past two in the afternoon of 8 May 1945, Winston Churchill, the Prime Minister, rose in his place in the House of Commons and announced that Germany had signed an Act of Unconditional Surrender. On this day Lovell was with me at Whaddon Hall, a country house near Bletchley in Buckinghamshire which had been taken over during the war by the Foreign Office. It was the Secret Service Centre where agents were trained and briefed and to which they communicated when operating in enemy territory. Some of the radar equipment used for locating their exact dropping and pick-up positions had been developed unknowingly by Lovell's group in TRE. Responsibility for its provision had been Bomber Command's, as was that for the two squadrons used for these subversive activities. I had taken Lovell to Whaddon to meet Brigadier Gambier-Parry, the head of this branch of the Secret Service, together with some of his officers, so that they could thank him for his contribution to their work, albeit made unwittingly. It was just before Churchill's announcement that, in company with Gambier-Parry, Lovell and I heard the news of the German surrender. It was fitting that we should have been together on this memorable occasion.

Lovell's last entry in his record of his work at TRE was written a week after VE Day (Victory Europe Day). It reads as follows:

These 50 pages contain only scraps from nearly 3½ years of deepest depression and ecstatic joys. It tells nothing of big bomb doors and nose H2S in Lancasters, of perspex in scanner barrels, or of the 99 other telephone calls which arrived every day. But H2S lived, and it seems that so few people really helped it to live, and so many through jealousy or bloody mindedness tried their damndest to hinder it and malign it, by action, non action or word of mouth. If they had helped, how much energy and worry would have been saved, and how much better H2S could have been! But *this* is *Thursday May 17th 1945* and VE Day is gone more than a week. Others are worrying and arguing about whether K band, IIIE or Mark IV should go to the Pacific. 8 Group (Pathfinder Force) is scarcely any more and the Air Vice-Marshal [D. C. T. Bennett] who caused us so much trouble, but who nevertheless was one of our staunchest friends, has grown into an MP.* So that is that, and may the next scrap book be about electrons, neutrons and Professors, and not about scanners, cathode ray tubes, and Air Marshals.'

The ease with which the Allies swept across the German-occupied territories and Germany itself, from 6 June 1944 until the collapse of German resistance in the first week of May, after Hitler's suicide on 30 April 1945, was unquestionably due to the long and sustained strategic bomber offensive which effectively began at the beginning of 1942. The truth was that production in Germany had been so progressively devastated by Bomber Command in 1942 and 1943, and by Bomber Command and the US Eighth Bomber Command in 1944, that German losses of weapons on all fronts were by 1944 and 1945 in excess of replacement rates from production. Bombing had denied not the men but the weapons with which to defend the Fatherland, despite the excellent management of German military production by Albert Speer, the German Minister for Armaments Production.

Between the beginning of the war on 3 September 1939 and 3 May 1945, when the last bombing raid was made on Germany in an attack against enemy shipping at Kiel, Bomber Command despatched 389,809 sorties against enemy targets in Germany, German-occupied territory and Italy, for the loss of 8,655 aircraft, a loss rate of just over 2.2 per cent. Of these sorties, 336,037 were despatched on bombing raids, dropping a total of 955,044 tons of bombs; 19,025 were despatched on sea-mining missions, laying 47,037 mines, a total tonnage in mines of 33,237 tons; the remainder were despatched on radio counter-measure flights, fighter support, decoy flights, intruder activities against enemy aerodromes, meteorological flights, reconnaissance and special operations such as agent-dropping and pick-up. By far the greatest proportion of this effort was undertaken between February 1942 and May 1945 under the command of Air Chief Marshal Sir Arthur Harris. During this period, 331,001 sorties were despatched, dropping 906,973 tons of bombs and laying 45,428 sea-mines, and of the total tonnage of bombs dropped, it is interesting to note that 865,715 tons were dropped in 1943, 1944 and the four months of 1945, during the period that H2S, OBOE and G-H were available to the bomber force.

Whatever documentary evidence one researches, German, British or American, it is evident that the strategic bombing of Germany was a decisive factor in the defeat of Germany. Since this was undertaken almost entirely by Bomber Command from February 1942 until the beginning of 1944, and largely by Bomber Command from the beginning of 1944 to the end of the war, Bomber Command's contribution to victory on its own was unquestionably decisive. Equally unquestionable is the fact that the Bomber Offensive would have been an abysmal failure in the absence of the vital contribution the scientists made to the effectiveness of the bomber. Without GEE, H2S, Fishpond, G-H and OBOE, Bomber Command could never have succeeded in its task. At the beginning of the war it had few adequate aircraft and no scientific aids to night operations, although at all times it had courageous air crews and efficient and determined ground staffs and maintenance crews. By 1942 it was beginning to expand with the right type of aircraft and the right bomb capacity, and it was in receipt of GEE, its first radar aid to navigation. By 1943 and through to the end of the war it was receiving the full benefit of scientific assistance to navigation, precision target-marking and blind bombing.

The contribution of the scientists and engineers of TRE was of inestimable value, and without it the war might have ended in a negotiated peace or even have finished with the ignominious defeat of Britain. It was not only the contribution made by TRE to the success of the Strategic Bombing Offensive that was vital but also that made to successful defence in the 'Battle of Britain' by the invention and development of ground radar and the fighter aircraft's airborne AI system. In the case of the 'Battle of the Atlantic' against the German Navy and its U-boats, success was achieved again by shipborne radar and by the airborne radar known as ASV. Many names were associated with these developments, and on the airborne side they include R. J. Dippy, Dr W. B. Lewis, A. H. Reeves, Dr F. E. Jones, Dr Alan Hodgkin, Dr S. Devons, Dr E. G. Bowen, Dr P. I. Dee and Lovell. But taking count of the exceptional importance of AI, ASV, H2S and Fishpond, the names of Dee and Lovell stand out prominently.

Lovell himself is particularly notable because he never allowed disasters and setbacks to deviate him from his tasks, and because of his dedicated and almost mad application to work which was always supported by his scientific genius. It was not enough for Lovell to have ideas; he had to carry them forward to a state where they could be put into practice and, due to his great sense of perfection, he was never satisfied with what he achieved and constantly sought to improve the original product of his imaginative mind. A major reason for the success of ASV, H2S and Fishpond was Lovell's readiness to study at first hand the problems that confronted an aircrew. This had to be confined to flying with his own experimental equipment and with prototypes of final versions, and to frequent visits to Bomber Command operational stations to meet and talk to crews returning from night raids over Germany. If he had been permitted to accompany aircrews on operations over enemy territory to gain first-hand experience of the conditions under which navigators had to operate his equipment, he would have gone without hesitation. But he knew too much, and he was too valuable to be put at risk.

Lovell's contribution to victory must be rated, alongside Dee's amongst the greatest from any man. H2S was not only an indispensable aid for navigating to and bombing targets in Germany which were beyond the range of other systems, targets which were considerable in number and industrially, from a military point of view, amongst the most vital to Germany's war effort; it was also essential to accurate navigation to Ruhr and other shorter-range targets where Pathfinder marking-techniques were used with the aid of OBOE. Moreover, it assisted follow-up crews to identify the Pathfinder marking and to avoid being led astray by decoy markers and fires. It is sometimes forgotten that the greater part of Germany lay outside the range of OBOE and G-H, added to which there were further important target areas in Poland, Czechoslovakia, Austria and northern Italy which could be attacked only with the aid of H2S. It is interesting to note that from July 1943 until April 1944, after which Bomber Command was switched to invasion targets, more than 75 per cent of the strategic bombing was dependent upon the navigation and bombing facilities of H2S. Indeed, from October 1943 to March 1944, inclusive, 93 per cent of the bombing effort depended upon H2S. The percentage from September 1944 to the end of the war was over 70.

9

Return to Manchester

As early as February 1945, Lovell was receiving offers from industry to take up senior research posts as soon as he could be released from his war work, appointments which offered substantial financial rewards. The first came by a letter from the Christie Hospital and Holt Radium Institute of Manchester. In April came an approach from Imperial Chemical Industries Limited, Dyestuffs Division, as a result of a contact by Professor Bragg with Lord Hankey's Committee on Higher Appointments to Industry. In May came another approach from ICI, but this time from the Explosives Division, which had been stimulated by a recommendation from Dr C. P. Snow. There were others, all of which were financially tempting. Efforts were made, too, to persuade Lovell to remain at TRE and to become a Government Scientist in the Civil Service. As a Principal Scientific Officer, he was now in receipt of a salary of £950 per annum, and although this was not as high as he could acquire in industry, he could, nonetheless, look forward to swift and attractive increases. Some people assumed that he would follow Dee to Glasgow University, where Dee had been offered and had accepted the Chair as Professor of Natural Philosophy, an appointment which he would be taking up as soon as he was released from his war work.

In fact, by a letter dated 26 January 1945 from the Registrar of the University of Manchester, Lovell was advised that he had 'been appointed Lecturer in Physics for a period of three years as from September 29th, 1945, subject to the usual conditions as to notice, at a stipend of £550 per annum, rising according to scale'. This was almost half his TRE salary. Then, by a letter dated 16 February, he received the 'Conditions of Appointment' form for his signature of acceptance. It had been, and still was, Lovell's firm intention to return to work on cosmic ray research under Blackett at Manchester, but there were two matters which made him hesitate to sign his acceptance. One was the very considerable drop in salary and the consequent reduction in living-standards which his family would have to face. The second was his uncertainty as to whether Blackett would himself return to Manchester, even though he had indicated that this was his intention. Lovell therefore stalled. By a letter dated 21 February, he told Blackett at the Admiralty of the approach that had been made to him by the Holt Radium Institute but that, in his heart of hearts, 'I am so anxious to return to Manchester Physics Dept., that I think it extremely unlikely that anything would divert me from that path . . . unless you have any objection I could arrange to visit them in March.' This he hoped might cause Blackett to confirm to him expressly that he, Blackett, would be returning to Manchester and would want Lovell with him. Lovell then continued in his letter to tell of Manchester's offer of the post of Lecturer in Physics at £550 per annum, and asked him if he knew of any family allowances on top of this salary. With a certain shrewdness he asked if he should sign the official appointment forms on 'probability grounds, or delay until I have visited the Radium Institute'. He concluded by saying: 'I am suffering from acute fatigue and have been told by a specialist that I shall collapse unless I stop work. I am therefore leaving TRE for 4 weeks beginning on Saturday, 24th February next. If you want me I shall be at Limpley Stoke with my family, but we are hoping to visit Manchester to get ourselves a home!'

Blackett's reply, dated 28 February, renewed Lovell's desire to return to Manchester, for it seemed to imply that Blackett would certainly be returning to resume his post as head of the Physics Department. He told Lovell that in addition to the stipend there was a family allowance of £25 per annum for each child. He had, he said, 'hoped to get your starting salary a bit higher, but it was not possible. . . . There is of course a regular increase of salary. . . .' He saw no harm in looking at the Holt Radium Institute job and if necessary holding up his reply to Manchester until after he had visited the Institute, but he very much hoped that Lovell would 'find it possible to accept the Manchester job in spite of the somewhat disappointing salary'. He went on to say that he had asked the Vice-Chancellor about initiating action for an early release of both Lovell and Wilson, but the view was that it would be best to await the outcome of the after-effects of the German counter-offensive in the Ardennes which might delay the expected imminent collapse of Germany. The last paragraph probably had the greatest effect upon Lovell, because it seemed to be almost a guarantee that Blackett would return to Manchester: 'I am terribly sorry that you have got so overtired and hope that a good rest will soon put you right. We must meet again soon to discuss future cosmic ray experiments. I am beginning to champ at the bit to get started. The radio detection of big showers and the distance to the moon must be fully thought out.' It was a baited hook to keep Lovell nibbling!

However, now that Lovell was resting and recuperating, he was able to consider his future a little more dispassionately. He arranged to see A. M. Tyndall, his old professor at Bristol, on 13 March. He also wrote to Dee at TRE to seek his advice. He held Dee in great respect. Generally speaking, the advice from both was go back to Manchester as his allegiance to Blackett would always prove greater than any other he could make. There

were three letters from Dee in March and April. In the first he enumerated university salaries at Glasgow and suggested that by these standards
Manchester levels were not at all bad; although he deplored in general
that something much better could not be done by the universities, with
Government aid, for the scientists who had done so much for the country
in the war. He refrained from advising Lovell on making a decision until
he had seen Blackett, who was due to visit TRE that week, and had spoken
to him about Lovell's future. 'I will pump him discreetly,' he wrote, 'not
only as to his own plans, but also to discover his real degree of enthusiasm
about having you back, not that I personally have any doubt on the latter
score.' In his second letter he assured Lovell that he knew 'nothing of a
lack of intention on Blackett's part about returning to Manchester', but he
went on to explain that he had not seen Blackett because his visit to TRE
had been postponed indefinitely. Just prior to receiving this letter, Lovell
wrote to Dee and told him he had finally made up his mind to return to
Manchester and would be writing to Blackett accordingly. This prompted
the third letter from Dee. He wrote: 'I don't expect you are waiting to hear
from me after my last letter which crossed yours, before replying to
Blackett. I think I agree with you about what you should do. The
"Radium" job seems to be research rather than application, and if you are
going to research you would probably be wiser to do so in Physics rather
than in a new subject. Not that I think you shouldn't research, it's merely
that I feel you are so good at "doing" things (dare I say à la Renwick?) that
I have sometimes felt you should do such things post war. . . .' The
reference to Sir Robert Renwick implied the latter's ability to cut through
red tape, break every procedure laid down by officialdom and improvise to
the maximum in order to meet urgent requirements without any delays.
Lovell had researched and then emulated Renwick in his determination
to see that his developments were swiftly translated into practical systems
for use by the Royal Air Force. He had transgressed every law in the book
in his clandestine efforts to take care of Bomber Command's desperate
needs, admittedly encouraged and assisted by Bennett and me, and by
Renwick himself. Dee's assessment was not only correct: it was prophetic.
Lovell's future research and application 'à la Renwick' was soon to
produce one of the greatest scientific achievements and engineering feats
of the immediate post-war period in Britain.

Referring to Lovell's release from TRE, Dee promised to take the
matter up with Renwick and Watson Watt. He seemed confident that an
early release could be obtained if Manchester officially asked for his
return to the University at the earliest possible date. At the time, Dee was
standing in for Rowe, who was sick.

Lovell's decision to return to the work he loved, and which he believed to be of the greatest importance to the future of mankind's knowledge, was not an easy one to take when he had his family to think about. It was not just a case of turning down lucrative offers; it was also a matter of taking a drastic reduction in his existing remuneration. But if any doubts remained, they were dispelled by Joyce. She rightly judged the importance to her husband of his return to cosmic ray research, and she understood that in such work he would find real satisfaction. Joyce encouraged him to the full in making his decision, even though she knew, better than he, what sacrifices would have to be made in order to live within their new and very limited means. On 7 April Lovell signed the 'Conditions of Appointment' to the University of Manchester, accepting the position of Lecturer in Physics with effect from 29 September 1945. In fact, due to Blackett's endeavours, he was released earlier than anticipated.

The Lovell family soon found a home on the outskirts of Manchester at Timperley, a house with a fair-sized garden and a stream running through it, which offered great possibilities for development under Bernard Lovell's expert care, for gardening had become another of his hobbies over the years. They moved in the early autumn, Lovell himself arriving at the University of Manchester in much the same manner as he had arrived from St Athan at TRE, when it was at Swanage in 1940, with lorry loads of equipment. He had never lost sight of those sporadic echoes he had first seen on the radar screens at Staxton Wold, Perth and St Athan in 1939 and 1940, and many times later when testing new radar systems, he had seen echoes which he associated with cosmic ray showers. Clearly, radar was a means of assisting his researches into cosmic rays, and with the war over and the probable abandonment of expensive and useful equipment to rot in the face of the elements, or to succumb to the steamroller of some diligent and unintelligent disposals authority, Lovell had decided to help himself. With the aid of Dr J. S. Hey of the Army Operational Research Group, he acquired two trailers full of radar equipment, including a $4\frac{1}{2}$-metre Army GL (Gun Layer) apparatus, which only a few months previously had been used to direct anti-aircraft guns at enemy aircraft, together with a portable diesel generator. Lovell had in 1940 drawn Blackett's attention to the possibilities of obtaining radar echoes from the ionization caused by large cosmic ray showers. But by the end of 1940 all thoughts of cosmic ray research by old or new techniques had become lost in the emergency of the struggle for survival. Now, in the autumn of 1945, Lovell returned to his interrupted academic career, complete with apparatus to try out new techniques—apparatus acquired for the price of a glib tongue and an engaging smile! As when he arrived with his lorry loads of equipment at TRE Swanage from St Athan, acquired by means unknown to anyone other than Bernard Lovell himself, eyes boggled with envy and disbelief as he pulled into the quadrangle outside the Physics Department of the University.

Lovell had arrived back in Manchester.

10

On the Track of a Meteor

Lovell's first plan when he returned to his academic career in civilian life was to substantiate his belief, derived from watching sporadic echoes on wartime radar equipment, that radio echoes from cosmic ray showers could be observed with radar. From such observations he hoped that more could be learned about these fast-moving particles which continually enter the upper atmosphere from interplanetary space and whose origin was uncertain. The idea of embarking upon astronomical research was not strictly in his mind, although his inquisitiveness about the Universe and its structure had never been assuaged since it had first been stimulated when as a boy, returning from that Tyndall lecture on 'The Electric Spark' in the winter of 1928, a lecture which had fundamentally redirected the course of his life, he had looked up at the stars and wondered what they were.

In 1945 radio astronomy was not yet a known science. So far, knowledge of outer space had been acquired through the eyes of man which are sensitive to radiations in a small region of the spectrum from the violet to the red. Radiation from the stars in this part of the spectrum penetrates the Earth's atmosphere without any significant absorption, and therefore this region provides a kind of window through which the Universe can be observed. At wavelengths shorter than the violet or longer than the red, the radiations are absorbed by the dust and water-vapour in the atmosphere. Since it was well known from the basic laws of physics that the Sun and the stars gave out most of their energy in the visible region of the spectrum, the inability to study the radiations from Space beyond this region was not believed to be a serious deterrent to a comprehensive study of the heavens.

If by the end of World War II radio astronomy was unknown, the subject certainly had its origins in events as far back as 1930-31 when Karl Jansky of the Bell Telephone Laboratories in the USA discovered that there were radio emissions from the Milky Way. At the time, he was investigating atmospherics as a source of interference with long-distance wireless communications. His radio receiving-equipment operated on a wavelength of several metres, and he noticed during his investigations a significant amount of noise even when there were no obvious sources of atmospherics such as thunderstorms. He then observed that the noise level reached a maximum once a day, but the period was not 24 hours, but

23 hours 56 minutes, which is the period of rotation of the Earth with respect to the stars, i.e. a sidereal day. He was thus able to conclude explicitly that this noise which he was receiving had its source not only outside the Earth's atmosphere but actually outside the Solar System, and he therefore decided that the stars must be emitting energy in the radio-wave part of the spectrum as well as in the optical. Jansky would have liked to continue his investigations, but Bell Telephone considered that he had completed his studies with regard to atmospheric influences on radio and wireless communications and would not support further research in connection with radio emissions from stars. Extraordinarily, neither did the astronomical community of that era react to Jansky's discovery. In fact, the only person to follow Jansky's work was a young amateur enthusiast, Grote Reber, who built his own 31-foot parabolic reflector and receiving-equipment in his private yard at Wheaton, Illinois. With this early, if not first, radio telescope, he plotted the first radio maps of the Milky Way, but by the time he published his results in 1940, the world had already begun to go to war and soon there was no interest in the Universe, only in the survival of the inhabitants of this speck of dust called Earth.

Whether Lovell in 1945 was aware that he was about to embark upon an extensive study of the Universe using radio techniques, thereby laying the true foundations of radio astronomy by which man was soon to probe deeper and deeper into Space almost to the very beginnings of creation, is a debatable point. He claims that it was more by accident than intent, but somehow one feels that he subconsciously permitted the accident to happen! At any rate, no sooner was he back in Manchester than he was working away furiously to get his radar equipment into operation, hoping to begin the search for cosmic ray echoes without delay, but as soon as he was 'on the air' he was to discover that his efforts were being sabotaged by an old-fashioned enemy. In 1945 Manchester still proudly operated its electric tram service, and the trams cavorted past the University with such persistence that they constantly swamped the cathode ray tube with their electrical interference, covering it with bright flashing spikes of light that made it impossible to detect any other signals such as echoes from cosmic ray showers. Even in the early hours of a Sunday morning, when all was apparently quiet, the interference was far too great for Lovell to be able to contemplate research under such conditions. Clearly a site outside the city was needed, and a determined Lovell sought out R. A. Rainford, the University Bursar, to see if the University could provide any land outside the built-up area where he could take his trailers. He met Rainford in the Staff House and on the same afternoon went to inspect a site in the area of

High Legh, near Lymm, to which Rainford had directed him. The land was traversed by high-voltage grid lines and offered even less sanctuary from interference than was available alongside the trams.

Six centuries ago, a Cheshire archer named William Jauderell, whilst fighting with the Black Prince at Poitiers, learnt that his house in England had been destroyed by fire. Because of this misfortune, the Black Prince gave him leave to return to England to look after his affairs, and to make his journey possible he provided him with a pass which was inscribed on a roll of parchment and from which hung the Great Seal of the Prince. William Jauderell made the journey home safely, and the parchment is still in the hands of his descendants, the Jodrell family, as the name is now spelt. The few acres of land above a small brook near the village of Lower Withington, twenty-five miles south of Manchester, which had been a part of Jauderell's estate, became known as Jodrell Bank—'Bank' being the Cheshire name for a small rise or hill. These few acres and certain adjoining acres were acquired during the early part of the century by a local farmer by the name of Ted Moston. Then just before the outbreak of World War II, the University of Manchester purchased from Moston eleven acres of land, including Jodrell Bank, for the use of the Botany Department. It was to this area that Rainford next directed Lovell when he rejected the High Legh site as utterly useless. Lovell recalls how this happened, in the Staff House. Rainford said: 'You see that man with the beard over there drinking beer? That's Sansome, the botanist, who runs a place called Jodrell Bank—try him.'

As luck would have it, Sansome was an amateur radio enthusiast and a keen radio experimenter, quite apart from being a professional botanist. The match was ideal. Lovell was by profession a physicist whose principal work in the last five to six years had been concerned with the most advanced radio research and techniques in the world, but one of his hobbies was gardening. Sansome was immediately ready to help by welcoming Lovell to his domain, and soon a friendship was forged between the two men through their mutual interests. Lovell says, 'There were some occasions when I felt we were better at each other's job!'

Early in December 1945 Lovell's trailers with their radar equipment and diesel generator left the quadrangle outside the Physics Department and were towed southwards from Manchester to their new site at Jodrell Bank. The prime movers that towed them were nothing to do with the University or, for that matter, any civil transport contractor. Lovell had more economical ideas. Somehow he managed to persuade the Army to undertake the transfer, and thus the equipment he had begged, borrowed and acquired was taken to its final location in military style. The accommodation at this new 'research centre' was not exactly palatial. It consisted of two wooden huts full of fertilizers and spades; there was no electric power within miles, and at the time there was thick fog in the first few days and a bitterly hard frost. But there were compensations. There were two friendly gardeners from Sansome's Botany Department, Alf Dean and Frank Foden, who were only too anxious to help in any way they could, and if it had not been for them, the start of operations at Jodrell might have been long delayed.

The first problem was to get the generator going so that the mobile equipment could have the power to go 'on the air', but even with Alf and Frank to help crank the diesel engine it remained morosely silent. However, Lovell's two new friends were well acquainted with Ted Moston, the farmer, who was a competent engineer with tractors, diesel engines and the like, and he was swiftly co-opted to the team. In no time he had the diesel in pieces—only to discover that the trouble was the simple one of the fuel pipes being blocked with ice! On the third day the diesel burst into song, and electricity was being generated at Jodrell Bank; Lovell was able to switch on his radar transmitter and receiver. It was 14 December, and he was greeted with the echoes from what he took to be extensive cosmic ray showers. He was in fact wrong, because he had switched on at the time of the maximum of the Geminid meteor shower.

A meteor is a small body moving around the Sun in the manner of a dwarf planet. If it enters the upper atmosphere of Earth, it becomes intensely heated by friction and destroys itself in the streak of luminosity known as a shooting star. It is now estimated that about one hundred million meteors enter the atmosphere daily and move at velocities of up to 45 miles per second relative to Earth. They are usually destroyed before they penetrate to 60 or 70 miles above the ground. The most spectacular are what are known as shower meteors which travel round the Sun in shoals, and when Earth passes through these shoals, the result is a shower of shooting stars. There are many annual showers named after the constellations in which their radiants lie, and amongst these are the Geminids, which can be observed from about 9–15 December of any year.

In December 1945 Lovell knew nothing about meteors or Geminids, but his equipment was working, and in one of the huts there was a coke stove in front of which Alf, Frank and Lovell could thaw themselves out in the cold winter months, brew tea and eat their packed sandwiches at lunchtime. Soon the two trailers with their diesel generator were transformed into a research laboratory, and the primary object of the Jodrell Bank excursion, observing echoes from cosmic ray showers, was supplemented by other researches. It was reasonable for Lovell's superior,

Patrick Blackett, to permit him to engage in a short field expedition in the interests of his work, but few other professors in his position would have encouraged the growth of this foray into the fields of Cheshire, with money and any other assistance he could muster, to the level of a permanent research centre. There has always been a certain amount of traditional freedom in university researches, but Blackett had the power to stop Lovell undertaking any research he personally wanted to undertake with the apparatus in his possession. However, within a few months of 14 December 1945, Blackett was as excited as Lovell at the string of discoveries that were soon pouring into the wartime radar equipment at Jodrell Bank, and even when it was quickly obvious that Lovell was not pursuing the original plan in connection with cosmic ray research, Blackett supported him wholeheartedly.

By early 1946 Lovell was convinced that the echoes he was receiving by day and by night were not from cosmic ray showers but from meteors. Pre-war literature and reports on ionospheric conditions contained many references to meteors and to the possibility that the trail of electrons left by a meteor burning up as it plunged into the Earth's atmosphere scattered radio waves back to Earth to give short-lived echoes. But the astronomical textbooks contained little about the phenomenon of meteors and shooting stars, and to correlate the radar echoes with meteors burning up required more knowledge about the behaviour and the presence of meteors. In the spring and early summer of 1946, Blackett's laboratory at the University of Manchester was beginning to take on a cosmopolitan atmosphere as scientists from all corners of the world began to visit the Physics Department for short or long periods. Amongst these young visiting scientists was a Norwegian by the name of Nicolai Herlofson,* an ex-wartime meteorologist. There is no connection between meteors and meteorologists, but on the assumption that meteorologists do sometimes look at the skies, Lovell asked Herlofson if he knew anything about the behaviour of meteors. In fact, he did not, but he was able to tell Lovell that the study of meteors did not form a great part of the activities of professional astronomers because it was considered to be a waste of telescope time to observe phenomena which could be seen by the unaided eye. Consequently the investigation of meteors was conducted mainly by amateurs, such as those organized by the British Astronomical Association. The director of this section was J. P. Manning Prentice, a Suffolk solicitor by profession. It was not long before Lovell had made contact with Prentice and thus taken another step towards satisfying his curiosity about the structure of the Universe.

For the first few months at Jodrell, Lovell was on his own, with Alf and Frank to help him start the diesel, to keep him company over a mug of tea and to munch their sandwiches together with him at lunchtime. However, he was quickly to receive Blackett's permission to recruit some of his wartime associates to work in Blackett's physics laboratories in Manchester and to help him out at Jodrell. The first and most important scientifically was Dr John A. Clegg, who arrived in the spring of 1946, together with two others, to join the embryo laboratory in the green fields of Cheshire. For technical reasons, Lovell had separated the trailer containing the receiving-equipment from the one with the transmitter by a distance of several hundred yards. With the diesel generator also sited apart from the transmitter and receiver, and with no connecting roads, it made life a little difficult. As Lovell recalls, 'To start a night's observation Clegg and I often began by wading in gumboots through two fields to our trailers and wrestling with the diesel, unprotected except by a flimsy canvas on its trolley.' The discomfort inspired them to make an apology for a road, which was nonetheless effective. They started the project armed with spades, but it was a daunting task for they wanted it to go from the main road to the trailers, about a quarter of a mile, and to connect the trailers and the diesel. Alf and Frank again came to the rescue with the knowledge that farmer Ted Moston had a scoop attachment to his tractor which could easily carve out two tracks about a foot deep and spaced to suit the gauge of a car's wheels. Moston's tractor was immediately pressed into service, and the resulting tracks were filled in with lorry loads of stone from a nearby quarry, the filling being done by hand by Lovell and Clegg. It was a great improvement and was to save the problems of getting bogged down in the wet weather when trying to deliver further apparatus and spares.

Following on Lovell's contact with Manning Prentice, the Suffolk solicitor hastened to visit Manchester to find out what were Lovell's interests in meteors. He first came to the Lovell home at Timperley and then, after a survey of the Jodrell laboratory out in the wilds, declared his interest in co-operating in a programme of research, combining visual and radar observations. The idea was that, if the echoes being received on the cathode ray tube in the receiving trailer appeared at the same time as the visible trail of a meteor in the sky, this would confirm the source of the echoes. But Manning Prentice warned Lovell and his three colleagues that meteors were irregular in their rate of occurrence, although there was always a sporadic background with a daily variation in rate which at 6 a.m., when the rate was a maximum, should give five to ten meteor trails per hour which were visible to the eye under clear sky conditions. The next major shower, Manning Prentice advised, would be the Perseids due between 30 July and 17 August, and since this was a reliable and regular shower, and the richest annual shower, it was decided that observation of the Perseids should be the object of their first joint venture.

The rest of 1946, through to 1950, was a period of the evolution of a new destiny for Lovell and Jodrell Bank, and it was marked by a number of milestones, some of which were personal or essentially of a family nature. On 23 June 1946 'Operations Perseids' was preceded by another important event. On that day Joyce Lovell presented Bernard Lovell with a second daughter, Judith Ann.

Shortly before the Perseids were due to appear, Manning Prentice arrived at Jodrell in an open Morris car, the back of which was piled high with celestial globes, star atlases and other paraphernalia which he used for his observations, including a deckchair, various instruments and, the most mysterious of all, a flying-suit. The deckchair proved not to be for leisure but, set up in as near a horizontal position as possible, to provide him with the means to lie with some comfort in a position from which he could keep the sky under constant observation and, with a piece of string stretched at arm's length along the line of a transient meteor, read off the stars which marked the beginning and end points of the meteor's track. His findings he recorded on a writing-board strapped to his thigh. The flying-suit was simply to keep him warm in the cold night air! It was arranged that, when a meteor appeared in the sky, Prentice would announce its arrival by a shout from his deckchair, whilst Lovell, and whoever was accompanying him, would watch the cathode ray tube in the trailer and thus establish any correlation between the echoes and the meteors. These early experiments provided much valuable information but were far from conclusive. There were shouts without echoes, echoes without shouts, and sometimes shouts which were followed by an echo some seconds later. The echoes, too, were 'a mixed bag', as Lovell recalls, 'some so short lived that they were scarcely visible, and others of many seconds duration, generally showing violent fluctuations in strength'.

After the Perseids, Manning Prentice promised to return in mid November for the Leonids, which were the next regular shower worth investigating and which were due between 15 and 17 November. In the meantime, however, he advised Lovell that on the night of 9–10 October there was a chance that Earth would pass through the tail of a periodic comet, the Giacobini-Zinner Comet, and that there might be an enormous but short-lived shower.

During 1946 Lovell was able to add to his equipment, thanks to some of his old friends at the Air Ministry. His acquisitions consisted of several trailers of radar equipment, for which he paid the nominal sum of £10. The *pièce de résistance* was a prime mover, consisting of a large cabin packed with electronic equipment and known in the Royal Air Force as a

'Park Royal'. This masterpiece of scrounging was delivered by Clegg, who drove it up to Jodrell from the south of England. Following the famous tracks constructed by Moston's tractor and the hands of Lovell and Clegg, it was carefully driven towards the site in the fields which had been appointed for this exceptional piece of booty. But disaster struck: half way there it slid into the mud and became bogged down and totally immovable. Thus its operating site was determined by fate, and the position of several aerial systems was automatically resolved. Oddly enough, the building which some years later was erected to take over the apparatus from the prime mover became known as the 'Park Royal', by which name it is officially still known today. But more immediately it was from the Park Royal vehicle that, on the night of 9–10 October 1946, Lovell and his colleagues mounted watch in the hopes of observing the Giacobinid meteor shower. Lovell described the incident thus:

The hours dragged on to midnight 9 October. We were seeing two echoes an hour which was quite a normal background rate. The sky was clear but nothing visual was evident. Then in a flash, it seemed, everything was transformed. Just after midnight our echo rate began to rise dramatically and simultaneously meteors streaked across the sky. The rates of echoes and visible meteors continued to soar. Soon they were coming so fast that we were unable to write down any details and by 2.30 a.m. there were so many that we could not even count them. We were glad of our cine-camera. By 3 a.m. the sky was streaked with trails and looked like the drawings of the great meteor showers of the eighteenth century which we had always thought to be imaginative. That was the peak. Our echo rate (on the cathode ray tube), which had been nearly a thousand an hour for a few minutes at 3.10 a.m., decreased and by 6 a.m. all was normal. . . .

In fact, it was the Giacobinid shower that provided conclusive evidence of a correlation between meteors and radio echoes, thereby demon-strating the fact that meteor trails reflect radio signals. Another interesting feature of these echoes was discovered thanks to Clegg's expertise in aerial design. Lovell managed to scrounge an Army searchlight, not for the light but for the mounting, which was an excellent turning-mechanism upon which the searchlight was operated in order to scan large areas of the sky. On this mount Clegg built a broadside array which could be turned to any part of the sky. With this arrangement Lovell and Clegg discovered that an echo from a meteor was present only when the ionized column of the trail passed through the aerial beam at right angles to the direction in which it was pointing. During the Giacobinid shower the aerial was maintained at right angles to the position of its radiant point—in Draco—as it moved across the sky, and the echo rate was many hundreds per hour as it reached its maximum. But when the aerial array was turned so that it was directed in line with the radiant point, the echoes disappeared from the cathode ray tube even though the sky remained brilliant with meteor trails. This method proved important in determining the radiant points of meteors as well as the correlation between meteors and their echoes. After this success, Manning Prentice became more and more enthusiastic about co-operating in the visual/radio experiments, and he not only arrived for the Leonids in mid-November but in mid-December took up his position at 4 a.m. on a snow-covered field in his deckchair, clothed in his flying-suit to protect him against the bitter cold, and observed the Geminid shower. This time, the shouts and the echoes were almost entirely in harmony.

During 1946 and 1947 Lovell and Clegg were almost lone hands, except for physical help from Alf Dean and Frank Foden and periodic tractor assistance from farmer Ted Moston. The main external research support came from Manning Prentice, whose enthusiasm led him to give up much of his spare time—and probably business time—to co-operate at Jodrell in the studies of meteors. His contribution was later to be recognized by the University of Manchester's awarding him the honorary degree of MSc. As Lovell says, his influence was cardinal to their early development and education in astronomy.

Although the early echoes received on the ex-Army and RAF radar equipment led Lovell deep into the study of meteors, the original intention of searching for echoes from those cosmic ray showers which entered the Solar System from outer Space was not abandoned. Lovell's calculations on the problem of receiving echoes from cosmic ray showers indicated that, for any reasonably successful study of this phenomenon, they would need much greater sensitivity in their equipment. The only way to achieve this at that stage of their technique was to build a much larger aerial. The first idea of Lovell and Clegg was to build a huge tower from hired scaffolding tubes upon which they could mount the aerial array. Without any professional constructional engineering experience, it was a pretty crazy idea. The plan was that it should be at least one hundred feet high, which meant that it would require some very substantial ground footings, so they decided to anchor the bottom scaffolding poles in concrete. Cement, sand and stones were soon collected for the task, but the acquisition of a concrete-mixer was beyond their resources, and so they had to resort to spades and muscle-power. Part of the tower was eventually erected before this scheme was dropped in favour of constructing a giant wire paraboloid on the ground, a much better proposition because it could be more easily fed with a powerful transmitter and, additionally, it would be easier to change the working wavelength. Once more, Lovell, with Clegg's assistance, worked out plans for what came to be known as the 'transit telescope'. The size of the wire bowl was determined by the distance between the bogged-down Park Royal prime mover and the boundary hedge of the field which they had been allotted for their work. This permitted a diameter of 218 feet. They planned on constructing this paraboloid of wire so that it looked vertically upwards to the sky. In order to be able to reach the edge of the bowl at its periphery with a ladder, this height was fixed at 24 feet. Since the diameter and depth of the bowl determined the focal length, this meant a focal length of 126 feet. How to build something which would carry the aerial at 126 feet above the centre of the paraboloid was beyond their ingenuity. In the end contractors were brought in for this part of the task with the backing of Blackett and with financial help to the tune of about £1,000 from the Department of Scientific and Industrial Research (DSIR). The contractors erected a 126-foot-high steel tube pivoted at the base and held by guys. With this steel tube hinged at the base, it was possible to lower it by manipulation of the steel guys for easy access to the aerials when adjustments or alterations to them were required. Originally, however, Lovell and his team had to ascend in a 'bosun's chair' to reach the aerial.

The construction of the paraboloid bowl was completed during the spring and early summer of 1947 and, with a few extra people now allocated to Lovell, the twenty-four perimeter scaffolding poles for anchoring the framework of the wire bowl were fixed in concrete by Lovell and his small staff, concrete-mixing being effected in the good old-fashioned way—with muscle and spades. The main framework of the bowl was then formed by 3/8 inch steel wires radiating from the centre to the tops of these poles and tensioned to the ground outside the perimeter by being held to the ground by more vertical posts set in concrete along the radius. On this framework miles and miles of thin sixteen-gauge wire were wound to form the reflecting screen. The family helped in tying this wire to the supports after it had been looped over them. Susan Lovell, barely nine years old, was press-ganged into helping. She recalls winding pieces of wire round the sixteen-gauge wire and helping to secure it to the supports. 'We were still at Timperley at this stage, and these days out at Jodrell, helping Daddy, were more like a family picnic. I don't think we realized we were doing anything important, except for Mummy. She was more or less in charge of operations. On the family front and in matters where the family were required to help, even at Jodrell, Mummy always acted for both of them—she was a terrific support for him—always was, and still is.' In fact, the whole family acted like a close-knit tribe, and still do—and God help anybody who dares to attack any one of them. Joyce Lovell stands out as a remarkable colleague, friend and wife, who gave

Bernard Lovell her unwavering support at all times but accompanied by intense criticism when needed.

By a letter dated 13 May 1947, from Professor M. L. Oliphant,* Professor of Physics at the University of Birmingham, Lovell was offered the post of Professor of Physics at the University of Sydney, Australia. Oliphant wrote: 'The University is a large one but physics therein has not been in the forefront for some time. The place needs a man who is prepared to go into it in rather a bull-headed fashion and drive through the apathy which has gripped it. . . . I think a man of your ability and drive could have a great deal of fun out there and could play a vital part in the scientific work of Australia. . . . The University is prepared to pay up to £2,000 a year to secure a good man. I have been asked to propose someone to whom an invitation could be sent, and I should very much like to be able to say that I believed you would go.' It was a tempting offer but, after consulting with Blackett and after discussing the matter with Joyce, he turned it down in the interests of continuing with his research work at Manchester.

Jodrell Bank, which by 1947 was beginning to resemble a fairground with its now numerous trailers, diesel engines and networks of aerial arrays, was still without any adequate permanent or even semi-permanent accommodation. Moreover, there was no real blessing from official quarters at the University that the research work at Jodrell should continue, let alone become an established extension of the Physics Department. Nevertheless, Blackett was taking an interest in all that went on, and with visions, like Lovell's, of extensive studies of the Universe at some later date, he was encouraging Lovell in his early work and setting about the task of whetting the appetite of the Vice-Chancellor of the University, the medical scientist Sir John Stopford,* with the possibility of Manchester's taking a national lead in this new science. The promise of a continuing research in the fields of astronomy, which Lovell was beginning to probe, together with the provision of permanent buildings, increased equipment and more scientific staff, seemed a likely way of holding Lovell in Britain.

On a glorious June morning in 1947, Blackett arrived at Jodrell with Sir John Stopford to introduce him to the activities of Lovell with his 'transit telescope'. In May an extraordinary high echo rate which had been observed in the previous year had returned, and Clegg had located the radiant point of a vast region of debris through which the Earth was moving, providing meteor showers in daylight which were invisible to the human eye but entirely detectable on the equipment at Jodrell. As the echo rate had continued to increase, Lovell persuaded Blackett to bring Sir John early in the morning when these meteor streams could be displayed on the cathode ray tube, and not in the afternoon when the radiants would have set. The occasion was perfect, and when Sir John stepped into the darkness of the trailer, he was confronted with a screen full of echoes.

The Vice-Chancellor's interest, now stimulated by both Blackett and his own observations, soon brought about the construction of the first permanent buildings, to preserve the precious apparatus from the now leaking trailers and to provide proper accommodation for the new and increasing team of researchers and engineering and technical staff, the latter including A. W. Smith (Fred) as the Chief Engineer, and Edward Taylor (Ted) who became Chief Technician until his retirement many years later in 1966. Then, towards the end of the year, Lovell was appointed the Director of the 'Jodrell Bank Outstation' at a salary which, with the addition of children's allowances, brought his income within fighting distance of half the Sydney salary.

The next move in Lovell's status came by a letter dated 23 January 1948 from the University Registrar. It advised him that, as from 29 September, 1948, still eight months away, he had been appointed Senior Lecturer in Physics in lieu of his present appointment as Lecturer.

Coincidentally Lovell received an air-mail letter, dated 8 February, from A. P. Rowe, now the Vice-Chancellor of the University of Adelaide, Australia. It arrived a few weeks later and offered him the Chair of Physics at an annual stipend of £1,500 per annum. It was a very flattering letter. Rowe had known Lovell throughout his brilliant war career, and he wanted him badly. This was certainly the period of Lovell's personal meteor shower, for he received yet another letter, dated 28 February 1948, from the bursar and secretary of the Board of Governors of McGill University, Montreal. It read: 'McGill University is at the present time seeking a successor to Dr A. Keys in the position of Professor of Physics and Director of the Electronics Research Laboratory. Your name has been suggested. . . .' The salary, although not stated, was known to be in excess of £2,000 per annum. Again Lovell sought Blackett's advice. In a letter dated 5 March, Blackett wrote: 'Thank you for telling me about McGill University and Adelaide. I do not see what more I can do about your position here but will let the Vice-Chancellor know that you have had these calls. You are now in the rather tantalising position of having a field of work which is so productive as to bring you many offers, and, at the same time, to be made rather immobile by virtue of the size and scale of your apparatus.' This was only too true, but what good would the apparatus be to Manchester without Lovell?

On 8 March he signed the official 'Conditions of Appointment' to Senior Lecturer with effect from 29 September following.

Lovell replied to Rowe and McGill saying that he had decided to remain with Blackett at Manchester. 'Since the war,' he said, 'we have created a large experimental station in the country and considerable sums of money are involved. The University have backed me so generously that I feel I must stay until it is so well established that it will run itself when I leave . . .'

Then, late in the morning of a sunny May day, after seeing an advertisement in the *Manchester Guardian* for a property in Swettenham, a village which was close to Jodrell Bank, Bernard and Joyce Lovell drove out to see the house in question. It was a large Edwardian house set in several acres of land and situated in beautiful countryside above the Dane Valley. That same afternoon, they purchased their new home, which was called The Quinta, a name which they inherited. It was to be their home till the present day. They moved in just one day before Judy Lovell's second birthday, 23 June. Blackett must have breathed a sigh of relief at this definite pointer to Lovell's intention to stay in Britain in the face of the latest temptations.

Since Lovell had originally set up his various equipments at Jodrell Bank to look for radio echoes from cosmic ray showers, it was not surprising that he and his slowly growing team should also spend time investigating the sources of the other echoes which they received. With the addition in December 1946 of C. D. Ellyett* from Canterbury University College, Christchurch, New Zealand, to take a PhD, and John G. Davies,* a young Cambridge graduate from the Royal Aircraft Establishment in January 1947, work began on developing methods for measuring the velocity with which meteors enter the Earth's atmosphere. This was assisted by the improvement of observation techniques by virtue of the visual watch on the tube being replaced by automatic camera recording systems, which had already resulted in the collection of important information about the physical properties of the high atmosphere and ionosphere in addition to the study of the astronomy of the meteors. For example, it was found that the variation in amplitude of the echoes was caused by the contortion of the meteor trail by the ionospheric winds. The stimulus for measuring the velocity with which meteors entered the Earth's atmosphere was the interest in discovering the source of all meteors. The meteors such as the Perseids and Geminids, which are concentrated in showers, were known to be closely associated with comets, and since the comets, and therefore these meteor showers, were known to be moving in elliptical orbits around the Sun, it was accepted that they were confined to the Solar System. In the case of sporadic meteors, however, which can be seen on any night, measurements from reliable astronomers had led to the opinion being held by some astronomers that these were not confined to the Solar System but came from interstellar Space, being only temporarily captured by the Sun and moving around it in a hyperbolic orbit. Astronomically, it was of importance that the origin of the sporadic meteors should be definitely determined, since if they were from interstellar Space they would provide significant information about the size and distribution of interstellar dust. Methods of observation at that stage could not settle the dispute. To deduce the orbit in which a meteor is moving in Space it is necessary to measure both its velocity and its direction with considerable accuracy. Visual methods of measuring the velocities of meteors were not at this time accurate enough, and at Jodrell Bank they devised methods, using radio techniques by which these velocities could be measured with unerring accuracy. Their success attracted the interest of a number of observatories, including the Royal Greenwich, the Armagh and the Smithsonian Astrophysical Observatory in Massachusetts, USA. In due course the researches at Jodrell showed that the hyperbolic theory was untenable and that sporadic meteors, like shower meteors, moved in closed orbits in the Solar System.

During these early days other phenomena made themselves known on the cathode ray tube such as aurorae, the violent radio emission from a solar flare, and the detection of radio waves from as yet undetermined sources. By the spring of 1948, when the transit telescope was in operation, and shortly after the tempting offers from Australia and Canada, Lovell became obsessed with the possibilities of a programme of research which would cover cosmic rays, meteors, aurorae, the Moon and the planets, the Sun and radio waves from outer Space. His dreams even led him to contemplate an exploration of the Universe. But his ambitions were now limited by the apparatus available to him. On wavelengths of a few metres the transit telescope had a beam width at least six or seven times smaller than any other instrument which had so far been used for astronomical studies, consequently the variation in strength of the signals received from the sky were very considerable and on the chart recorder 'stood out like humps on a camel's back', as Lovell described them. But the disadvantage of the transit telescope was its immobility. The paraboloid of wire looked up vertically into the sky, but the beam could not be moved to scan the sky. If only it could be, then it would be possible to build up a map of the sky. Indeed, all kinds of research possibilities came to Lovell's mind if only he could have a vast steerable telescope that could look at any part of the heavens at will.

However, the fact was that, despite the status Lovell had achieved in wartime research, he was a nonentity when he returned to Manchester for fundamental research, except to Blackett. Nevertheless, he was painstakingly asserting himself, and in 1948 he planned with the help of Blackett an international conference on Meteor Astronomy to be held at Manchester University on 9 September. It was a great success and was attended by a number of eminent astronomers. The opening paper was delivered by Dr F. L. Whipple* of Harvard, (later Director of the Astrophysical Observatory of the Smithsonian Institution, Cambridge, Massachusetts, and Professor of Astronomy at Harvard University) on the subject of 'Harvard Meteor Studies'. In his lecture he congratulated Lovell and his colleagues on their most remarkable contribution to meteoric astronomy by means of radar, and he expressed the hope that this work would continue for as long as possible in the interests of meteoric astronomy. He stated that the mapping of new radiants, both day and night, and the measurement of their velocity were of the greatest importance to a full understanding of the origin of meteors. 'Such data obtained by radar, by photography and by visual means,' he said, 'should finally enable us to state with some assurance the age of each meteoric shower and to delve deeply into the problem of the origin both of meteors and comets. The significance of these bodies in the evolutionary framework of the Solar System is not yet clear, but most probably is of prime importance.'

The highly complimentary reaction to this conference was a turning point in the University's interest in radio astronomy and perhaps was the beginning of Lovell's being accepted as an astronomer. Today, when radio and Space astronomy form such an important part of fundamental research, it is difficult to remember that in 1948 the achievements in war of scientists like Lovell counted for little when they returned to peacetime activities. In particular, astronomy was dominated by the optical astronomers who had to be convinced that any useful information about the Universe could be acquired other than by the use of conventional telescopes. The few radio astronomers were strangers in the official astronomical bodies and could command little financial or scientific support. However, after the 1948 conference on meteor astronomy and with the enthusiasm of distinguished American astronomers such as Whipple, attitudes changed rapidly. A year later, with Blackett's agreement, a meeting of the Royal Astronomical Society was convened in Manchester, and the visit of the members to Jodrell Bank on 1 July 1949 can now be seen as a great event for Lovell and radio astronomy. The complimentary letters which Blackett received enabled him to convince the Vice-Chancellor and the scientific establishment that this new science deserved support and encouragement.

11

A Dream Begins to Come True

Lovell cannot remember when he actually summoned enough courage to approach Patrick Blackett about his visions of a telescope of at least the size of the transit telescope but having the facility of being steerable in azimuth and elevation. He was not so naïve as to be unaware of the complexity of the engineering that would be involved in designing and constructing a 250-foot paraboloid, with its associated aerial, which could be steered towards any part of the heavens. The height of the mounting of the paraboloid so that it could scan through the vertical to the horizontal meant that it would have to be in excess of half the diameter of the paraboloid, and this in itself posed a serious engineering problem. Clearly, the project was not going to be one which could be financed by expenditure of £1,000. His approach was made sometime in the early summer of 1948, after his decision to remain at Manchester despite the offers from elsewhere. It was in the form of a conversation in which he enumerated all the research possibilities into the Solar System and the Universe which could be exploited with such an instrument as never before. Lovell says: 'I should have known better than to have had any doubts about the outcome of such a conversation with Blackett . . . without a second's hesitation he said that, if I could find some means of building such a device, and the cost, he would back me to the hilt.'

After the initial elation, Lovell was left like a man in the wilderness. He and his staff had no knowledge of constructional engineering, or indeed of civil engineering companies who might be competent to discuss such an imaginative idea or who would be interested in involving themselves in the technical study and costing of a scheme as complex as this and which might not, as a one-off task, be worth the effort financially. Undaunted, however, he began his search early in 1949 by writing to a few large engineering firms describing what he had in mind and asking if they would be interested enough to discuss the matter further. They were not. In fact the replies fell into two categories: those who professed to have too much work of 'national importance' on their plates to divert any effort to Lovell's problem, and those who declared, unequivocally, that the project represented an impossible engineering undertaking. It was, of course, true that Lovell was asking for a staggering feat of engineering and construction, but the problem of industry's disdain for such a madcap scheme acted only as a spur to prove them wrong and to achieve what he wanted. He had met the so-called impossible too often in the war period, only to discover and to prove that the reverse was true, to be intimidated by a few 'fainthearts' in peacetime. And so he continued his search for someone who could be so excited by such a challenging task as he was presenting that they would find the impossible a source of inspiration.

Then in the summer of 1949 a glimmer of interest in the giant telescope project was suddenly detectable. The first candidate to be found was through a senior member of an engineering company whose business included large optical telescopes. After discussions on site in July, this man wrote on 21 November to the effect that his own firm could not undertake such a project. He suggested to Lovell the name of Head Wrightson Limited who had a special projects department for unusual tasks. In his letter he enclosed a most ambitious-looking drawing and added that it was his opinion that the device could not be built for anything like £50,000. The implication seemed to be that it would cost very much more—a worrying thought because, in talks with Blackett, Lovell had discussed an outside figure of £60–70,000.

Meanwhile, however, Lovell had also been in touch with a Mr Roberts of Coubro & Scrutton, the firm which had supplied and erected the 126-foot-high steel tube mast for the aerial of the transit telescope and which had assisted in problems associated with strengthening the 30-foot paraboloid of a naval coastal defence radar which Jodrell had acquired earlier. This contact finally resulted in Roberts regretting that the design of a steerable telescope with a 250-foot paraboloid and its associated structure was too great an undertaking for Coubro & Scrutton. But on 20 May 1949 Roberts wrote that a Mr Linder, a director of the company, recommended an approach to one of the leading structural companies such as Dorman Long or Vickers Armstrong. He went on to say: 'However, as you know, the construction of the actual wire framing of the Paraboloid itself is well within our scope and we should be happy to assist you in any way you require.' In July Lovell again pressed Roberts for guidance because Dorman Long was one of the companies which had exhibited no interest when approached earlier. This resulted in a communication from Roberts dated 21 July stating that Coubro & Scrutton had been in touch with a firm of consulting engineers who had expressed great willingness to undertake the design work of the overall structure and to be responsible for obtaining tenders for the work from specialists. Impatiently, Lovell begged Roberts to make the necessary introductions, and on 8 September 1949 Roberts duly arrived at Jodrell Bank with H. C. Husband* of Husband & Company, the firm of consulting engineers in Sheffield which had expressed its interest.

So it was that Lovell met Husband on the perimeter of the transit telescope. It was to prove a memorable encounter and the starting-point of an enterprise which was to put Britain in the forefront of the new science of radio astronomy. Indeed, what transpired from this first meeting ultimately produced an engineering and electronic marvel with a capability far exceeding even Lovell's initial dreams. Lovell recalls that Husband asked him, 'What's your problem?' There were no polite preliminaries. 'I want a telescope of at least this size,' Lovell replied, pointing to the transit telescope, 'mounted like that small 30 ft. paraboloid over there so that we can steer it to any part of the sky. I've now been trying for over a year to persuade someone to do it but I'm told it's impossible,' he added. Husband looked at the device for a few moments, gazed up at the focal point 126 feet above the ground, and then said calmly: 'Oh, I don't know. It should be easy—about the same problem as throwing a swing bridge over the Thames at Westminster!' Four months later in January 1950 he produced a sketch of his proposal. Lovell now had two drawings to illustrate his requirements, but as yet no idea of costs.

In the meantime, through Patrick Blackett's initiative, a Radio Astronomy Committee of the Royal Astronomical Society was formed at the end of 1949 with Greaves,* the Astronomer Royal for Scotland, as Chairman. The first meeting of this Committee was held in London on 10 February 1950, with Greaves, in the chair, and attended by, amongst others, Patrick Blackett, J. A. Ratcliffe* (who in 1960 became Director of the Radio Research Station), Martin Ryle,* future Astronomer Royal and Nobel Prize winner for Physics in 1974, J. S. Hey* (formerly of the Army Operational Research Group and later in charge of radio astronomy research at the Royal Radar Establishment, Malvern), Manning Prentice and Lovell. At this meeting the members of the Committee were requested to express their views as to what was required to ensure that Britain's lead in radio astronomy could be maintained. At this time there were three radio astronomy research teams active in the country: J. S. Hey's at the Army Operational Research Group, Martin Ryle's at the Cavendish, Cambridge University, and Lovell's at Jodrell Bank. Hey was unable to come forward with many views because of his close ties with the armed services. Ryle at the time was primarily concerned with the improvement of his interferometer aerials which presented no major financial demand. He took the view that it was best to carry on working with small aerials until his team had a better idea, from further experience, of what they really required. It then fell to Lovell to come forward with a strong plea for the expenditure of a very large sum of money on the construction of a steerable paraboloid 250 feet in diameter. Minute 11 of this meeting reads: 'Dr Lovell then asked for consideration of his project for building in this country the 250 ft parabolic receiver so mounted that it could be swung round to any region of the sky. Preliminary drawings and a memorandum were submitted. After some discussion it was agreed that this was a matter of great importance for the future of radio astronomy in Britain and that the matter should be placed first on the Agenda of the next meeting.'

The second meeting of the Radio Astronomy Committee was held in Sir Edward Appleton's* rooms in Edinburgh University on the afternoon of 27 February 1950, Those present on this occasion were Greaves, Appleton, Blackett, Hey and Lovell, and Appleton took the chair. Ellison, who had taken the minutes of the previous meeting, again acted as Secretary. Prior to this meeting Lovell had circulated a memorandum in support of his proposal to build the radio telescope with the 250-foot paraboloid. Amongst the many important reasons was the argument that such an instrument would enable a complete survey of the position and distribution of radio stars to be made, 'yielding crucial information for the establishment of the nature of these sources and any relation with known astronomical objects.' The existence of the phenomenon of radio emissions from Space was accepted by astronomers. In 1946 J. S. Hey's team in the Army Operational Research Group had observed, with the use of the receiver of an Army radar equipment, radio emissions from the direction of the constellation of Cygnus which varied in strength with a short time period, from which he deduced that there existed a star-like object in that direction which was emitting radio waves. In June 1947 a research group in Australia also detected radio waves from the direction of Cygnus, and they too concluded that these waves were emanating from a local source in the constellation. In 1948, Martin Ryle's group at Cambridge confirmed the existence of the source in Cygnus. In addition, they discovered an even more intense source in the constellation of Cassiopeia. The remarkable feature of these discoveries, and of others which followed, was that there was no correlation between the radio sources and known optical objects such as bright stars or nebulae. Only in one case was there a significant correlation, and that was the source discovered in Taurus by the Australians, which was associated with the Crab nebula, the remnants of the supernova of AD 1054, now an expanding gaseous shell. But if astronomers accepted that there were such phenomena as radio emissions from Space as indicated by the dozen or so small diameter sources which had at that date been located, they were firmly convinced that they emanated from the Milky Way and that the sources were 'radio stars', that is, a hitherto unknown type of dark object in the Milky Way capable of emitting radio waves, but not visible even to the largest optical telescopes. In fact, few astronomers believed that these radio waves came from outside the Milky Way, but those who did were soon to be proved right.

Lovell's case for a radio telescope extended beyond the research into radio emissions from Space. It included extended studies of meteors, the Moon, the planets, and other investigations of the Solar System, and his memorandum was based on a very comprehensive programme of work. This second meeting of the Radio Astronomy Committee was, as Blackett and Lovell knew, to be a very critical occasion. Lovell recalls that he left home late on the evening of Sunday 26 February to drive to Manchester to meet Blackett and to catch the night train to Edinburgh. They had to change at Carstairs, where they were deposited upon the platform at 6 a.m. on a bitterly cold day. On the journey from Carstairs to Edinburgh, Blackett revealed his proposed tactics for the meeting, which at the time left Lovell aghast. He started off by announcing that he thought Lovell's memorandum a 'disaster', the implication seeming to be that he thought it far too ambitious, but nonetheless he hoped the Committee would not think so. He then declared that Lovell should not put forward his proposal for the telescope to be built as an instrument for his use at Jodrell Bank but as a project for Britain, the location of which was a matter for the Committee to recommend and to decide upon. It was a bitter pill for Lovell to swallow. After all, the Committee might well select some other site, although it was his idea. In fact, Blackett was planning a shrewd move. Indeed, after Lovell had outlined his proposals at Appleton's request, and after he had explained that the project was for a radio telescope for the UK and that its site was a matter for the Committee, the Chairman interrupted his discourse and made it emphatically clear that, if any such device were to be built, it must be built at Jodrell Bank, where the techniques already existed and where Lovell, who was proposing the building of such a telescope, was available to control its activities. After Lovell had been asked various questions, the crisis of the meeting was reached. The Chairman requested each member attending the Committee to state his opinion as to whether the Committee should support the proposal to construct such a vast fully steerable radio telescope, and whether a serious effort should be made to obtain money for this very considerable project, a sum which was then estimated at between £50,000 and £100,000. As each member gave his decision, Lovell was in such a state of suspense that he hardly dared to breathe, but when the last one to answer completed a unanimous and unequivocal support, his suspense turned to elation as Appleton said: 'I am impressed by the wide list of problems in astronomy and geophysics which Dr Lovell has listed as capable of solution by a radio telescope of this size; but I am even more impressed by the possible uses of this instrument in fields of research which we cannot yet envisage.' They were to prove truly prophetic words.

Without hesitation the Radio Astronomy Committee agreed to ask the Council of the Royal Astronomical Society to pass the following resolution:

The Council of the Royal Astronomical Society strongly endorses the proposals put forward by the Physical Laboratories of the University of Manchester for the erection in the United Kingdom of a steerable paraboloid aerial of 250 ft diameter. The Council considers that by the erection of this apparatus the prestige of science in Britain would be considerably enhanced. In giving its support the Council places on record its opinion that the investigations to be undertaken are of high scientific importance including, as they do, the systematic survey of both the isolated centres and the general background of galactic radio emission, the study of the radio spectrum of the galactic and solar radiations, the extension of the meteor programme to meteors fainter than the 6th magnitude, the further investigation of auroral phenomena and the measurement of reflected pulses from the moon, planets, gegenschein and solar corpuscular streams. The Council is impressed by the consideration that the construction of the proposed paraboloid would permit the continuation in the United Kingdom of new methods of astronomical research, which have been so greatly developed by the skill of scientists in the United Kingdom, and which are independent of climatic conditions.

The Committee also agreed that the University of Manchester should make an application to the DSIR for a grant to cover the cost of a design study, followed by an allocation of money to build the paraboloid when estimates were completed.

In the case of the Head Wrightson contact, it was quickly established that this company required £900 to undertake the necessary preliminary design work in order to arrive at an estimate for the construction of the paraboloid. Rather than put this cost to the DSIR, Blackett persuaded the University of Manchester to vote £1,000 to fund this initial task. The guessed figure by Head Wrightson's Special Projects Department now suddenly shot up to £500,000. Then, within a few months, Head Wrightson closed their Special Projects Department, and so Lovell was now left with only one string to his bow—H. C. Husband. The University of Manchester was, at the same time, spared the £1,000 expenditure. On 14 June 1950, after a businesslike initiation of the exploratory work, Husband quoted in accordance with standard fees a sum of £3,000 to complete design work, and a further £300 to sink a bore hole on the site to determine the state of the land upon which the structure was to be built. He estimated at this stage that the cost of the instrument as now visualized would be of the order of £120,000. On the same day, the University sent

off Lovell's formal application to the DSIR for the sum of £3,300 for the
design study and, eight days later, the DSIR gave its authority for the
payment of this sum, and noted the probable final cost of £120,000.
However, Sir Ben Lockspeiser,* who was Secretary of the DSIR,
mentally doubled the final sum when he interviewed Lovell about the
proposal. From experience he tended to doubt the amounts of money
which any enthusiastic scientific research worker estimated as necessary
for a new enterprise. But he was impressed by the idea of the project and
felt it was worthy of £200,000 to £250,000.

On 5 July 1950 a meeting took place with H. C. Husband at Jodrell
Bank at which the first detailed specification for Husband to work on was
agreed. There then followed constant liaison and visits with Husband
throughout the remainder of the year, including one at Blackett's instigation to the Admiralty's Gunnery Establishment at Teddington where he
thought the naval gunnery experts might be able to offer advice on
methods of steering the telescope. This, in turn, led to a visit to the
breaker's yard where Husband secured the 27-foot-diameter internal
racks and pinions from the 15-inch gun turrets of the battleships *Royal
Sovereign* and *Revenge* at a bargain price. They were items which were to
prove invaluable in the construction of the telescope as will be seen later.
Also during the remainder of 1950, Blackett insisted that Lovell should
prepare a comprehensive memorandum on the scientific aspects of the
proposal for the telescope to accompany the engineering submission
which was being drawn up by Husband. This memorandum was a substantial document covering the researches at Jodrell Bank which had led
to the concept of the telescope, the tasks which the telescope could
undertake, the scientific basis for the shape, size and focal length, and
other data upon which Husband had been asked to base his design. It
included comments on the problems of siting the instrument and providing proper power supplies. Helping Lovell in this task was Dr J. A. Clegg,
who wrote the chapter providing the calculations about the beam shape
and power gain of the telescope, and Dr J. G. Davies, who was assigned
the task of building a bench prototype of the analogue computer which
was to supply the information necessary to drive the telescope in sidereal
motion. Davies was therefore responsible for writing the chapter on this
subject for the memorandum.

Early in 1951 the memorandum was complete. So too were Husband's
proposals, together with a cost figure based on tenders which had now
been obtained. The price was £259,000! Lovell recalls that Blackett was
perturbed and annoyed at this enormous cost and complained bitterly at
Lovell's 'obtuseness in insisting on such a large paraboloid'. He took the
view that the chances of getting a quarter of a million pounds were less

than slim. He also felt that a great deal could still have been done for British astronomy with a smaller telescope costing something in the region of £100,000. Nevertheless, Blackett supported the scheme, and on 20 March 1951 a formal application for a grant of £259,000 was made to the DSIR. For the rest of 1951 there was a stunned silence in response to the request, although many influential friends were working behind the scenes on behalf of the project, including Blackett and Sir Henry Tizard, who was at this time Chairman of the Defence Research Policy Committee at the Ministry of Defence, and Chairman of the Advisory Council on Scientific Policy. The fact was that at the time grants for helping university and other fundamental research were of the order of only £45,000.

If 1950 and, more particularly, 1951 were nail-biting periods for Bernard Lovell, there were moments of excitement and pleasure to ease the suspense of waiting to see if his dream was to materialize or to fade into oblivion. Work with the 218-foot fixed-transit telescope continued, and R. Hanbury Brown* and Cyril Hazard,* two of Lovell's assistants, used the transit telescope to study radio emissions from the region of the sky containing the M31 extragalactic spiral nebula in Andromeda. Their results showed unmistakably that M31 was a radio-emitter. Although the signals received on Earth were extremely weak—M31 is at a distance of two million light years—it appeared that the radio-emitting properties of M31 were similar to those of the Milky Way. It was early proof that radio waves were emanating from objects in the Universe outside the confines of the Milky Way system. Further work with the transit telescope was also rewarding and whetted the appetite of Lovell and his team even more for the realization of the 250-foot steerable telescope.

The uncertainty over the outcome of the application for a grant to build the telescope continued into 1952. Worse still, the cost of steel rose substantially during 1951, as did the price of other materials, and fresh estimates were requested by the DSIR. The revision now shot the estimated price up to £333,000 a sum which the DSIR could not possibly provide on its own. For Lovell it was a deeply disturbing situation. Then, unexpectedly, the Nuffield Foundation, encouraged by Lord Nuffield himself, stepped into the breach. Always anxious that Britain should maintain her prestige as a great nation in many fields of endeavour, including science and technology, the Foundation foresaw the lead that this country could take in radio astronomy—and in engineering, by virtue of the exciting concept of the huge and skilled construction of the telescope itself. It therefore offered to share the cost with the DSIR pound for pound.

On a spring afternoon, a few days before Easter, Blackett telephoned

Lovell and, with two words, sent Lovell's emotions soaring to the heavens. 'You're through,' he said, and rang off! On 10 April 1952, the day before Good Friday, Lovell received a letter from I. G. Evans CBE, the Assistant Secretary of the DSIR, who was in charge of grants, advising him that an official letter announcing the grant was on its way to the Vice-Chancellor of the University of Manchester.

It was the third piece of good news that Lovell had received during the past twelve months. On 1 August 1951 Joyce presented him with the Lovell twins, Roger and Philippa, thus bringing the population of the clan up to seven. Then, on 29 September, Lovell was appointed the first Professor of Radio Astronomy at the University of Manchester.

12

The Crises Begin

Lovell's euphoria over the decision to proceed with the giant telescope was soon to be tested by the problems, setbacks, politics and national criticism that lay ahead, and the problems appeared on Jodrell Bank's D-Day + 1. In truth they had begun much earlier, particularly in respect of the site for the paraboloid of this massive instrument, together with its control centre.

As early as 1949 the few acres of land at Jodrell Bank which belonged to the University of Manchester had become inadequate for the purposes of the 'Jodrell Bank Outstation', which was already encroaching, by 'borrowing', onto the Botany Department's preserves. Even Lovell's private renting arrangement with a neighbouring farmer for a part of one of his fields still left him with a land shortage for his meteor aerials and other arrays and equipment, an arrangement which was promptly discovered by the vigilance of the University's finance department when he tried to pay the farmer the rent. The episode brought things to a head, for Lovell was told in no uncertain terms that land negotiations were the prerogative of the appropriate University department, and he was instructed to remove his aerials and equipment and to hand back the land to the farmer. This was easier said than done. Lovell had already sunk over fifty blocks of concrete into part of the field in question! Lovell says: 'I doubt if there has ever been an instruction which I had less intention of carrying out.' Actually, there had been plenty during the war which he had ignored with disarming innocence, thus adding to the success of Bomber Command! Lovell adds: 'Not for the last time had I acted impetuously and irresponsibly in order to get on quickly with research. The building of the aerials had been a hard job and we were in the midst of the excitement of the daytime meteor streams.' Lovell was rescued from his predicament by Sir John Stopford, the Vice-Chancellor. One sunny afternoon Sir John visited the outstation to find out for himself what all the trouble was about. He was entirely sympathetic towards Lovell's land problems and agreed that what had been installed in the farmer's field could not easily be removed. He suggested, to Lovell's delight, that he should ask the farmer whether he would consider selling the field to the University. Fifty blocks of concrete had clinched the deal! The final outcome was that the farmer agreed to sell the land together with another field known as Field 80 on the Ordnance Survey large-scale map.

In 1950, when the initial plans for the giant telescope were in their embryonic stage and under discussion, Field 80 was presumed to be the site for this vast instrument. However, for a variety of scientific and aesthetic reasons, Lovell had cast his eye covetously upon an adjacent field which belonged to a large neighbouring farm—a farm which had nothing to do with the farmer who had sold the University Field 80. Enquiries by Lovell had elicited that there was no hope of acquiring this land from the elderly widow who owned the property, which was known as Blackden Farm and which was farmed by her youngest son and his wife. Consequently plans went ahead on the assumption that Field 80 would be the site for the telescope. Then, during the latter part of 1951, when negotiations were proceeding for the finance of the telescope, the owner of Blackden Farm died, leaving, apart from her youngest son, three other sons who had moved away from home some years earlier. Shortly after the old lady's death Lovell learnt that the entire farm would have to be sold in order that her estate could be divided amongst her family in accordance with her Will. Without delay he informed R. A. Rainford, the University Bursar, who was aware of his desire for a particular field on this farm, that the field in question, or even the entire farm, might well be available for purchase. Rainford immediately asked the University agents to look into the matter, and the University indicated its willingness to purchase not only the field known as Field 132 on the Ordnance Survey map but the whole of Blackden Farm. Thus began the first problem in connection with the building of the telescope which, although relatively minor when compared with those that were to follow, was nonetheless frustrating.

As soon as authority was received for the project to go ahead, H. C. Husband, the consulting engineer, began the process of obtaining estimates for the foundation work. To make any progress in this matter it was essential for him to know in which field the telescope was to be sited. In addition, he was anxious to get ahead with the piling for the foundations before the autumn so that as much foundation work as possible could be completed before the winter set in. Lovell's insistence on the Blackden Farm field in lieu of Field 80 was now to cause serious delays due to the fact that the family involved in the Blackden Farm affair could not agree upon its future. The youngest son, who was resident on the farm and who had been farming it after his father's death for his mother, could see no reason why he should not continue to occupy the property and continue farming there after his mother's death. On the other hand, the other three brothers wanted their share of the inheritance and were in favour of a sale to the University of Manchester who, by May 1952, were offering generous terms in that they were prepared to purchase at a vacant possession price and yet permit the youngest brother to continue his tenancy at a very attractive rent. The only stipulation was the occupation by the University of Field 132 for the site of the telescope.

The youngest son was, however, opposed to the sale, and negotiations became protracted. Indeed, it was not until 21 August that contracts were exchanged and 3 September that materials for work on the foundations were moved onto the new site. By 1 October the building of the radio telescope, one of Britain's greatest contributions to post-war science, had truly begun.

However, the delay in the choice of site due to the protracted negotiations in respect of Field 132, the abnormally wet weather in the last three months of 1952 and in January 1953, followed by snow blizzards in February, conspired to put plans well behind schedule. The hope that all piling would be complete by the end of 1952, and the whole foundation for the telescope by the spring of 1953, was by November 1952 a forlorn one. In fact, the last pile was not completed until 21 May 1953, and it was not until 31 July that Whittals, the contractors for the foundations, completed the 350-foot-diameter circle of concrete of the ring beam which was to support the construction of the giant telescope. Ten thousand tons of reinforced concrete were now in the ground at a cost of £50,000.

Whilst the delayed progress on the foundations had certainly destroyed the chance of completing the telescope in the estimated time and having it ready to go into operation—within 2½ years—Lovell was less concerned with progress to date than he was by the financial problems arising from increased costs which now began to threaten the whole project. He was beginning to wonder not whether the telescope would be finished in 1954 or 1955 but whether it would ever be built at all.

The design of the steerable radio telescope allowed for a 250-foot-diameter paraboloid, that is 32 feet larger than the paraboloid of the fixed-transit telescope. The transit telescope had a long focal length, the wire paraboloid on the ground being shallow purely for practical reasons and the focus being at the top of the 126-foot steel tube upon which the aerials were mounted. This arrangement exposed the primary feed aerial to unwanted sources of interference and, if applied to the new steerable telescope, also seemed likely to present unnecessary problems to the engineers. Lovell, in consultation with his team and Husband, therefore decided to plan for an increase in the depth of the bowl over that of the transit telescope and to design a paraboloid with the focus in the plane of the aperture. For a 250-foot-diameter bowl, this meant that the tower arising from the apex of the paraboloid upon which the aerial systems would be mounted would be only 62½ feet.

The extreme accuracy to which Lovell required the paraboloid to be constructed and to be maintained at all operating angles was a very demanding feature of design. The radio emissions from Space had in the past been studied only on relatively long wavelengths, and the only known surveys of the heavens were those of Grote Reber, made prior to World War II, who with his own 31-foot parabolic reflector and receiver operating on a wavelength of 1½ metres with a beamwidth of 8 degrees plotted the first radio maps of the Milky Way from his garden in Wheaton, Illinois, USA. After the war, J. S. Hey of the Royal Radar Establishment had begun sky surveys on a wavelength of 4 metres with a beamwidth of 13 degrees. Lovell's transit telescope had surveyed the zenithal strip at much greater definition on 2 metres with a beamwidth of ±1 degree. Since there was negligible evidence of the radio waves from Space on wavelengths shorter than 1 metre, and since research into radio waves from Space formed part of the planned research, it was decided that the shortest working wavelength of the telescope should be 1 metre at which its beamwidth would be ±½ degree. With a working wavelength range of 1 to 10 metres, it was recognized that the new telescope could produce sky surveys of far greater definition than any other telescope available in the world and would be, indeed, the pre-eminent instrument in the world for all astronomical activities in that waveband. The decision to design for a working wavelength of 1 to 10 metres led to the specification for the shape of the paraboloid bowl to be within ±5 inches of the true shape relative to the focus, an exacting requirement to say the least. The size of the mesh of the reflecting surface of the paraboloid was determined by the 1-metre wavelength limit, and it was specified that it should be 2 inches square. With these parameters the efficiency of the paraboloid was expected to approach closely the theoretical value at the shortest operating wavelength. The basic problem presented to H. C. Husband, the consulting engineer, was, therefore, to construct such a gigantic paraboloid wire mesh bowl and mount it high in the air so that it could be driven separately in elevation and azimuth to give full coverage of the sky with continuously variable speeds from 2 degrees per hour to 36 degrees per minute with an accuracy of ±1/5th degree. Lovell also specified that the telescope must be able to move simultaneously in azimuth and elevation with the rates of movement determined by an analogue computer so that the instrument could track a star or planet automatically. The stringency of these specifications was inevitably to determine the strength and rigidity of the instrument and, hence, the weight and cost of the steelwork.

All of these requirements were contained in Husband's proposal of February 1951 for building the telescope. In this, he proposed driving the bowl in elevation through the two battleship gun racks, already purchased, mounted on trunnion bearings supported on two steel towers 186-feet high. The azimuth motion was to be obtained by mounting the towers themselves on twelve bogies, six under each tower running on a 320-foot-diameter circular double railway track. He also took account of the requirement for the bowl to be capable of complete inversion so that the aerial tower could be made to point to the ground in order to facilitate the changing of aerial systems. To provide access to the aerial on inversion, a mobile electrically driven small tower was planned to be mounted on top of a cross girder between the base of the two 186-foot towers and capable of moving along this girder to the inverted aerial tower and to be stowable at one end when not in use. It was this scheme which Husband had anticipated could be completed in 2½ years. It was also this scheme which in February 1950 had been loosely estimated to cost between £50,000 and £100,000, then estimated by the DSIR to be nearer £200,000 to £250,000, and in March 1951 to rise to £259,000 on the basis of some real estimates from Husband, only to shoot up yet again to £333,000 in 1952 due to price increases—and this without a single nut or bolt being changed in the design. As has already been mentioned in Chapter 11, it was this last figure that, but for the foresighted generosity of the Nuffield Foundation, might well have brought about the abandonment of the project.

In the autumn of 1952 Lovell wanted a change of design which, whilst having no effect upon the foundation work completed to date, would require considerable alterations to the structure of the 250-foot paraboloid. The request arose out of new information on the researches being undertaken by other radio astronomers around the world. In 1944, the Dutch astronomer J. H. Oort of the Leiden Observatory, in describing the earlier activities of Karl Jansky and Grote Reber and their measurements of the radio emissions from the Milky Way, drew attention to the advantage that would accrue to this type of investigation of the heavens if a spectral line existed. It was this statement that stimulated H. C. van de Hulst, a young Dutch astronomer, to study this problem and from his calculations to predict in 1945 that it should be possible to observe the 21-centimetre line of neutral hydrogen. Extraordinarily, this research was undertaken clandestinely during the German occupation of Holland. Then, in 1951, H. I. Ewen and E. M. Purcell of Harvard University, Cambridge, Massachusetts, successfully detected and observed this 21-centimetre spectral line. Six weeks later W. N. Christiansen and J. V. Hindman in Australia also successfully detected the spectral line emission from neutral hydrogen gas in the Milky Way on the wavelength of 21 centimetres, and they were quickly followed by Oort and C. A. Muller of Leiden University. The discovery of radio emission on this wavelength was of great importance because it was the only line emission known in the radio spectrum. The radio emissions which had so far been studied were over a broad band of wavelengths. On the other hand, this 21-centimetre emission was a line spectrum, and changes in wavelength of the signal received on Earth, because of the relative motion of the source and the Earth, enabled deductions to be made about the velocities of the gas clouds and hence the spiral structure of the Milky Way. The strength of the line would also give information about the mass of hydrogen in other galaxies.

Lovell immediately recognized the importance of this discovery to astronomical research, and he was therefore anxious to find ways and means of adapting the telescope to be able to operate on this 21-centimetre wavelength. There were, however, two major problems. First, the shape tolerances of ±5 inches already stipulated for the bowl were quite inadequate for work on this short wavelength. Then, the mesh size of 2 inches square was too open, and the radiation of 21 centimetres wavelength would leak through.

To meet this new operating requirement, Husband had increased the tonnage of steel in the structure to provide the necessary strength to offset the increased wind loading resulting from these changes. The original tonnage of steel based on provisional drawings of February 1951 had been 959 tons, but when the design was drawn in final detail, the tonnage increased to 1,000 tons. With the new specification the tonnage required now rose to 1,177 tons. Into the bargain the price of steel had risen substantially by the beginning of 1953. In fact, the increase in price and the increase in quantity of steel was resulting in a £39,000 increase in the cost of the structural steel work. But steel costs were not the only shock. All costs had risen, and by the beginning of the spring of 1953 it was evident that the £333,000 was going to be substantially exceeded. At the end of February 1953 Lovell faced the DSIR officials on the subject of obtaining an increase of the order of £100,000 in the grant to offset rising costs. At this meeting it was made clear to him that a figure of £100,000 extra was from the point of view of the DSIR out of the question. They just did not have that sort of money to dispense. Evans, the Assistant Secretary in charge of grants, promised to do his best to help but saw little hope of an answer for at least two to three months. It therefore became an anxious phase for Lovell, who was now left seriously wondering whether the telescope could be constructed in its present design. However, to assist the DSIR in their efforts to raise the extra money, Lovell, with the help of Rainford, the University Bursar, and Husband, set about preparing a more detailed story of why the extra money was needed.

By 23 April revised estimates were complete and contractors' tenders for all major items were available, including those for the control building.

The new estimated price was £439,616—a 31 per cent increase over the money already allocated.

The Nuffield Foundation had already been approached for further funds and had agreed to contribute another £32,000, making their total gift £200,000. But this still left a sum in excess of £60,000 to be found by the DSIR.

On 28 April Rainford met the DSIR finance officials armed with the revised figures, and although he reported them to be 'helpful and anxious to overcome the present dilemma', the actual result of the meeting was a request to the University to make a formal application for a meeting with the DSIR Scientific Grants Committee on 6 May to put their case for the increase in the original grant. This meeting was attended by Lovell and Rainford, and it went sadly awry from the beginning. To begin with, the Committee was composed of different members to those who had originally recommended the award of the grant, and now included Sir George Thomson,* Master of Corpus Christi College, Cambridge, Dr R. V. Jones,* Aberdeen University's Professor of Natural Philosophy, and Dr Willis Jackson.* In his diary of events, under 'Wednesday, May 6th', Lovell wrote: 'A. H. Wilson was Chairman and it (the Committee) included G. P. Thomson and R. V. Jones. G. P. immediately seized on the wind loading problem as it affected the extra steel and took us back four years to arguments about wind tunnel tests. The attack was completely unexpected and really no business of this Committee. The Chairman was most reasonable and tried to stem the arguments. Finally it was agreed that we should obtain an assessment of the position by an independent aerodynamic expert—Mair* [Professor Mair formerly of Manchester University] was suggested as one who had earlier been associated with the project. It was further emphasised that the structural strength calculations of the consultants were not in question—only the basic wind pressure assumptions. . . .' A much greater matter for concern arising from this meeting was, however, the emphatic suggestion by the Committee that the University should show its own backing for the project by making a financial gesture itself. Since the University had no capital available to help in this manner, and since it was already heavily committed to Jodrell by way of staff and running-expenses, Rainford protested strongly at this suggestion.

The outcome of this meeting was a state of gloom for Lovell, despite the fact that later in the day the permanent officials of the DSIR assured him that they were of the opinion that the Committee, in fact, wanted the project to proceed as quickly as possible.

In the meantime Lovell had to clear the matter of wind pressure on the telescope with Professor Mair. This he did without delay, and on 12 May he wrote to Sir George Thomson saying: '. . . we have prepared a short note regarding the wind pressure on the radio telescope in consultation with Professor Mair. I have handed the original, signed by him and the Consulting Engineer, to the DSIR. No doubt you will receive a copy officially, but I should like to take this opportunity of sending a copy to you with some additional observations. . . .' He went on to explain in some detail the reasons for believing that the design not only contained adequate safety factors on the basis of the average wind experienced throughout the year, and even took account of exceptional conditions experienced the previous year, but erred on the side of too large a safety factor. 'Mair is perfectly satisfied that the basis of the wind pressure used in the calculations is correct . . . I very much hope, therefore, that the independent assessment by Mair will alleviate your concern.' It did, and at a meeting of the DSIR's Advisory Council on 20 May it was agreed to provide the extra money, but the Council advised that it might not be possible for 'DSIR to provide the necessary money for any further such increases in costs should they arise. In the unfortunate event of more being required it may be necessary for the University to raise it by appealing to another source.'

This warning note from the DSIR caused some panic and subsequent delay in placing the contract for the steel and for the steel structural work with United Steel Structural Company Limited. Not surprisingly, Rainford was concerned about the liability with which the University would be landed if the price did increase when the telescope was half finished! Lovell was naturally anxious to have no more delays, and Husband had advised on 19 May that if the steel contract could be placed within the next few weeks delivery of steel would commence in February, 1954, and be complete by May . . . gabbards and cranes could be erected in January, 1954, the steel work erection would begin in March, 1954 and be completed in September, 1954.' To get a quick decision on placing the steel contract, Lovell suggested to Rainford that the construction of the control building could be delayed, thereby keeping £30,000 in reserve. His attitude was 'that a control building without any steel work was useless, but that the steel work without a control building would still be a great deal of use'. It was a doubtful argument, but it helped, and on 18 July the contract was placed. By the end of July the steel for the telescope was being rolled.

By September 1953 there seemed to be a little less worry about the future financial situation, and on the 9th Husband was given the go-ahead to place the contract for the control building. Unfortunately, the contractors who had offered the lowest price immediately began to procrastinate over their acceptance and on 24 September advised that 'after investigating the local labour position' they had found that, due to demands for labour arising from other large contracts in the area, they estimated additional labour costs of £1,050. Fortunately Husband was able to interest another contractor, Z. & W. Wade of Whaley Bridge, who submitted an even lower tender than the one which had been originally accepted, and in mid-October the contract was finally placed with Wades.

For the moment Lovell was relieved temporarily of some of his anxieties about the telescope. His family had been his refuge and continued so to be. The Quinta provided a relaxation with its garden which he was now actively developing and to which he was applying his botanical knowledge. The arboretum had been commenced and many varieties of trees had been planted, a multiplicity of which were of rare species. A further diversion from his worries was cricket, a long-held passion which he now indulged by playing for the local village team of Chelford which he captained for many years. Then there was music. Almost as a ritual he would play the piano first thing in the morning before he set off to work, and then again last thing at night before going to bed. In the garden everybody helped. Susan says: 'When he came home from work, he would blow his top to Mummy for ten minutes about what wasn't being done at Jodrell and about inefficient contractors and workmen. There was so much that went wrong and a feeling that the telescope would never get built. The sheer exhaustion caused by the project did reflect on our family life, and sacrifices were made by the whole family—Mummy in particular. But when he was working in the garden, we all helped and everything was much happier.' Lovell did not neglect his parental duties to his children at this time, or at any time. He took a keen interest in their school progress and demanded a high standard. Susan recalls the ceremonial rites of being taken to the local station at Goostrey on a Monday morning to catch the train to Manchester where she was a weekly boarder at Withington Girls' School in Fallowfield.

He would get there at least ten minutes early for the train, and then he would walk up and down the station and you would be expected to keep up with him walking at about thirty miles an hour! And there would be a great tirade about, for example: 'For the next six months you have got to think what the inside of a rat looks like, whether you like it or not. And no more parties and no more going out until the standards in all your subjects improve!' And it certainly had effect. For the next six months one just did what was expected. He expected a high standard academically from Bryan and me, and a very high standard of behaviour was expected of all of us—we all had to help in the house and the garden, but somehow we did it willingly and enjoyed it. And when we did do well or did the right things, he didn't exactly praise us, but he looked so happy it was enough.

To offset the worries over the building of the telescope there was the astronomical research which was continuing very actively with the transit telescope. Measurements of extra-galactic radio emissions continued, and the radiation from the bright spiral Ursa Major Nebula, M81, was measured at a frequency of 158.5 megacycles, the ratio of radio flux to light flux being found to agree well with that observed for other late-type spirals. The detection of a very weak system of irregularities in the background radiation at high galactic latitudes was extended, and many other measurements were made, including those of radio stars, in particular two intense sources which had been detected in Cygnus and Cassiopeia. Studies of solar radio emission, and aurorae observation, had been continued, as had been the meteor survey and the study of the radar reflections from the meteor trails to investigate the upper atmospheric winds. A new series of experiments had begun in connection with the Moon. Lunar echoes received from pulse transmissions from Jodrell were being observed using a small aerial array with the aim of making a detailed study of the deep fading which had been found, so far, to be characteristic of lunar echoes.

All of this work was stimulating Lovell's interest in the Universe and his desire to know more about the beginning of time. He was becoming curious about the origins of the Universe and questioning the theory of the accident in Space which had created the Universe. 'Quite simply,' he says, 'I had a passionate feeling that the telescope was going to be an immensely powerful instrument for the exploration of the whole range of astronomical phenomena which we had been studying during the last few years.'

13

The Telescope Rises—and So Does the Price

By the beginning of 1954 the programme of construction of the telescope was well behind schedule. The foundations were admittedly complete, and the power house was almost complete. The control building, however, which had been expected to be well advanced by the start of 1954, was by March not even showing above ground level. But the major delay was the date of delivery of the central pivot, which was to have been on site in April 1953. This in turn was to set back the erection of the towers and the huge paraboloid which they were to support. The central pivot was the key to the mobility of the telescope, carrying the cross girder which was to connect the two towers at their bases, which in turn were to be mounted on bogies running round a circular railway track thus enabling the telescope structure to be rotated, as required, through 360 degrees in azimuth. The dead weight of 2,000 tons in the structure, and the large variations in bearing pressure caused by heavy wind loads, was to be distributed over the central pivot and on the multi-wheeled bogies on the railway track. The central pivot alone was to take the entire horizontal wind forces to which the telescope could at anytime be subjected from any direction, together with a vertical loading of 200 tons, plus a share of the dead weight of the cross girder to the bogies and the driving machinery housed in it. The design allowed for about one half of the dead weight of the telescope to be taken on four of the driving bogies, two of which were located under each of the vertical towers, with much of the remainder being distributed over light, undriven 'wind' bogies. Therefore, the central pivot and the bogies were fundamental features of the construction of the telescope and had to be available before the contractors could embark upon the erection of the steel superstructure.

It was not until 11 May that the central pivot was delivered to the site. It was November before the driving bogies were all delivered, and mid-April 1955 before the last of the 'wind' bogies arrived. However, by the beginning of October steelwork erection was under way, which was some consolation, but a far cry from the expectation in mid-1953 that the steelwork erection would begin in March 1954 and be completed in September of the same year.

By the spring of 1954 it was obvious to Lovell that the telescope would never be in operation by 1955. Worse still, it was becoming clear that, with escalating prices and unexpected snags, the increase in the grant allowed by the DSIR in the previous year was never going to be sufficient. The truth was that an instrument of the size of the Jodrell Bank Radio Telescope, with a bowl 250 feet in diameter, had never previously been envisaged as a practical proposition from an engineering point of view anywhere in the world. It was a pioneering development, and no one should have ever considered it on the basis of a firm cost estimate, but without such a basis, however inaccurate it might prove to be, no sanction to go ahead with the project would have been received. Here was an apparatus which was to stand as high as St Paul's Cathedral and which was to be capable of being moved smoothly and controlled in all directions with a high degree of accuracy by instruments on a panel in a remote control room. Husband and Lovell had a designing problem of the greatest magnitude, particularly as no other such instrument of similar operating complexity and size had ever before been contemplated—not even in the USA or the USSR at that time. Because of this, the design changed as work progressed. And as time passed, both experience and increased requirements added to cost, quite apart from the inevitable increases in material prices and labour costs.

Although Lovell's vision was of a giant radio telescope as an instrument for extensive scientific studies of the Solar System and the Universe at large, he was enlightened enough from his wartime work to recognize that the telescope would be perhaps the most powerful radar equipment in the world, let alone in Britain. He foresaw that the V2 rockets of World War II might well be developed into mighty weapons. Werner von Braun, the German rocket engineer and father of the V2, had been taken by the Americans at the end of the war and was already working on Intercontinental Ballistic Missiles (ICBMs) for the USA military forces. Other German scientists associated with rocketry, who had been captured by the Russians, were known to be working on similar weapons for the USSR. Moreover, it was known that attention was being devoted by the USA and almost certainly by the USSR to the practicability of launching Earth satellites into Space. Indeed, on 4 October 1954 such a prospect was indirectly confirmed when a special committee of the International Council of Scientific Unions, whilst acknowledging the usefulness of rockets for investigating the atmosphere in connection with the reliability of world radio communications, weather forecasting and other matters of interest to Earth's inhabitants, made a recommendation, as follows, that Earth satellites should be considered: 'In view of the great importance of observations, during extended periods of time, of extraterrestrial radiations and geophysical phenomena in the upper atmosphere, and in view of the advanced state of present rocket techniques, CSAGI[1] recommends that thought be given to the launching of small satellite

12   Members of the Royal Astronomical Society photographed during their visit to the meteor aerial built on an Army searchlight at Jodrell Bank, 1949

13   Bernard Lovell (*centre*) photographed with his staff under the meteor aerial on the day in 1951 when he was elected to the first Professorship of Radio Astronomy at the University of Manchester

14　The transit telescope with the small original radio telescope in the background, 1951

15　Professor Fred Whipple (*left*) of Harvard University, USA, and Bernard Lovell, the latter demonstrating how easy it is to turn the central pivot upon which the giant telescope was to be built; 1953

16   The Jodrell Bank radio telescope, at that time the largest in the world, nears completion in April 1957

17, 18   *Below left*: One of the bogies on which the telescope structure rotates on rails laid in a circle with a diameter of 360 feet. There are twelve bogies in all. Photographed in June 1957. *Below right*: The elevating gear for the paraboloid or reflecting bowl which is 250 feet in diameter. This rack was taken from the 15-inch guns of HMS *Royal Sovereign* when she was broken up. Photographed in June 1957

19 Welding the steel plates that form the reflecting surface of the bowl, June 1957

20 The finished paraboloid with the aerial erected in the centre, June 1957

21 The historic moment in July 1957 when the bowl of the telescope was first tilted under power. Sir Charles Husband, the consulting engineer who designed the telescope (*left*) with Bernard Lovell

22 A view of the Jodrell Bank radio telescope from the controller's desk, August 1959

23 Lord Renwick of Coombe, formerly Sir Robert Renwick Bart, KBE

24   At the White House, Washington DC, 7 July 1960—*left to right*: President Eisenhower, Lovell, Dr T. Keith Glennan (Head of NASA)

25   *Left to right*: Lovell, Congressman Fulton and Dr Fred Whipple, photographed at the time of Lovell's testifying before a Senate Committee in Washington DC, July 1960

26   The author talking with Valentina Tereshkova, the first woman in Space, at a reception at the Russian Embassy in London in 1964

27   Sir Bernard Lovell with the famous radio telescope at Jodrell Bank (the Mk 1A version) in 1977

28   Sir Bernard and Lady Lovell in the garden at The Quinta, November 1983

vehicles, to their scientific instrumentation, and to the new problems associated with satellite experiments, such as power supply, telemetering and orientation of the vehicle.'

It was, in fact, this pressure from the scientific community that led to the announcement by President Eisenhower on 29 July 1955 that the United States would launch a satellite during the International Geophysical Year of 1957–8, an announcement which was capped the following day by the Russian statement that the USSR too would launch a satellite for the IGY which, it claimed a few weeks later, would be heavier than the proposed American satellite.

If in the spring of 1954 no statements on satellite launchings had yet been made, Lovell's foresightedness recognized that, with rocketry in such an advanced state of development, the probability that satellites were just around the corner was a near certainty. Moreover, despite his normally idealistic outlook, he was pragmatic enough to recognize the possibility of the development of Space techniques for military purposes as well as for pure research. So who was to be the first to watch and monitor what might soon become a secret race for the utilization of Space for aggressive practices? Why not his radio telescope? In which case, should not the Air Ministry, the Admiralty and the War Office be interested in the possible applications of the telescope for defence purposes? It was, after all, going to be a colossal radar set, as well as a telescope for exploring the Solar System and the Universe, and one which the military might wish to support financially.

Lovell was not lacking friends and ex-colleagues in the higher and appropriate echelons of the Ministries concerned with defence, and he shrewdly submitted memoranda on the subject of defence uses of the telescope to those concerned. If there was to be no hope of further funds from the DSIR, as warned by this body when it approved the 1953 increase, he had to find other sources which would be prepared to offer financial assistance to cover the capital cost of the telescope.

The idea of getting some money out of the Ministry of Supply[2] arose from a discussion in 1953 at the Air Navigation Committee, of which Lovell was a member, on the problems of navigating aircraft. This dealt mainly with inertial navigation, but it was stated that as a long-term measure the Air Staff were interested in the use of radio emissions from the Sun and the stars for astro-navigation. Lovell was asked his view on

[1] This was a Special Committee, formed by the International Council of Scientific Unions, to make plans for the third international Geophysical Year (IGY) scheduled for 1957–8.
[2] The Ministry of Supply replaced the Ministry of Aircraft Production after the war and became the provider of research, development and equipment for the Armed Services. Ultimately, its duties became a part of a new Ministry—the Ministry of Defence.

the feasibility of such a proposal and gave it as his opinion that the Sun might well be used but that it was doubtful whether radio stars would be a practicable proposition. At the time, he promised to stage a demonstration to assess the chances of 'locking-on' to the Sun with radar equipment, but due to lack of assistance in getting suitable apparatus from the Royal Radar Establishment, formerly the Telecommunications Research Establishment, he let the matter slide until towards the end of the year he was reminded by the Committee of his promise. This drew from him a second promise that he would write a paper on the subject and submit it early in 1954. Late in January he settled down to the problem at a time when he came into possession of some very surprising and exciting news: Dr John Hagen of the US Naval Research Laboratory, using a 50-foot paraboloid, had succeeded in measuring the radio emission from Cassiopeia, Cygnus and Taurus on 10 centimetres. The surprising feature of Hagen's results was the unexpectedly high intensity, especially the relative increase in strength of Cygnus and Taurus to Cassiopeia. This meant that radio stars could probably be used for astro-navigation. The telescope had already been modified in design to operate down to 21 centimetres at an embarrassingly large extra cost. Obviously it would increase research capabilities to modify the design of the bowl of the telescope to enable it to work in the 10-centimetre band, and if the Ministry of Supply would cover the further additional expenditure to enable research in this band to proceed in its own interests, perhaps some of the previous excess expenditure could be covered at the same time. It was, as the Americans say, good thinking!

On 4 February 1954 Lovell despatched his memorandum to the Air Navigation Committee, and on 23 February this paper was discussed by the Committee, whose recommendation to the Ministry of Supply was that support should be given to Manchester University to undertake a programme of fundamental research into the centimetric emissions from Space and their potentialities for use as a navigational aid. At the same time, Lovell was to give some details of the amount of money required to fund such a programme, including any capital costs required for modification to the design of the telescope. Following this meeting, Lovell had a discussion with Dr Robert Cockburn,* who was then in his last days as Scientific Adviser to the Air Ministry prior to taking up a new appointment as Controller of Guided Weapons and Electronics at the Ministry of Supply. This was the same Cockburn who had been at the Telecommunications Research Establishment in charge of counter-measures research during the war and who had been one of the implacable opponents of the use of H2S, Lovell's brainchild which had revolutionized the effectiveness of RAF Bomber Command, as has been related earlier. At this meeting Lovell records that: 'Cockburn was not particularly interested in the navigational aspects but was particularly interested in the possibilities of using such a high gain instrument for other work connected with defence against guided weapons.' This was a possible application of the telescope which had previously been hinted at by Lovell. The outcome was that Cockburn asked for an accurate assessment of the cost of modifying the telescope for such purposes, and a scientific assessment of its performance.

The interest shown encouraged Lovell to believe that, without doubt, there would be financial support forthcoming from the Ministry of Supply, and he immediately consulted with Husband on the new requirements. It was quickly clear that operation in the 10-centimetre band could be achieved with modifications to the bowl, including a decrease in the size of the mesh to ¾ inch, extra steel for stiffening purposes, fitted bolts and certain other changes, bringing the increase in cost to £46,000. On 2 March a memorandum detailing the extra costs and containing an assessment of the performance of the modified telescope was sent to Cockburn by Lovell. So sure was he that rescue was at hand that on the same day he advised the DSIR that help from military quarters was likely to be available for modifications to extend the performance of the telescope to meet certain defence requirements. At the same time he told Rainford and Mansfield Cooper,* who was acting as Vice-Chancellor of the University during Sir John Stopford's absence on leave, of the new plans and the resultant expected support for further funds, if needed, from the Ministry concerned. Alas, Lovell's hopes were soon to be dashed. A letter from Cockburn dated 15 April 1954 advised him that after considerable thought he could not justify providing such a large sum as £46,000 from the defence budget. It was a bitter blow. As Lovell recorded in his diary: 'I suppose I expected him to say £60,000 was on the way'. In fact, it was an example of the astonishing blindness of officialdom to the needs of the future.

Disappointedly Lovell had to confess to the University authorities that he had been over-optimistic. He also had to tell Husband to abandon the proposed modifications as no alterations to design which would increase the cost over the present estimate could now be contemplated, but to his consternation he discovered that it was too late and that much of the extra cost was already committed.

His next effort to obtain Ministry of Supply assistance arose from a realization of the real weakness in Britain's defence against air attack. Lovell was a member of the Air Warfare Committee, and at a meeting on 27 July 1954 he was horrified to learn that no one had any idea how to detect the approach of Intercontinental Ballistic Missiles either from trajectories which took them high into the Earth's atmosphere or from stacked positions in Space which he foresaw as a future possibility. Additionally, there was even an inability to detect supersonic bombers! Lovell again pressed hard for Ministry of Supply support for the telescope in order that it might provide the very instrument that was needed for such urgent defence purposes until such time as purely military equipment could be developed and produced. Willis Jackson brought Sir Harry Garner, Chairman of the Guided Weapons Advisory Board, to Jodrell to discuss the matter; Sir Ben Lockspeiser, the then Secretary of the DSIR, visited Jodrell with the Chairman of the Public Accounts Committee to learn at first hand of Lovell's proposals. Both Willis Jackson and Lockspeiser were horrified at the sterility of the approach to the problems of defence against ICBMs and supersonic aircraft. Finally, at the end of September, Lovell despatched his memorandum on the subject of the detection of ballistic weapons and supersonic aircraft to Cockburn at the Ministry of Supply. In his diary he wrote: 'What will he do? What will Garner do? Will they see Lockspeiser? If so, what will Lockspeiser do? The cards seem to be falling splendidly at last. Unless one of these players is incredibly stupid, without any feeling of safety for the country, I can scarcely believe that urgent instructions to finish the telescope regardless of over expenditure will not be given very soon.'

But Lovell's *cri de cœur* fell on deaf ears. Someone in the midst of the 'Establishment' was incredibly stupid, or was there an element of professional jealousy?

From now onwards the financial problems increased. Indeed, the telescope seemed to arise out of the ground far more slowly than the price rocketed upwards. By November 1954 £165,000 out of the £390,866 allocated for the project had already been spent, yet there was little to be seen above ground level. This £390,866 was the increased sum approved by the DSIR in 1953 for the capital cost; the total figure of £439,616, which was approved, included non-recurrent costs of £48,750. Typical of new increases at this time was that of £30,000 in the driving system estimate over the £79,000 already allowed. Then there was an additional £15,000 expected to be overspent on the structural steel, £2,000 on the foundation contract, £2,500 on the control building and £1,000 on the control system; a mere increase of £50,500 compared to what was to come in 1955.

On Christmas Eve 1954, whilst Lovell noted the gloom in the financial outlook, he also wrote in his diary of events:'Since the dreary note on the eve of Christmas a year ago the site of the telescope has been transformed. Then there was nothing above the ground, not even the railway track, and Wades were only digging the drains of the control building. Now the steelwork of the two telescope towers rises 140 feet above the ground. . . .'

Certainly some good progress had been made in November and December, and 1955 began smoothly, but not for long. In August 1954 Husband had considered the question of re-designing the bowl of the telescope due to problems connected with its construction using a wire mesh, and in September of that year he came up with the idea of using a solid sheet reflector as a way out of these troubles. The solid membrane added no new problems to the safety of the telescope, since calculations of wind loading in bad winter conditions had already assumed that complete icing of the mesh would make it as solid as a sheet of steel, permitting no spaces through which the wind could pass, thereby lessening its impact. Lovell liked the idea, provided there was no relaxation in the performance of the telescope as detailed in his specifications. The need for a definite decision was urgent in order to avoid further delays in the time schedule. Husband's keenness to re-design was dictated by structural considerations; a solid membrane for the vast 250-foot bowl would provide greater stiffness than would be the case with the original wire mesh concept. Moreover, he estimated that it would increase the tonnage of steel required only marginally. Lovell's interest lay in the operational advantages, because there would be no loss of signal by leakage through the mesh and no leakage of unwanted interfering signals through the mesh from behind the bowl. The decision to proceed was taken and by the spring of 1955 it was to provide the beginnings of a series of new escalating costs over and above the increase of £50,500 occasioned by the driving system estimate, additional structural steel, control building, control system and foundation contract, a sum which the DSIR had, with reluctance, promised to meet.

The first signs of trouble began with wind-tunnel tests of a scale model of the solid membrane bowl at the National Physical Laboratory (NPL) which revealed problems of structural flutter at wind speeds of only 40 m.p.h. By April 1955 Husband had overcome this by introducing a design for braking or damping the flutter of the bowl in high winds. This pushed up costs by an estimated £15,300, almost entirely occasioned by an increase of 100 tons of steel in the construction of the bowl. Lovell was shaken, as was Rainford, the Bursar; moreover, he believed the £15,300 to be an under-estimate. But this was only the beginning of the financial shocks of 1955. The hopes in early April that by giving the contract for the driving system to Siemens of Germany would make substantial savings were dashed, partly because of an import duty which had not been foreseen. Then, by June, the emergency arrangements for damping the structural flutter of the bowl were regarded as inadequate, and further strengthening was estimated to increase the cost by yet another £5,000. In September came the next batch of bad news. Lovell's diary records on Friday 9 September:

> This morning a letter from Husband to the Bursar's Office gave the dreadful news that Dempsters (contractors for the solid membrane for the bowl) wanted £33,000 to do the membrane. Husband says that the cost of the sheet was only £5,000 and that the high cost was entirely due to labour. Apparently Dempster's first figure was in the £40,000 to £50,000 region. To this must be added £2,000 for the painting. . . . Even worse, Cannon [Chief Administrative Officer in the Bursar's office], said there was a certificate from Husband asking for a further payment of £56,000 to United Steel, making £165,000 in all for work completed. It is not clear how much of the steel for the bowl this includes, but it is already far in excess of the contract price of £131,000.

Dempster's quote also contained the information that the order for the solid membrane for the bowl would have to be placed without delay in order to obtain delivery of the steel sheet to enable them to start work in April 1956 and to complete the contract in six months from the starting-date. Lovell exclaimed at this news: 'So much for any hopes we may have had of starting research work with the telescope this autumn!' He could have added: 'And bang go any hopes of starting before the end of 1956!'

Strangely, the unfolding of the financial disasters in 1955 occurred at a time of the most noticeable progress in the growth of the structure, even if this growth was sadly behind the original schedules. When the snow and ice of January and February faded away, work at the tops of the two towers re-started, and by late March the structural work had reached a stage where Lovell felt hopeful of realizing the United Steel Structural Company's February promise that now they had the steel work for the bowl in their shops they were expecting to erect it during the summer. That turned out to be wishful thinking. However, mid-June brought encouragement with the arrival on site of the steel work for the central 20-foot ring of the bowl together with the main trunnion-bearing assemblies through which the bowl was to be driven in elevation. On 13 June the central ring was being assembled on the ground. Lovell records in his diary that the erection of the trunnion-bearing assembly 'has still to await the pedestal bearings and these are now in some firm in Manchester'. However, it appeared that, if the pedestal bearings were ready reasonably quickly, both of them could be hoisted into position at the top of the towers and made ready for the beginning of the erection of the main bowl framework before the workers on site closed down for their holidays in July. On this time-scale it was possible to visualize the commencement of work on the bowl framework by the end of August. But this was not to be. The pedestal bearings did not arrive on site until early

August. Further delays ensued in the delivery of various other parts, including the two gun racks which had been purchased for a song from the breaker's yard at Inverkeithing in 1950 and which were being modified to drive the bowl in elevation as effectively as they had once driven the 15-inch guns of HMS *Royal Sovereign* and HMS *Revenge*. In fact, it was not until the middle of September that the first trunnion-bearing assembly was hoisted into position on the northern tower, and it was the last day of September before the first great gun rack was lifted to take up its position on this tower. Its twin for the southern tower, although available, was not raised into position until 13 February 1956. The hopes of operating the telescope in 1957 were now looking rather forlorn. But it was the disastrous state of the financial situation, which was revealed so starkly by October 1955, that even raised doubts as to whether the entire project of the telescope would be abandoned.

The lead-up to costs far in excess of original estimates has already been traced. Following the bad news on costs of the membrane on 9 September, together with the request from Husband to make a further payment to United Steel of £56,000, making over £160,000 paid out for steel work when the last estimate had been a total of £131,000, there came another bombshell. On 17 September 1955 Husband advised that the weight of steel work required for the project had gone up from 1,177 tons to 1,700 tons and that the cost of this item would now be £221,000, or nearly £100,000 up on the previous estimated increase for steel arrived at in the early part of 1953. Rainford, the Bursar, promptly prepared a memorandum for the Officers and Council of the University in which he concluded that an additional £160,000 was now needed to finish the telescope over and above the £390,866 approved for capital cost by the DSIR in 1953. Lovell commented in his diary: '. . . one thing only keeps me reasonably calm, it is that so much of the structure is now complete that it really is inconceivable that the country won't finish it.' By the beginning of October, Rainford had increased his figure to £170,000 and on Saturday the 8th this was the figure revealed at a meeting with Sir John Stopford, the Vice-Chancellor, and Sir Raymond Streat,* the University Treasurer, to which Lovell, Rainford and Husband had been summoned. The outcome of this meeting was an instruction to Lovell, Rainford and Husband to prepare a detailed document on the situation for the information of the Officers of the University. Lord Simon of Wythenshawe, the governing director of the Simon Engineering Group of Companies, who was also Chairman of the University Council, was not present at the meeting, but he demanded and obtained a full report of the proceedings on the same day. Then on the next day, Sunday, Lord Simon, accompanied by Sir Hugh Beaver, the Chairman of the DSIR Advisory Council, went over to Jodrell Bank to see Lovell. Unexpectedly, Lord Simon was more comforting than Lovell had anticipated and, despite expressions of horror at the situation, he actually discussed ways of raising the money from industry.

But even worse was to come!

In order to prepare the document detailing the financial situation for the Officers of the University, Rainford and Cannon met Husband at his offices in Sheffield to review the latest estimates and the expenditure committed to date. They did not get very far, and although Husband was due in Ceylon the following week in connection with a major contract in which he was involved as consultant, it was decided to continue the meeting with Frank Betts, a mechanical engineer in Husband's consultancy, who was closely concerned with the design of the telescope, and T. Holmshaw, Husband's senior structural engineering assistant, on the following Thursday, 20 October. It might have been more appropriate if the day had been a Friday the 13th!

At this meeting the true situation was revealed, and it was more disastrous than even Lovell or Rainford had imagined. Once again it was the steel situation which produced the most deadly blow. The weight of steelwork had gone up, as already warned by Husband, to just short of 1,700 tons, and the price from £114 per ton to £135 per ton. With other increases, some straightforward price increases and some arising from inevitable modifications and additions to design, not at all inconsistent with such a pioneering project, the new estimate for the capital cost of the telescope had risen to £630,000 against the figure of £390,866 estimated in 1953. In effect, without the DSIR's further help, or the ability to raise money from industry, the University was heading for a debt of £240,000, less the additional £50,000 already promised by the DSIR. In his diary, Bernard Lovell records the details of this 'ghastly mess' and adds: 'All the old worries about the work being stopped return, alleviated only by the thought that this would not rectify the situation since all the steel is now cut and waiting for transport to Jodrell.' The Vice-Chancellor, he concluded, would clearly have been justified in dismissing him with ignominy.

It was a depressed Lovell who arrived home on the evening of Friday 21 October after hearing the awful details.

At the Vice-Chancellor's reception on Wednesday the 26th, Lovell felt 'things seemed a little brighter'. The following day Rainford brought S. H. Smith, the Finance Officer of the DSIR, out to Jodrell Bank to see the progress and to have a preliminary talk about the financial difficulties. Gazing out of the control-room window, Smith observed: 'The strength of your position, Lovell, is that huge mass of steel!' The situation was, in fact, somewhat reminiscent of the fifty blocks of concrete sunk in a field which he had rented without authority in 1949 and which had forced the purchase of this field for his research work. Smith also gave it as his opinion that the Advisory Council of the DSIR might well be persuaded to make a pound-for-pound offer to assist with the completion of the telescope. This would mean anything from £100,000 to £130,000 from either side and implied that the University would have to raise over £100,000 itself. To Lovell, this seemed a daunting prospect, even though it raised his hopes that the telescope would now surely be completed. With a sense of euphoria, tempered with caution this time, he felt that the DSIR contribution of £100,000 plus would be put into immediate effect, thus enabling certain urgent contracts to be placed. But this confidence also proved to be ill-judged. On 5 December 1955 came the news from the DSIR that, before any further grant could be considered, there would have to be a Committee of Inquiry into the financial state of the project. On 6 December Lovell wrote in his diary: '. . . full of depression and anxiety about the proposed Committee of Inquiry—one might as well have embezzled the money or be a pedlar! . . . the evening brightened by a letter from Blackett which I expected to be a blast, but which was actually a very understanding one . . .'

Blackett, who was now head of the Department of Physics at the Imperial College of Science and Technology, and a member of the DSIR Advisory Council, said in his letter: 'I had a talk with Cawley* [Sir Charles Cawley, CBE, the Director of the division at DSIR concerned with University grants] about the Jodrell business. I gather that the independent enquiry is to be made into the events leading to the present situation. . . . When the matter was brought up to the Grants Committee and to the Council I felt personally that everybody knew that ultimately the Government would have to be asked to fork out more money to finish the project, but it is quite clear that this cannot happen until the enquiry is over.' He went on to declare his doubt that the extra money could be found from existing DSIR funds, which were already below the level required for the support of other University research subjects. But he added, 'As far as I can see, and this is purely a personal view, the Government will eventually produce some more money for Jodrell, but how much I cannot say. Since it is clearly of the utmost importance that the project goes on without any check in time, I think the only possible course is for Manchester to place the necessary further contracts themselves and hope for the best. If the worst should happen, and of course the present is the worst possible time to get more money out of the Government, Manchester would presumably have to get the money on loan and repay out of income over years in the future. . . .' On 9 December

Rainford advised Lovell that there was not the slightest chance of the University Officers agreeing to place contracts on the basis of Blackett's proposal, which added once again to Lovell's depression.

1955 had been a bad year for Lovell and one which was full of serious worries and great mental stress. There was, however, one compensation in this year which was a source of great consolation. He was elected a Fellow of the Royal Society, the greatest honour that Britain can bestow upon a scientist.

14

Inquiry, Report, Inquiry

The dates for the DSIR Inquiry were set for 18, 19 and 20 January 1956. The constitution of the Committee, which was announced a few days earlier, was Mansfield Cooper, the future Vice-Chancellor of the University of Manchester, as Chairman, Professor J. A. L. Matheson* (Manchester University's Professor of Engineering), Dr R. L. Smith-Rose (Director of the DSIR's Radio Research Station), H. L. Verry (Assistant Secretary in the Overseas Liaison Division of the DSIR), C. Scruton (a senior member of the staff of the Aerodynamics Division of the DSIR), Dr J. A. Saxton (of the Radio Research Station; from 1966 Director of the Radio and Space Research Station), Dr F. G. Thomas (MICE of the Building Research Station), S. H. Smith (DSIR Finance Officer) and P. D. Greenall of the DSIR Grants Division as Secretary.

There were preliminary visits to the telescope by some members of the Committee on 5 and 6 January, and then on Wednesday the 18th the entire Committee assembled at Jodrell, where, after a brief inspection of the telescope, control building and power house, it began its deliberations. Lovell was asked to be present at 2.45 p.m., but on that Wednesday he was left alone in an anteroom until 7.30 p.m., when the Committee adjourned for the day, treatment which profoundly irritated him for he was not accustomed to having the affairs of the telescope discussed without his being present. The next day, however, it was his turn to be investigated, and he was not 'released', as he puts it in his diary, until 6.30 p.m., 'after being investigated for 8½ hours with an hour for lunch—almost the entire morning alone, and then with Husband and Rainford'. It was a gruelling experience, and at the end of it all he was exhausted, but nonetheless he felt satisfied that the Committee was sympathetic about the financial problems. In his diary he noted that everything was discussed thoroughly and that Husband frankly conceded that the Defence intervention, which had fallen through, but not before some design changes had been committed, was not directly responsible for the change in design. What had happened was that it had stimulated rethinking which had led to the design being altered for other sound reasons, and this, in turn, had increased costs. There was also an extensive discussion on the decision to change from a wire mesh for the bowl to a solid membrane, and on the matter of ensuring the availability of the steel and necessary components for this part of the design which were now in immediate danger of being disposed of elsewhere. Dr Smith-Rose emphasized on this score, as well as on others, the urgency of finishing the telescope in a steerable condition in time for the International Geophysical Year which was scheduled for July 1957 to December 1958, during the period of maximum sunspot activity. Forty nations had agreed to participate, including Great Britain, and Smith-Rose drew attention to the fact that a major contribution by Britain was dependent upon the use of the Jodrell Bank telescope.

From Lovell's point of view, one of the most cheering moments during the inquiry was when he learnt that Mansfield Cooper had received a letter from the DSIR Advisory Council stressing their 'continued faith in the timeliness and promise of the telescope'. This augured well for the outcome of the inquiry, and both Lovell and Rainford were confident that the DSIR would find half the balance of the outstanding excess above the 1953 approved figure, leaving the University to raise the rest from other sources. Indeed, there were immediately good omens supporting this view. On the Committee's final day the Chairman asked Rainford, the University Bursar, whether the University could take action to place orders for the materials for the solid membrane of the bowl to avoid any hold-up in that direction. Within hours, the University Estimates and Finance Committee authorized the letting of the contract for the membrane with Messrs Orthostyle, who had been chosen by Husband in preference to Dempsters on grounds of their lower tender. However, there was a condition that the University's liability should be limited to the cost of the steel—£5,000—until such time as instructions were given for the assembly and erection, estimated to be in June 1956. Another good omen was P. D. Greenall's advice to Rainford to write officially to the DSIR asking for an extra grant of £250,000 in order to complete the telescope. Finally, after the Committee of Inquiry's report was completed and signed on 23 February 1956, and considered at a special meeting of the DSIR on 15 March, Lovell heard through Rainford that the DSIR had recommended a contribution of half of the outstanding £¼ million on condition that the University found the other half. However, there was one snag. The DSIR could not implement their recommendation until Treasury approval had been obtained, and this proved to be a long-drawn-out affair.

A further study by the Committee of Inquiry had finally assessed the outstanding figure at £260,000, which meant that the DSIR were proposing to contribute £130,000 extra towards the telescope, leaving the University to find the other £130,000 by whatever means it could devise.

With the knowledge that the University would have to find a substantial sum to contribute towards the telescope, a fact that was realized as early as the previous autumn, Lovell had already sent begging letters to companies, institutes and personal acquaintances. His action had been triggered by a comment at a luncheon party on 31 October 1955 with the University Officers, at which the disastrous state of affairs was discussed. Lord Simon had left Lovell in no doubt as to his opinion of the deplorable state into which he had landed the University and indicated that it was up to him to set about raising the money required from outside sources. Simon was, however, fascinated by the telescope project and hinted that contributors might well include the Simon Engineering Group of Companies and Simon himself. However, the approaches, apart from those to the Simon contingent, were at this stage abortive and, in any case, the University was now anxious to avoid a public appeal until after the DSIR Committee of Inquiry had been finally assessed and Treasury approval granted for the DSIR's £130,000 contribution.

By June there was still no news of a Treasury decision, only rumours that the Treasury were anxious about the reaction by the Parliamentary Public Accounts Committee to this over-expenditure and, therefore, to the possibility of an investigation by this Committee. In the circumstances the Treasury wanted to be seen to be cautious and difficult about agreeing to the DSIR's contributing an additional £130,000 towards completion of the telescope, and they began to cover themselves by asking the DSIR why the over-expenditure could not be recovered by legal action against Husband, the consulting engineer. What the Treasury were doing, in fact, was to read into the findings of the Committee of Inquiry that the major portion of the over-expenditure was occasioned by design changes made by the consultant without reference to Lovell or to officers of the University of Manchester.

Then, on 15 August, came the news that the Treasury had at last agreed that the DSIR should make an additional grant of £130,000, the remaining £130,000 to be found by the University by appeals to non-Government sources. But there were conditions. Whilst the Treasury had dropped its original view that the consultant should be sued for the over-expenditure, it now stipulated that the University must give a written guarantee, with Counsel's opinion, that this sum of £260,000 over-expenditure was not greater than it would otherwise be if legal action to recover the money from the firm of consulting engineers had been taken. It was a shock for the University, and all concerned with this highly advanced technical and scientific project which, ironically, was soon to become the pride of the nation and a vital asset to the Western world. This condition was typical of the petty bureaucracy of men whose horizons were limited by the four walls of their Whitehall offices and whose only concern was the preservation of their own skins. In fact, they were not protecting the taxpayer against extra expenditure of money, for the Treasury was not being asked by the DSIR to provide additional money; the DSIR had made it perfectly clear that it intended to find the sum of £130,000 from funds already voted to it by the Treasury for the purpose of scientific and technological research.

Lord Simon and the Officers of the University found the Treasury conditions totally unacceptable, and their immediate reaction was to explore other avenues for the money whilst, at the same time, trying with the University's Counsel and the DSIR to find some formula by which the Treasury conditions could be made acceptable. On the subject of raising money from alternative sources, Lovell immediately made approaches to some of his fellow American astronomers. Amongst these was Professor Fred L. Whipple, the Director of the Astrophysical Observatory of the Smithsonian Institution, Cambridge, Massachusetts, and Professor of Astronomy at Harvard University. Fred Whipple was an international authority on comets and meteors, and Lovell had come to know him in the late forties through his collaboration with him during the earlier meteor studies at Jodrell. Then, only the previous year, they had met in Manchester at a Radio Astronomy Conference when Whipple had stayed with the Lovells at The Quinta. Whipple had been in Britain during the war and had made some valuable contributions to radar research. He had also become a true Anglophile, and on receipt of Lovell's letter he was immediately anxious to help. On 31 August he wrote that he 'was devastated to learn of the financial difficulties that you now have with the 250-foot telescope. . . . My immediate reaction, and the one I have maintained all during today while thinking about your problem, is that you would do best to contact Dr Alan T. Waterman, who heads up the National Science Foundation.' The function of this Foundation was to study the needs of basic science and to finance these in so far as its budget permitted. Whilst Whipple did not think that Lovell could obtain any appreciable sums of money from that source, he emphasized that 'Dr Waterman has an intimate knowledge of the sources of funds for basic research in this country.' But Whipple thought that the best chance of raising money was from the Department of Defence. 'I have no idea,' he wrote, 'whether you should make that contact through your own Defense Organization, or through the assistance of Dr Waterman. . . . With regard to the probability of success, I think it is reasonably good (at least a 50–50 bet) with regard to the Department of Defense, but I have no idea of the price you might be asked to pay, or the price that you would be willing to pay in terms of "selling your scientific soul". I gather that Manchester is not willing to make heavy concessions in this direction. . . . The use of your telescope as an unbelievably powerful radar might be of huge interest to the Defense Department.' It was an encouraging response, and Lovell was quick to acknowledge the letter. But for the moment this was not a course to be pursued until other fields had been explored and, in any case, it would need a visit to the United States Defence Department by Lovell, and this might produce a delicate situation with the British authorities.

An interesting aspect at this time was the fact that the National Science Foundation of America had just obtained a grant of $7 million—about £2½ million at the then rate of exchange—for the construction of a precision radio telescope, smaller than that at Jodrell Bank. Construction was due to start at an early date. In a letter dated 29 October, Lovell drew Lord Simon's attention to this in the hope that it would provide him with ammunition to attack the Treasury. In his letter he added that: 'One serious aspect of this is that our own manpower is being drained. Three of my own people are already in America, and one of the Directors of Scientific Research in the Ministry of Supply is leaving in a few days to supervise the construction of this telescope.'

Despite all the financial troubles, the telescope structure arose inexorably into the sky. It was like Jack's beanstalk. It just grew and grew. It even seemed to shrug off the problems of industrial disputes on site, and delays in delivery of materials, as mere temporary inconveniences. Its growth had now acquired a momentum which was uncheckable. In February 1956 the second gun-rack was hoisted to the top of the southern tower. By the middle of March the great framework of the bowl had been hoisted into position. Lovell wrote in his diary: 'It looks enormous now that the full parabola can be seen in position.' On 11 June work on the bowl had proceeded so far that, as Lovell put it, '. . . the telescope now looks terrific. At last one can begin to see what a 250 ft bowl looks like suspended 180 ft above ground.' The 62½-foot aerial tower, which was to rise upwards from the centre of the bowl and which had been erected on the ground, was lifted into position in mid-July. By 1 September all the ribs of the bowl were in position. By 10 September the telescope bowl steelwork was finally ringed around the outer circumference, and the work of the cranes and the vast encasement of scaffolding around the entire structure was now nearly at an end. Only a number of miscellaneous items had still to be lifted, including cladding for the tower tops which supported the bowl, walkways and the steelwork for the stabilizing girder and for the swinging laboratory which was to be sited underneath the bowl. By mid-December the scaffolding was steadily disappearing and more and more of the telescope was being revealed in stark grandeur. Even 80 feet diameter of the steel membrane of the bowl had been completed.

But still no signs of the money, and still the Treasury's unacceptable conditions remained. Moreover, the state of the financial affairs of the telescope were beginning to filter through to the public via Press rumours, particularly in the Manchester area, and this soon led to snide attacks on the Lovell family. But this close-knit tribe knew how to deal with the critics of their father, at whatever level. Susan recalls the incident at school in Manchester of the girl who criticized the 'stupid telescope' as a waste of money which could have been spent on more schools. Susan was not the kind of adversary with whom the wisest young girl would choose to cross swords. She promptly attacked the critic of her father, knocked her off her bike and treated her to some potent feminine fisticuffs! For her aggressive foray in defence of her father she says: 'I got a rocket for this action from the headmistress, but I refused to apologize.' She added: 'We were always defending Daddy at this stage of the telescope. We felt that any criticism of the telescope was a direct attack upon him which had to be dealt with!'

Another memorable incident also occurred in the latter part of 1956, which is remembered by all the family. At that time Judy and the twins, Roger and Philippa, were at school at nearby Brereton, and Joyce Lovell took the children, including Susan and Bryan, to Brereton Church for a special school service one Sunday. Susan and Bryan recall that on this occasion there was a visiting vicar who, in his sermon, likened the telescope to a goldfish bowl, and the scientists to 'open-mouthed goldfish searching gaumlessly for things they have no business to be sticking their noses into, because the Universe is God's province and not man's'. At the end of the service Joyce waited with her brood outside the church, and when the vicar eventually appeared, she surrounded him with the family and, to his acute embarrassment, she introduced them to him as 'some of the fish in the goldfish bowl'!

About the only truly cheerful note in 1956 for Lovell was sounded in a letter from the Royal Institution dated 26 November. It read: 'I have much pleasure in informing you that the Managers, at their recent meeting, decided that the Actonian Prize for 1956 should be divided between you and Mr Martin Ryle for your researches on radio astronomy which have so greatly extended our knowledge of the Universe.' Lovell had joined the ranks of celebrated persons such as Sir George G. Stokes, Madame Curie and Sir Alexander Fleming who were included in the list of recipients of this honour, which is awarded only once in every seven years.

Lovell closed the year with a note in his diary written on Christmas Eve. 'Yes, yet another Christmas without the telescope! But to repeat last year's remark—surely this really is the last. . . . It looks as if January and Feb. will be pretty inactive and thus if the telescope really has got to be ready by July 1st some pretty fast work will have to be done. Still, it is possible to repeat again, as on Christmas Eve 1955, that we've got a good deal more than a year ago and, more important still, the shadow of the inquiry doesn't hang over us, although we still haven't got the money!'

But if one inquiry no longer hung over Jodrell, another was only just around the corner, and this one even more ominous.

The Jodrell Bank radio telescope was the largest and most expensive single item of research equipment that had, to date, been undertaken by a university and, from the points of view of design, engineering and construction, it was a pioneering project. It was a grave misfortune that the timing of its erection should have coincided with a period when there was a tide of rising criticism about the traditional freedom of universities to use their financial grants without any demand for public accountability. The sums being provided by the Exchequer for university purposes were rapidly becoming larger and larger. These grants which came directly from the Exchequer reached the universities through the University Grants Committee and were not routed through a ministerial department. Therefore, the university's books were not open to inspection in spite of the considerable amount of public money voted for the use of universities. Voices were already being raised in the Parliamentary Public Accounts Committee about the Committee's inability to criticize university expenditures. Whilst the over-expenditure of £260,000 on the telescope was 'chickenfeed' when compared with the discrepancies which the PAC normally investigated—figures running into millions—it was a godsend to those who were seeking a confrontation on university spending as a pathway towards gaining more public control of university affairs. The financial problems of the telescope offered a chance to indicate that universities were incapable of controlling the expenditure of large amounts of money, and the opportunity was seized upon. The PAC decided to investigate, and on 21 March 1957 Dr H. W. Melville,* who had just replaced Sir Ben Lockspeiser as Secretary of the DSIR, had the unenviable task of appearing before the Committee and being interrogated on the findings of the DSIR's own inquiry into the affair.

Two weeks earlier, on 5 March, the report on the DSIR's inquiry prepared by the Comptroller and Auditor General at the Treasury, Sir Frank Tribe, KCB, KBE, was published. This document contained the facts about the increasing cost of the telescope but was somewhat unfairly balanced because it contained no explanation of the circumstances which had led to increased costs. The Press promptly had a 'field day', throwing bricks at the unfortunate telescope and at all those concerned with the project. In particular, the report, by virtue of its absolute factuality, left open the question of individual blame or whether there was any reason to blame anyone at all. This, ironically, left the possibility that blame lay with

H. C. Husband, the consulting engineer, and to a lesser extent with
Lovell, and this was the line adopted by the Press. Nothing could have
been more deplorable, for the Vice-Chancellor of the University of
Manchester and the Treasurer had only just completed negotiations with
Husband on the subject of his fees, and he had been most co-operative
and generous in agreeing to forgo some of the fees due to him in order to
help out the University. Fortunately the Press comment was limited and
brief and was not pursued. But this was not the only adverse effect of the
Tribe report. Undoubtedly it had some influence on the PAC investigation which was conducted by seven MPs with Sir Frank Tribe and A. T.
K. Grant, an Under-Secretary at the Treasury, in attendance. The MPs
were Mr Benson in the chair, Mr Arbuthnot, Mr Hoy, Mr Oliver, Mr
Peyton, Mr Steele and Mr Thornton-Kemsley.

The PAC, in its summary of its 'Minutes of Evidence' reported that: 'It
was stated in evidence that the engineering consultant changed the design
without the concurrence of the University; new structural features were
introduced into the instrument and the complexity and cost were thereby
materially increased. Although the University professor, who was
primarily responsible for the outline design, lived on the spot, he was not
consulted so far as the Department were aware.' The 'Department'
referred to was the DSIR. This accusation, which was a travesty of the
truth, arose from questions by Mr Benson to Dr Melville, the Secretary of
the DSIR:

Benson: In October, 1955, the University told the Department that the
design had been changed substantially without their approval?

Melville: Yes.

Benson: If this was a University project, who had changed the design without
obtaining the approval of the University, the engineer or Professor
Lovell?

Melville: Oh, no, quite clearly the engineering consultant changed the design
without the concurrence of the University.

Benson: He made it solid instead of mesh? [A reference to the decision to
change from a wire mesh reflector to one of solid steel.]

Melville: Yes, he introduced new structural features into the instrument to
make it more rigid and, in his opinion, I think, a more safe structure.

Benson: Without even consulting the University?

Melville: Without consulting the University.

Benson: Is that transverse circle one of the things he introduced? [This was a
reference to the stabilizing girder which had been introduced after
the wind tunnel tests to dampen flutter.]

Melville: Yes, that is one of the new features which, of course, has added to the
complexity of the instrument.

Benson: He designed that on his own without consulting anyone?

Melville: Yes.

Benson: And without advising them that it would materially increase cost?

Melville: Yes.

Benson: That is rather unusual, is it not?

Melville: It is unusual, but this is an unusual structure.

Benson: It may be, but even with unusual structures the engineer does not go off on his own responsibility and enormously increase the expense without telling anybody?

Melville: Quite.

Benson: What line has been taken about this?

Melville: Well, of course, directly this became known to the Department immediate action was taken and a Committee was set up to inquire into the whole basis of the design and for the reasons for the change, and a report was in fact published setting out all these matters in some detail. I do not mean published in the ordinary way. It was confidential to the Department and the University.

Benson: It was confirmed that this alteration was made entirely without consultation?

Melville: Yes.

Benson: Professor Lovell lives on the spot presumably?

Melville: Oh, yes, he lives in the apartments.

What Lovell's apartments were, is a mystery. He lived in his own house, 'The Quinta, three miles away!

The investigation by the PAC went on in this vein for hours, and even raised the question of suing the consulting engineer. But the entire evidence pointing to lack of consultation between Husband and Lovell was far from the truth, as was to be revealed sixteen months later.

The extraordinary aspect of this PAC investigation was that the question of increases in material costs from price rises and increases in labour costs from wage awards, both of which contributed substantially to the over-expenditure, were never discussed. Also, that the £260,000 should have become the subject of such pointed attention was droll, to say the least, when compared with the *sotto voce* revelations in the following months that, for example, 'in the three years 1953–54 to 1955–56 works so started by the Army and Royal Air Force without express Parliamentary sanction were estimated to cost £4.62 million and £26.2 million respectively.' Then, again, there was an expenditure of '£3.5 million on works other than those for which provision had been made in the Estimate. . . .' In the case of the Royal Air Force expenditure, Sir Maurice Dean, KCB, KCMG, the Permanent Under-Secretary of State for Air, with true Civil Service aplomb, was able to claim 'urgency' and 'national interest'!

The PAC report upon all its Sessions from the period 1956 to 1957 was not completed until 24 July 1957, and it was not published until Tuesday

13 August. Before its publication there was spectacular progress in the construction of the telescope, and by the end of May all the cranes had vanished from the site, the painters were hard at work, the riveters fixing the steel plates of the bowl membrane had nearly completed their task, the driving system had been installed, the swinging laboratory had been hoisted into position underneath the bowl, and all the walkways were complete. However, by this time Lovell was nearly prostrate with exhaustion. It was not just the telescope, with all the delays and financial worries, which had taken its toll; there had also been the programmes of research and the preparations for Jodrell's commitments to the International Geophysical Year, which had been part of the daily work throughout the past years and which had added to his onerous burdens.

On 1 June, having decided to take a brief rest, he went to North Wales for a holiday with the family. Joyce, with Judy and the twins, had departed a few days earlier, and Bernard Lovell followed with Susan and Bryan. Susan and Bryan, respectively eighteen and sixteen years old at the time, recall that their father was terribly low, and so they teased him throughout the journey to cheer him up. 'We talked the whole way,' Susan relates, 'with a thick Scottish accent. How ridiculous it sounds now—but how he laughed. And when we got there, he said to Mummy, "Gosh, I was depressed and miserable when we set out on this journey, but these two—really, they are just the end!" He was a jolly good sport and you could always cheer him up by teasing him.' On 12 June, Lovell relates, he climbed Snowdon with Susan, Bryan and Judy, and when they returned they found the remainder of the family in a state of immense excitement. Husband had phoned from Jodrell to say that the telescope had moved in azimuth under power!

Back at Jodrell on Thursday 20 June, Bernard Lovell was to witness a great moment. In his diary on that day he recorded: 'The bowl has been tilted! A marvellous Summer morning and after much clearance of the site and general preparations the bowl began to move at about 10.30. The transition from no movement to movement was imperceptible, the motion was superb—only a quiet hum from the motor room like a great ship. After about 10 degrees they stopped to regrease the gear racks and then at about 12 o'clock it was put right over to 30 degrees. A majestic sight in the hot sun. Husband delighted; the power consumption so small that the people in the power house were unaware that the movement was on.' Patrick Blackett, who heard the news the next day, wrote a letter dated 21 June: 'Very many congratulations! This is great news. . . .' Indeed it was, and for the moment all the past worries and troubles were forgotten.

By the end of July the solid membrane of the bowl was complete, and in August Lovell and his team began their early tests of the instrument. On

Friday night, 2 August, they made their first recording—160 megacycles with the bowl in the zenith. Lovell wrote: 'A remarkable run completely free from interference although the galaxy was half scale. Hazard reckoned that the sensitivity was at least 6 times up on the transit telescope, and Hanbury said it was the finest record he'd ever seen.' On 9 August they began measurements of the polar diagram of the reflector on various frequencies.

But their joy was soon to end.

The dreaded PAC report appeared on the afternoon of 13 August with its pointed criticism of Husband for making substantial changes in design, resulting in increased costs, without consultation with Lovell or the University. Lovell says of this moment: 'I do not think any of us expected this personal attack. It was utter nonsense. For the previous seven years scarcely a day had passed without a personal, mail or 'phone contact between Husband and myself.' The newspapers seized on the report and castigated everyone for lack of general co-operation, Husband in particular, and for the lack of responsible care in handling public funds. They also questioned the necessity for this expensive research toy. 'The irony of this situation,' Lovell wrote in his diary, 'is quite unbelievable. To be slashed by a Government committee when this marvellous instrument is beginning to work is a most strange business.'

On the evening of the 13th, Husband, who was understandably furious at the accusations in the report and the Press, telephoned Lovell and demanded that he should immediately write a letter to *The Times* denying the allegations, otherwise he would sue him personally. After consultation with Rainford, the Bursar—the Vice-Chancellor was away on holiday—it was agreed that it would be most unwise to concede to Husband's request at this stage. Then on Wednesday the 14th Rainford called Lovell and said that Husband had threatened that he would drag the information out of him in the witness box and, in the circumstances, he—Lovell—had best see Husband in company with the University solicitors.

15

Help from Many Sources

The University officers had already rejected the Treasury condition under which the DSIR could make a further grant of £130,000 towards the telescope, leaving £130,000 to be found by the University. The condition was that the University must, with Counsel's opinion, guarantee that the £260,000 over-expenditure was not greater than it would otherwise be if legal action to recover the money from Husband was taken. Now, too, the University officers rejected the findings of the Tribe report and the PAC report that Husband had acted on his own in matters of design change without consulting Lovell and without the knowledge of the University. Husband was quickly to learn of the University's firm stand and, within hours of making his threats, he simmered down and relented. Moreover, the day after the publication of the report John Maddox, the Science Correspondent of the *Manchester Guardian*, came out to Jodrell Bank and the following day, Thursday, published a very complimentary piece about the performance of the telescope together with photographs. It was a consolation to Lovell and Husband after the other unfavourable Press comment.

But if Lovell was relieved for the moment from threats of Courts of Law, he was still in the doldrums over the question of finances. If the DSIR were not to be permitted to come up with their £130,000 without the Treasury's conditions being met, then the University needed to find £260,000 from outside sources as a matter of urgency. This had been emphasized by the Vice-Chancellor to both Lovell and Rainford.

Since the war, Lovell had maintained contact not only with ex-TRE colleagues but also with several of those Royal Air Force officers with whom he had been so closely associated. When the PAC report was published and the financial situation became instantly more acute because of the criticisms it contained, his thoughts turned to those persons who might have the necessary influence in both political and industrial circles which would materially assist in raising substantial sums of money. Sir Robert Renwick* was obviously one. During the war Renwick had been Controller of Communications at the Air Ministry and Controller of Communications Equipment at the Ministry of Aircraft Production; under Churchill's direct control, he had been in charge of all radar research and development and responsible for the production of the heavy bombers of Bomber Command. Undoubtedly he had been one of the most powerful of Churchill's 'lieutenants'. Now, in the post-war years, he had returned to the City and become a leading industrialist and financier with an excellent reputation and a not inconsiderable influence in political circles, particularly those of the Conservative Party. I was amongst those wartime friends with whom Lovell had maintained contact and he knew that I had also remained close friends with Renwick since the war.

Lovell was also aware that I had just recently joined Texas Instruments of Dallas to form a UK subsidiary. During the 1950s this company had become sole supplier of silicon semiconductor components (transistors and diodes) to the US aerospace industry. From 1958 Texas Instruments (UK) in turn became sole suppliers of silicon semi-conductors to British aerospace companies manufacturing guided weapons, e.g. ground-to-air and air-to-air missile systems being developed and produced by such firms as de Havillands, Vickers and Plessey, including the de Havilland ICBM Bluestreak. At this time Texas Instruments of Dallas and its UK subsidiary were the only company in the world making silicon semiconductor components and applying these to military and Space projects.

On the morning of 15 August, two days after the publication of the PAC report, Lovell talked with Rainford, the University Bursar, about the possibilities of enlisting Renwick's aid. That same afternoon he wrote to Rainford: 'With reference to paragraph 2.B of the Vice-Chancellor's note dated the 1st August on the radio telescope appeal, and as a result of our telephone conversation this morning, I have asked Group Captain Saward about getting Sir Robert Renwick to Jodrell Bank. He hopes to see him some time during the next few days, and will arrange a date—probably in the second half of October—and he has promised to drive him up personally to see us. I will let you know as soon as any further arrangements are made. . . .'

On 23 August, just before leaving for Boulder, Colorado, to attend a meeting of the International Scientific Radio Union (URSI), Lovell replied by letter to my request for further information about the telescope:

My Dear Dudley,
    In response to your telephone call I am sending you the following documents:–
    1. A note on some practical implications of the telescope which I have written specially, and which I hope will give Sir Robert some indication of its practical importance to the electronics and aircraft industries.
    . 2. A note on the financial situation which has been compiled by the Bursar of the University. This is not for circulation but I have obtained the permission of the Bursar to send it to you for transmission to Sir Robert. . . .

3. A photocopy of the main editorial comment in the current issue of the New Scientist which I was delighted to read.

4. Two general articles on radio astronomy which I have written. . . .

When you next speak to Sir Robert would you say that I sincerely appreciate his interest, and shall look forward with very great pleasure to an opportunity for showing him the telescope in action. Thank you also for your tremendous assistance. It is by far the best way to handle this if you can spare the time to drive him up.

Yours ever,
Bernard.

In effect, Lovell left it very much to me to liaise with Renwick on his behalf.

The note on the practical implications of the telescope described its design and explained that it had been built for two main functions: firstly for use purely as a receiving aerial for the study of radio waves emitted from the remote parts of the Universe, the Sun and the planets, and secondly as a radar instrument for the transmission and reception of radio waves for the study of meteors, the Moon, the planets, the aurora borealis and Earth satellites. Whilst much of the future programme of work would be fundamental research, Lovell pointed out that in the radar applications the research would be closely related to many practical problems facing the electronics and aerospace industries, including those connected with the ballistics of future man-made missiles. The studies, he emphasized, could provide knowledge essential to the control of guidance systems needed for rockets and missiles travelling beyond the atmosphere. He continued: 'The telescope is certainly the only instrument which exists at present in Great Britain which will be able to detect and track the Russian and American Earth satellites by radar. The significance of the telescope in this role is great, particularly in the information it will yield about the detection and tracking problems.'

The reference to the detection and tracking of the Russian and American Earth satellites by radar was in connection with the claim in July 1955 by the Russians and Americans that they would launch such satellites during the International Geophysical Year of 1957–8.

I had little difficulty in persuading Renwick to take an interest in the problems of Jodrell Bank and to use what influence he had in an attempt to urge the Conservative Government of the day, which was under Harold Macmillan's leadership, to take steps to alleviate the University's financial embarrassment over the telescope. However, in the first instance Renwick suggested it would be best if Lovell could come down to London for a preliminary discussion. 22 October was finally arranged for this meeting, the venue to be the Savoy Grill where the three of us were to have lunch together.

Then came an unanticipated miracle.

On his return from Boulder, Colorado, Lovell had expected to find work at Jodrell virtually complete and a fully steerable telescope at the disposal of his team. But this was far from the case. In his diary on 2 October he wrote: '. . . I was infuriated at the impotence of the Site Committee which met on Tuesday Sept. 24. . . . Husband has continued to find every possible excuse for not doing things. At the Site Committee he said that 14 days intensive work was required to link up [the driving system] with the control room. After 7 days Brush appeared and succeeded in driving it [the telescope] backwards.' The Brush control equipment had been scheduled for completion by 21 August! 'Brush due to come again on Tuesday, but on Monday night there was a blow up because their Chief Engineer refused to come back with "University people breathing down his neck". . . . However, some Brush people did appear yesterday and by the evening the telescope was being driven satisfactorily from the control room computer. . . .' In fact, it still seemed that ages separated Lovell and his team from any reasonable use of the telescope for scientific purposes. This was a depressing thought when the International Geophysical Year had already commenced and Jodrell Bank was expected to participate actively in the various programmes of related research.

Amongst the proposed research uses of the telescope was its employment as a radar device to study radio echoes from the Moon and the nearer planets. It was evident, early on in the planning of the IGY, that this kind of research would fit well into the IGY programme. Lovell's team were already obtaining echoes from the Moon with some of their existing smaller equipment and had developed a technique for the measurement of the total electron density in the Earth-Moon space. These measurements were expected to be a particularly important contribution to the IGY. Bearing in mind the announcement in 1955 that the Americans and Russians intended to launch Earth satellites, Lovell had included the tracking of these as a further useful experiment, and he had considered the possibility of using the Earth satellite as an artificial moon close to Earth and measuring the electron content in the Earth-satellite space. Then by comparison with the lunar results he believed it would be possible to measure the electron density in the interplanetary space between the satellite and the Moon. But the important part of the contribution to the IGY programme was the official proposal that Jodrell Bank should use the telescope as a radar device to track the Earth satellites, and Lovell was naturally anxious that the instrument should be ready to tackle this task the moment the first satellite was rocketed into orbit. At this time the date was unknown, although Lovell had been informed by the

Americans at the International Scientific Radio Union meeting at Boulder that it would be several months before the USA would be ready to launch their satellite and that the Russians were known to be encountering severe difficulties with their launching plans and that there was not the slightest chance of a Russian satellite being the first in orbit. On the face of it, Jodrell Bank still had some breathing-space.

Then, dramatically, on Friday 4 October of this year 1957, in the early hours of the morning, the USSR launched man's first artificial Earth satellite. Lovell says that, 'the telephone bells which aroused me from sleep carried a message which I had been expecting at any time, but I had no conception of the impact which this historic feat would have on the world, or of its consequences for me personally and for the telescope.' This remarkable Soviet success stunned the West, which had persistently failed to recognize and to take note of the advancement of the Soviet Union in science and technology since the end of the war. More particularly it shocked the USA, which had refused to believe the Russian pronouncements in 1955 that the USSR would launch a satellite at the beginning of the IGY. Then, in June 1957, the Americans had dismissed as propaganda the announcement by A. N. Nesmeyanov, the President of the Soviet Academy, that both the carrier vehicle and the instrumentation for the first Soviet satellite were ready and that it would be launched 'within a few months'. Even on 1 October, when the Russians broadcast the frequencies on which their satellite would transmit, no one in the West really believed that the Russian attempt to put a satellite into orbit was a matter of hours away. But the most galling news about the Soviet success was that the satellite, called *Sputnik I*, which had been placed in an orbit ranging in altitude from 140 to 560 miles, weighed 184 pounds against the 3.25 pound 6-inch sphere of the American planned satellite *Vanguard*, which was superseded as the first American satellite by *Explorer I* weighing 31 pounds, which was placed in orbit on 31 January 1958. Moreover, the carrier rocket which launched *Sputnik I* was an Intercontinental Ballistic Missile (ICBM). Clearly, contrary to Western belief to date, the Russians had successfully developed these powerful long-range weapons that could carry devastating warheads to enormous distances with great accuracy. On the day of the launching, one sceptical highly placed American militarist, who would not concede the victory of the race into Space to the Russians, announced that 'Anyone can fling a lump of old iron into Space.' But on 7 October the *Manchester Guardian* reported a comment from Alistair Cooke, the well-known journalist and American radio commentator, couched in a rather different vein: 'The White House assurance, given out by Mr Hagerty, the President's press secretary, that it did not come as a surprise, is drowned by the astonishment of the scientists, the defensive surprise of the Pentagon, and the angry cries of the Democrats. Senators Morse of Oregon, Jackson of Washington, and Symington of Missouri, were quick to blame the Administration's defence economics for the shame of the Soviets' palpable superiority in the long-range missiles field. And Senator Symington applied the classic American poultice to every wound in the body politic. He "demanded" a Senate investigation.'

On the same day, in a leading article, the *Manchester Guardian* also summed up the situation succinctly: 'Thinkers, technicians, and manu-facturers must have been given their fullest scope. Their achievement is immense. It demands a psychological adjustment on our part towards Soviet society, Soviet military capabilities and, perhaps most of all, to the relationship of the world with what is beyond. . . . What of Russia's war capacity on Earth? There, little doubt can remain. Mr Krushchev was speaking no less than the truth. The Russians can now build ballistic missiles capable of hitting any chosen target anywhere in the World.'

Initially, Lovell had no intention of using the telescope to observe *Sputnik I*. The instrument was incomplete, with the contractors still in possession, and it was not yet possible to drive it continuously from the control room. Moreover, the radar equipment which it was intended should be used on the American satellite as soon as it was launched was not on the telescope, nor were there immediate plans for installing it because the launch was not expected for several months. In fact, it was still in the laboratories several hundred yards from the telescope itself. However, a barrage of questions and telephone calls from the Press deluged Lovell, demanding to know whether the telescope was or would be tracking the *Sputnik*. This was quickly followed on Saturday and Sunday by a positive state of siege of Jodrell Bank by journalists, BBC and ITV personnel and members of the public, eager to have first-hand news of the progress of Russia's orbiting satellite. As Lovell said, 'Maybe our Press relations were so bad and our public image in such disgrace that there was a feeling that some vague demonstration of the usefulness of the telescope should be forced.' But he had no intention of connecting a simple receiver to the telescope and then steering the telescope to receive the *Sputnik*'s bleep-bleep signal, which it was transmitting continuously, when the bleep-bleep was already being received by simple receivers on the ground and being broadcast to those who wanted to listen. Indeed, he absolutely refused to indulge in such a pointless demonstration for the sake of effect. As he said: 'For me it was either the radar experiment already planned for the telescope or nothing.' Lovell was, in fact, only interested in tracking the satellite by radar, and this he could not do with the telescope still in its unfinished state.

On Monday 7 October, however, there was a dramatic change in the situation. He was to learn from telephone calls from certain Government Ministries in London that there was no defence or other radar in the country capable of detecting and tracking the carrier rocket which had injected the *Sputnik* into orbit! And this was the rocket of a Russian ICBM! Although the news confirmed a suspicion he had held for some time, he had been unable to believe that those responsible for the defence and security of the nation could have been so blind as to neglect the requirement to detect ballistic missiles. Then, by the end of that day, he received the incredible news that in the free Western world, including the USA, not a single radar equipment had succeeded in locating the carrier rocket!

With the vast gain of the telescope, Lovell knew that, even with the low-power radar transmitter Jodrell Bank had already been using on their Moon echo experiments, it should be easy to obtain a radar echo from the carrier rocket.

The miracle required to establish the immediate necessity for the telescope for national security, in addition to researches into the Universe, was there for the asking.

In the meantime, Husband, the consulting engineer, had informed the Press that the telescope was 'fully operational', which was quite untrue. He had then expressed to Lovell his annoyance, and that of the contractors, that he, Lovell, was not taking advantage of the situation by demonstrating the potential of the telescope by using it to receive the *Sputnik*'s signals. They were eager for some good publicity for a change! Lovell seized on their desires on that Monday to get what he wanted. He told Husband that, if he would summon those parties concerned with the completion of the work necessary to enable the instrument to be driven through the computer from the control room, he, for his part, would attempt to detect and track not the *Sputnik* but the carrier rocket with the telescope. The ploy paid off. Work which had previously been estimated to take weeks was now completed within forty-eight hours. The idea of the telescope being the only instrument in the Western world—and later it was discovered to be the only one in the whole world—capable of detecting and tracking the Russian rocket was a fantastic stimulus. At 6 p.m. on Wednesday 9 October, 'the servo loop to the telescope drive was closed and for the first time the instrument was moving automatically under remote control from the control room,' Lovell recorded.

The next problem was to link up the radar equipment which was still in the laboratories hundreds of yards away from the telescope. To move it bodily onto the telescope at short notice was regarded as impossible—it weighed several tons. It was therefore decided to connect it by transmission lines across the intervening field and then by flexible cable onto the telescope. The cable was a part of the schedule of equipment required for the instrument, but with the present financial embarrassment there was no money to purchase it at this time. The Press, now aware of Lovell's plans which could provide the scientific scoop of the post-war years, were subtly made aware of the telescope's predicament, and they were quick to make sure that everybody knew the situation. Their publicity was effective, and Sir John Dean of the Telegraph Construction and Maintenance Company immediately offered to send Lovell any high-frequency cable that was required as a matter of priority. He was as good as his word, and miraculously the cable arrived at nearby Crewe Station on the Wednesday evening just as the servo loop on the telescope was being closed. A few minutes after midnight, with the entire place seething with reporters, TV crews and anyone else who could get near Jodrell Bank, the telescope, under test, was transmitting to the Moon, and the first radar echoes from the Moon were being obtained on this remarkable instrument. The test revealed a need for some modifications. By 11 October, when the rocket was estimated to be above the horizon, all was ready for an attempt to detect it. The equipment functioned perfectly, and the cathode ray tube was full of radar echoes from meteor trails, but with nothing to guide Lovell and his team as to what an echo from a rocket would look like, they were uncertain whether one of the echoes was at such a range and of such a character that it was a response from the rocket.

Then, just before midnight on Saturday 12 October, there was, as Lovell describes it, 'an unforgettable sight on the cathode ray tube as a large fluctuating echo, moving in range, revealed to us what no man had yet seen—the radar track of the launching rocket of an Earth satellite entering our telescope beam as it swept across England a hundred miles high over the Lake District, moving out over the North Sea at a speed of 5 miles per second. We were transfixed with excitement!' Lovell had the only instrument in the world that could detect and track an Intercontinental Ballistic Missile. He recalls turning to Bryan,* his elder son, who had asked to be present to witness the event and who was showing more interest in the arts than in science in his school education, and saying: 'If the sight of that doesn't turn you into a scientist, nothing ever will!'

The reaction of the Press was tremendous. From criticism of the project the newspapers turned to unrestrained praise. Night after night the lecture room at Jodrell Bank was packed with reporters and cameramen. Almost as a ritual, Lovell had to give two Press conferences each evening, one at 6 p.m. and one at 11 p.m. Joyce Lovell, with help from Bryan and Judy and from the families of other members of the Jodrell team, served hundreds of cups of tea throughout those nights. Suddenly the telescope was no longer a dirty word. It had been transformed into a national asset, even if it was still in debt! Susan, who had started her nursing training at the Middlesex Hospital shortly before this event, said: 'He became a hero overnight and it was wonderful. At the hospital everybody said "Oh, you're Miss Jodrell Bank 1957." It was lovely.'

On 14 October I drafted a letter for Sir Robert Renwick which appeared in *The Times* on the 16th under the heading 'Lessons of the Satellite', the same day that the telescope, just after midnight, tracked the rocket out to a distance of 930 miles over the Arctic Circle. It read:

> The Russian satellite, following on the announcement of possession of the Intercontinental Ballistic Missile, is a salutary warning that the Soviet Union is a leading power technologically. A remarkable point about this latest achievement is that the Russians have launched the 'moon' on a near polar orbit instead of on the easier equatorial orbit planned by the United States of America. This in itself implies immense superiority in rocket development.
>
> The cost of penetrating space is too prohibitive for the United Kingdom to contemplate at present and therefore we have fallen sadly behind in technical development in this field. Faced with this situation one might expect that those aspects of science in which Britain has established an ascendancy should receive the backing which is essential to our prestige and, indeed, to our survival. Even if we cannot make a satellite we might at least ensure that we have the means of detecting and observing those objects launched by foreign Powers, and thereby acquiring at little cost vital scientific information.

Referring to the fact that the research station of the University of Manchester at Jodrell Bank appeared to have in the radio telescope the only instrument in Britain, and probably the world, capable of detecting and tracking *Sputnik I* and its carrier rocket by radar, the letter continued:

> The astonishing thing about this new use of the telescope is that the Director of Jodrell Bank had to depend on the timely gift from industry of some polythene cables in order to bring the instrument into operation for this purpose.
>
> The publicity which the satellite has drawn to the radio telescope has, in fact, revealed a depressing financial situation and it is disturbing to learn that Manchester University, which has had the courage and the initiative to proceed with the erection of this instrument, is now under stricture from the Government because the expenditure on this project has exceeded the original estimate by some £250,000, a sum considerably less than that expended on a single modern bomber aircraft. It should not have been necessary for Professor Lovell to depend on last-minute charity on this vital occasion and it will be a disgrace if funds for the perfection and operation of this telescope remain so short that further recourse to charity becomes necessary. . . .

It was with this background that the meeting with Renwick on 22 October took place. Renwick had studied carefully Lovell's note on some of the practical implications of the telescope and the Bursar's note on the financial situation. He had also had a number of discussions with me, and I had left him in no doubt about the defence importance of the instrument. He was aware of the Public Accounts Committee report and the refusal of the Treasury to authorize the DSIR to contribute another £130,000 to the cost, leaving Manchester University to find the other £130,000 unless certain impossible conditions were guaranteed. However, whilst Renwick questioned Lovell about all of these matters with his usual thoroughness, it was on the subject of the future capabilities of satellites to provide a continuous surveillance of Earth, and the threat this posed to national security, and about the possibilities of ICBMs being stacked in orbit and controlled by future sophisticated satellites, that he concentrated the conversation. Indeed, he was looking at the necessity of having the telescope as an effective defence weapon, as well as an instrument for the exploration of outer Space by the study of signals from radio stars hundreds of millions of light years away, until such time as the military had their own radars capable of giving early warning of enemy missiles. It was this aspect which he believed would carry most weight with the Conservative Government under Harold Macmillan. Never one to waste time, and impressed by Lovell's information, Renwick acted promptly. After lunch the three of us hastened back to Renwick's office, where he immediately telephoned No. 10 Downing Street and suggested to Harold Macmillan, who was on the eve of his departure to the USA to discuss matters of concern to the two countries, including defence, that he should meet Lovell and myself for a briefing. Whilst the Prime Minister was not sure that he would personally be able to see us that afternoon, he requested Renwick to despatch us to 10 Downing Street right away, and if he himself could not be there, he would arrange for his Private Secretary, P. F. de Zulueta,* to be briefed on his behalf. He also requested that a note about the operation of the telescope should be prepared for him to take to Washington. This Lovell wrote on the spot for typing by Renwick's secretary, whilst Renwick dictated a covering note to the Prime Minister. These two documents are recorded below:

Note on Jodrell Bank Telescope

The Radio Telescope at Jodrell Bank which has recently come into operation is a giant radar aerial consisting of a steel bowl 250 feet in diameter. The superstructure holding this bowl weighs two thousand tons and is built so that the radar beam from the telescope can be directed with precision to any part of the sky.

The telescope has been built for two purposes. Firstly to receive the radio emissions which are generated in the remote parts of the Universe and, secondly, as a giant radar system for the study of the Moon and other bodies in the Solar System by the method of radar echoes. It has been realised for some time that this instrument would be the most powerful radar equipment in the Western world and would be particularly well suited to the location and tracking of satellites by radar. It had been intended to use the telescope in this way to track the American satellite in order to obtain fundamental data which would be necessary as a first stage in the detection and tracking of enemy long range missiles.

The potentiality of the instrument has now been demonstrated on the Russian rocket and satellite and the attached photograph shows a part of the radar trace as the instrument tracked the rocket from the Arctic Circle into Russia a few nights ago. The Russian rocket and satellite have therefore provided an unexpectedly early opportunity for obtaining this basic information which is urgently needed for the design of Britain's and America's defence systems.

> A. C. B. Lovell.
> Professor of Radio Astronomy at
> Manchester University
> and
> Director of Jodrell Bank
> Experimental Station.

22nd October, 1957.

22nd October, 1957.

Dear Prime Minister,

I enclose a note by Professor Lovell on the Jodrell Bank Telescope. I personally feel that the country is very lucky to have had ready a radar instrument which is capable of detecting and observing the Russian satellite and rocket independent of any signals emanating from the device and therefore being able to give us much vital information.

The sad part of this otherwise great story is that Manchester University has now used all the funds allocated to them and are short of some £250,000 with no money for running expenses or for further development.

It appears to me that apart from ourselves, the Americans will be extremely interested in the information that can be gathered for defence purposes from these early radar contacts with the rocket and satellite. Provided Manchester University is relieved from its financial embarrassment and supplied with sufficient funds to operate effectively you have, I suggest, something of immense value for defence purposes to offer the Americans.

> Yours sincerely,
> Robert Renwick.

The Rt. Hon. Harold Macmillan, PC, MP,
10 Downing Street, Whitehall, S.W.1.

Armed with these two documents, Lovell and I went out into Park Lane and hailed a taxi. When I said, 'Ten Downing Street,' the driver stared at both of us and raised his eyebrows in complete disbelief. Admittedly

Lovell was looking his usual distraught self and I appeared a bit wild on this occasion. The taxi-driver waited to see what happened when he dropped us outside the entrance to No. 10, and when we approached the policeman and knocked on the door, he seemed to expect that we would be swiftly propelled out of Downing Street and into Whitehall, but we were unable to see the look of disappointment, or dismay, on his face when the door opened and we were ushered inside!

We did not meet the Prime Minister, but, instead, we spent something over an hour briefing de Zulueta, to whom we also entrusted Lovell's memorandum with the photograph of the radar trace of the rocket, together with Renwick's letter. That same evening, before his departure for the USA, Harold Macmillan wrote to Renwick from No. 10 Downing Street:

Dear Sir Robert,
    Thank you so much for sending me the very interesting note by Professor Lovell on the Jodrell Bank telescope. I was very glad to have this paper on the eve of my departure for Washington.
    Thank you too for your kind message of good wishes.
                                        Yours sincerely,
                                        Harold Macmillan.

I reported to Renwick on the 10 Downing Street visit and expressed disappointment at the absence of the Prime Minister but hoped that every possible effort would be made behind the scenes to relieve Manchester University of its financial worries. I agreed to keep Renwick informed of events.

On his return from Washington, the Prime Minister was subjected on 29 October in the House of Commons to questions about the Russian satellite:

Mr Arthur Bottomley (Labour) asked the Prime Minister if he will arrange for an inquiry to consider why this country, which pioneered the development of radar and jet propulsion, should lag behind the Union of Soviet Socialist Republics in launching the first artificial satellite to circle the world.

Sir I. Fraser (Conservative) asked the Prime Minister what official scientific bodies in Britain have made observations of the Russian earth satellite; how soon they began their observations after its release was announced; if he will make a statement as to the Government's policy in relation to this phenomenon; and how far it is the intention of the Government to carry out similar experiments.[1]

The Prime Minister in his reply referred to the United Kingdom contribution, for what it was worth, to the International Geophysical Year.

[1] From *Hansard*, Volume 575, No. 156, Tuesday 29 October 1957.

On the subject of Britain's plans for its own satellite he was emphatic: 'There has, however, never been any intention that this country should launch an earth satellite and only two countries, the Union of Soviet Socialist Republics and the United States of America have stated their intention to do so. I do not consider that this situation calls for any inquiry by the Government. . . . Hon. Members will have seen that within the last few days our great radio telescope at Jodrell Bank has successfully tracked the Sputnik's carrier rocket.'

Bottomley persisted in his questioning:

Mr Bottomley: If the Prime Minister will not cause inquiry to be made, will the Government consider the views expressed by Field Marshal Lord Montgomery two years ago that the country which launched a satellite that could circle the world would have an immense strategic advantage over all others?

The Prime Minister: Of course, I always consider with respect the views of the Field Marshal, and I think all members of the House do so, but I think he was probably referring not so much to the satellite as to the control of the arc of the rocket which is part of this operation. That was the part that might have the strategic effect, not the satellite itself.

The Prime Minister was only partially correct. He could have learnt from Lovell that satellites in orbit would soon be able to maintain constant reconnaissance of all parts of the world, without infringing national airspace, using highly sophisticated cameras. In addition he would have known that control of the arc of the rocket was of small importance compared to the control by the satellites, manned or unmanned, of the delivery of ICBMs with devastating accuracy. Also, he would have been made aware of the potential peaceful uses of satellites to provide navigational aids, better meteorological information, mapping for detection of Earth resources, and world-wide communications systems, quite apart from scientific research into the Universe of the utmost importance. Unquestionably Field Marshal Lord Montgomery had correctly visualized the military possibilities of constant reconnaissance and control of weapons stacked in orbit and was not just referring to rocket trajectories.

In fact, it seemed at the time that there was divided opinion about the impressiveness of Russia's technological feat and the remarkable capability of the telescope at Jodrell Bank. But there were those outside Government circles who were greatly impressed by Britain's ability to make a unique contribution to the Space Age. The success in tracking the rocket generated enormous public interest.

Also appreciative of the telescope's power were the Russians. During the last week in October the signals from *Sputnik I* became less and less distinguishable, and finally inaudible. On 26 October the Soviet

Astronomical Council sent a telegram to Lovell requesting the help of Jodrell Bank in tracking the *Sputnik* and in locating the carrier rocket of the satellite and advising them of its position at regular intervals. On the same day it was announced in Moscow that no more signals were being received from the satellite itself as its batteries were exhausted. There were further Soviet requests to Lovell for help during the rest of October.

16

Grubbing for Money

Early in the morning of Saturday 2 November 1957, the telephone rang at The Quinta and was answered by Judy, now 11½ years old. It was the London Press Association. Being the first day of a weekend which had followed yet another week of hectic activity at Jodrell Bank, Judy, with commendable discretion, decided to leave her parents in peace to sleep off their exhaustion and to take the message herself. She wrote: 'London press acosshien rang up at 25 past 7 to say the russians had launched anover satolite. It weighs eight times as much as the other. The London press said they were not given the time it was launched at. Going to try to get it. Added that it had a dog on bord.'

Sputnik II weighed 1,120 pounds and did, indeed, carry a dog, which went by the name of Laika. Moreover, the dog was equipped with complete life-support equipment. When Bernard and Joyce Lovell awoke to read Judy's note, they realized that the weekend was no longer to be one of hoped-for rest. The telephone was soon ringing continuously, and demands for information of the whereabouts of the satellite came pouring in from the Press. A satellite with a dog on board had stimulated interest to even greater heights. The telescope was again diverted from its astronomical researches, and further success in locating the rocket by radar encouraged Lovell to feel even more confident that at least £130,000 worth of his financial troubles would now soon be over, but he was taking no risks, as he was well aware that the further £130,000 required to cover the cost, over and above the DSIR's hoped-for contribution, had somehow to be raised by the University from non-government sources.

In a letter to Sir Robert Renwick with a copy to me, dated 12 November, he wrote:

You asked me to keep in touch with you about our progress at Jodrell Bank, and I am therefore writing to give you our latest news, particularly with regard to satellites and rockets. You may remember that when we last met I said the Jodrell Bank telescope appeared to be the only instrument capable of locating the rocket and satellite now that the batteries had failed. Apart from Russia, where the position is very uncertain, this still appears to be the case. It has been reported that the Ministry of Supply establishment at Malvern obtained a radar echo from the rocket but there is no record of their success on the satellite, and in any case their installation, which is on 10 cms., has such a narrow beam that they have to be told where to point their instrument beforehand.

We have, therefore, had to assume national responsibility for keeping track of satellite one and its rocket, and now we are faced with the same task on satellite two, which has just ceased transmission. We are, of course, delighted to be in a position to assist the Ministry of Supply and many other interested bodies at home and in America in this manner, but our resources are strained more than ever. . . . I am still very distracted by the financial worry over the cost of the telescope . . . it would appear that the Treasury is only prepared to make the additional grant of 50% of the remainder (50% of the outstanding £260,000) on conditions which the University will find very hard to accept. For example, because of the unfortunate PAC report I am informed that even legal action in respect of the consulting engineer is contemplated. . . . If we had built a white elephant instead of one of the most magnificent instruments in the world then one would understand and be prepared for this attitude. I only wish someone would force the interested parties to get round a table, settle the differences and arrange for the telescope to be paid for. . . .

The Russians will soon send a rocket to the moon and no doubt all eyes will once more turn to Jodrell Bank. With this present radar apparatus we should stand no chance of tracking the rocket by radar for more than about 5,000 miles which is less than a fortieth of the distance to the moon . . . even if the rocket carried its own transmitter like the satellites we should need the radio telescope in order to pick up the radio signals at that distance. I am not aware of any radar apparatus in the world which, even if connected to our radio telescope, could track the moon rocket by radar for any appreciable part of its journey. . . .

For some time we have been constructing an apparatus to obtain radar echoes from the planet Venus. If we used this on the moon rocket we could track it for about 150,000 miles which is over half the distance to the moon. Unfortunately like most other things this project is being delayed because of shortage of money although in this case only £2,000 or so is involved. Beyond this we are sure that an apparatus could readily be built to extend the range of the telescope so that the rocket could be tracked to the moon . . . we feel that the cost would be considerable—probably £100,000. . . . This would, indeed, be a magnificent apparatus capable of radar research on other planets as well as its immediate application to the tracking of the moon rocket. . . .

In a letter dated 18 November, I told Lovell that Renwick had received his letter and was sending a copy to the Prime Minister's personal secretary. I continued by saying: 'Bob has suggested that I ask you to keep either one of us advised of any exceptional things of interest which might occur during your watch on Space, so that such information may be passed to the PM without delay. I think he is working on the basis that the "hotter" the information the more likely it is that speedy action will result.'

On Saturday 30 November Jodrell Bank added another feather to its cap by observing the final orbits of the carrier rocket which had launched *Sputnik I* into orbit around Earth. In this exercise it co-operated with the USA by passing information to Professor Whipple, the Director of the Smithsonian Astrophysical Institute at Cambridge, Massachusetts. The telescope had located the rocket during four of its circuits on that afternoon, the last of these being number 873. On the telephone, Whipple agreed with Lovell that, since the rocket had already descended by twenty or thirty miles during this Saturday, it was unlikely to survive the night. He therefore arranged for a concentration of visual observers in America to take over the watch when the orbits disappeared below Britain's horizon, and the rocket was located over America on circuits 877 and 879. On the 879th circuit, the period of orbit was only 88 minutes and its height above Earth about 100 miles. A few minutes later, a brilliant fireball was seen over California which Whipple concluded to be the burn-up of the rocket as it entered the atmosphere. This was confirmed by the fact that on Sunday Jodrell Bank could detect no trace of the rocket still in orbit. Unable to track the Russian rocket by radar themselves, the USA had gratefully leaned on Jodrell Bank for information to enable them to pick it up visually on its last circuit. Professor Whipple told me that 'it was a fine piece of transatlantic co-operation.'

Renwick not only sent Lovell's letter of 12 November to the Prime Minister's personal secretary, de Zulueta, but he also sent a copy to Dr Charles Hill,* the then Postmaster General who was about to take up his new ministerial appointment of Chancellor of the Duchy of Lancaster. By a letter of 6 December, Hill replied to Renwick in cheerful vein, saying he had made inquiries at the Treasury and had been informed 'that the Telescope is substantially completed and that the Department of Scientific and Industrial Research, which is the Department responsible, should be in a position to provide the rest of the money needed, when certain points of accounting have been cleared'. Renwick was not all that sure, as he put it to Lovell, 'how far it takes us', and he wrote again to Hill on 9 December saying he was delighted to hear the excellent news that the DSIR were in a position to provide the rest of the money when certain points of accounting had been cleared. Being aware of the notorious PAC report and the Treasury's impossible demands upon the University in respect of Husband, he added, 'I think it would be excellent politics if, in view of the bad publicity there has been with reference to the finances of the telescope, an announcement could be made as soon as possible that the finances are now all clear and that there is ample money for the future running of the telescope.' Hill's reply to this was that he thought it would be wisest 'to wait until the money has actually arrived before we begin publicly to chortle!'

In the meantime the Americans were accepting a bid of $6 million for the construction of a radio telescope half the size of the Jodrell Bank instrument; in American eyes, a 'mere' £2,150,000 at the then rate of exchange!

When Lovell received from Renwick copies of the correspondence with Hill, he wrote in reply on 17 December that the reference to the DSIR providing the rest of the money required was in respect of only 50 per cent of the outstanding debt of £260,000 and that Manchester was still faced with 'finding from somewhere the rest of the money'.

The series of events which now followed were remarkable, the only cheerful elements being praise from the USA and a telegram from Moscow to Lovell conveying New Year good wishes and adding: 'Every success in your work. Best thanks for satellite operations.' From the British Government came nothing but apathy. Only Renwick held out hopes of forcing the Government to redress the situation, but even this had its element of risk, as Lovell was soon to be advised by the Vice-Chancellor of the University.

With Renwick now pressing for information on the prospects of raising the £130,000 which Manchester was being left to find, and declaring his view that the Treasury should find all of the £260,000 plus any more that might, within reason, be needed, Lovell wrote to Sir Raymond Streat, now Chairman of the University Council, on 24 January. He told him that he was being pressed by Renwick to agree to his taking some exceptional action to persuade the Government to provide the entire balance of the money required to pay off the telescope's debts. 'He has immediate access at the highest level,' he wrote, 'and would, I think, in the first instance, try to force the government to pay the balance. If this failed he would be by far our most powerful advocate for raising the money from industry. Would you be kind enough to let me know what I can tell Renwick about the current situation.' This brought a swift reply, not from Streat but from the Vice-Chancellor, dated 30 January 1958, in which he wrote that he was hoping the University Officers were going to be able to solve major problems concerning the telescope within the next few weeks. He admitted that they had been hoping for this for months without much success, but now he believed there were one or two propitious signs. 'In view of this,' he concluded, 'would you kindly hold your hand from contact with Sir Robert Renwick or anyone else about unorthodox approaches to the financial powers. I think we must work at the moment through DSIR and no one else. . . .'

Lovell attempted to 'stall' Renwick as a result of the Vice-Chancellor's letter, an action which had little effect, for Renwick continued to seek assistance for Jodrell Bank, but, now, with great discretion. His efforts to persuade the Prime Minister to make some personal intervention with the

Treasury through the Chancellor of the Exchequer, however, had very little immediate effect, if any at all. Indeed, the last communication to Renwick from the Prime Minister's office came in a letter dated 4 February 1958, from the Prime Minister's secretary, de Zulueta. After referring to the departure of the PM on a Commonwealth tour, de Zulueta said he had collected more facts about the situation as a result of his own enquiries at the Treasury. 'As you know, the financing of the original telescope was a matter of great financial difficulty largely because the final cost is certain to be several times the original estimate. Very large payments towards the cost were made by Her Majesty's Government through the Department of Scientific and Industrial Research, and these payments have led to criticism by the Public Accounts Committee. However, the Department of Scientific and Industrial Research have more recently agreed, under certain conditions which have been accepted by Manchester University since Professor Lovell wrote to you, to make a further contribution to the cost of this valuable project. . . .' This information was inaccurate. The Officers of the University of Manchester certainly had not accepted the conditions which attached to the further £130,000 contribution by the DSIR to the telescope debt. In fact, they were fighting to have removed the accusation by the Treasury and the PAC that the over-expenditure on the instrument had been occasioned solely by Husband, the consulting engineer, making expensive alterations to design without discussing such matters with Lovell and the University authorities.

Renwick's approaches to the Prime Minister and other influential members of the Government and the Conservative Party could not, in fact, have any direct effect upon the findings of the PAC. The membership of the PAC consisted of representatives from both the Government and the Opposition, and it possessed autonomous powers. Its findings could be debated in the House but not influenced by the Government or Opposition except in debate. Certainly Renwick's activities enabled the Prime Minister and others to be well briefed on the importance of the telescope to the nation, but at that point his intercession on behalf of Lovell and Manchester University reached its limit. The University Officers were therefore well advised to warn against further unorthodox approaches and to conduct their negotiations with the DSIR alone, the only body which had any hope of persuading the PAC to reverse its findings on the part played by Husband in the alterations to design which had caused the substantial over-expenditure. Certainly, in the final outcome, the University Officers proved that their approaches to the problem were the effective ones and, together with the DSIR, in particular Charles Cawley, were soon to convince the DSIR's new Secretary,

Dr Harry Melville,[1] that his evidence to the PAC had been inaccurate. Nevertheless, from inquiries in the political circles of that period the author discovered that the Prime Minister and certain other Ministers did what they could to encourage the finding of a favourable solution to the telescope's financial problems.

In the meantime, on Sunday 9 February, Sir Raymond Streat visited Lovell at 'The Quinta'. It was another moment of shock. Over tea in the study, Streat told Lovell, in the kindest way, that it was his unpleasant duty to warn him that he was in a 'perilous situation'. It was his opinion, and that of the University Council, that a writ by Husband might well be served on him in the near future for something in excess of a quarter of a million pounds. To say the least, Lovell was shattered. He virtually gasped out the question that, since he did not possess such a sum of money, or indeed any money at all apart from his remuneration and a house which still bore a mortgage, what would happen? Streat answered that he was sure the University would bear the legal costs of the action, but as long as the PAC record was allowed to stand, it was believed that the case would be lost, in which case failure to pay would mean imprisonment! Poor Lovell hit the depths of despondency. The radio telescope was an instrument that had become the symbol of Britain's continuing greatness in scientific and technological achievement, and her contribution to Space research. It was the only equipment in the Western world capable of detecting and tracking ICBMs, and of providing the basic know-how for the speedy development of military equipments for such national security purposes. It was the sole system available and capable of providing the USA the co-operation essential to its newly developing Space programme. And for enabling the British nation to possess this superb and scientifically important instrument, the only major scientific research instrument produced in Britain since the war, the British Government were ready to leave Lovell to face a court case, brought by Husband, which might well result in imprisonment!

Following this talk with Lovell, the Vice-Chancellor and Sir Raymond Streat, accompanied by the University's solicitor, had a meeting with Husband and his solicitor on Friday 14 February. At this meeting Husband made it clear that he felt his reputation as a consultant had been so jeopardized by what had been published in the proceedings of the PAC that, even if it cost him a fortune, he would pursue Lovell and the University by every process of law unless he received a letter from Lovell or the University admitting that he had consulted with them fully at all stages of the contract. He was, in fact, unrepentant and not to be dissuaded from this threat which he had already made previously.

The agony for Lovell about his future was, however, soon to be

[1] Later Sir Harry Melville.

diminished. By a letter dated 28 February 1958, the Secretary of the DSIR, Sir Harry Melville, who had been the person who was interrogated by the PAC in March 1957, conveyed to the Clerk of the PAC fresh evidence about the affairs of the telescope. After referring to the evidence which he gave before the Committee on 21 March 1957, when he said that Professor Lovell was not consulted as to alterations in design, he wrote: 'It was my understanding at the time of giving evidence that Professor Lovell was not consulted by Messrs Husband and Company on the major changes of design although, as stated in the Treasury Minute dated 21st January, 1958, I did not intend to imply that no discussions on the scientific aspects of the design took place. I attach a memorandum submitted to me by Messrs Husband and Company. After discussing the matter with the University of Manchester I am now satisfied that there was extensive consultation between Messrs Husband and Company and Professor Lovell on questions of design. The University of Manchester have authorised me to say that they associate themselves with this con-clusion.' It had been a difficult situation for Melville. He was new to his appointment and had had time to visit Jodrell Bank for only about an hour before attending the inquiry. Although he was carefully briefed by Charles Cawley, the Director of the division of the DSIR concerned with university grants who had been closely associated with the progress of the construction of the telescope, he had misunderstood the situation at the time of the inquiry. Courageously Sir Harry Melville now stated: 'So far as my previous evidence may have been misleading, I wish to offer the fullest apology to the Committee.'

This letter resulted in the Vice-Chancellor of the University, and Rainford, the Bursar, being asked to appear before the PAC on 18 March to give evidence. Coincidentally, on the same day, Lovell was asked to address the Parliamentary and Scientific Committee on the work and future potential of the telescope. Lovell recalls that the Vice-Chancellor and Rainford emerged from a room in the House at the same time as he emerged from another room having completed his lecture and that 'they were unhappy and not hopeful as to what the Committee would say in its report.'

As a result of this pessimism and on the advice of Sir Raymond Streat, the Vice-Chancellor called together a meeting of the University Officers on 30 April with Streat in the chair. The purpose was to discuss how the University should set about raising all of the £260,000 in the event of the DSIR not being permitted to make good their generous offer of £130,000 towards the increased costs. In the event, other matters took precedence. Streat, supported by the others, felt that a public statement by the University, in agreement with Husband, to the effect that the University had been kept informed by its consultant about increases in costs might ease the situation and remove the threats of legal actions by Husband. This, in turn, might make it easier for the DSIR to give the financial assistance it wished to give. Lovell recalls that the Vice-Chancellor, a Professor of Industrial Law, was of the opinion that the University should accept the Treasury conditions which implied that Husband was solely to blame, and then take counter-legal action against him if he should sue. 'The Treasurer, A. V. Symons,' Lovell relates, 'quietly said: "Vice-Chancellor, I suggest we take no action; time is a great healer!" ' It was decided to follow his advice, which proved to be a wise course. The pessimism was soon shown to be unfounded for the PAC report of their latest meeting, which was published on 24 July, stated that: 'In view of further evidence, it is clear that evidence given to the Committee of last Session was gravely inaccurate and misleading, and that there was in fact the fullest collabor-ation on scientific and technical matters between the consultants and the University professor.' It went on to record that extensive consultation on design had at all times taken place and that the University authorities associated themselves completely with this conclusion.

No longer were the Treasury conditions referred to in correspondence as 'certain points of accounting', implicit in connection with the payment of the DSIR's further contribution of £130,000, which then became immediately available. Part of the financial problem was now lifted from the shoulders of the University, and the threat of a legal action against Lovell disappeared into thin air. Husband was satisfied that he had been exonerated from the accusations levelled at his integrity. Even so, the situation remained difficult, for the additional £130,000 still had to be raised by some form of appeal to industry and private individuals. In fact, it could have been worse still, because an entirely unexpected excess above the previously calculated total deficit of £260,000 came like a bolt out of the blue. The final bill from the United Steel Structural Company, the main contractor, came to £124,405, bringing the total to £417,016. In October 1955 the figure had been reliably estimated at £292,611. Husband contested the claim, and in the end, by a generous decision of Sir Walter Benton-Jones, the Chairman of the United Steel Companies, United Steel abandoned its latest demand by way of giving a substantial contribution to the radio telescope. They had rated the final achievement above purely financial considerations. Sir Raymond Streat put it well when he officially offered the University's gratitude: 'Indeed we know full well that from the Company's point of view their association with the University in this venture has not been financially profitable, but in view of the novel character of the structure and its great importance to scientific developments in this country, they have never failed to meet our requests.

We are greatly their debtors on this account and in my opinion the nation and world of science are also in their debt.'

As the way ahead began to clear for Lovell and his telescope, so did the demands for its use increase—an increase that was to bring welcome revenue in the form of hard-currency dollars. This prospect started just before Easter 1958, when Lovell received a secret and highly confidential message that a certain Colonel of the United States Air Force wished to visit him as a matter of urgency. A date was arranged and at the Colonel's request Lovell met him personally at Goostrey railway station, just two miles from the telescope. From then onwards the whole affair became like an episode out of Ian Fleming. As soon as they reached Lovell's office at Jodrell Bank, the Colonel asked that the windows should be shut and the doors locked and that the conversation should be conducted *sotto voce*! It was then that the astonished Lovell became even more astonished, as he learned of the incredible progress the USA had made in the matter of a few months, since the launching of the first Earth satellite, *Explorer I* (weighing only 31 pounds as compared with Russia's *Sputniks* of 184 pounds and 1,120 pounds), and as the Colonel revealed the reasons for his urgent transatlantic crossing. The US Air Force had decided to use their highly secret Atlas Intercontinental Ballistic Missile to launch a rocket to the Moon and planned to be ready for this project by the coming August. However, they had one major obstacle in the way of proceeding with their plans: they had absolutely no means of tracking the rocket! Therefore they had decided to ask Lovell if they could use the telescope at Jodrell Bank for this purpose! Some of the radio equipment that needed to be linked up to the telescope to enable it to continue tracking over the whole 250,000 miles to the Moon would be provided by the US Air Force.

This was another of those miracles which had a habit of turning up for Lovell when he had just hit 'the slough of despond'. He agreed with alacrity to the request but told the Colonel that he would be obliged to seek some formal authority from the University and from the DSIR. However, the Colonel was insistent that the matter must remain a secret at this stage and that an instant decision was imperative. Lovell's agile mind, well trained in the war years in the art of undertaking clandestine action in the interests of research, decided that he could join in the exercise on the basis that he was doing something in connection with the IGY programme for which he had funds from the Royal Society. In this manner, no payment from the US Air Force, which would require explanation, need be forthcoming, although Lovell, ever with an eye to the future, hoped that success in this venture could ultimately lead to substantial dollar earnings for the telescope. With agreement reached on initial secrecy, details were discussed and the Colonel advised Lovell that a complete trailer load of tracking equipment would be flown over from the Space Technology Laboratories in Los Angeles about a month before the launch together with a small party of technicians. In the meantime, Lovell was to organize the necessary supplies and means for connecting the US special equipment to the telescope.

Within hours of this meeting the mysterious American colonel was 'winging' his way back to Los Angeles.

'For three months,' Lovell records, 'the arrangements made in my office remained a complete secret.' This was apart from a few members of his staff whom it had been agreed would have to be advised of the plans if Jodrell Bank's co-operation were to be effective. However, late in July it became known to the public at large that something was afoot. A sharp-eyed journalist from the *Manchester Guardian* had spotted an enormous trailer on the road from Burtonwood, at that time a US Air Force base, marked in large letters 'Jodrell Bank, US Air Force, Project Able.' A few days later, after this zealous reporter had done some good homework, knowing that it was already hinted in the USA that an attempt to reach the Moon was contemplated, a calculated guess appeared on 25 July in the *Manchester Guardian* with the headline 'Jodrell Bank Joins in Journey to Moon.' It read:

> The United States Air Force will make a serious attempt to get a rocket to the moon in the next few weeks. . . . The radio telescope at Jodrell Bank will be used as an essential tool in the tracking of the rocket after its launching from Cape Canaveral. This can be inferred from the appearance of a United States Air Force van full of electronic equipment. . . . The van at Jodrell Bank appears to have come directly from the United States and is staffed by three or four American technicians. . . . Its presence there can be explained only if it is proposed to use the Jodrell Bank telescope as a means of following the broad outlines of the path followed by a rocket. . . . The Jodrell Bank telescope is uniquely suited to this task. . . . That the United States Air Force should have fallen back on the use of Jodrell Bank for this purpose is a telling tribute to the versatility and power of the great telescope.

The launch date was planned for Sunday 17 August, which from Lovell's point of view could not have been a more inappropriate time. He was due to participate in a symposium on Radio Astronomy in Paris from 29 July until 6 August, and then to proceed to Moscow for a meeting of the International Astronomical Union. Since the date for the launch had been conveyed to him in strictest confidence, he could not contemplate changing his plans because it would have been interpreted by the Press that the 'go' for Project Able was imminent.

·In Moscow, whilst Lovell's mind was very much centred upon the event scheduled for Sunday 17 August, being anxious about Jodrell Bank's performance in tracking the American Moon rocket, he nonetheless tried to concentrate on establishing good links with Russian astronomers and those concerned with the Soviet Union's Space programme. Amongst these was Professor Alla Massevitch,* Professor of Astrophysics at the University of Moscow, who was in charge of the satellite optical tracking network in the Soviet Union. But his efforts to establish any rapport with this attractive and accomplished lady were largely unsuccessful at this stage, although later she was to visit Jodrell Bank on a number of occasions and to become a good friend of the Lovell family. In her diary of this Moscow visit Joyce wrote of Alla Massevitch: 'She doesn't give anything away. No, not even to B. Too good for him and Fred (Whipple) and Uncle Tom Cobley and all. Footnote. On leaving Moscow B had achieved two things – (a) found out the telephone number of her flat in Moscow, (b) left a letter in her locker saying 'Why don't you co-operate?'

On 17 August Lovell learned by telephone from Jodrell Bank that the Moon rocket had been launched but had exploded eighty seconds after launch. It was a misfortune for the Americans, although they had several reserves. For Lovell it was a lucky break because the second attempt was scheduled for October, which meant that he would be there to supervise Jodrell's activities.

At 8.42 a.m. on the morning of Saturday 11 October 1958, the Americans launched their 88-foot rocket *Pioneer I* in their second attempt to reach the Moon. After 'blast-off' at Cape Canaveral in Florida, it was picked up at 8.52 a.m. by Jodrell Bank, just ten minutes later, an occasion that was witnessed by a fascinated crowd of reporters and cameramen, including BBC radio and TV and ITV teams. As the rocket appeared over the Jodrell Bank horizon, the great bowl of the telescope began to move, swinging up from pointing at the horizon and then turning towards the south as the rocket climbed over the Atlantic and above North Africa at a speed approaching 25,000 m.p.h. with all its main rockets fired. The velocity achieved at the burn-out of the fuel was, in fact, 23,180 m.p.h. instead of the 24,033 m.p.h. required for escape from the Earth's gravitational field, and so the rocket failed in its purpose and, after reaching a distance of 79,000 miles into Space by Sunday, closely tracked all the time by the radio telescope, it began to fall back to Earth. Observers at Jodrell Bank were also able to determine that the launching angle was incorrect and that the rocket, had it continued on its journey, would have missed the Moon by 12,000 miles. In the early hours of Monday 13 October, *Pioneer I* burnt up as it re-entered the Earth's atmosphere over the South Pacific. Although *Pioneer I* failed in its primary objective, it was a striking scientific success, producing the first information about the nature of the zones of trapped particles and the magnetic field out to nearly 80,000 miles from Earth.

For Lovell and his telescope it was a monumental triumph. The Americans had had to rely entirely on Jodrell Bank for news of the rocket and for the relay of the telemetry information coming to Earth from its scientific packages. At Cape Canaveral there was nothing but praise for the scope and efficiency of the Jodrell Bank equipment, and one American official was quoted as saying: 'You British ought to shout out a bit more loudly about your achievements.'

Shamefully, the British Government continued to ignore the remaining financial plight of the telescope in the face of its latest feats. By contrast, the members of the United States House of Representatives Space Committee immediately began to consider a recommendation that some form of grant should be made by the USA to the funds needed for relieving the University of its problems and to enable the telescope to continue in operation. The Committee, as a result of a visit to Jodrell Bank in September by James G. Fulton, a Republican member of the US House of Representatives, accompanied by two staff advisers, were proposing that the National Aeronautics and Space Administration (NASA) should support Jodrell Bank by giving contracts or sub-contracts to the telescope and pay for such invaluable assistance as had been provided during the *Pioneer I* exercise. In addition, they felt that the Pentagon's Advanced Research Projects Agency should also provide funds. Dr Charles Shelton, the Assistant Staff Director of the House of Representatives Space Committee who had accompanied Congressman Fulton, stated that he felt 'sympathy' for the position of Professor A. C. B. Lovell, and it was reported in Washington that 'Dr Shelton felt it was unfortunate that a great scientist like Professor Lovell should have to go around grubbing for money instead of concentrating on his scientific work.'

The reaction of the British Press to this news was extensive, and carried banner headlines. 'Jodrell Bank May Get U.S. Grant' announced the *Manchester Guardian* on 16 October 1958; 'US May Aid Jodrell Bank With Money—Congress Proposal' was how the *Daily Telegraph* blazoned its report; 'US To Buy Into Our Space Eye' was the reaction of the *Daily Express*.

The eventual result of the US proposals was that Rainford, the University Bursar, was able to negotiate an attractive arrangement with NASA for the telescope to be used in co-operation with American Space programmes with payment on an hourly basis. It was an arrangement which helped Jodrell Bank significantly with its financial problem, and Britain with its dollar earnings. It also meant that the telescope was soon to become an integral part of the US deep Space instrumentation facility.

And still the British Government shrugged its shoulders and left Lovell to go around with a begging-bowl.

17

Pioneer V

On 28 November 1958 the appeal to industry and the public for the University of Manchester's portion of the outstanding debt on the telescope was launched. The target figure had been set at £150,000, £20,000 above the actual sum needed to clear the deficit. The expectation that the successes of the telescope would make it easy to raise the money was not realized. Lovell's hopes of being clear of debt by the end of 1958 proved to be over-optimistic. The successful co-operation with the US did, however, bring in income at this time, even though American attempts in the autumn of 1958 to reach the Moon with *Pioneer I* and *Pioneer III* failed. Moreover, during a visit in late November to Jodrell Bank by two eminent Russian Space scientists, Lovell elicited the information that the Soviet Union had no equipment capable of tracking a lunar rocket, which led him to think, erroneously, that the Russians were not contemplating a lunar launching in the near future. If they were, however, they would have to lean on Jodrell for tracking-facilities—which would earn even more recognition of the importance of the telescope, even if it brought in no roubles.

In the spring and summer of 1959 money-raising parties were held at Jodrell Bank to which industrialists and private persons were invited in the hopes of persuading them to contribute towards reducing the outstanding debt. In addition hundreds of letters were written and every conceivable contact was explored. But the results were disappointing. Lovell wrote of these attempts to raise money: 'In spite of these efforts, which personally I found increasingly distracting and exhausting, the appeal fund had reached only £65,523 by July and had increased by a mere £530 by the end of the year.' Apart from £20,000 coming from Simon Carves Limited and Henry Simon (Holdings) Limited at the instigation of Lord Simon of Wythenshawe, there was one gift of £5,000 from Imperial Chemical Industries Limited, five of £2,000 and over from Pye, Associated Electrical Industries, of which Renwick was a director, Bowater Paper Corporation, Renold Chains and Marks & Spencer, eleven of £1,000 and over, thirteen of £500 to £700, and fifty-one of £100 and over. The rest were in small sums of £50 or less, many from private individuals. In the list of amounts under £5 were: 'my pocket money for this week' from an 11½-year-old girl, 15 shillings from Form 4A of a school, 10 shillings from a family of three who gave up their midweek bar of chocolate for a few weeks to save this sum, £1 from an old-age pensioner, and 2 shillings from a disabled man. There were many other similar contributions from young persons and the elderly who could ill afford a single penny.

On 3 December 1959 the *Manchester Guardian* was constrained to write in its leader about the telescope: 'The creation of this superb instrument has given Britain a place in Space research that no other country yet has: we may have no satellites but we can tell the Russians and the Americans just what is happening to theirs. It is a shameful fact that the Jodrell Bank telescope is still in debt and that the prestige it achieves for Britain still depends on borrowed money. . . .'

On 6 December the *Sunday Dispatch* displayed the headline 'The Shame of Jodrell Bank' followed by a sub-headline 'Schoolboys send pocket money to save our face.' Then came the criticism: '. . . The Chancellor of the Exchequer, Mr Heathcoat Amory, is to be asked in the House of Commons to save Britain the embarrassment of relying upon little school boys to uphold her prestige in the eyes of the world. . . . Sir Arthur Vere Harvey MP for Macclesfield will urge him to pay off the debt. . . .'

But the Government remained unmoved, even in the face of the telescope's further triumphs which had been achieved earlier in September and October.

Just after lunch on Saturday 12 September 1959, as Lovell was about to depart from The Quinta in his car to captain the Chelford Cricket XI in a local match, he was stopped in his tracks by frantic signals from the family. It was a telephone message from Jodrell Bank to say that word had just been received that the Russians had launched a rocket which was due to reach the Moon on Sunday evening. At almost the same time, another call on the external telephone came from a member of the national Press with the same information and asking what Jodrell were going to do about it. Lovell's answer was short and to the point. He was going to play cricket! He added that in any case it would be more than thirty hours before the rocket would reach the Moon. This blasé attitude was occasioned by an episode at the beginning of the year, on 2 January, when the Russians made their first attempt to reach the Moon with *Lunik I*. Although it missed the Moon by 4,600 miles and moved into an orbit round the Sun, it was a clear demonstration of the lead which the Russians had over the Americans in rocketry. However, Jodrell failed to locate *Lunik I*, due to lack of information from the Russians which would have enabled the telescope to locate the rocket initially and track it on its 235,497-mile journey into Space. As a result, Lovell had written to his contacts in the Soviet Union complaining of the lack of warning and information on transmitter frequencies and other helpful data. He had pointed out that, without Jodrell Bank's confirmation of what was happening to their rockets, there could be doubts in the West about their claims, as indeed there were about *Lunik I*. Now, once again, the Russians had launched a rocket to the Moon with no forewarning and information about frequencies.

And so, for the first six hours of *Lunik II*'s journey into Space, Lovell led his village cricket team to victory, whilst Jodrell Bank continued with its existing two research programmes which were currently using the telescope. But on his return to Jodrell in the early evening he was met by the American contingent, which was still there for co-operation on further US Space efforts, reporting that they had been harassed all afternoon by Washington demanding that an attempt should be made to locate and track the Soviet rocket. Their complaint was that the only information they were able to give Washington was the news that Professor Lovell was playing cricket, and therefore nothing could be done until the game was over! Washington was apparently incredulous but could only wait impatiently for the return of this eccentric professor who played games with a bat and ball when a momentous event of world-wide importance was taking place. Lovell was unmoved by the consternation of the American team until he had unlocked the Telex machine office on the off-chance that the Russians had sent information on their latest Moon attempt. In seconds his blasé attitude mercurially changed to one of excited action, for there in the Telex was a message from Moscow giving precise details of the frequencies of the transmitters in *Lunik II*, the exact co-ordinates calculated for latitude and longitude of Jodrell Bank, and giving an estimated time of impact on the Moon as 10 p.m. BST on Sunday evening.

Within no time the telescope was prepared for the tracking of the rocket, and without difficulty *Lunik II* was located on the precise co-ordinates supplied by Moscow—at a distance, at that moment, of 100,000 miles from Earth. Dr J. G. Davies, a senior member of the staff, had meanwhile located the *Lunik*'s signals on the second beacon frequency in the 19-megacycle band on another equipment. Lovell recorded: 'this turned out to be of cardinal importance'; as we shall presently see. After some cabling alterations, the *Lunik II* signals on both frequencies were, by midnight, being received in the control building.

By Sunday afternoon, as the Moon rose over the Jodrell Bank horizon, the telescope's observations confirmed that the rocket was on the correct course for a lunar impact. During the day the place had become packed with Press, radio and television men from all over the world. By early evening the excitement was intense. Two hours before the predicted time of impact, there was an urgent call from America. The American team at

Jodrell had reported that the telescope was receiving signals from *Lunik II* and that it was on course for the Moon, but they were not being believed on the other side of the Atlantic. They asked Lovell to take this call. After the distant spokesman had again expressed his disbelief, Lovell held up the telephone in front of the loudspeaker, thus transmitting the sound of the *Lunik* across the Atlantic.

Despite the seething turmoil of chattering reporters and TV men, the Jodrell Bank staff went about their various duties methodically. During the last hour of the rocket's flight, now more than 200,000 miles away, J. G. Davies measured the doppler shift as the rocket fell under the gravitational field of the Moon by comparing the frequency of the received signal on the 19-megacycle equipment with a standard in the control room. It was a crucial measurement which left no doubt about impact and made it possible to calculate the general area of arrival. With the variation in frequency being measured over the final hour, the acceleration of the rocket as it approached the Moon's surface could be accurately determined. If this acceleration over the last twenty minutes or so was equivalent to that which had already been calculated for an object within the Moon's gravitational field, proof of the rocket reaching its destination would be implicit.

The predicted time of impact was 40 seconds after 10.01 p.m. BST. By 9.55 p.m. the babble of conversation in the hall and corridors outside the control room had died to a whisper. Outside in the forecourt the silence quickly cast its net. Only the relayed sound of the *Lunik*'s bleep-bleep, bleep-bleep broke the stillness which had descended upon everyone. In the control room all eyes were fixed on the clock. Lovell wrote of this moment: 'The excitement and the tension remains vivid in the memory as the time approached. At 10.01 the bleeps were still loud and clear, at 10.02 we began to think that it may have missed, but 23 seconds later the bleep ceased—the first man-made object had reached the Moon!' When Lovell announced the Russian success, pandemonium broke loose as reporters stampeded for telephones, cameras clicked and the TV cameras whirred. The *News Chronicle* reported that at 10.00 p.m., 'Prof. Lovell took a handkerchief from his pocket and mopped his brow.' When the bleep-bleep ceased, it said that '. . . he rushed from the control room exclaiming "It's there! They've hit the Moon!" In his excitement he tripped over television and sound cables strewn over the floor ready to record this moment in history.'

It was a remarkable feat. The rocket had reached its destination just 83 seconds later than predicted after a journey of 235,497 miles, landing in the area of Mare Tranquillitatis, Mare Serenitatis and Mare Vaporum. Its speed of impact was 2.05 miles per second. However, there were the disbelievers, particularly in the USA. Richard Nixon, the Vice-President, said: 'None of us know that it is really on the Moon.' Harry Truman, the former US President, stated that the Russian achievement was a 'wonderful thing—if they did it!' One of Britain's astronomical representatives in America told the Press that, 'It would be quite easy to have a clock mechanism installed in the rocket so that the signal could be shut off at about the time the Russians said it was to hit the Moon.' But a further remarkable feat was the part played by Lovell and his team with the telescope. With the only instrument in the world capable of tracking the *Lunik*'s voyage, and with J. G. Davies' measurements of the doppler shift as the rocket fell under the Moon's gravitational field, they were able to substantiate without any question that *Lunik II* had arrived on the Moon at the time stated and in the area indicated. Indeed, some weeks later the director of the American Moon programme remarked to Lovell that J. G. Davies' measurements were a flash of genius. In fact, the technique was refined and used in all subsequent Moon experiments to establish the motion of rockets under the gravitational field of the Moon.

In Britain, every newspaper, national or otherwise, carried the news on their front pages of the Russian success and the tremendous part played by Jodrell Bank. The praise for Lovell and his mighty instrument was unstinted. Only in Government circles was the reaction almost non-existent. Symptomatic of the Government's attitude was the comment by the Foreign Secretary, Selwyn Lloyd, on the sensational exploit of *Lunik II* and the notable accomplishment of Jodrell Bank in monitoring its journey over such a vast distance. He said: 'I don't think many people are terribly interested in it.' No doubt the Government was too preoccupied with a forthcoming General Election which was timed for 8 October. Even the swift follow-up to Russia's success on 4 October with the launching of *Lunik III*, for the purpose of circling the Moon and photographing the far side, left the Conservative Government uninterested in Space and Jodrell Bank, despite the fact that by 9 October the Conservatives had been re-elected for a third term of office with an overwhelming majority of more than a hundred seats. Sir Robert Renwick's lobbying behind the scenes at the end of 1959 and early in 1960, which included discussions in company with myself and the Chairman of the Conservative Party Sir Toby Lowe, the Minister for Science and Technology, and the Minister of Aviation, failed to raise a spark of interest, or at any rate sufficient spark to send off the money necessary to discharge Jodrell Bank's debt.

Apart from HRH Prince Philip, Duke of Edinburgh, no one of prominence in this country had bothered to visit Jodrell Bank after its 1959 successes. Prince Philip, on 11 November, called in accompanied by the late Lord Woolton, who was at that time Chancellor of the University. Lovell wrote: 'Prince Philip's great interest and understanding of our work created a memorable impression on all who were present.' For further encouragement, Lovell and his team had to look to Russia and the USA, and from these two nations it was effusive.

Another triumph for Lovell and his Jodrell Bank telescope was to follow in the spring of 1960, when the first striking success for the Americans in their Space programme was at last to be realized. This was a probe into deep Space without a specific planetary objective but with a number of important major scientific experiments in view, including the measurement of cosmic rays in Space over a wide energy range, the measurement of the ionization and electric charge in a given region of Space, the measurement of magnetic fields far out in Space, and micrometeorite detection. If data from these experiments could be obtained as the probe penetrated millions of miles into Space, much invaluable scientific information would be obtained. Moreover, vital experience would be gained for America's later plans to send a probe to Venus. But the success of the *Pioneer V* deep Space probe was absolutely dependent upon the co-operation of Jodrell Bank. In all previous tasks with Space vehicles Jodrell Bank had acted in a passive capacity, only receiving the signals transmitted by the previous *Pioneer* probes. This time the telescope was required to transmit to the probe to command its various functions, as well as to receive the probe's transmitted information. The telescope was still the only instrument in the world capable of transmitting with adequate signal strength over tens of millions of miles to command the probe's functions. Modifications were, however, required, including a re-design of the aerial system and the use of a powerful transmitter. This was done during the months prior to the launching-date. At the same time, more trailers of equipment were flown over from Los Angeles, and the American contingent at Jodrell Bank was increased. The plain fact was that, if America was to show any semblance of catching up on Russia's now acknowledged lead in Space technology and rocketry, she had to have the co-operation of Lovell, his team and the telescope!

By March 1960 all was ready, and a few minutes after 1 p.m. BST on 11 March *Pioneer V* left its launching-pad at Cape Canaveral. Twelve minutes later it came over the Jodrell horizon, and its signals were immediately received by the telescope. At precisely 1.25 p.m., when the probe was 5,000 miles from Earth, a signal was transmitted from Jodrell to the probe which fused the explosive bolts holding the payload to the carrier rocket. Immediately *Pioneer V* was released from the carrier rocket and continued on course and transmitting as planned. For the rest of the day it continued to respond to the commands of the telescope. By evening, as it sank below the horizon, it was 70,000 miles away. The following evening it was beyond the Moon. Day after day the telescope commanded and recorded vital information from *Pioneer V*. On 18 March HRH Princess Margaret on a visit to Jodrell Bank pressed the button which initiated the command signals to the probe, then 1,400,000 miles away in the Solar System. On 8 May, when *Pioneer V* was 8,000,000 miles away in Space, it was commanded to switch on its 150-watt transmitter which was to be used when the probe's distance was reaching the limits of the range of the 5-watt transmitter used for the first weeks of travel. It responded immediately, allowing for the 1½-minute interval for the signals to travel to and from the probe. Jodrell Bank continued to command *Pioneer V* and to receive its information out to 22,462,000 miles when, on 26 June, the probe's batteries, which were being charged by solar energy collected by silicon cells mounted on four paddle-wheels, became so weak that contact was lost. (Pioneer V is now in orbit around the sun with a period of 312 days, and it will remain in this orbit indefinitely.)

A statement issued by NASA in May, whilst Jodrell was still in contact with *Pioneer V*, was the first major recognition of Lovell's contribution to Space exploration. It said: 'This is truly an historic event,' and it quoted Dr T. Keith Glennan, the Head of NASA, as saying: 'To our British colleagues we extend our heartiest congratulations on their magnificent tracking and communication achievement.' But the greatest accolade was yet to come. In July Lovell was invited to go to America to be received in the White House by President Eisenhower and to receive from the President his personal gratitude for the unique and valuable contribution made by him and his colleagues at Jodrell Bank to the US Space research programme. On 7 July 1960, the day of Lovell's welcome at the White House, he was presented by NASA with a silver replica of *Pioneer V* in which a small instrument had been constructed which played two tunes 'dear to the hearts of the people of both nations', as Dr Glennan explained. They were 'My Country, 'Tis of Thee' and 'God Save Our Gracious Queen'. Together with this model he was given a scroll from the US Government expressing its gratitude for his invaluable services. Also on the same day, a NASA Press release announced that efforts to communicate with *Pioneer V*, which was then 27.5 million miles away, had been terminated and that a six-minute message received from the probe by Jodrell Bank on 26 June 'was the last communication from the 94.8-pound Spacecraft'. After reporting that *Pioneer V* had established the greatest range over which man had maintained control of an instrumented vehicle, the greatest range over which man had tracked a man-made object, and the greatest range from which man had received telemetry, it went on to record the impressive technological and scientific 'firsts' which had been achieved. These included:

1. The first use of an interplanetary guidance system.

2. The first probe to carry its own self-sustaining power supply—the paddle-wheels with silicon cells for collecting solar energy.

3. The first spacecraft to provide attempts to control and compensate for the increased heating associated with the motion of the probe in towards the Sun in its orbit towards Venus.

4. The first quantitative mapping of interplanetary Space magnetic field.

5. The first quantitative measurement of the interaction of the solar wind and the geomagnetic field.

6. The first real verification of the ring current circulating around Earth at from 30,000 miles to 60,000 miles. The current flowing inside this region of Space was computed to be 5 million amperes.

7. The discovery that the Forbush decrease, a measure of the decrease in the cosmic ray intensity at the beginning of a solar flare, is wholly an interplanetary phenomena and is not associated with the magnetic field around Earth as previously believed.

8. The discovery that the intensity of the outer van Allen radiation belt around the Earth is not produced directly by the injection of electrons from the Sun, but that electrons are somehow accelerated to higher velocities after being caught in the Earth's magnetic field.

9. The first measurement of the size of the Solar System by means of a Space probe.

There followed a separate release which announced that the instrument which had been an essential part of controlling the probe and receiving its information in the course of its 22.5 million mile journey into Space was the British Radio Telescope at Jodrell Bank, '. . . .conceived by Dr A. C. B. Lovell and designed and constructed by the engineering firm of H. C. Husband'. It went on to make it quite clear that America's success was only possible due to Jodrell Bank's co-operation and reported that the British Telescope now 'assists NASA under contract'. It described the telescope's construction in some detail and finished by stating:

Dr Lovell believes that the Jodrell telescope will be able to identify radio-wave sources one billion to two billion light years away. Studies by radio astronomers with a telescope such as the Jodrell Bank facility eventually may lead to a decision between the two major scientific theories of the origin of the Universe according to Dr Lovell. One theory is that all matter in the Universe once was concentrated into a small mass which exploded to form the galaxies as we now know them. The second proposes that matter constantly is being created and that, as old galaxies fly apart, new ones are created in the space between them.

Observations of the distances between galaxies as they were billions of years ago will lead according to Dr Lovell, to a resolution of the two theories.

A charming way of expressing the vital contribution of Jodrell Bank to America's Space programme came from Dr J. A. van Allen,* Professor of Physics at the University of Iowa, in a telegram to Dr T. Keith Glennan, regretting that he could not be present at the NASA reception for Lovell. It read: 'Having survived recent celebration of our 184th year of independence from the British I regret I cannot join you in greeting Professor Lovell and celebrating our second year of dependence on the British.'

Another honour accorded to Lovell was for him to testify before the Senate Committee on Space. Moreover, President Eisenhower put his helicopter at Lovell's disposal so that he could visit a number of the installations associated with the USA's Space activities.

On both sides of the Atlantic the headlines blazoned forth: 'Pioneer Tracker Visits Ike'; 'Eisenhower Thanks Professor Lovell'; 'Eisenhower Tribute to Professor Lovell'; 'Eisenhower Thanks Jodrell Bank Men'. But the British Government, with the exception of Lord Hailsham, the Minister for Science and Technology, maintained a profound silence. It was left to President Eisenhower and the Americans to shower Lovell with well-deserved praise.

In the course of the *Pioneer V* experiment, as the probe penetrated further and further into deep Space at a velocity relative to Earth of 21,000 miles per hour, there was, however, one man in Britain who was impressed by Jodrell Bank's performance and Lovell's vision. When the probe was 'blasted-off' from Cape Canaveral, the telescope was still saddled with a debt of £50,000, but a few days after the launch Lovell was called to the telephone. It was Lord Nuffield's private secretary to say that Lord Nuffield wished to speak to him. Lovell records the conversation in these words:

'Is that Lovell?'

'Yes, my lord.'

'How much money is still owing on the telescope?'

'About £50,000.'

'Is that all? I want to pay it off.'

Lovell was almost speechless, and in trying to thank Nuffield he referred to the fact that the telescope could never have been built but for the generosity of the Nuffield Foundation, to which Lord Nuffield replied:

'That's all right, my boy, you haven't done too badly.'

And so, in May 1960, the debt was cleared at last, and the news of a gift of £25,000 from Lord Nuffield and a further contribution of £25,000 from the Nuffield Foundation was announced on 25 May. The *Manchester Guardian* said, 'If ever there was a State investment of which a British Government could be proud it is the great radio telescope at Jodrell Bank.' Then, after castigating the Government for its niggardly behaviour, it praised Lord Nuffield and the Nuffield Foundation for their foresighted generosity. 'It is a splendid gesture and we may take pride in the fact that there remain private citizens who are ready to shoulder Britain's debts. But for the Government this was a debt of dishonour and remains so.'

A few days later, Joyce Lovell wrote to Lord Nuffield to thank him for his magnanimous gesture which had brought such great relief to the whole family. Nuffield replied personally in a letter dated 9 June 1960:

Dear Mrs Lovell,
Thank you very much indeed for your kind letter, and I would like to assure both you and your husband that I was happy indeed to have been in a position to be able to discharge the outstanding debt on the telescope, and thus relieve the strain and worry, and lighten the Professor's burden.

Yours sincerely,
Nuffield.

18

The Case for Blue Streak and Black Knight

Following the launching of *Pioneer V* on 11 March, there was a series of notable Space events provided by the USA and the Soviet Union. On 1 April the USA, using a three-stage Thor-Able rocket, placed *Tiros I* (Television and Infra-Red Observation Satellite) into orbit. This was the first ever satellite to provide detailed photographs of the world's weather. On 13 April they launched *Transit* into orbit, a navigational satellite, again using the Thor-Able combination. On Sunday 15 May the Soviet Union launched *Sputnik IV* into orbit, a 4½-ton spaceship containing a pressurized cabin carrying a dummy pilot. Its orbit was a near circular one, with an apogee of 230 miles and a perigee of 194 miles, circling the Earth every 91.2 minutes and passing over Paris, London, San Francisco, Melbourne and Ottawa in the course of its gyrations. The cabin itself weighed 2½ tons and carried 1½ tons of apparatus, including the necessary equipment for manned Space flight, power sources and radio transmitter. Then, on 24 May, the USA put the 5,000-pound *Midas II* into orbit (Missile Defence Alarm System), a satellite designed to give speedy warning of a missile attack by detecting with infra-red sensors the heat given off by the exhausts of a missile engine. *Midas I* had been launched in the autumn of 1959 but had failed to go into orbit.

The contrast between the USA and the USSR on instrumentation at this time probably favoured the Americans, but the immense weight which the Russians had been able to launch into orbit on 15 May was a startling pointer to the power of their propulsion systems. Moreover, the success of the dummy in Space, and its final recovery, was indicative that the USSR was close to achieving manned Space flight.

The question of US superiority of instrumentation had certainly been in doubt until *Pioneer V*. On 4 October 1959 the USSR had launched *Lunik III*, the historic Moon-probe, which had photographed the hidden side of the Moon, the cameras in the probe being operated by a command signal transmitted from Earth. The direction and velocity of launching the rocket had been critical, since it had to be placed in an orbit which made it an Earth satellite with its major axis so large that at apogee it just passed around the Moon. But the success of the US *Pioneer V*, launched five months later, redressed any question of disparity in instrumentation and seemed to put the Americans ahead.

The contrast in Space activities between the US and the Soviet Union on the one hand and Britain on the other was almost non-existent. Britain was a 'non-starter' except for the outstanding work of Lovell, his team and the Jodrell Bank telescope.

But Lovell's success, and his tremendous enthusiasm, had stimulated a few of his old wartime colleagues into taking some action to attempt to persuade the lethargic Macmillan Government that Britain should play its part in this new and important—important commercially, scientifically and militarily—exploration of the atmosphere around Earth and of the Solar System as a whole. The most influential individual was Sir Robert Renwick.

Towards the end of 1959 Group Captain E. Fennessy,* Managing Director of Decca Radar Limited, Dr F. E. Jones,* at that time Technical Director of Mullards Limited, and I met on several occasions to discuss defence matters and the absence of any serious plans for the United Kingdom to embark upon a national Space programme. We had all been wartime colleagues, associated with the development and use of radar in the war. By the nature of our post-war work, particularly at this time, we were well aware of the trends in scientific development for military and commercial purposes. As Deputy Director of the Royal Aircraft Establishment (RAE) in the fifties, F. E. Jones was fully acquainted with the design studies that were being undertaken by a department in the RAE to assess the possibilities of Space exploration, and of the very detailed proposals for a reconnaissance satellite for military purposes which had been submitted to the Air Ministry in the middle fifties. Fennessy, as head of Decca Radar, knew of the radar guidance systems required for launching purposes and of the instrumentation plans for proposed satellites of the immediate future. I, as Managing Director of Texas Instruments (UK), was well versed in the plans for Blue Streak, Britain's ICBM then under development and under prototype construction by the De Havilland Aircraft Company, as Texas were the only company in the UK, at that time, making silicon transistors and diodes of the degree of sophistication required for the guidance systems of Blue Streak and other guided weapons. Indeed, the Applications Division of Texas Instruments was working alongside De Havillands and other major companies working on guided missiles, to develop those electronic designs which were essential to the major functions of such systems. With Lovell we recognized the possibilities of having the vehicle to launch satellites into orbit already to hand by a combination of Blue Streak and Black Knight, the latter being a British-designed rocket which had been used as a probe into the upper atmosphere for research purposes. In fact, we knew that De Havillands had in the latter part of 1959 submitted to the Ministry of Aviation a paper on the use of Blue Streak and Black Knight as

a launching-vehicle for British satellites. But we were seriously concerned at the 'confidential' rumours in circulation at the end of 1959 that
the Government intended to abandon Blue Streak as a carrier for a
nuclear warhead, for which it was being designed, and in the Space
research field to rely upon limited design work for British satellites which
would be injected into orbit by courtesy of the USA.

At the end of 1959, when I was assisting Renwick with his lobbying
activities to persuade the Government to allocate the money required to
discharge Jodrell Bank's debt, I also advised Renwick of the fears of
Lovell, Fennessy and F. E. Jones, together with those of others in the
aviation and electronics industries, that the Macmillan Government was
considering withdrawal from development of powerful rockets, whether
for military or Space requirements. It was rumoured that it was the
intention to rely upon the USA for the supply of ICBMs and Space
facilities and to concentrate only upon conventional weapons, including
delivery of nuclear bombs by the strike aircraft of what was known as the
V-Bomber Force. On Monday 7 December 1959, the day before I
departed for Dallas, Texas, to attend my company's annual planning
conference, I talked with Renwick, in company with Fennessy, in an effort
to persuade him to take some positive action to dissuade the Government
from pursuing any course which could lead Britain into an inadequate
defence policy and deny her the capability of conducting her own Space
programme. Renwick reacted favourably and promised that, if Lovell, F.
E. Jones, Fennessy and I could collect together a team of experts in the
various fields related to Space exploration, he would arrange, in the first
instance, a meeting with Sir Toby Lowe, now Lord Aldington, the
Chairman of the Conservative Party; then, when Sir Toby's advice on how
best to present the case to the Government had been received, he would
arrange a meeting between the team and those Ministers, including
members of the Cabinet, who would be most concerned with such a
project.

Early in February 1960 the Government published its Defence White
Paper, and on 1 March the Government's Defence Policy was debated in
the House of Commons. The debate disclosed, as Sir Harold Watkinson,
the Minister for Defence, put it in his reply for the Government, 'a wide
measure of vacillation and confusion' among the Labour Opposition
about what their defence policy should be. The Labour Party was, in fact,
totally divided on Defence Policy. It included those who wished to
abandon the nuclear deterrent altogether, those who felt it worthwhile to
keep it for the moment based on aircraft delivery and to scrap Blue Streak
and any development of further ICBMs, and those who were ready to
disarm Britain, come what may. Only Hugh Gaitskell, winding up for the

Opposition, showed any sense of responsibility from the Labour benches when he said that the real case for Britain having its own independent nuclear capability was fear of excessive dependence upon the USA and the doubt as to whether the Americans would be ready to risk the destruction of their own cities on behalf of Europe.

Whilst the Government's policy was to retain the nuclear deterrent as the key to defence, it was clear that it had no firm idea as to the future method of delivery and was hoping the V-Bomber Force of Bomber Command—the Victor and Vulcan aircraft—would undertake the task into the '70s. In the debate, Christopher Soames the Secretary of State for War, did, however, emphasize that the Government were 'rigid in our view that we should continue to contribute to the deterrent, but . . . flexible in our view as to . . . the instrument on which we will be dependent after the V-Bombers'. The actual timing, he said, would depend on the expectation of the effective life of the V-Bombers with respect to the newer weapons. This was confirmation of the terms of the Defence White Paper which stated that the V-Bomber remained the principal British contribution to the strategic power of the West. However, after stating that the American Thor fixed-site ICBM had joined the operational front line of the RAF in 1959 and that development of Blue Streak, Britain's own ICBM, was continuing, it added that the Government might decide not to rely on fixed-site missiles as successors to the V-Bombers. Instead, the possibility of mobile launchers, whether aircraft or submarines, was being considered. The only submarine-launched missile was the American Polaris which, if acquired for the British deterrent, would leave its use under the control of the Americans—an undesirable situation. Reference was also made to the new Mach 2 aircraft TSR2 for a strike/reconnaissance role, but it was not clear whether this new design was for the proposed future aircraft delivery of nuclear bombs after the demise of the Vulcans and Victors. What Soames and the Government failed to say was that the continued development of a British ICBM means of delivery of atomic warheads must be a matter of priority if the effectiveness of a British deterrent was to be maintained.

It was against this background that the Renwick meeting with Sir Toby Lowe took place on 30 March. Lovell, Fennessy, F. E. Jones, Dr H. M. Finniston* (later Sir Monty Finniston, Chairman of British Steel), Dr W. F. Hilton,* head of Hawker Siddeley's Astronautics Division, G. K. C. Pardoe,* of De Havilland's in charge of the development of Blue Streak, and I attended for the purpose of airing our views to Sir Toby on the need for a British Space Programme and independence in rocket capability. Although our reasons differed, they nonetheless knit together to produce a potent case for the exploitation of Space for military, commercial and long-term research reasons. But whilst we were aware of what was going on in the world, and what was not going on in Britain, only Lovell had personal knowledge of the capabilities of and likely advances by the USA and the USSR in the exploration and utilization of Space, and his arguments for Britain playing her part in this new medium were weighty indeed.

The outcome of the meeting was that each of those present should write a memorandum on his reasons for advocating a British Space Programme and circulate these papers amongst each other, and then we should meet again to decide upon the basis for a common memorandum to be submitted to Sir Toby Lowe, who would circulate it to selected Ministers prior to a meeting with them in the House of Commons. It was agreed that Lovell and I should draft the final combined memorandum.

Just two weeks later, on Wednesday 13 April, Sir Harold Watkinson announced in the House of Commons the Government's decision to cease development of the Blue Streak long-range ballistic missile as a military weapon. 'The technique of controlling ballistic missiles has rapidly advanced,' he said. 'The vulnerability of missiles launched from static sites, and the practicability of launching missiles of considerable range from mobile platforms, has now been established. In the light of our military advice to this effect, and of the importance of reinforcing the effectiveness of the deterrent, we have concluded, and the Australian Government have fully accepted, that we ought not to continue to develop, as a military weapon, a missile that can be launched only from a fixed site.' He went on to say that Britain's strategic nuclear force, based on the V-Bomber Force, was an effective contribution to the deterrent power of the free world and that in due course some other vehicle in lieu of Blue Streak would be required to replace the V-Bomber Force. He then went on to state that the Government were considering the idea of 'prolonging the effectiveness of the V-Bomber Force by buying supplies of the airborne ballistic missile Skybolt which is being developed in the United States'. He concluded his statement by announcing that the Government would now consider whether the Blue Streak programme could be adapted for the development of a launcher for Space satellites.

This news caused an uproar in the House, with criticism of the Government's policy coming from both sides. George Brown, the principal Opposition spokesman on defence, whilst welcoming the abandonment of Blue Streak as a military weapon—'the Opposition have been pressing this for three years . . .'—rightly criticized the proposed alternative action. Skybolt, he pointed out, was a vehicle which did not yet exist, and 'nobody can yet know whether it ever will exist.' Events proved him right. It never did come to fruition and was dropped by the Americans before it ever got off the drawing-board. In general, however, the Opposition were delighted to see the beginning of the end of Britain's credibility as a major military force with an independent nuclear deterrent capability. The Liberals were of the same opinion. Jo Grimond, the Liberal Leader, asked: 'Will the Minister give up this pretence that Blue Streak can be used as a launcher for a Space satellite; and will he give up this preposterous policy of an independent British deterrent?' He suggested, like George Brown, that there should be an inquiry 'into this waste of £65,000,000'. This was the cost of development of Blue Streak to date. It was Mr Farey-Jones, a Conservative back-bencher (MP for Watford 1955–64), who perhaps summed up the situation in the wisest terms and with remarkable foresightedness. He was highly critical of the Government's decision to abandon Blue Streak. 'Those who are properly informed,' he said, 'will regard this as a calamitous decision. This is not a question of financial expenditure, it is a question of Commonwealth participation in the scientific progress of the next 100 years, compared with which a figure of £65,000,000 is a bagatelle. As a result of this decision the Minister has put in pawn to the United States British Scientific progress in the exploration of outer Space for the next 25 to 50 years.' Mr Farey-Jones had understood the economic necessity of military, commercial and scientific interests to be linked closely together if research and development in these new fields of rocketry and Space vehicles were to be adequately funded.

The official abandonment of Blue Streak lent added urgency to the work of the Renwick 'pressure group'. Whilst some hope had been held out that Blue Streak might well be used in conjunction with Black Knight to provide an initial launcher for a British Space Programme, rumour persisted that the Government was lukewarm about such a proposition and ready to confine the nation to modest satellite experiments launched by American rockets when the Americans could find room for the occasional British equipment. Interestingly, it was understood that there was considerable opposition inside the Conservative Party to the Defence Policy and it was hinted in certain circles that Sir Harold Watkinson himself had been forced to adopt measures which he found unpalatable. If there was a major difference of opinion in the Government over development of ICBMs and Space exploration, the sooner those who supported continued development could be properly briefed, the better. They should be made well aware of the enormous benefits which would derive from a Space programme.

By the latter part of May the memoranda from all of the members of the Renwick 'pressure group' had been completed and circulated, and on Wednesday 1 June they met with Renwick to discuss the form and contents of the memorandum that was now to be prepared and submitted to selected ministers. Each individual had concentrated on his area of specific knowledge. Fennessy had developed his reasons for a British Space Programme around the revolution that the use of satellites could create in the field of communications and facilities for navigation, and the stimulus this would provide for the electronics industry. Finniston and I tended to emphasize the military importance of Space, but I did include a commercial justification for a Space Programme, although this had military connotations in that I drew attention to the use of satellites for Commonwealth communications links and for aerial survey, navigation and mapping, all of which would also satisfy growing military require-ments for defence. G. K. C. Pardoe naturally concentrated on the state of the art of rocketry, presenting a clear and detailed survey of the develop-ment progress of Blue Streak and Black Knight, enumerating the facili-ties that existed for testing and launching these systems, including those at Woomera in Australia where test firings of Black Knight had already achieved 100 per cent success. He also outlined the studies which had already been undertaken into the combination of Blue Streak, Black Knight and a third stage for injecting 2,000 pounds of satellite payload into near Earth orbits of 300 miles in altitude, 600 pounds into more distant orbits, and 100 pounds or more as probes into Space or into a 22,300-mile 'stationary' orbit rotating once in 24 hours in an equatorial plane in the same direction as the Earth's rotation, an ideal orbit for a telephone communication system and for television broadcast covering a vast area of the world.

But it was Lovell, who knew more about the progress of the USA and the USSR in the field of Space research, due to his liaison with these countries in their Space efforts since October 1957, who compiled the most weighty paper on the subject under the heading 'Space Research and the UK'. He reviewed the new techniques for research in astronomy astrophysics, geophysics and related sciences during the last fifteen years and emphasized that, although Britain had exhibited a progressive outlook immediately after the war, she was rapidly falling behind America and Russia. Now, the only major efforts in Space research were those provided by the activities of Martin Ryle at Cambridge and scientists at RAE making use of emissions from the satellites of the two great post-war Powers. In addition, there was the unique part being played by the radio telescope at Jodrell Bank in connection with some of the American NASA deep Space programmes. After referring to the arrangements then being made for British scientists to instrument the American Scout Satellites, he commented: 'It cannot be seriously argued that the long drawn out negotiations with the USA to adjust our experiments to fit in with space and weight, which are always likely to be far less than is technically possible at any time, can be conducive to a healthy British Space effort. In other words, it is certain that the best that can be negotiated with the USA will always be far below what they are themselves capable of doing; and, incidentally, will be far below what the UK could accomplish with Blue Streak and Black Knight. Our scientific policy in major fields of research will be effectively controlled by another nation.' On the subject of personnel, he was scathing about Government suggestions that the UK could not mount an independent Space programme because it did not possess enough scientists and technicians. 'The supporters of this argument overlook the present practical situation which is that a significant drain of our young people is taking place to the USA. It is erroneously believed that the higher USA salaries are responsible, but practical day-to-day association with this problem indicates that the best people go because they genuinely feel that facilities for research in the USA are superior.'

Whilst his paper concentrated mainly on research, he gave his prognosis of the foreseeable commercial benefits arising from active research. Recognizing that adequate funding of a British Space Programme would necessarily depend upon a military interest as well as commercial and research interest, he also supported Finniston's and my emphasis upon the need for development of a military capability in Space if Britain were to remain a Power in the world with a significant influence on international affairs: '. . . a decision to make an entire cancellation of Blue Streak would imply that the UK will never re-enter the field as a major partner in world strategy.'

The meeting finally decided that the memorandum for submission to Government Ministers should place the commercial justification for a Space Programme as first priority, followed by scientific research as second, and the military justification as third priority. The commercial justification was to concentrate on the use of satellites for a UK and Commonwealth telephone and teleprinter network based on three satellites at 22,300 miles rotating once in 24 hours in an equatorial plane in the same direction as the Earth's rotation. It was to be emphasized that a far greater number of circuits could thus be provided at a much lower cost than would be the case with submarine cables. The other commercial uses of satellites were to include the broadcast of sound and television programmes to a world-wide coverage, navigational facilities for air and sea transport and air traffic control, and for meteorological short-and long-range forecasting.

It was left to Lovell and myself to produce this document. It was completed on 14 June 1960, under the heading 'Memorandum in

Support of a United Kingdom and Commonwealth Space Programme'. It contained cogent reasons for a British effort. After enumerating the commercial applications, it concluded this section with the statement:

If the United Kingdom and Commonwealth wish to remain a first-rate military, political and commercial power, they must, above all, have Space knowledge and they must develop a vigorous aerospace industry. Such know-how cannot be obtained at second-hand—it must be worked for by direct effort in the field of Space exploitation. Space exploitation and research involve the development of new technologies which will become the industrial techniques of the future and which will provide us with the ability to maintain our position in the commercial markets of the world during the next two decades. It is significant that Space involves highly advanced technologies in the power, metallurgical, electronics, physics, chemical, biological and medical fields. . . .

The scientific justification was a repetition of Lovell's own paper on the subject and drew attention to the necessity of Britain's national science being free from the restrictions that would inevitably be imposed upon it if it had to rely on foreign vehicles to enable it to explore the Solar System and, at some time in the future, the regions of outer Space. Emphasis was placed on the discoveries springing from such research which would have important commercial, biological, medical and military implications. It concluded by reminding the reader that the voice of the UK in international scientific gatherings had always been prominent, but at present Space research was controlled by the USSR and the USA alone.

The military section was brief, but to the point. After accepting that ballistic guided missiles would be the most powerful long-range vehicles for delivering warheads, it turned to the future: '. . . the rapid development of orbiting satellites, manned or unmanned, for use as reconnaissance satellites, attack platforms, early warning systems and navigational guidance stations, together with vehicles for operation to and from Earth and between satellites is likely to start a revolution from conventional warfare to three-dimensional strategy. . . . National survival will, in future, depend upon the rate of scientific and technological progress in the new field of aerospace armaments. . . .' Attention was drawn to the fact that it was already possible for the orbiting satellites of the USSR and the USA to make constant unauthorized observations of UK and Commonwealth territory.

The memorandum concluded with a detailed proposal for a British Space Programme based on its own launching-vehicles and concentrating initially on the commercial applications. It recommended that a United Kingdom and Commonwealth Space Authority (UKCSA) should be created on similar lines to the American Space Authority, NASA, for the co-ordination of all British Space activities. It was proposed that the aim should be to launch six satellites over the next three to four years, commencing with a first launching within two years. It was estimated that this initial programme could be undertaken within a budget of £15 million per annum over a period of several years, 'by which time the commercial advantages alone, of exploiting Space, are certain to be so compelling that further finance would be readily available'. With regard to the military aspect, the recommendation was that the Authority should make available to the Chiefs of Staff the outcome of all its works to assist them in their own studies of the military implications of Space. The last paragraph of the recommendations stated that, by the time the first phases of such a Space programme had been completed, further development would almost certainly have opened up new applications for orbital vehicles and new approaches to power plants.

Renwick delivered copies of the memorandum to Sir Toby Lowe without delay, and by the end of the third week in June the memorandum was in the hands of Sir Derek Heathcoat Amory, Chancellor of the Exchequer, Sir Harold Watkinson, Minister of Defence, Mr Duncan Sandys, Minister of Aviation, Viscount Hailsham, Minister for Science, and Sir Keith Joseph, Minister of State, Board of Trade. A copy also went to the Prime Minister.

On Monday 27 June the Renwick 'pressure group' met over dinner in a private room at the House of Commons arranged by Sir Toby Lowe. Those present, apart from Renwick's team, were Sir Derek Heathcoat Amory, Sir Harold Watkinson, Mr Duncan Sandys, Viscount Hailsham, Sir Keith Joseph and Sir Toby Lowe. It was a stimulating affair. The clarity and enthusiasm with which Renwick's 'pressure group' argued the case for a British Space Programme were impressive. No one had an axe to grind, and each as an individual, and all as a team, held the deep and sincere belief that a Space programme was a key to the future authority and prosperity of the United Kingdom and Commonwealth. Again, Lovell's contribution was of particular interest because of his close relationship with the USA and the USSR in their Space programmes, and because Jodrell Bank had up to that date been responsible for the communications to and from and for the control of the American deep Space probe, *Pioneer V*, which only the day before, at 27.5 million miles from Earth, had passed a six-minute message to the Jodrell radio telescope. Whilst dwelling on the scientific research aspects, he produced convincing reasons under constant questioning why there would be substantial commercial and defence 'spin-offs' arising from the research aspects.

From early reports it was believed that the meeting had brought some measure of success. Indeed, it was soon known that limited work was to continue on Blue Streak and Black Knight pending a decision by the Government on a Space Programme, a decision that would be reached in October when Parliament reassembled after the summer recess.

Just over a week after the House of Commons meeting, Lovell was in the USA to receive the grateful thanks of President Eisenhower and NASA for the help and co-operation of Jodrell Bank which had been indispensable to the success of *Pioneer V*. At a Press conference on that occasion, held on Thursday 7 July, Lovell was closely questioned about his views on the idea of an independent British Space Programme using the Blue Streak and Black Knight rockets, rather than Britain relying upon facilities being made available by the USA in American rocket vehicles. Lovell, with some confidence in a favourable outcome of the House of Commons meeting, but cautious to avoid any show of a lack of 'faith and friendliness in American co-operation', as he put it in his reply, explained his own view and that of others in Britain on the necessity for the UK to have an independent stake in Space exploitation.

> I think that the arrangements which have been made for the instrumentation of United States payloads is extremely valuable [he said], but this isn't good enough for a country which wants to have a thriving science and technology of its own. [This was a reference to America's offer of facilities in its Scout vehicles for British experiments.] The demands which the further development of the Blue Streak and Black Knight with their own payloads place on engineering and industry in Great Britain will not be faced if we merely have to instrument American payloads. I would also, personally, take an extremely serious view of a nation like Great Britain which voluntarily, for the sake of a few million pounds, opted out of its immediate association with the development of rocketry, even though at the present time a military decision has been made not to use them. I think it would be a grievous error not to keep one's engineers and scientists in touch with these developments, because the whole military strategy is clearly in a phase of being transformed. And at the moment no one can see where we should be in the next one or two decades.

19

Britain Rejects Space

Early reports indicating that the meeting between Government Ministers and the Renwick 'pressure group' had altered the attitude of the Government towards a British Space Programme proved to be over-optimistic. Some sort of favourable decision had been expected soon after Parliament reassembled in October after the summer recess. There had been exciting enough events in the world of satellites to stimulate interest. In August the Russians launched a spaceship containing two dogs, Strelka and Belka, and successfully brought this ship out of orbit to land within six miles of the pre-planned point on 20 August with the dogs still alive and in good condition. They were, in fact, the first two living creatures to orbit the Earth and return to bark the tale. On 12 August the USA launched *Echo I*, a passive satellite injected into a 900-nautical-mile nearly circular orbit. The carrier rocket contained a 182-pound payload consisting of a container into which a 100-foot-diameter reflecting surface in balloon form was folded. After injection into orbit, the two halves of the container were separated by a small charge, and the balloon, made of ½-milli-metre-thick aluminium-coated mylar, inflated in the vacuum of inter-planetary Space under the influence of the sublimation of 10 pounds of benzoic acid placed within the sphere. This Space effort was to test the feasibility of using a passive satellite to reflect signals for long-range communications. On 22 August Jodrell Bank co-operated with the USA in these experiments, continuing with its assistance for three nights. Then, on 4 October, the USA successfully injected its first active com-munication satellite, *Courier*, into orbit, transmitting messages to it from one part of the world and receiving the stored messages from it on demand from the ground when it passed round the other side of the globe.

On 12 February 1961 the Russians announced the launching of a probe aimed towards Venus, using a new technique whereby a heavy satellite was placed in orbit around Earth, the probe being launched from this Space platform. This method was to be adopted later by the Americans for deep Space launchings because it enabled the maximum advantage to be obtained of the Earth's own orbital velocity. In June Professor Alla Massevitch and Dr Khodarev, who had designed the equipment in the Russian Venus probe, arrived at Jodrell Bank to co-operate with Lovell and his team in locating the probe after their own equipment had lost contact, and they were therefore unable to receive the information transmitted by the probe when it was near Venus. This collaboration was highly successful.

Finally, on 12 April 1961, as a climax to this first era of the Space Age, the Russians launched their manned spaceship, *Vostock I*, into orbit, carrying Yuri Gagarin. It completed one orbit of the Earth and then re-entered the atmosphere and landed safely. Gagarin had proved that man could survive the entry into Space and had opened the way to manned Space flight.

In the face of these remarkable feats, despite the fact that Britain had the ability and capability to exploit the opportunities of entering the Space Age, the Government remained impassive and virtually inactive. The only move it made was a half-hearted approach to the Commonwealth and Europe to sell the idea that Britain was prepared to offer Blue Streak and Black Knight as its contribution to a British Commonwealth and European Space Programme if Europe and the Commonwealth provided the rest of the money needed for such a project.

Renwick, however, was not prepared to give up hope of a British Space Programme altogether. Constantly fed with information from Lovell direct, or through myself, about the activities of the USA and the Soviet Union, and impressed by the idea of a satellite communications system on a global basis, providing greatly increased circuits across the Atlantic and throughout the Commonwealth at a probable lower cost than by laying more transoceanic and transcontinental cables, he determined to press harder for a more enlightened Government outlook. He was intrigued by Lovell's statement in his memorandum advocating a Space Programme where he referred to communications: 'The estimates of cost already made indicate that the capital investment in the satellite communication system is less than or comparable with the proposed Commonwealth cable link and has infinitely more flexibility. . . . Apart from the sheer communication facility considered above, the satellite communication system would make it possible for the UK broadcasting and television interests to achieve world wide coverage. For example, how much per minute would advertisers pay the ITA for world-wide advertisement? . . .' He was also impressed by the statement in the Lovell/Saward combined memorandum referring to the brochure prepared by Hawker Siddeley on the subject of reconnaissance and communication satellites which had been submitted to the Ministry for Science: 'One single example might be a system of three Satellites at a height of 22,300 miles, rotating once in 24 hours in an equatorial plane in the same direction as the Earth's rotation which could provide global communications covering the entire world except for the polar regions. This widespread communication network, linking the Commonwealth with itself and with the rest of the world could revolutionise the telephone and teleprinter systems with incalculable effects on the business world, an aspect which the United Kingdom and Commonwealth cannot ignore financially and politically. Telephone calls and teleprinter links could be provided at a fraction of their present cost . . .'

By the end of 1960 Renwick had decided to create an organization that could examine the prospects offered by mounting a Space Programme and put forward concrete proposals for the utilization of active satellites for the extension of communication facilities as a first priority, followed by other commercial applications such as navigational satellites, Earth surveys, meteorological forecasting and air-traffic control. On 10 February 1961 the British Space Development Company Limited (BSDC) was formed and incorporated, a consortium supported by such companies as Hawker Siddeley, Rolls-Royce, Mullard, Associated Broadcasting Development (ATV), Plessey, Pye, Rank Television and General Trust, Ferranti, GEC-AEI (Electronics) and British Insulated Callender's Cables. Its Chairman was Renwick.[1]

The first major study undertaken by the BSDC was a comprehensive proposal for global communications with a British Commonwealth Satellite System. This was submitted to the Government in August 1961 and included a detailed system proposal, an examination of research and development costs and capital and operating costs, and an assessment of revenue based on carefully researched and prepared estimates of traffic over the period 1961 to 1985. The BSDC's 'Summary of Probable Income and Expenditure' for the period 1961 to 1985 estimated £89 million for research and development costs over the years 1961 to 1968, £145.9 million for capital and operating costs for the period 1966 to 1985, making a total outlay for the period 1961 to 1985 of £234.9 million. Revenue beginning in the year 1968 was estimated to bring in a total of £712.6 millions by 1985, a net profit before tax of £477.7 millions. The figures and the proposals were good enough to stimulate the interest of certain merchant banks in the City, but the problem was that all telephone and teleprinter activities in the UK were statutorily confined to the domain of the General Post Office and, therefore, the Government. Consequently, however much private enterprise might be ready to take the risks attending such an advanced approach to future methods of

[1] The Directors of BSDC were Lord Renwick (Chairman), Dr F. E. Jones, Group Captain E. Fennessy, Group Captain Dudley Saward, G. C. I. Gardiner, CBE, FRAeS, MIMechE (Managing Director of Hawker Siddeley Dynamics), A. A. Rubbra, CBE, FRAeS, MIMechE (Technical Director of Rolls Royce) and G. K. C. Pardoe as Chief Executive and Chairman of the Technical Committee. Professor A. C. B. Lovell was the Scientific Consultant.

communications, it was not prepared to take them if denied the rewards. Therefore the problem for the BSDC resolved itself into one of persuading the Government and the Post Office to take the step towards the future communications technology.

In the USA it was a different matter. Private enterprise, under certain federal laws, operated the internal and overseas communication systems. Even so, for an international operation there had to be some form of federal co-operation. The launching problem for the USA companies interested in developing communication satellites was resolved by the facilities offered by NASA. For example, AT & T paid NASA $2.5 million to launch its two Telstar communication satellites in 1962 and May 1963. The Telstar and RCA relay satellites demonstrated the possibilities of transatlantic television and telephone facilities but were in near-Earth orbits and therefore of limited use, giving only a few hours of transatlantic coverage per day. Nevertheless, this limited success enabled the Americans to recognize the enormous profit potential, despite considerable costs, as well as the political importance of developing a satellite communication and television broadcast system that would provide a continuous world coverage with a vastly increased number of speech and teleprinter circuits and an appropriate number of television channels. Recognizing that an international network would require the collaboration of other countries, the American Congress first of all passed a Bill in 1962 to create a Communications Satellite Corporation, known as Comsat, for the purpose of developing a world-wide satellite system. A provision of the Bill was that half the stock would be owned by companies who acted as carriers and the other half by the public. Then in 1964 an interim agreement was reached with nineteen interested nations to form an International Telecommunications Satellite Consortium to be known as Intelsat. The stock holding in the company was finally settled at 38.3 per cent for US investment and 61.7 per cent for the other countries who by 1972 numbered fifteen. (The other countries were the UK, Australia, Japan, Canada, France, Italy, West Germany, Pakistan, Spain, Israel, Philippines, Argentina, Brazil, Taiwan.) The UK's share was 10.9 per cent.

The system adopted by Intelsat was three satellites at 22,300 miles above the Earth in equatorial orbit rotating once in 24 hours in the same direction as the Earth's rotation, thus effectively remaining over the same point of the Earth's surface. One was to be over the Atlantic, one over the Pacific and one over the Indian Ocean, thereby providing world-wide coverage. These satellites were named Syncoms. Syncom was a Hughes Aircraft Company development, and the first was launched in February 1963 but failed. The second was successfully launched into orbit in

August 1963, and the third in 1964. By 1969 global coverage was achieved. By 1970 there was dual satellite capacity available across the Atlantic. At the present time Intelsat is providing more than 60 per cent of the world's intercontinental circuits between 76 countries.

Interestingly, Intelsat was one of the systems proposed originally by Hawker Siddeley to the British Government and by the Renwick 'pressure group' in 1960, and by the BSDC in 1961. In November 1962 a further proposal was put forward by the BSDC in collaboration with Eurospace, a group of European industrial companies. This also estimated a substantial cumulative revenue over an eight-year operating period after all research and development, capital and operating costs. But no interest was shown by Government. In 1973, referring in a speech to Britain's lost opportunities, Lovell said: 'Successive UK Governments have adopted a lamentable attitude to this issue during the last fifteen years. It is possible to understand, even without acceptance, the arguments about involvement in national launchings for scientific research. But it is hard to understand the ineptitude of those who were responsible for the neglect of this communications market, even considered as a straightforward business proposition apart from the clear advantages to national defence. In spite of strong pressure from responsible individuals, the appropriate industries, and eventually the Eurospace organisation, nothing was done. In a few vital years the UK lost control of the communications market which this country had created a few decades earlier. . . .'

Indeed, the UK lost more than control of the commercial communications market. It now has to rely on the USA for the provision of defence satellite communications. Moreover, the proposals and technical studies by BSDC for direct television broadcasting from satellites in March, 1966 were ignored, as were other detailed proposals for the use of satellites for international airport handling, meteorological forecasting and reconnaissance for Earth resources. By October 1964 the Conservative Government had completed its term of office, and a General Election returned a Labour Government, a government which was even more resolutely opposed to 'dabbling in Space' and to continuing with any ideas of developing and building launching vehicles for satellites or any modern defence weapon of the ICBM family. And Labour's attitude to defence measures did not stop at rockets. By January 1965 Dennis Healey, the Minister of Defence, was planning major cuts in the aircraft industry. On 2 February the P-1154, a vertical-take-off supersonic ground-attack and interceptor aircraft was cancelled in favour of the American Phantom, and the HS-681 short-take-off transport plane was dropped for another American aircraft, the C-130E. Then, on 6 April, Mr Callaghan, the

Chancellor of the Exchequer, announced in his budget speech the cancellation of TSR-2, a supersonic strike aircraft capable of delivering nuclear weapons at tremendous range and with a performance and electronic systems that far exceeded anything that was for many years due from the aircraft stables of the USA and the Soviet Union. The cancellation was particularly odious because Harold Wilson, the Prime Minister, had given a pledge that the TSR-2 programme would continue if Labour were elected to office. The only major aircraft project which survived was that of the Anglo-French supersonic Concorde which the Government also intended to cancel but which was saved by the French Government insisting on such enormous damages under their contract that Britain was forced to allow it to continue.

The fact was that by 1965 Britain had withdrawn from the field of Space for commercial exploitation and for military strategy. Furthermore, she had abandoned any serious attempt to have a credible future defence and, therefore, a voice of any weight amongst the great Powers.

In 1970 Lord Renwick wrote in his Chairman's Report from the BSDC:
In the nine years since its formation the work of BSDC has always suffered from the lack of interest and support from the various Ministries with which we have been in touch. This, itself, perhaps caused largely by inter-ministerial jealousies. It has never, therefore, been possible for BSDC to achieve the objectives for which it was set up and which it was so admirably fitted to achieve. . . . The future objectives of BSDC will therefore be to continue to exert pressure on the Government and its Departments towards a more constructive and extensive UK Space development. In this connection the Company may expect to discharge further study contracts with particular reference to communications systems and, indeed, specifically those related to national telecommunications and television requirements as referred to above. [This was a reference to a study contract undertaken for COMSAT.] We would also address ourselves to the new tasks that will emerge in the use of data derived from Earth resource satellite systems. . . . We would now expect to maintain a large effort at BSDC Company expense. . . .

But within another two years, with continuing Government apathy, now on the part of the newly elected Heath Conservative Government, the BSDC had to go into voluntary liquidation. Britain had clearly decided to leave the field open to the USA and the USSR, except for begging a ride in an American rocket for the occasional satellite which she hoped to construct to show some semblance of interest in the new technology, and apart from playing a very modest role in any European Space consortium which might be established in the future.

For Lovell it was evident, even by 1963, that any chance of adequate British facilities in Space to help astronomical researches was doomed.

Without an early British-controlled commercial and defence programme, there could be no rockets for launching research satellites into orbit and probes into deep Space. Therefore his best hopes for such facilities lay, immediately, in collaboration with the USA and the USSR until a European Space Programme was established at some nebulous date in the future.

However, Lovell's efforts outside the Renwick 'pressure group' were not without some limited success. A letter dated 3 April 1960, from Sir Solly Zuckerman,* the Chief Scientific Adviser to the Secretary of State for Defence, requested his assistance. He explained that he no longer attended meetings of the Scientific Advisory Council on 'Scientific Research and Technical Development of the Ministry of Aviation' but occasionally read the minutes. He indicated that he was disturbed at the attitude adopted to the subject of anti-ballistic missile defence. Asking Lovell if he could possibly meet him when he was next in London to discuss the matter, he wrote: 'I have always been impressed by your realistic attitude to this problem, and disturbed by the over-optimistic estimates which are sometimes made—occasionally even by my people. I should like to know whether you think it enough for an official such as Cockburn to say "that the UK attitude to ballistic missile defence was an extremely reserved one". What people like myself want to know is whether a defence system is or is not scientifically conceivable.'

Lovell met Zuckerman on 15 August. Following this meeting and the Renwick 'pressure group' meeting of 27 June with certain Cabinet Ministers, including the Minister of Defence, Lovell was invited at the instigation of Zuckerman to join a small panel of scientists to advise the Minister on the possibility of defence against ballistic missiles. He accepted on 12 September. As early as May 1958 the use of the Jodrell Bank telescope had been considered by the Air Ministry for use as an early warning system. Now, as a member of this special panel, Lovell was able to influence thought towards the development of the Fylingdales early warning system against ballistic missiles emanating from the USSR in the event of war. Moreover, he was able to arrange for the use of the Jodrell Bank telescope in time of 'Alert' to act as the secret early warning system until Fylingdales came into operation in September 1963. Indeed, throughout 1962 and 1963 Britain's early warning defence against ballistic missiles was totally dependent upon Jodrell Bank under a 'smoke-screen' of a programme of meteor-detection. So secret was the arrangement that at Jodrell only Lovell and J. G. Davies knew what was happening.

Following his activities on Zuckerman's panel of scientists, Lovell was approached by Sir Maurice Dean, the Permanent Under-Secretary of

State for Air, to ask him if he would consider joining a committee of scientists which was studying the various requirements of the Royal Air Force. After an informal lunch in May 1962, Dean wrote to Lovell giving him more information about the activities of this committee. The letter was dated 28 May. It listed the composition of the committee as Professor Hawthorne,* Professor of Applied Thermodynamics at Cambridge, as Chairman, and Sir William Cook,* of the UK Atomic Energy Authority, Mr Lighthill,* Director of the RAE, and Sir Graham Sutton,* Director-General of the Meteorological Office, as members, with Hayne Constant, the Ministry's Scientific Adviser, and the Deputy Chief of the Air Staff acting 'in all respects as members'. Dean said: 'As I told you at lunch recently I very much hope that you will consider becoming a member of this committee [known as the Air Ministry Strategic Scientific Policy Committee]. One of the points I had in mind is of course that sooner or later the Royal Air Force is likely to want to enter Space. Another point—among many others—is the future of military communications.'

Lovell was quick to respond on 1 June: 'I think there is no doubt that it should be both a duty and a pleasure for me to join this party . . . your conversation raised my spirit about the possibility of the country's Space activities, and it would make me most happy if I could help in any way. Presumably you saw the paragraph in The Times yesterday to the effect that France is about to launch its own satellite. What an indignity for the UK this will be.'

Apart from the close co-operation on the use of the Jodrell Bank telescope as a 'stand-in' for defence against ballistic missiles, Lovell's contribution to this committee and to Zuckerman's panel of scientists was significant in respect of his advice on the design of Fylingdales. Moreover, he persuaded the Air Ministry to press for a military communications satellite system, but due to the massive reorganization of the three Services under the one Ministry—the Ministry of Defence—coming at the critical moment, the idea of any independent Space activities was lost in the confusion and then abandoned by the incoming Labour Government in October 1964. In fact, Lovell was advised by a letter dated 30 June 1964 that, due to the creation of a unified Ministry of Defence, the Air Ministry Strategic Scientific Policy Committee was to be dissolved. This letter went on to thank him for his 'most valuable contribution to the Committee's deliberations and for the benefit this has brought to the Royal Air Force'.

Lovell's suspicions, held earlier, that Britain was going to opt out of its own independent Space Programme were soon to be irrevocably confirmed.

20

The Rainbow Bomb

From August 1957 to August 1970 the radio telescope, known as the Mk 1, gathered information from 68,538 hours of operational use. 4,877 hours were categorized as 'miscellaneous use', consisting of assistance to Government agencies, both British and foreign—7.1 per cent of the telescope's operational time. Of this 'miscellaneous use' 2,498 hours, or 3.6 per cent, were employed directly in collaboration with the USA and USSR in their Space Programmes. From the advent of *Sputnik I* in October 1957 up to the early sixties, the proportion of time spent in connection with the USA and USSR Space activities was relatively very small, but it was nonetheless the main reason for the immense public interest in the Jodrell Bank radio telescope. Whilst this interest arose from a use of the telescope for which it was never intended, it was of considerable importance to the support gained for radio astronomical activities in the United Kingdom.

By 1960 Lovell was having dreams of more and bigger radio telescopes, an optimism which was quite undaunted by the financial problems associated with the existing instrument which were still unresolved, and stimulated by the very considerable demands upon the existing instrument which were becoming excessive. At the end of 1959 and the beginning of 1960 he had informal discussions with H.C. Husband on the possibilities of designing a telescope with a 1,000-foot paraboloid. In 1959 Lovell, jointly with Martin Ryle of Cambridge, had put forward a paper for consideration by the DSIR on 'The Future of Radio Astronomy in Great Britain'. This had been discussed by the Astronomy Sub-Committee of the DSIR in the spring of 1960, and it was at this meeting that Lovell pressed his proposal for a much larger telescope. Remarkably, the DSIR agreed to make a grant of £10,000 for a 'design study to be made of a steerable radio telescope of significantly greater size than the 250 ft. instrument now in operation at Jodrell Bank.' In fact, there were major problems associated with the idea of a telescope expanded from 250 to 1,000 feet in size, Husband being particularly concerned about the height at which the 1,000-foot paraboloid would have to be mounted in relation to wind effects, a height considerably greater than that of the present telescope. As a result of design studies, an application was made to the DSIR on 19 December 1960 for £173,228 for the construction of a prototype telescope with an elliptical aperture of 125 feet × 83 feet 4 inches. Husband had felt that it would be practical to build a telescope elliptical in shape with the height limited to between 300 and 600 feet, and the horizontal dimensions of the bowl extended to 1,000 feet. In the application Lovell explained that the prototype was required for two reasons. First and foremost the new approach in design to accommodate the much enlarged bowl, or paraboloid, was so radically different that it was necessary to build a scaled-down instrument to test the practicability of the new concept before embarking upon what could well be a £10–20 million project. The second reason was that it would be many years before the grandiose scheme could be completed, financial considerations apart, and in the meantime new research facilities were required at Jodrell Bank because the existing telescope was so overloaded with work. This tele-scope was to be called the Mk II.

Two months later, on 21 February 1961, Lovell, with outrageous optimism, applied for £109,850 for a Mk III instrument with a bowl of the same size and shape as the Mk II but constructed with a wire mesh as opposed to one of solid steel. It was to be a less accurate but a transport-able version of the Mk II and was to act as an essential part of the interferometric facilities in combination with the Mk I telescope for the measurement of angular diameters of radio sources in the heavens. It was therefore necessary for it to be transportable to provide varying baselines.

It is doubtful whether an event at the beginning of 1961 encouraged Lovell in his confident, almost presumptuous, approach to the DSIR for two substantial sums of money when the Government's strictures over the financial problems of the Mk I telescope were still fresh in everyone's mind. Regardless of the wonderful news affecting his personal prestige, he would almost certainly have proceeded in the same manner, but he may have been slightly encouraged by the unexpected recognition of his activities. In the New Year's Honours List of 1961, Lovell was created a Knight of the Realm. In February Queen Elizabeth, the Queen Mother, deputizing for Queen Elizabeth II, touched with her sword the shoulders of this kneeling buccaneer of the twentieth century—a buccaneer in the interests of Britain's exploration of the Universe—and pronounced: 'Arise, Sir Bernard.' It was most appropriate that Elizabeth II should have conferred this great honour, thus emulating her predecessor, Elizabeth I of England, who had knighted other notable buccaneers, explorers of the uncharted world in the interests of their country.

However, it was not until December 1961, after much wrangling over finances and after Lovell had rewritten the application for the Mk II telescope emphasizing its requirement for increased researches and no longer calling it a prototype for a much larger future telescope which had Treasury circles worried, that the DSIR gave the go-ahead. Moreover, it was not until the summer of 1964 that the new telescope was completed on the site of the original 218-foot transit telescope which the Lovell family, Clegg and other members of the early team had erected in 1947. Since 1964 the Mk II has played a significant part in the Jodrell Bank researches both on its own or as an interferometer with the Mk I.

The DSIR grant for the Mk III telescope did not fare so well. It was not that the DSIR was lacking in enthusiasm for the Mk III but rather that they felt a further large grant on top of that for the Mk II, when there was so much competition for funds for other projects such as those associated with nuclear physics, would be frowned on by the Treasury. Nevertheless, early in 1962 the astronomy sub-committee of the DSIR expressed the opinion that £40,000 might be found from their allocated funds as a contribution towards the project, leaving Lovell to find a sum in the region of £70,000 from other sources. Lovell was undaunted and set about trying to interest some of his friends in the USA in joining his project, taking immediate advantage of his visit to America in March 1962 when he was due to give the Condon Lectures in Oregon on 'The Impact of Modern Astronomy on the Problems of the Origins of Life and the Cosmos'.

But none of Lovell's attempts to obtain outside assistance succeeded. Fate was to smile on him later, however, when in August 1963 Treasury approval was given to the DSIR to make a grant of £115,000 for the construction of the Mk III telescope which was ultimately completed by the beginning of 1966 and initially sited at Wardle near Nantwich in Cheshire.

The 'giant' telescope that was to follow the Mk II prototype, and which was called the Mk IV, never did materialize. Instead, the Mk I was modified to give a greatly superior performance and was named the Mk 1A; but that was much later.

1960 to 1964 were years packed full of variations for Lovell, quite apart from his knighthood and his successful struggles to increase the facilities for researches into the composition of the Universe and to determine its beginnings. A major research programme since the Mk I telescope had come into use had been, and still was, the study of radio emission from certain types of stars in the Universe which are close to the Solar System. A long period of observation had already yielded results which seemed likely to open up a new avenue for the exploration of the atmospheres of the stars. Moreover, it was beginning to appear that the galaxies with which astronomers had been familiar over the past twenty years might not be the only type of galaxies existing in the Universe, and that a new breed of galaxy might exist consisting of an extremely dense nucleus in which the processes of radiation are not only those associated with hot stars but might be a radiation of a synchrotron type both in the optical and radio regions. But in 1960, whilst Lovell's interest covered all these areas of research, as well as co-operation with the USA and the Soviet Union in their Space activities, his immediate concern was with 'radio' stars.

Late in the summer of 1960 Professor Fred Whipple made a trip to Britain. His prime interest on this occasion was Jodrell Bank, and whilst staying with the Lovells discussions took place on collaborative research into flare stars, phenomena which two years earlier in 1958 had begun to attract Lovell's attention. These were what were known as 'red dwarfs', stars which are normally very faint but which are characterized by the occurrence of sudden irregular and short-lived increases in brightness, increases of half a magnitude occurring every few hours and of one to two magnitudes every few days. Some outburst on the star's surface is responsible for these sudden increases in brightness, not unlike the flares which the Sun exhibits on a much smaller scale. Indeed, in 1948 an American astronomer, W. J. Luyten, discovered the binary star U V Ceti, the second nearest star to Earth in Space, and observed in December of that year a variation of two magnitudes in brightness of the star. He estimated the flare energy to be 4×10^{24} joules, which was in excess of the energies of the most violent solar flares, and 100 to 1,000 times in excess of the energies of the more frequent solar flares. Observations of flares on other red dwarf stars gave similar energies. It was on the basis of these estimates that Lovell began investigating flare stars in the metre waveband in 1958 with the radio telescope at Jodrell Bank.[1] However, corroboration that the bursts of radio emission were actually associated with the flares was necessary because the short-duration signals for which the telescope was searching were often produced from many terrestrial sources. Simultaneous visual or photographic observations were needed for correct identification. Lovell managed to stimulate Whipple's interest in a collaborative programme, and Whipple suggested using the Baker-Nunn cameras of the Smithsonian Satellite Tracking Network, which in Iran, South Africa, Spain, Curaçao and the Argentine were conveniently distributed around the longitude of Jodrell Bank. This collaborative programme began on 28 September 1960 and continued with considerable success into 1963, the details of the observing programme and the handling and study of the photographic results being conducted by Whipple's staff at the Smithsonian Astrophysical Observatory at Cambridge, Massachusetts. By the autumn of 1963, as a result of a visit by Lovell to the Soviet Union, Russian astronomers were also collaborating

[1] For those interested in the more detailed scientific astronomical studies of Jodrell Bank, *Out of the Zenith—Jodrell Bank 1957–1970* by Sir Bernard Lovell, published by the Oxford University Press, is strongly recommended. It is not the purpose of this biography to go into scientific details.

with the USA and Jodrell Bank in this extensive scientific study of flare stars.

Collaboration with the Russians on some aspects of Space research had already begun, as the reader will have realized, although it had not been on such a frank and open basis as that with the USA. However, despite the excellent relations which Lovell had established with the astronomical fraternity in the USA and with NASA, there were moments of serious conflict about American activities in Space in 1962, the most notable being the controversy over the 'Starfish' explosion. This was a 1.5 megaton nuclear bomb, known as the 'Rainbow Bomb', which was launched from Johnston Island in the Pacific on 9 July and exploded at an altitude of 250 miles. It followed another US experiment in Space which had caused the scientific community deep concern. The military need for secret communications via Space led the United States to experiment in 1961 with a system by which it was proposed to encircle the Earth at an altitude of a few thousand kilometres with 350 million pieces of wire which were to act as reflecting dipoles. The project was known as the 'West Ford' or 'Needle' project, and a test belt was placed in orbit. It was evident to Lovell and Martin Ryle that an operational system would prove to be a serious interference with some astronomical researches of import-ance, and in 1962 they published a paper in the Quarterly Journal of the Royal Astronomical Society under the title 'Interference to Radio Astronomy from Belts of Orbiting Dipoles (Needles)'. It was a strong protest which included detailed calculations of the disruptive effects to astronomical research. Fortunately the US Defense Department aban-doned the plan in favour of the more conventional satellite systems of today.

The announcement of the H-bomb test was made at the beginning of May, and it brought a torrent of criticism and counter-criticism from the scientific world. The most outspoken voice against such tests was that of Lovell. His protest was, however, directed against the test because of the destructive effect it was likely to have on astronomical research with radio telescopes, and he was careful to emphasize that he was not taking part in the controversy about atmospheric tests leading to nuclear fall-out as he had no professional competence to speak on such a matter. In the London *Observer* of 6 May, recounting the disruptive effects of the 'Project Argus' tests in the South Atlantic in 1958, when nuclear devices of one to three kilotons were exploded at an altitude of 300 miles, he asked what a megaton—a thousand times the power—would do. The particular inter-ference with the environment of the Earth to which he referred concerned the belt of radiation trapped in the magnetic field of Earth which was discovered by Professor J. A. van Allen in 1958 and which is known as the 'van Allen Belt'. This radiation consists of atomic particles such as electrons and protons bouncing backwards and forwards under the influence of the Earth's magnetic field. Lovell predicted that the explosion would either disrupt the existing van Allen zones or give rise to a new zone of trapped particles which could seriously affect long-range communications and the operation of communications satellites such as Telstar, Transit and the experimental British Ariel satellite which had been launched by an American rocket, and cause serious interference with radio astronomical research. He emphasized that there was a possibility that the inner part of the 'van Allen Belt', denuded of radiation, might not be restored for several years, resulting in scientists being robbed of the opportunity to study this region of Earth's environment in its natural state. He was not alone in voicing alarm at the idea of a nuclear test in the atmosphere of substantial proportions without a full international scientific study of the likely effects. Whilst he dismissed any likelihood of 'fall-out', he accused a small group of military scientists, unknown and unidentified to the world at large, who had persuaded their masters to take a series of huge gambles under the guise of defensive necessity. 'On the scale of the cosmos they are dealing with fireworks,' he wrote. 'Nevertheless the Earth is so minute on the cosmic scale and its environment is controlled by the delicate balance of such great natural forces that one must view with dismay a potential interference with these processes before they are investigated by the delicate tools of the true scientist.' He went on to point out that both Russia and America had subscribed to the resolutions of the International Astronomical Union that no group had a right to change the Earth's environment in any significant way without full international study and agreement.

On 29 May, whilst conceding that the Americans had announced their intentions quite openly, which was in marked contrast to the secretiveness of the Russians, he stated that they were proposing to take 'unilateral action, against the accumulated wisdom and advice of those who still have freedom to speak in the international community, with an utter contempt for the grave moral issues involved.' He added that the much-vaunted dedication of the USA to the peaceful use of extra-terrestrial space would now be seen as a veil which could be torn asunder at the convenience of the American militarists and their attendant scientists.

Professor S. Fred Singer of the University of Maryland, an American authority on high-altitude physics, was quick to enter into dispute with Lovell, but in balanced and constrained fashion. He wrote in the London *Observer* of 3 June that such phrases in Lovell's criticism as 'a series of huge gambles' and 'grave moral consequences' implied that the proposed 'Starfish' explosion would 'somehow upset nature and cause calamities here on Earth. Nothing,' he continued, 'could be farther from the truth. The effects are closely predictable, small and harmless. Basic physical considerations show that the Earth's natural radiation belt will be only slightly perturbed: and even this perturbation will be temporary.' He insisted that even a major temporary modification of the radiation belts should not be cause for objecting to high-altitude nuclear tests. If it were, he said, 'then we must object to solar flares, which produce changes of a factor of 10 within the inner radiation belt. And we must object to magnetic storms which occur occasionally, and which will change the intensity in the outer radiation belt by as much as a factor of 100.' These natural fluctuations, he averred, were far greater than any man-made effect. Indeed, he claimed that a controlled modification of the trapped radiation, not necessarily as a result of bomb explosions, was 'precisely what one needs to determine some important properties of the radiation'. Singer then criticized Lovell's opinion of America's military scientists as 'uncharitable' and 'unjustified'. Whilst admitting that high-altitude tests were conducted purely for military reasons, he said that: 'It is evidently important to evaluate the effects of nuclear weapons exploded at various altitudes so that better defences against ballistic missiles can be constructed. . . .'

Singer did, however, agree with Lovell on the matter of principle that no government has the right to change the environment in any significant way without prior international study and agreement. On this score he believed that the USA had, so far, done reasonably well in giving 'full advance announcements', whereas the Soviet Union had 'never made any prior announcement of Space launchings or other Space experiments, or even made detailed disclosures following the experiments'. In the face of this persistent Soviet attitude of complete secrecy, Singer felt it might prove difficult for scientific groups to persuade the American Government to release more information than it was already doing. But it is to be hoped, he said, 'that the open discussion initiated by Professor Lovell and others will help to improve the situation in this respect'.

Professor J. A. van Allen, and Dr Herbert Friedman of the US Naval Research Laboratory, both specialists in cosmic rays and solar research, added their defence of the proposed American nuclear test. They announced their opinion that the bomb explosion would have no serious or lasting effect on the radiation zone and added their belief that it would yield important scientific knowledge about radiation and cosmic phenomena. Dr Friedman, who was a member of the Committee on Space Research—Cospar—for the Third International Space Science Symposium, went further. In referring to the fact that the USA, through the Academy of Sciences, submits its proposals for Space experiments to Cospar, he made the statement: 'We welcome comments, suggestions and views of all members; and these are given serious consideration in all planning and programming. However, we will not yield the authority for final decision to any international body.' He added that in deciding on any Space experiment a competent group of US scientists weigh the knowledge expected to be gained against any of the risks which may result in interfering with other areas of scientific research. 'When the gains overbalance the risks,' he said, 'the decision is made to experiment.'

Metaphorically, Lovell was to have the last word. In Washington, on 20 August, just over a month after the high-altitude explosion, van Allen admitted that the new belt of high-energy radiation which had been formed around the Earth as a result of the test had increased the potential danger for manned Space flights. This was a matter for concern in America. On 21 February 1962 Colonel John Glenn had successfully undertaken America's first manned space flight, completing three orbits as compared to the one orbit by Russia's Yuri Gagarin in April 1961. Anxious to stay ahead of Russia in Space activities, further manned flights were scheduled, but now the hazards of the new radiation belt, and the duration of the potential dangers to man in Space, threatened the schedule for such experiments. By September three experimental satellites had had their communications systems knocked out completely. They were Transit IVB and its companion satellite Traac, and the British satellite, Ariel. Telstar also failed, and although it revived temporarily, it became completely dead a few months later.

This was not all. Also in September Dr George C. McVittie, of the University of Illinois Observatory, said experiments with the Observatory's radio telescope had been seriously damaged. Dr J. Allen Hynek, the director of Northwestern University's Dearborn Observatory, reported that the radiation resulting from the bomb was a matter of serious scientific concern and agreed with McVittie that Lovell's views had been vindicated and that the explosion should not have been carried out. Hynek observed to a Chicago newspaper, however, that 'at least the government is honest' by publicly reporting that the bomb's radiation was much stronger than anticipated. McVittie, in fact, wrote a letter to Lovell, dated 2 September, in which he said: 'You were right and I was wrong—and how! I am particularly enraged at having been so naïve and trusting. . . .' He went on to say that he had been taken in by the US Government's assurances that the bomb would not contaminate Space and affect research. He was not the only one to write apologetically. As reported in *Topic* on 3 November 1962:

America continued her high altitude nuclear tests last week, but only at a height of 20 to 30 miles. President Kennedy's scientists seemed to be deferring to Sir Bernard Lovell, director of Jodrell Bank Experimental Station in

Cheshire. Before the rainbow high-altitude test of July 9, Lovell warned of the serious threat to the future of radio astronomy research. His strictures annoyed America and, apparently, embarrassed scientists and politicians in Britain. The effects of the bomb have proved him right, and he is still receiving written apologies from American Space Scientists who criticised him then. Lovell says: 'It seems that one cannot raise one's voice without being accused of being what the Americans call pink—a fellow-traveller. That has hurt me very much. I am not pink or anything like it. I was extremely upset by the bitterness with which some close American friends attacked me, but I have since been delighted by their letters of apology. They have been most generous about it, and admit that I was right and they were wrong. They agree that the effects of the explosion were not predicted even approximately'. . . .

Lovell's outspoken criticism of the 'Starfish' explosion, better known as the 'Rainbow Bomb' explosion, echoed throughout Government circles to no mean effect. Shortly after his outburst in the London *Observer* on 6 May, he received a letter from P. L. Woodfield of the Prime Minister's office, dated 17 May, stating that the Prime Minister 'has of course read your published views about the proposed high altitude nuclear tests. He has, however, asked me to write to you to say that he would be very grateful if you would be so good as to send him a memorandum setting out your considered views on this question.' Lovell promptly prepared a paper on the matter and despatched it on 21 May. It was a very comprehensive and explicit paper, in three parts. Part I summarized present knowledge of the regions of Space likely to be influenced by the nuclear explosion; Part II discussed the probable effects of the proposed explosion of a 1.5 megaton bomb, referring, as an example, to the disruptive effects of the September 1958 'Project Argus' experiment in which nuclear devices of only one to three kilotons were exploded at an altitude of 300 miles; and Part III covered the more general issues affecting international science which were raised by the proposal to go ahead with the project. It was emphasized that the memorandum was 'concerned solely with the geophysical and astronomical aspects of the problem'. On 30 May the Prime Minister, Harold Macmillan, acknowledged receipt of Lovell's communication, saying: 'I am grateful to you for your prompt response to my suggestion that you might send me a memorandum setting out your views on the high altitude nuclear explosions . . . I have studied your views myself, and have taken steps to see that the attention of the appropriate United States authorities is drawn to them.'

Despite protests to the United States Government, and consideration being given to bringing the question of high-altitude nuclear tests before the International Court of Justice at The Hague, nothing was done. In fact, the Prime Minister, in the end, admitted that the British

Government had consistently given public support to the decision of the United States to conduct a series of high-altitude tests. 'We have based our support,' he wrote, 'on the great importance of these tests to our defence.' Nevertheless, after the explosion of the 'Rainbow Bomb' on 9 July 1962, Lord Hailsham, the Minister for Science in the Conservative Government, was instructed by the Prime Minister to call upon the Government's steering-group on Space research, which was under the chairmanship of Sir Edward Bullard,* 'to set up a working party to consider on the basis of available unclassified information the effects of high-level nuclear explosions on scientific experiments, and to report their views to the Minister through the steering group'. J. A. Ratcliffe, the director of the DSIR's radio research division, was appointed chairman, and Lovell was co-opted as a member. In their report it was stated that the artificial release of large numbers of charged particles in localized regions of Space can have very damaging effects on scientific experiments. Whilst the release from nuclear explosions in the high atmosphere was the only topic dealt with by the working-party, they wanted it noted 'that there are inherent dangers to science in other recent proposals, for example, to make nuclear explosions on the moon, or to release radioactive debris from nuclear-powered rockets'. They went on to say that the explosion of 9 July 1962 had injected particles into the high atmosphere which had become trapped in the Earth's magnetic field in numbers sufficient to make an important change in the charged particle environment of the Earth. 'It will not now be possible,' they said, 'to observe some aspects of the original natural environment until it is clear that the artificial content has effectively disappeared, and on present estimates this may not be until one or more years have elapsed.'

The main conclusion of Bullard's steering-group, after studying the working-party's report, was that high-altitude nuclear explosions of the US Rainbow Bomb type have serious adverse effects on scientific research and other Space activities such as communications, meteorological and navigational satellites and, therefore, any further proposed experiments of this kind should be openly discussed—as far as defence considerations permit—with the scientists whose work might be affected. Their recommendation was that, when any more high-level nuclear explosions were contemplated by any country, they should first be discussed by an international group of scientists who should be given the task of advising how the explosion should be planned, (a) so as not to interfere with any known scientific researches and (b) so as to produce the most valuable scientific results. A body under the International Council of Scientific Unions, such as Cospar, was proposed as a suitable international group.

The findings of the working-party and the main conclusions of the steering-group were published in a White Paper on Thursday 16 May 1963 and discussed in the House of Commons at Prime Minister's question-time on the same day. Harold Macmillan, the Prime Minister, said that the report of the working-party and the steering-group's conclusions had been sent by the Government to the United States Government. He also stated that the British Government were always closely informed by the US Administration about such experiments as those under discussion, which were of the greatest importance and significance to vital aspects of defence. When pressed by MPs to take the initiative to try to establish some degree of international control over nuclear experiments in Space, Macmillan said: 'The only final and satisfactory action would be if we could abolish these tests altogether by both sides.'

In the House of Lords, on the same day, Lord Hailsham announced the conclusions of the Bullard steering-group. The question of persuading the US Government to agree to some form of international control of nuclear experiments in Space was, he believed, a difficult one. Whilst there was no doubt that scientific opinion in Britain considered that these experiments were a matter of international concern which required discussion, he emphasized that, on the other hand, the government of any country was concerned with national security, and in the present state of disarmament negotiations it was uncertain how far one could proceed successfully in this matter. 'There have been Russian nuclear high-altitude tests as well, which equally could cause trouble,' he said. 'One has to face the fact that tests in the high atmosphere are one of the consequences of the failure of the Powers to reach a test ban agreement or a disarmament agreement. In the absence of this the most one can do is to make representations when one knows of anything in the air.'

Nevertheless, Lovell's outspoken campaign had a dramatic effect in influencing scientific opinion in America and Russia, and, in turn, in influencing the Governments of the US and the Soviet Union. In June 1963, after the report of the working-party on nuclear tests in the atmosphere, together with the conclusions of the steering-group, had been sent to the US Government, John F. Kennedy, the President of the United States of America, announced that three-power talks between the UK, USA and Soviet Union on nuclear testing would resume in Moscow. This was a continuation of talks which had begun during 1958 and which had resulted in a temporary moratorium on testing going into effect on 3 October 1958, a ban which had lasted up till 1 September 1961, when the Soviet Union had resumed atmospheric testing with thirty tests, including one with a yield of 60 megatons. The renewed talks in 1963 culminated in an agreement to ban all nuclear tests in the atmosphere, outer Space and underwater. Tests held underground were not banned. This Nuclear Test-Ban Treaty was signed on 5 August in the St Catherine's Hall of the Kremlin, in the presence of the United Nations Secretary-General, U. Thant, by the Soviet Union, the USA and the UK and, with the exchange of instruments of ratification by these three countries, came into force on 10 October 1963.

21

Eupatoria

Of the many visits Lovell made to foreign countries, those to the Soviet Union had a special feeling of pioneering. Some of the first Soviet scientists to emerge from the USSR after the war came to Jodrell, and these early contacts between individuals who hitherto had been merely names in scientific literature were unforgettable. These contacts and his first return visit in 1958, mentioned earlier, were to lead to many valuable collaborative scientific enterprises in astronomical and Space research.

The co-operation provided by Jodrell Bank when the Russians lost touch with their Venus probe, launched on 12 February 1961, had created an atmosphere of considerable goodwill. In June 1961, as related in the previous chapter, Professor Alla Massevitch and Dr Khodarev had visited Lovell and worked with his team in searching for the probe, liaison being maintained by telephone between the small laboratory at Jodrell Bank and a control centre in the Soviet Union.

Undoubtedly this collaboration was one major factor in stimulating plans for Lovell to spend some time in the Soviet Union in 1963. In March he received an invitation from M. V. Keldysh, the President of the Academy of Sciences of the USSR, to visit the Soviet Union for three weeks as the guest of the Academy. Keldysh wrote that he would be given the opportunity to see astronomical and radio-astronomical observatories in Moscow, Pulkovo, the Crimea and Bjurakan and to become acquainted with their work. Keldysh also expressed the hope that Lovell would 'agree to present several talks to the scientists of these observatories and inform them on some results of research work done at Jodrell Bank.'

At that time information reaching the West about Soviet facilities for astronomical and Space research was scarce, and Lovell eagerly accepted this invitation. On 25 June he left London for Moscow in a Soviet TU 104 jet.

Although Lovell was not a habitual keeper of a diary, he did so during the building of the Mk 1 telescope, and he did so now, so that he would not have to trust only his memory about the facilities and research he expected to see in the Soviet Union. Inevitably and fortunately this diary records many aspects of his visit that reveal the excitement and problems facing a visitor to the Soviet Union at that time.

'Today I woke up in Swettenham and went to bed in Moscow,' he wrote. 'With the heavens emptying I said goodbye to the children with

Roger adding to the downpour because we wouldn't let him cycle to school. Bryan still at Oxford [completing his third year] with the last day of exams but expected home tomorrow. . . . The Vanguard which should have left at 10.20 (from Manchester) actually left 15 minutes late and because of a queue over London we weren't down until 11.35. London looked miserable with little hope of the Test Match [with Australia] being resumed.' Lovell's obsession with cricket never waned.

His diary for the 25th continued: 'The TU 104 which brought us to Moscow left punctually at 12.20. Clearly the Russians are terrifically proud of the aircraft. A man from the Embassy who welcomed me aboard was at pains to explain that it was the first jet to fly in service. . . . The Captain looked as though he would be willing to take it into orbit if ordered to do so by the Kremlin! The hostess eagerly pointed out the speed and height and the landmarks "according to schedule".'

The arrival in Moscow was on time, and apart from the Russian welcoming party led by Dr Oraevsky of the Academy of Sciences, who was to be Lovell's constant companion during his visit, he was also met by Mr Garratt, the Scientific Attaché at the British Embassy. Alla Massevitch was in the Russian party to greet him, and it was from her that there came a surprising remark. Her first words were, 'But where is your wife?' In fact, a few days previously Lovell had received a message from Mikhailov, the director of the Pulkovo Observatory, and a cable from Moscow, that 'Academy extends invitation Lady Lovell accompany you as guest of the Academy.' In her greeting Massevitch seemed blissfully unaware that in Britain, as in the Soviet Union, many problems had to be surmounted and visas obtained. In the event Joyce arrived at Moscow airport on 5 July.

In the intervening days Lovell was to see many extraordinary facets of life in the Soviet Union, and scientific developments which were entirely new to him. Immediately on his arrival Oraevsky suggested that perhaps he would like to attend the press conference at Moscow University which was being given for the Russian astronauts, including Colonel Bykorsky and Valentina Tereshkova, who on 14 and 15 June had been launched into orbit, both returning to Earth on 19 June. He wrote: 'The Conference was in the great hall of the University which we used during the 1958 I.A.U. [International Astronomical Union] Assembly. It was crammed with a galaxy of TV and other cameras such as I've never before seen. The President of the Academy, Keldysh, was seated with all six astronauts on the platform. . . . We had already missed the first hour but even so were in time to hear Bykorsky and Tereshkova—I should think it would be quite a while before a more attractive astronautess goes into Space!'

The next morning Lovell attended a discussion at the Academy of Sciences with Academician V. A. Ambartsumian of the Bjurakan

Observatory, Professor V. V. Vitkevitch, the Chief of Department of Radio Astronomy, Khodarev, the designer of the Venus probe and Director of the Crimean deep Space tracking-station and certain members of the foreign department. Following a TV interview, he was given some idea of the programme that had been prepared for him. However, it was not until his meeting with Keldysh that he was to learn the more detailed plans for his visit. 'At 2.30,' he wrote in his diary, 'an audience with President Keldysh. A somewhat more impressive approach than [to] that of the President in the White House. Up the wide stairs through the palatial rooms of an ex-Tsar's wife, through enormous rooms of secretaries and telephones, guarding the President's rooms, who had 4 telephones on a side table and roses on his desk. . . .' Ambartsumian was also present with Vitkevitch and two others. After the pleasantries, the meeting got down to a discussion on Space in which Keldysh gave his view that the Russian programme for the future would include an extension of manned Space flights, a continuation of probes to the Moon and the planets, and the establishment of manned platforms in Space. Lovell was then closely questioned on his views about the necessity of putting a man on the Moon for really satisfactory research purposes as compared with relying upon instruments soft-landed on the Moon. It was clear to Lovell that the Russians were uncertain about a manned landing and that there was opposition to such a project, although he detected that Keldysh probably was in favour and in the midst of arguments about the idea. This was not so different from the situation in the West, which had led Lovell to conjecture that Russia would be first on the Moon. Now, however, he revised his ideas. 'At least I realise now,' he wrote, 'that to talk of a Russian Moon landing in 1968 or 1970 means nothing more than guessing at dates which they themselves are not even doing.'

Nevertheless, Keldysh expressed an earnest desire for international co-operation in a lunar programme, saying that the first step would be for scientists to agree in an international document on what they wanted to find out about the Moon and advise on the experiments to be performed.

On the question of prestige as a possible reason for the USSR's investments in Space, Lovell wrote: 'The President said that a country's scientific effort was a most significant contribution to the standing of a country in the eyes of other nations. He was good enough to illustrate this by pointing out that Jodrell had enormously contributed and added to the prestige of the UK in the USSR.' It was then that Keldysh delighted Lovell by informing him that he was to be shown the Soviet deep Space tracking-facilities in the Crimea, a station about which no information had emerged to Western ears. He said that he was anxious that Lovell, after seeing the deep Space tracking-centre, should discuss with the scientists involved, and with himself, the possibilities of co-operation by Jodrell Bank in these activities.

But at least some of Lovell's thoughts were still in Britain: 'Garratt phoned this morning [27 June] to find out if all was well and with the incredible news about the Test Match. They played after lunch and it was drawn with England's last pair needing 6 runs to win and with Cowdrey having had to come out with his broken arm.'

On 27 June Lovell, accompanied by Oraevsky, flew to the Crimea for the start of his tour. At Simferopol Airport they were met by Professor Severney, director of the Crimean Astrophysical Observatory, and then drove to the Observatory, which was high in the Crimean mountains, nearly 2,000 feet up at Nauchny.[1] There he was greeted by Alla Massevitch and her attractive young daughter Natasha, as well as by other well-known Russian astronomers, including Shklovsky, with whom Lovell had discussions on his interpretation of the newly discovered radio sources named quasars (quasi-stellar radio sources)—the most distant objects in the Universe yet discovered. (For an account of the discovery of these objects and particularly of the part played by Jodrell Bank see *Out of the Zenith* by Sir Bernard Lovell, published by the Oxford University Press.)

The following morning Lovell delivered his promised lecture to the summer school at the Observatory. Just after this lecture he was handed a telegram from his son Bryan announcing that he had gained a 'Top Second' in his degree and had been offered a £200 grant for research. Lovell immediately despatched his congratulations and advised him to accept the grant. He signed it 'Pater and all Soviet astronomers'. The rest of the weekend was occupied by visits to the 100-inch telescope at the Observatory, other installations and laboratories in the area, interspersed with sight-seeing at the ancient city of Bakhchisarai.

On 1 July, accompanied by Alla Massevitch and Severney in a chauffeur-driven car, Lovell was taken to the Soviet Union's deep Space tracking-centre. In another car were Oraevsky and Khodarev.

We proceeded through Simferopol along the airport road and then turned N.W. After about 2 hours we passed through the mineral water health resort of Saki and then soon reached the W. coast of the Black Sea where we bathed on a beach 10 km long, deserted except at the N end where it became Eupatoria. K [Khodarev] pointed to the peninsula W of Eupatoria and said his antennas were there but we could not see them. So we proceeded through

[1] During his visit Lovell was taken to the original site of the Crimean Observatory, at Simiez high above the Black Sea coast. The observatory had been destroyed by the Germans during World War II. The telescope mirror had been buried, but its location was betrayed by the Tartars and the invaders riddled it with bullets.

Eupatoria and then along a road past the railway station where a train from Moscow had just arrived. After 10 km we turned left along a rough, dusty road which was little more than a track through a cornfield. By this time the antennas were looming before our eyes and I was soon able to recognise the multiple array of 8, 16 m dishes which had been described to us. But there were 3 of them! (three of the multiple arrays)—one far away to the left of our road.

The next few hours were an absolute whirl during which Lovell was surrounded by at least ten and sometimes twenty Russians, many talking simultaneously whilst he tried to grasp the main features of this extra-ordinary place. The start of the tour took place in a rather roughly constructed building 'equal to our worst wartime construction' which was the control room of the telescopes. It was differently designed to the Jodrell control room but performed about the same function and was similarly equipped. From there he was shown the antennae consisting of eight 16-metre paraboloids or dishes, mounted on a 'bedstead' frame, each dish being accurate to 3 millimetres and aligned individually on a radio source, the whole completely steerable in azimuth and elevation. What Lovell could not deduce with his own eyes about these installations and their performance, he was able to discover from answers to his questions. The same frankness appeared to be the case when he was shown the receivers, the telemetry room, the tape-recording room and the radar-receiving system which had been successfully used in 1962 and early 1963 to obtain radar echoes from Mercury and Mars.

The transmitting site was 10 kilometres distant. Adjacent to one of the telescopes was the entrance to the air-conditioned underground warren of laboratories into which he and his escort descended. In his diary he recorded his observations. 'Master frequency is a quartz crystal in a special room with a temperature control to a few thousandths of a degree. The frequency is 100 Kc/s. Constant to 1 in 10^{10} over a 10 minute period and 1 in 2 or 3×10^{10} over 24 hour periods (and this has been maintained for 3 years). The multipliers are in an adjacent air conditioned room. . . . Another room contains the build up of the signal to 700 Mc/s at which level it goes to the transmitting hall, an enormous room containing six 20 kw klystron transmitters! The construction and plumbing into the waveguides is magnificent. Either or all of these transmitters can be paralleled to the telescope. . . . The control desk for the transmitters is in this hall. . . .' More than 100 kilowatts of energy at 700 MHZ (Mc/s) could be fed into the telescope for the control of space probes, so lethal to humans that it could never be used below 10 degrees elevation. Indeed, during operation the radiation from the aerial was such, Lovell was told, that all surrounding personnel were always evacuated to a safe distance.

This transmitting-site was also the headquarters of the deep Space tracking-station and contained a 'hotel' with living-quarters and excellent messing-facilities. It was here, late in the afternoon, that Lovell had lunch with his escorting party of many Russians, some of whom he knew well and could recognize and others who were unknown to him. Here there were discussions about the day's visit, and Lovell raised the possibility of co-operation, but it was agreed that these matters could best be discussed after their return to the Crimean Observatory.

Lovell realized that by arranging for this visit the Academy had greatly honoured him. He had seen the latest Soviet engineering and electronic developments, the details of which the authorities had not yet released. Indeed, his cameras were taken from him on arrival with the promise that he would be sent photographs when the details of the installation were made public. (The photographs have not yet arrived.)

The long journeys, the intense heat and the excitement of the tour were exhausting, and when he returned to the Crimean Observatory that evening, Lovell hoped that the day was over. But his hosts had other ideas. He wrote:

This was the last day of the summer school and M [Massevitch] had organised a concert followed by a banquet and dance. At 7.30 p.m. when one might reasonably be expecting to be eating and resting after such a day, M sent O [Oraevsky] to get me as the guest of honour to perform in the concert. I acquitted myself by playing a few pages of Cesar Franck's 3rd organ chorale which fortunately I had with me in case a keyboard came my way. The concert was really quite good, contributed by young people from the school singing and dancing, including a marvellous performance by Natasha [Alla Massevitch's daughter]. Surely she will become a ballerina! When we finally returned to the hotel it was 9.30 p.m. Dinner had been prepared for us at 5—heaven knows why because we were eating our lunch at Eupatoria then! So we went to the courtyard for the banquet—a buffet with much wine. The fountains were playing, it was floodlit, and as hunger was assuaged the beauty of the scene in the warm night materialised. There was much talking and dancing and my conversations were constantly interrupted by various ladies asking me to dance, during which conversation was impossible because they knew no English and I no Russian. . . . At 11.30 p.m. with Khodarev rather merry and all hope of co-operative talk disappeared, I betook myself to bed having noticed the absence of M and the rest. . . .

But Massevitch had not retired. The next day she reprimanded Lovell for leaving the banquet so early, during her absence to observe a Sputnik.

The next day Lovell had discussions with Khodarev and Oraevsky on the possibilities of collaborative efforts with Jodrell Bank in which the Eupatoria facility would transmit signals to Venus, and Jodrell would receive them after reflection from the planet—a round trip of some 60 million miles. Other co-operation between the two sites in the radio astronomical and radar work was also considered, and it was agreed to seek the approval of Keldysh and the Soviet Astronomical Council.

Returning to Moscow (where the temperature was 9°C compared with 30°C at Simferopol) Lovell gave various lectures and visited Serpuchov, south of Moscow, another developing Soviet radio-astronomical site which was to be the scene of much future collaboration with Jodrell.

On the morning of the 5th he met the Astronomical Council to discuss the proposals for collaboration with the Soviet Union on astronomical research which he wished to negotiate. These consisted of:

1. Combined studies with the Eupatoria and Jodrell Bank telescopes of the flare star radio emission, together with an extension of the simultaneous optical observations, already in progress, to other Soviet observatories, and the inclusion of US observers.

2. The initiation of bistatic radar observations of the planets Venus, Mars and Mercury, involving transmission in Eupatoria and reception at Jodrell Bank, and vice versa.

3. Simultaneous use of the Eupatoria and Jodrell Bank telescopes in the study of angular diameters and the structure of the radio sources. This would lead to an increase of 60 times in resolving-power over any then available. (The subsequent history of this idea, involving an entirely new technique of accurately controlled independent tape-recordings of the signals at the two sites, is described in *Out of the Zenith* by Sir Bernard Lovell, published by the Oxford University Press.)

4. The extension of co-operation between Jodrell Bank and the Soviet Union in the tracking of Russia's lunar and deep Space probes.

5. Visit of Soviet scientists to Jodrell in connection with these programmes.

These proposals were taken to Keldysh the same day, and he quickly endorsed them. There was, however, one specific condition. Nothing was to be disclosed about Eupatoria, except in very limited and general terms, and its situation was not to be revealed. It was agreed that Lovell could only say that this radio telescope facility existed 'in the Crimea'. Following this, there was a wider discussion on astronomical research of the future in which Keldysh again sought Lovell's views on the necessity for landing a man on the Moon, the advantages of building a telescope on an orbiting platform in Space, and the problems of orbital rendezvous.

The remaining nine days consisted of more visits to astronomical installations including optical telescope tracking-stations, Professor Mikhailov's Pulkovo Observatory near Leningrad and Academician Ambartsumian's Bjurakan Observatory at Erewan in Armenia, interspersed with plenty of sight-seeing. On all these visits Lovell was accompanied by Joyce, and on a number of occasions they were entertained at the homes of the scientists concerned. Amongst the eminent Soviet scientists whom Lovell had met on his visit in 1958 and whom he wished to meet again was Academician Peter Kapitza FRS, who lived just outside Moscow. Kapitza had spent a number of years in Britain, having left Russia in 1922 at the age of twenty-eight to study for his PhD at Cambridge University, where he worked under Lord Rutherford. From 1930 to 1934 he was the Director of the Royal Society Mond Laboratory, Cambridge. Then, during one of his visits to his Russian homeland, he was persuaded not to return to Britain but to accept the appointment of Director of the Institute for Physical Problems of the Academy of Sciences, Moscow. Ultimately he became the backbone of Russia's nuclear development, and many years were to pass before he was permitted to visit Britain again, on which occasion he stayed with the Lovells.

An appointment was made for Bernard and Joyce Lovell to lunch with Kapitza and his wife on Saturday 6 July at Kaputia, their country residence. They discussed many things, from Space research to life in Britain. Kapitza was reticent about Russia's Space programme, but frank. He said they hoped to send a man around the Moon in two or three years time. He discussed with Lovell the comparison of USSR and USA Space facilities. Kapitza was clearly of the opinion that the Americans were marginally ahead but said he found it difficult to understand why they were not greatly in advance of the Russians.

The following day Lovell and his wife went with Alla Massevitch and her daughter Natasha on a sight-seeing tour of Zagorsk. They had expressed a wish to see the monastery there. The square inside was thronged with people queuing for the blessing of the holy water. It was a surprising spectacle in this atheistic Communist nation, and the fervour of the crowd was, in the circumstances, difficult to comprehend. 'When photographing this scene,' Lovell wrote in his diary, 'I was accosted by an angry group of women who accused me of being an intellectual and having come there to laugh at them.' Having escaped the antagonism of the throng, Alla Massevitch led them to the museum which adjoins the monastery and which holds the relics of the church which had been seized in the revolution, interspersed with anti-God posters. The Lovells, however, were more interested in seeing one of the cathedrals and welcomed the offer of a young man to act as their guide. 'The first Cathedral,' Lovell wrote, 'was not in use. . . . The decorations and murals were marvellous. Our guide pointed out the house of the Patriarch where Ramsay [the then Archbishop of Canterbury] had stayed during his visit to Russia . . . He then took us into the main domed cathedral. This again was a superb piece of work and held the original coffin of Sergius. The original 13th century church was in use and crowded.' Before they departed, their guide asked Lovell to sign the visitors' book. When he saw Lovell's name, he commented that it was familiar to him, and then unexpectedly he asked Alla Massevitch if it was correct that Sir Bernard Lovell had given scientific evidence for the existence of God! It was an incongruous situation.

On their last day, 15 July, Lovell and his wife attended a farewell lunch in Moscow. On this occasion Lovell told Keldysh of his designs for a vast new radio telescope which was unlikely to be built for some time, if ever, because the estimated cost was in the region of £20 million, a sum which he hardly expected to be made available by the British Government. Keldysh thought for a moment and then commented that £20 million was only 50 million roubles, or just 1 per cent of the money he had at his disposal per annum for scientific research. 'You come to Russia, you come to us. We will build it for you,' he said jovially. Lovell replied: 'It is very kind of you, but I am an Englishman and I wish to work in England.' But he saw this as an opportunity to suggest a visit by Kapitza, so he added: 'I know Kapitza is anxious to come to England and to see Jodrell Bank, and if he came we would happily show him our plans.' Keldysh looked across the table and said that Kapitza had too much work to do, but when it was completed, he could go. A few years later, Kapitza and his wife were welcome guests at the Lovells' home.

After the lunch Oraevsky drove the Lovells to the airport, and at 6 p.m. they boarded the London-bound Comet after saying their farewells. 'We landed thankfully in a grey beautiful city at 8.10 p.m.,' Lovell wrote in his diary.

At 10 p.m. we made our final short flight to Ringway. The sky was beautiful with its many coloured lights—as good as San Francisco, J said. At Ringway [Manchester] the 'plane taxied close to the new airport building and in the main lounge we could see Bryan and Judy silhouetted against the light waving frantically to us. And so by midnight local time—by 2 a.m. Moscow time—we turned into Swettenham and The Quinta, unbelievably quiet and peaceful after the noise of the last few weeks. . . .

Tuesday, July 16. Neither J nor I could sleep much—the sudden contrast was too great, so we rose early and looked out over the rose garden and went through the accumulated mail. . . .

22

Venus and the Moon

By the autumn of 1963 the first three-way collaboration on astronomical research between the USA, the USSR and the UK, arising from one of Lovell's proposals during his visit to the Soviet Union, had begun. The collaborative programme for the study of flare stars conducted by Jodrell Bank and the Baker-Nunn cameras of the Smithsonian Satellite Tracking Network, which had started on 28 September 1960, was now joined on 18 September 1963 by the Russians. The link-up was between Jodrell Bank, the Smithsonian Baker-Nunn cameras and the observational facilities in the Crimea, Odessa and Abastumani, and these collaborative programmes continued uninterrupted through to December 1969, when they had to be temporarily suspended because of the major modifications to the Jodrell Bank telescope which were to be incorporated during 1970. (The scientific details of these important astronomical studies are related in Chapter XIII of *Out of the Zenith* by Sir Bernard Lovell, published by the Oxford University Press.)

On 23 July, eight days after his return from the Soviet Union and a few days before he left for a holiday in Ireland with Susan and John Driver, his eldest daughter and her husband, Lovell wrote to Lord Hailsham, the Minister for Science and Technology, with a copy to Dr Hugh L. Dryden, the Deputy Administrator of NASA, reporting on his visit. In this letter he detailed the co-operative programmes which he had discussed and agreed with Keldysh and Academician Kotelnikov, the Director of the Institute of Radio Technics and Electronics responsible for the deep Space tracking-station at Eupatoria. He also related the views of Keldysh on the future Soviet programmes for Space, referring to Russia's determination to perfect rendezvous techniques, to establish a manned Space platform for astronomical observations and to continue with plans to implement their existing programme on the instrumental exploration of the Moon, Venus and Mars. 'I think it can be assumed,' he wrote, 'that apparatus is now in process of assembly for the attempt to make a soft landing of instruments on the lunar surface, and that the launchings will be made in a matter of months.' He went on to explain that there was a rejection of plans for a manned lunar landing for three reasons: Soviet scientists could see no immediate solution to the problem of protecting cosmonauts from the lethal effects of intense solar outbursts; secondly, they could find no economically practical solution for transporting sufficient material to the Moon to mount a useful manned research exercise and guarantee a safe return of the crew to Earth; thirdly, they were convinced that the scientific problems involved in lunar exploration could be solved at less cost and as quickly by using unmanned, instrumented lunar probes. Lovell concluded these comments by adding that he had told Keldysh that he did not agree with this assessment since he believed that the human brain was essential to the efficient solution of the questions presented by the lunar surface. This drew from Keldysh the comment that the idea of a manned project might be revived in a few years if progress indicated hope of a solution of the problems associated with such a project. 'He (Keldysh) stated,' Lovell wrote, 'that the Academy believed that the time was now appropriate for scientists to formulate on an international basis (a) the reasons why it is desirable to engage in the manned lunar enterprise and (b) to draw up a list of scientific tasks which a man on the Moon could deal with which could not be solved by instruments alone.'

By a letter dated 6 August, James E. Webb, the Administrator of NASA, replied to Lovell in the absence of Dr Dryden on vacation. NASA, he said, found his account of his Russian visit most interesting and were pleased to have the benefit of his observations and thoughts with regard to the future ideas of Soviet scientists. The plan 'to orbit a manned astronomical platform is interesting in the light of our own project for an unmanned orbiting astronomical observatory; a comparison of results could be interesting'. He went on to say that it was encouraging that Lovell had been able to plan some co-operative programmes in radio and optical astronomy. With regard to Space research, 'Our present relationships with the Soviet Union,' he wrote, 'have developed directly from correspondence between President Kennedy and Chairman Khrushchev on specific possibilities of co-operation in this field. Dr Dryden's discussions with Academician Blagonravov over the past year or so have followed within this framework. There is already a current agreement between the Soviet Academy of Sciences and NASA. . . .' Webb concluded by saying that, if the Soviet Academy was truly interested in the matters described in Lovell's letter, NASA would look forward to further exploration by Dr Dryden with Blagonravov with a view to increased co-operation. 'I assure you that there has been and continues to be a strong desire on our part to maximize the areas of co-operation between this country and the Soviet Union with the fullest participation by other countries.'

Co-operation between the Soviet Union, the USA and Jodrell Bank proved to be more difficult than Lovell had hoped. Whilst the flare star programme got off to a flying start, the bistatic radar observations of the planets Venus, Mars and Mercury were much delayed. In September 1963 Lovell sent Kotelnikov a proposal, drawn up by Dr J. H. Thomson of his planetary radar group, for an experiment with Venus. The plan was for the Eupatoria facility to transmit signals to Venus and for Jodrell to receive the reflected signals. Intensive observations were to be made for a period of ±50 days around the time of the closest approach of Venus to Earth. From the frequency broadening of a continuous wave signal reflected from the planet, Lovell expected that they would be able to determine an accurate value of the planet's rotation period and of the direction of the rotation axis. He also anticipated that they would be able to detect individual surface features and make a more precise determination of the orbit and the astronomical unit. The Jodrell proposal additionally pointed out that Mercury and Mars should be readily detectable by this bistatic system.

To proceed with the experiment, Jodrell Bank needed information about the precise transmission frequency and stability of the Eupatoria transmitter and about the exact latitude and longitude of the system so that the doppler shifts during the periods of observation could be calculated. There was no immediate reply to the Jodrell memorandum. Indeed, it was not until 22 July 1964 that Lovell heard from Kotelnikov, and during the long waiting period he had the uneasy feeling that the Russians might not be willing to supply the information which he had requested. However, he was wrong, for Kotelnikov's ultimate reply welcomed the experiment and provided the required details of the Eupatoria transmitter.

Lovell replied immediately, suggesting that the first experiments on Venus should be scheduled for the beginning of 1965. But more delays were to follow, this time caused by Jodrell taking longer to modify equipment in order to receive the Venus reflected signals on the transmitter frequency divulged by the Russians. March or April 1965 now became the hoped-for date, but this did not suit the Russians, who suggested a starting-date of 1 July 1965, and carrying on with the experiment regularly in the course of the year with two-hour contacts two or three times a week. This suggestion by Kotelnikov for detailed periods of observation did not suit Lovell's programme of work for the telescope, and a string of new dates was proposed throughout 1965 with each side having genuine difficulties in fitting in with the other. Then, with a preliminary test on 21 December 1965, bistatic contact was made via the Moon but failed on Venus due to a misunderstanding about procedures for introducing the doppler frequency shift corrections. At last, however, on 6 January 1966. Lovell was able to advise Kotelnikov that strong signals had been received via Venus. By the end of March a stage had been reached where it seemed that the experiments should perhaps cease as sufficient information had been collected. Moreover, the USA had been undertaking similar experiments and were ahead with their findings, which by 1967 had been published, with the result that there was no real interest for further publication of similar findings. Had the Russian/ Jodrell Bank experiment been carried out in 1963, as originally suggested by Lovell, the conclusions would have proved to be exciting as they would have constituted entirely new information about Venus. Nevertheless, the liaison had proved that scientific co-operation with the Soviet Union was possible.

Another international experiment which included the USA, the Soviet Union and the UK also occurred in this period. Unfortunately it was not without its element of political suspicions. On 25 January 1964 the American *Echo II* was launched, a reflecting balloon similar to *Echo I* which had been launched on 12 August 1960, but which was 135 feet in diameter compared to *Echo I*'s 100 feet. Its orbit was near circular at an altitude of 750 miles. As early as 1961 the USA had suggested that the Soviet Union and the USA should communicate with each other via *Echo I* as a gesture of friendliness and a step towards co-operation in Space activities. Blagonravov had agreed, but since the balloon was not high enough to provide mutual visibility for communication purposes between the Soviet Union and the USA, it was decided to use Jodrell Bank as a terminal. In fact the experiment never went ahead because Blagonravov later advised NASA in the USA that 'difficulties had arisen'. These were almost certainly political. A year later, on 7 March 1962, President Kennedy sent Mr Khrushchev, the head of the Soviet Union, an invitation for Soviet scientists to participate in exploring the feasibility of inter- continental communications-satellite systems. On 20 March Khrushchev responded favourably, saying that the Soviet representatives on the United Nations Committee on the Peaceful Uses of Outer Space would be instructed to discuss with the US representatives 'concrete questions of co-operation in research'. Of the six areas which he listed for dis- cussion, communication satellites was the first.

Immediately a meeting took place between Dr Hugh L. Dryden and Academician A. A. Blagonravov at the United Nations in New York and, later, from 29 May to 7 June, the discussions continued at a meeting in Geneva, when agreement was reached on collaboration in meteorology, geomagnetic surveys and satellite telecommunications. The telecom- munications collaboration was to be via the future *Echo II* as *Echo I* had deteriorated, and yet again Jodrell Bank was to co-operate by acting as a terminal. The proposal was for Jodrell Bank to receive messages from the USA via *Echo II* and to transmit these to the Zimenki Radio Astronomical

Observatory of Gorki University. When *Echo II* went into orbit all was ready for the experiment to begin on 21 February 1964, including arrangements by the British Post Office for a direct teleprinter link between Jodrell Bank and Washington and between Jodrell Bank and Gorki. However, no account had been taken of the political suspicions that existed between the USA and the Soviet Union, despite the outward display of the two Governments' willingness to co-operate in some areas of Space research. On 7 February 1964 Dryden of NASA wrote to Blagonravov, saying: 'If both sides are to derive maximum benefit from the experience of working together with *Echo II* the experiment should involve both transmission and reception by each side. I would like, therefore, to ask the Academy of Sciences to give the most serious and urgent consideration to an expansion of the programme of tests you have outlined so that it will provide for similar transmissions from Zimenki to Jodrell Bank.' A copy of this letter was sent to Lovell with a covering note saying: 'We wish to wait for Academician Blagonravov's reply to Dr Dryden's letter prior to coming to any agreement on a schedule of tests from Jodrell Bank to Zimenki Observatory.'

Lovell, however, wanted to proceed as scheduled regardless of the outcome. As a result a US officer was sent over to dissuade him from such an action, and when Lovell said he intended to go ahead with the experiment, the officer informed Lovell that he would have to speak to the President of the USA and have him stopped.

Lovell was annoyed because he felt that the Americans had no right to prevent Jodrell Bank, a University establishment, turning its telescope onto the balloon, but he accepted that it was an American balloon and, therefore, it would be tactless to ignore the request. However, Dr J. G. Davies, one of Lovell's senior colleagues, had a brilliant idea. The Moon was still common property, and it could be used just as well as an orbiting balloon to bounce off an echoed message from Jodrell Bank to Russia. And so, on the night of 21 February, following a telex message to Zimenki advising that first contacts would be via the Moon, Jodrell Bank sent the following message: 'To Dr Ghetmantshev and Colleagues at Zimenki: We at Jodrell Bank take this opportunity of sending our warm greetings to you via the Moon. We hope that this co-operative experiment may lead to closer links in the future between the astronomers and scientists in our countries. With best regards. Lovell, Davies, Thomson, and the staff of Jodrell Bank.'

Without delay, the Americans withdrew their holding-action on the tests via the balloon, and on 2 February Gorki received Jodrell Bank's signals via *Echo II*. The response was immediate: 'Blagonravov and Ghetmantshev to Lovell, Davies and Thomson: Congratulations on success of first session of experimental radio connection via *Echo II* satellite as radio wave reflector. Glad emphasise importance of this practical step on international co-operation in field of exploration and utilisation of outer Space for practical purposes.'

There followed a message back to Gorki from NASA in the USA: 'To Academician Blagonravov. This teletype message is transmitted via the US active repeater communication Satellite Relay II, to the General Post Office terminal at Goonhilly Downs in Great Britain whence it is re-transmitted by the Jodrell Bank Observatory via the US passive reflector communication satellite, *Echo II*, to Zimenki Observatory in the USSR. We hope this modest beginning will lead to further association between our countries in international efforts towards development of a global satellite system to serve the communication needs of all nations. . . . With warm regards. Hugh L. Dryden.'

These experiments continued until 8 March and included facsimile picture transmissions. After the 8th they ceased, although Jodrell Bank continued until the end of April with further communication tests with the USSR, using the Moon as a passive reflector satellite. In fact, the idea of a joint US/USSR global satellite communication system, using passive reflectors, was superseded. The USA rightly committed itself, with western Europe, Canada, South America, the Pacific and the Middle East, to a system based on active geostationary communication satellites at 22,300 miles above the equator rotating once in 24 hours in the same direction as the Earth's rotation, thereby effectively remaining over the same point of the Earth's surface. With the appropriate number of satellites, global coverage was achieved, and an international consortium was formed, known as Intelsat, consisting by and large of all countries outside the 'Iron Curtain'. Partly for political reasons, but more particu-larly on practical grounds, the Soviet Union developed its own system. Because so much of Soviet territory lies far to the north of the equator, the geostationary satellite was not a satisfactory solution to its own communi-cation problems. Instead, it developed what is known as the Molniya series of communication satellites which are in highly eccentric twelve-hour orbits with perigee at about 500 kilometres in the southern hemisphere and apogee over the Soviet Union at about 40,000 kilo-metres. The satellites spend a large proportion of their orbit in communi-cation with Soviet territory, including the Warsaw Pact countries, and only a few are required for continuous coverage. The system also provides for communication with Soviet ships in the southern hemisphere entirely adequately, and it is extremely well suited to the USSR's requirements for military, deep Space and astronaut communication.

The collaboration on exploration of the Moon, suggested to Lovell by

Keldysh during the 1963 visit, never did materialize. Indeed, the Soviet Union seemed reticent to discuss its plans with the USA, and the USA was not that much more forthcoming on its intentions. Consequently no significant discussions took place on the advantages of manned exploration over unmanned but instrumented investigations. Neither was there any serious attempt to list jointly the tasks that a man on the Moon could undertake which could not be accomplished by instruments alone. But Lovell's assessment of the Soviet Union's near readiness to attempt a soft landing with instruments on the lunar surface proved to be well judged, even if first attempts were unsuccessful; there were five failures between late 1963 and 1965 (*Luna 4* to *Luna 8*). During the same period the USA with its Ranger programme succeeded in obtaining close-range photographs of the lunar surface with *Rangers 7, 8* and *9*. In fact, the USA and the Soviet Union were running neck and neck in their approach to exploration of the Moon, which certainly contributed to the lack of desire on the part of both sides to discuss their programmes together. Moreover, there were already military strategists proposing that nuclear weapons should be placed on the Moon as an inviolate second-strike capability. The theory was that no nation would dare to make a nuclear attack on another, however destructive its first strike, if the target nation had retaliatory capability based on the Moon. Therefore, priority of landing man on the Moon and taking possession of this territory may well have been the reason for the intense efforts of both the USA and the Soviet Union to be first on the Moon and to be able to colonize it effectively for military purposes. This, too, would have explained their reluctance to discuss their lunar programmes.

In February 1966 the Soviet Union launched its *Luna 9*, an unmanned instrumented probe which made a soft landing on the Moon on Thursday 3 February and which began to send back excellent photographs showing very fine details. These photographs were not available to the rest of the world and, but for an astute action on the part of Lovell, might never have been disclosed in full. Having tracked *Luna 9* to its soft landing with the telescope at Jodrell Bank, J. G. Davies recognized the familiar tones of a facsimile picture transmission emanating from the surface of the Moon, indicating that a camera was successfully in action. The problem was how to decipher these transmissions. J. G. Davies suggested that perhaps they could obtain a print-out by using a newspaper photographic wire machine. Lovell immediately decided to try out the idea, and after several hours of telephoning in a frantic search for such a machine, one was acquired from the *Daily Express* offices in Manchester. It worked, and by the afternoon of Friday 4 February immaculate pictures of the Moon's surface were being received from *Luna 9*.

The *Daily Express* generously agreed that the results should be distributed to all newspapers simultaneously, despite the fact that it was the loan of their equipment which had made possible the reception of the photographs. Assuming that the Russians would immediately release these pictures to their Press, Lovell released Jodrell's to the British Press. On Saturday and Sunday mornings, to the annoyance of the Russians, the British national Press carried a selection of pictures before the Russians had, in fact, released their photographs to their own Press and, indeed, before it was known that they had successfully transmitted photographs from the surface of the Moon. Their reaction was prompt. Blagonravov accused Jodrell Bank of 'certain motives of a sensational nature' and said it was somewhat surprising that Jodrell had been in such a hurry to publish results without asking Soviet scientific organizations for information in the first place. Lovell was unrepentant but replied in conciliatory fashion. The fact was that Jodrell Bank was an 'eye on the sky' and, at this stage, neither Russia nor America could be entirely secretive in Space.

From the British Press there came a wave of favourable comment, typical of which was a short leader in the *Sunday Telegraph* headed 'Proud of Jodrell'. It read:

Left out of the Space race because of their inability to work hard enough and save hard enough, the British can still feel great pride in the achievement of Jodrell Bank. By training its radio telescope on the Moon on Friday and feeding signals from the Russian Spacecraft into the kind of picture-receiving machine that newspapers use, Sir Bernard Lovell's men stole a march on the Russians who, by Saturday morning had still not released their pictures from Luna 9.

The existence of Jodrell Bank, let all the politicians note, is due more to private enterprise and public subscription than to Government assistance. This, under Mr Macmillan, was timid and niggardly.

23

The Mk IA and Mk V Telescopes

As mentioned in the opening paragraph of Chapter 21, of the total of 68,538 hours of operational use of the Jodrell Bank telescope from August 1957 to August 1970, only 4,877 hours were devoted to assistance to Government agencies, both British and foreign, for purposes other than strictly astronomical research. Of these 4,877 hours only 2,498, or 3.6 per cent of the total hours of usage for all purposes, were employed directly in collaboration with the USA and the USSR in their Space programmes. From 1970 onwards the telescope was used almost exclusively for research. Even so, the assistance given to both the USA and USSR had been vital to the success of their Space efforts during those years before they had developed and built their own radio telescopes of similar complexity and high performance to that of Jodrell Bank, and they were generous in their recognition of Lovell's contribution, showering upon him academic honours and awards.

A singularly great mark of recognition followed the epic landing on the Moon of the *Apollo 11*'s lunar module on 20 July 1969, at 4.17 p.m. US Eastern Daylight Time, when Colonel Edwin Aldrin and Neil Armstrong became the first men to set foot on the Moon. It was a milestone in human history, and a presidential dinner was held on 13 August at the Century Plaza Hotel, Los Angeles, to honour the three astronauts—Aldrin, Armstrong and Lieutenant Michael Collins. Lovell and his wife were invited to this function by President and Mrs Nixon as their personal guests. Unfortunately they were unable to attend. Another tribute to Lovell's past assistance to the USA came at the same time by way of a photograph of *Apollo 11* from George E. Mueller, the head of NASA, inscribed: 'Dear Bernie (Bernard), My thanks for all you've done for Space.'

But from a strictly scientific point of view it was what Lovell had done and was doing for astronomy that was of the greatest importance to Britain and, indeed, to international research in this growing field of science. The historic discovery by Karl Jansky of the Bell Telephone Laboratories, USA, in 1931 that radio waves were reaching Earth from outer Space, and the later work of Grote Reber who, with his 31-foot parabolic reflector and receiving equipment plotted the first radio maps of the Milky Way at the end of the thirties were neglected. This strange hiatus in the development of the science of astronomy was caused partly by World

War II, but the developments in radar during the war resulted in British and Commonwealth scientists rapidly applying these newly discovered radio techniques to the field of astronomical investigations. By 1960 Britain had achieved a pre-eminent place in radio astronomy thanks to the contributions of Lovell with his Jodrell Bank telescope, Martin Ryle with his radio telescope at Cambridge and J. S. Hey with his radio equipment at the Royal Radar Establishment at Great Malvern. The contribution from the Commonwealth team in Australia led by E. G. Bowen and J. L. Pawsey was equally significant.

During the 1950s important developments in radio astronomy also occurred in the USA, the USSR, France, the Netherlands and Germany, but it was Lovell's concept of a vast steerable radio telescope that could view all parts of the heavens and penetrate further into the Universe than any previous astronomical instrument that led the revolution in astronomical research. Even by the early '60s the steerable radio telescopes already constructed or being constructed were smaller and less powerful than the 250-foot telescope at Jodrell Bank. Moreover, their development had been principally for Space probe and satellite operations.

By 1960 the cosmological implications of the work of the research teams led by Lovell at Jodrell Bank (Manchester University) and Ryle at Cambridge had had a considerable influence on the development of theories of the origin of the Universe. Moreover, their work was moving into a new phase, with Cambridge concentrating on the distribution and number of what were then believed to be the most distant objects yet detected and which were certainly beyond the range of the most powerful optical telescopes, and Jodrell Bank addressing itself to the measurement of the angular diameter and precise location of discrete radio sources in outer Space. The observational data from Jodrell and Cambridge had interesting repercussions on theoretical astronomy generally, and in furthering the understanding of the nature and origin of cosmic radio sources in particular.

The successes of Jodrell Bank, Cambridge and the Royal Radar Establishment soon emphasized the necessity for some special consideration being given to the new era of astronomical research and for some kind of budget being provided to enable future programmes of research to be embarked upon and the necessary facilities to be made available. In fact, the parsimonious attitude of Government to the expenditure on Jodrell Bank, now the most envied scientific installation for astronomical research in the world, was fast giving way to a more generous and enlightened outlook, and on 20 December 1961 the Lord President of the Council, Viscount Hailsham, who was also Minister for Science, appointed a Radio Astronomy Planning Committee under the aegis of the

DSIR: 'To consider and advise on the nature and extent of the participation of HM Government in research and radio astronomy; in particular
to consider programmes, facilities, funds and organisation required to
support the UK interest in research in radio astronomy both nationally
and internationally.' The Chairman was Lord Fleck KBE, and the
Committee, which came to be known as the 'Fleck Committee', included
Sir Edward Appleton, Lovell, Ryle, Hey, Fred Hoyle* and Sir Richard
Woolley, the Astronomer Royal.

    This Committee set to work quickly, and by 1963 it had formulated an
initial plan in five fields of work: 'the Solar System; the Galaxy and
individual non-thermal sources associated with supernovae and radio
studies of certain types of stars; nearby normal galaxies; the radio galaxies
which exist with considerably greater intensity than our own galaxy;
cosmology'. It expressed the view that it was possible that the first phase of
radio astronomy, that of exploring anything detectable and devising some
explanation of its existence, had passed and that the greatest progress
would now probably be made by a careful integration of theory with
experiment. It admitted that, 'despite the research done in this country
and overseas in radio astronomy, our level of understanding is still at
present rudimentary.' It accepted that many fundamental problems,
although established, remained unanswered and that radical advances in
both theory and instrumentation would be necessary. 'There seems little
doubt,' it stated, 'that radio astronomy will remain a centre of interest in
modern science for many years to come. . . . The nature of the problems
in radio astronomy which will require investigation in ten or even five
years' time, and the design of instruments required to tackle them, will
depend to a large extent on the cosmological models derived from observations using the existing and planned radio telescopes. During this
period, there will almost certainly be considerable developments in Space
research and in ultra-violet and infra-red astronomy using satellites.'
Because of the advanced state of techniques at Jodrell Bank and Ryle's
radio telescope at Cambridge, the Committee recommended that the
existing research centres at Manchester and Cambridge Universities
should be especially encouraged and given an indication of the financial
resources likely to be provided for new instruments and services up to
1972.

    Based on the commitments as at 1963, expenditure by the DSIR on
radio astronomy had been estimated at £2 million over the ten-year period
1955–65. The Committee, whilst accepting that major progress could
probably still be made in this new science with instruments of about the
same size as those at present in use, considered that by 1972 more refined
techniques would be required, calling for instruments costing around

£1.5 million each for siting at Jodrell and Cambridge. Support and resources to use these facilities adequately was conservatively estimated at £1 million, thus giving a total of £4 million needed over the period 1963–72 at the then ruling prices. This represented 10 per cent of the £40 million of funds made available to the DSIR for research grants over the period 1963–72. The £4 million did not, however, take into account claims for capital investment in other branches of astronomy such as optical and theoretical astronomy. Nor did it cover a tentative proposal for a giant radio telescope at Jodrell Bank with a steerable paraboloid 1,000 feet in diameter which could give Britain a research facility unlikely to be surpassed in the foreseeable future. This was to be known as the Mk IV telescope and was a project that was likely to run into millions of pounds. Nevertheless, at this stage the £4 million seemed to be in line with the policy to give special encouragement to the new science of radio astronomy. Also, it was in excess of the £173,228 allocated in December 1961 for the Mk II telescope at Jodrell Bank, and the £115,000 approved in August 1963 for the construction of the Mk III telescope, also for Jodrell, but initially sited at Wardle near Nantwich in Cheshire. This Mk III was a transportable version of the Mk II (see Chapter 21) and was to act as an essential part of the interferometric facilities in combination with the Mk I Jodrell Bank telescope.

At the end of 1964 there was a considerable reorganization of the various scientific 'bodies' representing the different branches of science and technology, bringing them, in the main, under one central council to be known as the Science Research Council. Even before this Council was officially approved and in receipt of its Royal Charter, Lovell was approached by Sir Harry Melville in an effort to persuade him to permit his name to be put forward for membership of this extremely important and potentially powerful Government Council. After careful consideration and discussion with Sir William Mansfield Cooper, the Vice-Chancellor of Manchester University, he agreed to let his name go forward, accepting that election would surely place a heavy burden of national responsibility upon his shoulders and involve him in much extra work when his Jodrell Bank burdens were already more than onerous.

By a letter dated 25 January 1965, from the Right Hon. Anthony Crosland MP, Secretary of State for Education and Science, under whose Ministry the new Science Research Council was to be formed, Lovell received his official request to serve on the Council. Crosland wrote, 'I am writing to ask whether you would be willing to serve as a member of the Science Research Council, which will be formed when the Science and Technology Bill receives the Royal Assent. The Bill has completed passage through the House of Commons, and will be taken in the House of Lords shortly.' He went on to state that this new Council 'will take over the work hitherto conducted by the Department of Scientific and Industrial Research in relation to research grants, and postgraduate student awards; and the Radio Research Station of DSIR. To this will be added the control of the Royal Observatories, and the Rutherford and Daresbury Laboratories now under the National Institute for Research in Nuclear Science which will cease to exist as a separate Institution. The control of the Space Research programme, now vested in the Steering Group for Space Research, and the British National Committee will be transferred to the Council, and the Steering Group will be wound up.' Crosland's letter advised that the Council was to be formally constituted on 1 April 1965.

Lovell acknowledged Anthony Crosland's letter on 27 January, accepting the invitation to serve on the SRC, and by a letter from Crosland dated 24 March he learned that he had been elected. Melville had already advised him that if elected he would be the member with special responsibility for optical and radio astronomy in universities, the Royal Observatories, the Radio Research Board and Space Research finances. As the SRC settled down to its duties, these responsibilities were confirmed for Lovell by the formation under the Council of the Astronomy, Space and Radio Board (ASRB) of which he was appointed Chairman. Reporting to the ASRB were two committees, the Astronomy Policy and Grants Committee (APGC) and the Space Policy and Grants Committee (SPGC).

Prior to the formation of the SRC, the concept of the gigantic Mk IV steerable radio telescope with a 1,000-foot aperture paraboloid which had received some favourable consideration as a future project by the Fleck Committee, was dropped because of the almost certain opposition there would be from the Government to an expenditure of a sum of at least £10 million, and probably nearer £20 million. However, arising from the early thoughts on the Mk IV, there emerged the concept of a Mk V instrument which was to have a larger aperture than the existing Mk I and much greater accuracy. What was sought was maximum efficiency at a wavelength of 21 centimetres and useful performance at 10 and 6 centimetres. Early in 1964, due to hesitation on the part of the DSIR to make a grant for a feasibility study for a large telescope, entirely due to a Treasury embargo on the provision of funds for investigations of projects unless the DSIR could give an assurance that they intended to proceed with such projects and that the total money was available within their allocations, the University of Manchester decided to support a study itself. With the approval of the DSIR, the University entered into an agreeement with Husband & Company, the consulting engineers, on 17 April 1964 to undertake the necessary study. The arrangement with the DSIR was that the money would be refunded to the University if the project proceeded.

In July of the same year Husband submitted his 'Confidential Report on the Proposed Mk V Radio Telescope', setting out the essential parameters of the telescope which he would investigate. At this time, the study was to consider a range of apertures (size of paraboloids) 'not less than 375 ft (major axis) by 250 ft (minor axis), and a maximum size of 500 ft by 250 ft'. The concept was being based on the elliptical design of paraboloid employed on the Mk II and Mk III telescopes. In April 1965 Husband submitted a report on 'Proposals and Cost Estimates for the Mk V Radio Telescope'. The concept employing an elliptical paraboloid had been dropped, and the document included a curve giving the costs for a telescope of circular aperture from 260 feet in diameter to 400 feet. The estimate at 1965 prices was £1.785 million for the 260-foot version and £4.089 million for the 400-foot version. The report was confident of the practicability of constructing a radio telescope with a 400-foot-diameter paraboloid but indicated that the cost against size beyond 400 feet would rise so steeply that the recommendation was that 400 feet should be the ultimate aim.

In the light of this report Lovell applied in the summer of 1965 to the SRC, which had replaced the DSIR, for a grant of £45,000 in order to undertake a full design study. The money would be required, he indicated, to run from 1 October 1965 to 30 September 1966. Unfortunately the Treasury embargo on grants for design studies, unless it was certain that the final project would proceed and could be financed, applied equally to the SRC as it had to the DSIR. However, by 1966 the situation changed, and on 23 June 1966, in the expectation that authority to proceed with a design study would be given, the SRC, with Lovell, interviewed prospective organizations which might act as agents for the studies which were to be undertaken by Husband & Company and Freeman, Fox and Partners. The United Kingdom Atomic Energy Authority (UKAEA) was chosen, and at a Council meeting on 14 July the decision was taken by the SRC to make the grant of £45,000 for the design study of the MK V radio telescope. The instructions given later by the UKAEA to the competing consulting engineers on cost were precise. The cost was to be contained within a ceiling of £4.25 million at January 1967 prices, and it was required that the instrument to be built should have the largest possible aperture—believed to be 400 feet—with the specified tolerances as indicated in the guidelines set out in a memorandum by Lovell, F. G. Smith and J. G. Davies dated November 1966.

' During the course of this initial history of the Mk V, the SRC had replaced the DSIR, and Lovell himself had become a member of the

Council and, into the bargain, the Chairman of the Council's Astronomy, Space and Radio Board (ASRB). This position of responsibility was soon to land him in a dilemma. The ASRB had responsibility for projects other than those which were of specific interest to the future programmes of research at Jodrell Bank. In April 1967 the UK agreed to join with Australia in the building of a 150-inch optical telescope in New South Wales on a fifty-fifty basis. The Anglo-Australian Telescope (AAT), as it came to be known, was estimated to cost £4 million, of which Britain was to contribute £2 million from the SRC allocations. (It was scheduled to be completed by the end of 1973 but was not, in fact, completed until July 1975. The final cost was £7.5 million, of which Britain contributed £3.75 million.) By the end of 1967 the ASRB also had in its forward plans other important and expensive items such as the UK series of satellites, which fell into the multi-million-pound category, routine expenditure and minor developments for the Royal Observatories, and considerable sums required for the Radio and Space Research Station and various university departments. In the field of astronomy there were two major projects for the future: the Mk V radio telescope which, as already stated, was to be held within a ceiling of £4.25 million, and Sir Martin Ryle's proposal for a 5-kilometre aperture synthesis instrument at Cambridge which was expected to cost between £2 million and £3 million. As Chairman of ASRB, Lovell now had to consider the overall requirements for the scientific ventures which fell within his jurisdiction for advice to the Council. This demanded an impartial judgement of priorities if choices had to be made which, in turn, meant limiting his own desires if necessary. Lovell's integrity on this score was soon to be proved.

Another item of expenditure which suddenly arose at this time was in connection with the Mk I telescope. After the severe winter of 1963, parts of the concrete in the azimuth turntable showed signs of distress, and Husband, the consulting engineer, began to give warnings that an instrument of the size and complexity of the Mk I could not go on for years without a large-scale overhaul. By 1964 the 'overhaul' project had developed into a modification proposal to improve the performance of the telescope, converting it into what was designated the Mk IA. Husband estimated the cost of this job, which was an extensive one, at £268,400. At the time Lovell did nothing about the proposal because he was anxious to proceed with the Mk V project, and he realized that, if he started asking for this kind of money for the Mk I, it would surely prejudice any hope of proceeding with the Mk V. Indeed, he was already concerned in mid-1966 about finances for the Mk V. In his diary he wrote: 'Actually the future outlook for the project is full of gloom. The decision to proceed with the design study came on a day of economic crises (14th July,

1966)—Bank Rate up to 7% and threats of ever increasing restrictions to save the pound.'

From time to time, Lovell and his team looked at Husband's proposed modification to the Mk I to convert it into the Mk IA 'particularly in view of the fact that it would give an overall surface accuracy of ±1 in. with high efficiency at least on 21 cms'. Then, in the autumn of 1967, hairline cracks in the cones carrying the paraboloid to the trunnion-bearings were noticed by one of the maintenance engineers. Husband was immediately informed, and after inspection he judged them to be fatigue cracks and immediately arranged for them to be welded. But no sooner was the telescope back to its normal position for operation than the cracks appeared in the cones in another place. Husband now decided that these cracks had probably developed when the telescope had first operated ten years ago and had perhaps been rusted over and not noticed. Clearly this was another indication of fatigue which might mean that the Mk I, after ten years of constant operation, now had only a limited life unless a major overhaul was undertaken.

By December 1967 Lovell was driven to exercise his impartial judgement. The SRC budget was now subject to trimming because of the deteriorating economic situation in Britain. Lovell wrote in his diary: 'First of all Devaluation meant that we lost something like £1 million off the SRC budget, and there was an indication that our growth rates were not going to be what were necessary to maintain our programme.' In fact, it now became evident that, although the activities of the ASRB were receiving favourable treatment, it was going to be financially impossible to proceed with both Martin Ryle's telescope at Cambridge and the Mk V simultaneously. One of them would obviously have to be cancelled, or at best delayed in favour of the other. Shortly before Christmas Sir Brian Flowers,* who had succeeded Melville as the SRC's Chairman, consulted with Lovell and Ryle, advising them that a choice between the two instruments in question would have to be made and that if necessary he would 'toss a coin' to resolve the matter. Lovell was, however, conscious of the fact that throughout the past years the strength of radio astronomy in the UK had depended upon mutual understanding and co-operation between Ryle and himself, and he had no wish to jeopardize this situation. Being well aware that Ryle was ready to proceed with his design for the synthesis telescope, whereas there were still scientific arguments about the Mk V to be resolved with the result that the final design was far from complete, Lovell recommended that the Ryle telescope should take precedence over the Mk V. This made economic sense because the Ryle telescope was estimated at half the cost of the Mk V, and already there were indications that the Mk V was going to exceed substantially the £4.25

million estimated in 1966. Tied in with this recommendation was a condition that the Mk IA concept should proceed in parallel with equal priority and that the ASRB should write in a two-year delay on the beginning of the Mk V. The ASRB and its Astronomy Policy and Grants Committee under Fred Hoyle, the eminent astronomer, fully supported Lovell's recommendations, as did the SRC itself, regarding them as making 'both scientific and economic sense'.

These decisions emanating from Lovell's responsible and unselfish approach to the financial problems proved in the end to be to Jodrell Bank's advantage. If nothing were done about the Mk I telescope, it would soon be out of commission, and if deteriorating finances continued, the Mk V might never be built. In such circumstances, the University of Manchester would become a minor influence in the field of astronomy. But with the Mk I substantially renovated and upgraded in performance by various proposed modifications, the University was promised an instrument of greatly improved performance, if not actually equalling that of the Mk V. Moreover, this Mk IA telescope would be achieved at an estimated cost of £350,000 against a cost of at least £2.5 million if the instrument was to be built from scratch. On 3 February 1968 the University of Manchester submitted its application to the SRC for a grant of £350,000, to which would have to be added agent's and consulting engineer's fees, and early in June, after some hesitation, the Treasury gave its approval to the SRC to make a grant of £400,000 for the Mk IA project, the sum to include the fees of the consulting engineers and the agents who would supervise the task. The kind of timetable that Lovell now began to hope for was the completion of modifications to the foundation work and the railway tracks by the autumn of 1968, the major steel work during the summer period of 1969, with modifications to the paraboloid and to the computer and other instrumentation going on in parallel. But it seemed that all the 'hold-up' problems experienced with the original Mk I were now to be visited upon the Mk IA, together with a repetition of financial embarrassments.

In July 1968 Husband warned that the cost was now likely to be £374,000 excluding fees. This was disturbing because Lovell knew from the SRC that the Treasury were unlikely to extend the £400,000 grant by more than 10 per cent up to £440,000. The foundation work went ahead a little later than had been expected, but by September it was underway. The major financial shock was soon to follow. By December, due to increases in steel costs and in the labour costs associated with the steelwork, Husband was obliged to submit a new estimate. It was £504,000 excluding the fees. Lovell was most disturbed. The economic situation had continued to deteriorate badly, and devaluation of the pound had already meant a loss in excess of £1 million from the SRC budget. There was still no sign of the Treasury agreeing to the £2.5 million grant for Ryle's Cambridge synthesis telescope. The chances of agreement by the Treasury to spend ultimately £4.5 to £5 million for the Mk V were beginning to look forlorn. To ask for an additional £100,000 for the Mk IA at this stage, a sum which Lovell believed would escalate still further, would certainly have an adverse effect on the prospects for the Mk V. It was not that the figure of £0.5 million was in any way comparable to the £4.5 to £5 million estimated for the Mk V, but rather that the scale of inflation that was overtaking the Mk IA at this early stage could be insupportable in the case of Mk V, the commencement of construction of which was now envisaged for 1971.

Lovell's reaction was to send Husband back to his drawing-board to contain the modifications to the Mk I within the budget of £400,000 plus a variance of 10 per cent, excluding fees, even if this reduced the performance specification. At a meeting of the SRC on 19 December 1968, however, Sir Brian Flowers and J. Hosie (Director of the Astronomy, Space and Radio Board Division, i.e. the permanent SRC official parallel to the Independent Chairman of the Board, which post was held by Lovell) gave it as their opinion that the Treasury would have to be informed of any intention to accept less accuracy in performance than had been specified in order to keep within the budget. 'Together with the history of Mk I,' Lovell wrote, 'their view was that this in itself would have an exceedingly serious reaction on the Mk V proposal, even in the event that we did not go back for further money for the Mk IA.' Therefore, after every effort was made to find savings without affecting performance, an application was made in April 1969 to the SRC for a supplementary grant of £145,000, and in July the Department of Education and Science and the Treasury signified their approval of this additional sum. This brought the total grant to £585,000 including fees. This news arrived on 15 July 1969, and in his diary for 16 July Lovell wrote:

A very hot summer day, and it has just gone 5 o'clock. Two and a half hours ago we watched on the television screen the launching of *Apollo 11*; man's first attempt to land on the Moon. The excitement of this occasion has been heightened by the fact that early on Sunday morning the Soviets launched *Lunar 15* which we had been tracking and there is widespread belief that this *Lunik* will soft land and attempt to collect some rock to bring it back to Earth before the Americans bring theirs back. Certainly the *Lunik* is on an orbit which is taking 24 hours longer to reach the Moon than any previous Lunik and the telemetry is quite different from any which we have seen before. So it seems a good day to bring the diary of events respecting the telescopes up to date. . . . Well, it was with great relief yesterday that we received a telephone

call to say that the Treasury now agreed to the additional expenditure on the
Mk. IA. . . .

As a matter of interest *Apollo 11* succeeded in its mission as has already
been related. *Lunik 15* failed.

Some months later, on Friday 28 November, Lovell recorded in his
diary: 'Since the last entry was placed on tape, the *Apollo 11* astronauts
succeeded in their mission to the Moon and now, a few days ago, the
Apollo 12 astronauts returned safely to Earth after the second successful
mission. In the meantime there have been very active developments in the
case of both the Mk V and the Mk IA. . . .' Somehow Lovell's telescope
problems always seemed to diminish at the time of the Space 'firsts' of the
USA or USSR! The situation was that in the case of the Mk IA the
replacement of the railway track, the introduction of the inner bogies and
the steelwork up the diametral girder, all started more or less on time
following on the earlier completion of the foundation work, and were
completed on schedule on 12 November, enabling the telescope to
resume full operations until the final stage of the modifications began.
This was scheduled for 1 April 1970 perhaps an appropriate date, for
delays immediately occurred and, in fact, the Mk I telescope was driven to
the zenith for the last time at 09.00 hours on 14 August 1970. After
modifications to the paraboloid and introduction of new instrumentation,
it was to emerge on 14 November 1971 as the Mk IA, 'an instrument',
Lovell wrote, 'looking only marginally different to the casual observer, but
nevertheless a much improved telescope with stresses and strains
removed to give it a further long life of research'.

The cost of the Mk IA finished up in excess of £600,000. Added to the
original cost of the Mk I, which had already done 13 years' hard and
invaluable work, the total was still less than £1.5 million. At prices in 1971
it would have cost in the region of £7 million, or possibly more, and
therefore it was yet again a bargain for Britain. It is also interesting to note
that by the end of 1978 the combined operational time spent by the Mk I
and Mk IA on various researches amounted to 118,000 hours. Taking
into account the total costs of construction, repairs and overhauls, the cost
per hour works out at £10—and as each further year goes by the cost will
decrease. Also by 1978 more than 600 published research papers had
originated from Jodrell Bank, and 150 postgraduate students had
obtained their Master's or Doctor's degrees for their work with the
telescopes. The training of these young people who subsequently filled
many important research, industrial and teaching posts in many parts of
the world represents one of the most significant aspects of the activities of
the establishment. Of further interest is the fact that the cost of building

the Mk IA today is estimated at between £20 and £25 million, rising rapidly. Clearly, Jodrell Bank has been one of Britain's best post-war scientific bargains.

Unfortunately the plans for the Mk V telescope had a dismal ending, due to the rising costs which Lovell had feared would escalate as each year passed. However, even when it was evident that an application to the SRC for approval to go ahead with this instrument would now have to quote a figure of £6.2 million, against the previous limit of £4.25 million estimated in 1966, the University of Manchester submitted such an application on 6 November 1969. At the time, Lovell wrote in reference to this figure of £6.2 million: 'This sum of money is, of course, a considerable increase on the limits of £4.25 million to £4.5 million at 1967 prices and is arrived at in the following way. There is an extra £300,000 for the jacking system and my application makes it perfectly clear that this is a new concept and has not been before a committee before; there is £200,000 for ancillary equipment, i.e. parametric amplifiers, additional workshops at Jodrell Bank, and so on; there is about £600,000 for agent's fees and the design fees, and this leaves the actual prime cost of the Mk V telescope not very much above the scaled up figures of the 1967 prices to the January 1970 prices. We have, in fact, got just over £5 million entered in our Forward Look, so that over and above the Forward Look we are deficient by about a million pounds. . . .'

The official application listed the costs as follows:

Construction of Mk V Telescope	£5.380m
Design Fees	£0.470m
Agency Fees	£0.150m
Supplementary Items	£0.200m
Total	£6.200m

It was supported by the relevant design study documents, assessments of costs and a book detailing the work it would undertake, entitled *The Scientific Programme of the Mk V Radio Telescope*. This last document, 117 pages in length, was a weighty argument for proceeding with the project and made it very clear that the Mk V with its 400-foot aperture would place Britain ahead in astronomical research for many years to come, when considered in conjunction with Ryle's new Cambridge Synthesis telescope, which was now under construction. Indeed, the Mk V would be effectively the equivalent of the latest American instrument, the 440-foot radome telescope already proposed but not at that time financed.

On 18 November 1969, with Sir Fred Hoyle in the chair, the

Astronomy, Policy and Grants Committee considered the application. Apart from the members of the Committee, Sir Brian Flowers, Chairman of the SRC, was in attendance, and it was he who obtained a definite statement from the Astronomer Royal and from the other members of the Committee that the Mk V was the most important project in astronomy with which they would wish to proceed. The decision to proceed was therefore given by the SRC, and all looked set fair for this major project. But by the end of 1970 the prospects were turning sour. In November 1970 the cost was re-estimated at £7.8 million at January 1971 prices. In the 12 months since the application was made, the cost had risen by nearly £3,000 per day due to inflation. The stage of detailed design to tender was estimated to take 12 to 18 months so that construction could not be expected to begin before the end of 1971, which meant that £7.8 million was likely to be well short of the final cost.

On 1 December 1970 the revised cost estimates of the Mk V, together with estimates for different sizes of apertures, were submitted to the Astronomy, Policy and Grants Committee. These had been detailed by Lovell in a memorandum dated 30 November. The figures included consultants and agency fees and a sum for contingencies. The sizes of apertures covered were 400 feet—the existing Mk V project—390 feet, 380 feet, 370 feet, 360 feet and 350 feet. The Mk V figure was £7.8 million, the 390-foot version came out at £7.21 million, the 380-foot at £6.81 million, the 370-foot at £6.23 million, the 360-foot at £5.94 million and the 350-foot at £5.59 million. The APGC re-affirmed their intention to build the Mk V telescope with the largest possible aperture, i.e. 400 feet, but on 15 December the Astronomy, Space and Radio Board, of which Lovell was now no longer Chairman, took a different view. Two days after the meeting of the ASRB, Hosie acquainted Lovell with the Board's decisions, which were: (a) that they could not afford £7.8 million for the telescope; (b) that they would seek advice from UKAEA who had been appointed agents by the SRC, and Husband, the consulting engineer, as to the maximum aperture which could be built for a given sum which was to be about £5 million; (c) they would find out what would be the cost of copying the Bonn telescope. (The Bonn instrument was a German radio telescope with an aperture of 100 metres—(328 feet.)

Husband and the UKAEA were presented with the task of a new design study. By the beginning of 1971 Lovell was of the opinion that a firm decision should now be taken either to proceed or to abandon the project. In a letter to the Vice-Chancellor of the University of Manchester, dated 21 January 1971, he made the comment: 'In my view the University should before very long take steps to enforce a decision, one way or the other. I hope you will agree after reading the (enclosed) memorandum that the present hold up is intolerable and our future progress is being hampered both here and nationally in a manner which is far worse than an adverse decision against the Mk V.' But unbelievably the indecision continued throughout 1972 and 1973, with inflation constantly escalating costs. In a memorandum dated 28 February 1972, Lovell wrote: 'The Vice-Chancellor pointed out that if we held a pistol at the heads of the SRC then they would certainly withdraw. While acknowledging that, I made it clear that I would now set a limit to the time during which I would continue to be associated with this project, since I could not be held responsible for this continued state of indecision costing us between £1,000 and £2,000 per day at a time when even a year ago we had every reason to expect that we would actually be constructing the telescope.'

By 1974, costs had gone through the roof. In April 1974 the tenders for a telescope with a reduced aperture of 375 feet, known as the Mk VA, indicated a cost of a massive £20 million. The preliminary inquiries concerning an alternative German design appeared likely to lead to a cost of £15 million as the very minimum figure. There was no prospect of the SRC's obtaining such funds, and the project had to be abandoned, but not without a great deal of public criticism. Since its original conception in 1964 from the 1,000-foot Mk IV proposal, which had to be dropped for cost reasons, the MK V had by June 1974 cost £750,000 in feasibility and design studies, investigations, drawings and tenders. All for nothing. The Public Accounts Committee, after its investigation into this expenditure on a radio telescope that was never to be built, fully endorsed the 'step-by-step' approach of the Science Research Council to ensure that the project could be afforded within the Council's limited budget. In fact, the PAC endorsed an attitude which killed the project and which made it unlikely that any similar visionary scientific scheme could succeed under the then system of financing scientific research. The constant process of trying to ensure that costs would remain within a certain bracket and delaying the go-ahead month by month and year by year to look at fresh estimate after fresh estimate resulted in a magnificent research instrument, which for want of courage could have been built for £4.5 million in 1967, being abandoned in June 1974 because the cost had escalated due to inflation to £20 million. In fact the fruitless protective arrangements to safeguard the financial aspects had led to a complete waste of £750,000 and a great deal of precious manpower. Lovell wrote at the time, in a draft letter to *The Times*, a letter which he never sent: 'Not finance, but lack of vision and courage coupled with political pressures demanding that the available money should be spread amongst projects likely to be productive of knowledge useful to the State, combined to kill the Mk V telescope project. The creation of the great machines of fundamental research will remain in peril until the country recognises the need for appropriate funding without the bureaucratic entanglements now rapidly stifling the work of its creative scientists.'

Lovell was justified in his criticism. But it is evident that the real cause of the failure to build the Mk V was the indecision to proceed in the early years caused by the excessive caution of the Treasury in respect of fears of rising costs. By their irresolution, particularly from 1964 to 1967, they let inflation outbid them and, into the bargain, submit a bill for £750,000 for no return.

24

'Words Fail'

Astronomy and its associated instruments were not Lovell's only responsibility as a member of the SRC and Chairman of its Astronomy, Space and Radio Board. Space research was an item which offered a tremendous potential for increasing the astronomer's knowledge of those deeper regions of the Universe denied to the optical and radio telescope sited on Earth. The ability to place scientific instruments in orbit above the obscuring layers of the Earth's atmosphere had in early 1958 led to surprising discoveries. For example, the Geiger counters in the first American Explorer Satellite had revealed zones of protons and electrons trapped in the Earth's magnetic field, leading to the realization that interplanetary Space was not the near vacuum populated only by the planetary bodies, asteroids, meteors and comets as previously believed. On the contrary, interplanetary Space was found to be a complex of particles and magnetic fields with the planets and Earth enveloped in the attenuated solar corona. This meant that previous ideas about the relationship of major geophysical effects to disturbances on the Sun, such as magnetic storms and the aurora borealis, needed revision. Lovell foresaw the probable fund of knowledge that would be available to a telescope sited on a platform orbiting in Space, or operating from the surface of the Moon, and from probes despatched to the planets of the Solar System such as Venus, Mars and Jupiter. What was disappointing and disturbing was that Britain had opted out of the chance to conduct its own Space research, without dependence upon other nations, and had therefore denied itself the opportunity to take a significant part in exploring the Universe.

By 1965 Britain had effectively withdrawn from any independent exploitation of Space for commercial, military and scientific activities. When the USSR launched its *Sputnik I* in 1957, Britain had the ballistic rockets Blue Streak and Black Knight in an advanced stage of development for military purposes. However, the military arrangements with the USA to establish ballistic rocket sites in Britain and to arm them with American Thor ICBMs, thus saving Britain the cost of continuing with its own independent deterrent, a move considered by many to be an unwise one, led to the abandonment of Blue Streak and Black Knight as future military weapons. But the way was then opened for these two British projects to be integrated for use as launchers for Space vehicles for commercial and military objectives and additionally for Space research. The important and immediate commercial application could have been for communications. Unfortunately the official advisory committees of both the Conservative and then the Labour Governments adopted an antagonistic attitude to Space activities other than in concert with Europe. Indeed, the critical lead which Britain should have taken at the time of the cancellation of Blue Streak and Black Knight as ICBMs by using them in combination as Space vehicles·'evaporated almost entirely', Lovell said, 'as the politicians sought to ingratiate themselves with the European Community by the offer of British expertise and hardware'.

The political moves to curry favour with the European Community resulted in the creation of the European Launcher Development Organization (ELDO), with Britain offering Blue Streak as the first stage of a launcher and with the second and third stage being built by France and Germany. This was a dismal failure and by 1972, with its 'Europa' launcher, ELDO failed to place a single satellite in orbit. In fact, much money had been used to no avail.

A parallel European organization was created specifically for dealing with payloads for satellites, named the European Space Research Organization (ESRO). This was somewhat more successful. With Britain bearing one quarter of the cost of the organization, several satellites were designed and built successfully on a multi-national basis and launched by US rockets. But disagreements between the European countries concerned led to arguments about the role of ESRO, resulting in a reduction in the planning and construction of purely scientific satellites in favour of more commercial applications. This prompted Lovell, as Chairman of the ASRB, to submit to the SRC a highly critical attack upon the fact that a vast proportion of the Board's budget was absorbed by ESRO. In a statement to the Council dated 27 September 1968, Lovell began by stating:

> As Chairman of the ASRB it is my duty to convey to Council the recommendation of the Board that the UK participation in ESRO should continue. However, this endorsement of the recommendation of the SPGC [Space Policy and Grants Committee] was made in a form which still deepens the cleavage between the various activities of the Board. The members in favour, without significant further qualification of the recommendation, were Sheppard, Boyd, Eastwood, Saxton. The following members agreed "without enthusiasm"—Brück, Ryle, Redman, Lees. The Astronomer Royal declined to offer an opinion on the grounds that he was not competent to do so, and Hoyle, the Chairman of the APGC [Astronomy Policy and Grants Committee] opposed the resolution vigorously. Elliott, the remaining member of the Board, was not present, but has since informed me that he, too, would have opposed the resolution.

Lovell went on to report that the SPGC now absorbed 70 per cent of the Board's budget and that approximately 75 per cent of this share was accounted for by the subscription to ESRO. This percentage of the Board's budget created a disproportionate balance between the national and international activities of the Board, and because of ESRO's poor showing to date, Lovell stated: 'I simply cannot reconcile this distribution with the split in the Board. . . . Under these circumstances I am forced to enquire into my personal reaction to this situation.' He then went on to say that he had a deep faith and interest in the Space field and was well acquainted with the revolutionary impact which the researches in Space vehicles had so far had on knowledge of the Solar System. He was certain that many researches being initiated would have a profound influence in acquiring knowledge of the deeper regions of Space in the next decade. But he was critical of the lack of influence accorded to the UK by its European partners in ESRO, despite the substantial financial contribution made by the SRC:

Members of Council are well aware of the gloomy story of ESRO. 'As far as the ASRB is concerned the plain facts are:-
I.   that we have so far spent £20 million on the organisation;
II.   that if we continue at the agreed growth rate of 6% we will have spent by 1976 a total sum of at least £60 million;
III.   that for these sums of money we have so far managed to get 5 experiments into orbit and that our best expectation is that by 1976 we might have had about 15 experiments in orbit (based on a one-fifth share of the number estimated by Dinkespiler* [the Director of Planning and Programmes in the ESRO]);
IV.   that each UK experiment in an ESRO satellite will have cost about £4 million by 1976, plus a quite significant sum from the amounts distributed by the SPGC in the UK.

The vast cost of some of the ESRO proposals in relation to the possible scientific outcome, and to the limited influence of UK scientists in the choice of experiments, had led Lovell to the state where he felt he could no longer support continued participation in ESRO. Britain was, he felt, paying out its money solely to help finance the scientific desires of continental Europe. Another fact which disturbed him was the revelation that the more ambitious launchings could be undertaken only with the participation in payload and launching of the American National Aeronautics and Space Administration (NASA) and that ESRO was therefore actively seeking a more detailed integration with NASA. 'It was my understanding,' he wrote, 'that ESRO was to be the third independent power in the Space field.'

Lovell's overall conclusion was that, to improve the UK Space research situation the UK must remove itself from 'the incubus of ESRO' as a first step. 'We should then organise our research programme on a national basis and in bilateral collaboration with NASA when appropriate and possible,' he wrote. 'I take this view even if ASRB's budget were to be reduced by the whole amount of the ESRO subscription. I believe that the Space scientists of the UK have been trapped into an expensive mode of thinking before they have deployed their ability and brain power on the more elementary experiments. For example, there is a vast difference in cost of satellites which need a measure of orientation and those that are only spin stabilised. A tremendous amount of vitally important data remains to be obtained by the cheaper forms of satellite, some of the most important results of this decade have been obtained by the Chicago group in cheap spin-stabilised satellites.' He referred to the important work done by this group with three satellites costing $12 million and only $2.5 million each for launching, which was just about the equivalent of an 18 months' subscription to ESRO. He concluded by saying: 'The Government may wish to continue its contribution to ESRO for political reasons. In this case I consider that the Government should make it clear that it is doing so for those reasons; that it should not continue on the shoulders of an SRC recommendation and that any such move should not hinder the re-organisation of the ASRB on a more realistic financial basis.'

To Brian Flowers, the Chairman of the SRC, Lovell wrote that, since the views expressed in his statement to the Council ran contrary to the recommendation of the ASRB, 'I have little alternative other than to place my resignation as Chairman of the Board at your disposal. This I do with regret. Naturally, I understand that the extension of my membership of SRC to September 1970 was on the basis of my continued chairmanship of the ASRB and in order to simplify your action as much as possible under these unfortunate circumstances I will at the same time place my resignation from Council at your disposal and will await your advice as to whether I should make formal submission to the Secretary of State.'

Lovell was, in fact, dissuaded from resigning, as was Hoyle who had also decided to resign. Instead, he remained on the Council and as Chairman of the ASRB until September 1970,[1] when his tenure of office was due to expire. But his criticism of ESRO and of Britain's Space policy proved to be soundly based as the years passed. At all times he looked back to the end of the 1950s and the early 1960s and considered what the situation could have been in Britain alone had she had the good sense and courage to develop her own Space launcher by an integration of Blue

[1] Lovell's original appointment to the SRC was for three years, expiring September 1968. He was persuaded to continue for two more years to September 1970.

Streak, Black Knight and perhaps a third stage. The proposals had been put forward in 1960 by the Renwick 'pressure group'. Then, in 1961, the British Space Development Company, which had been formed by Lord Renwick as a consultative consortium of the leading British aerospace and electronic companies, had put forward a detailed and budgeted plan for a satellite communications system for the Commonwealth and the Atlantic. This was to be an entirely British system and British launched, and self-financing. Had these ventures been proceeded with, instead of being abandoned in the interests of the political desire, Conservative, Labour and Liberal, to ingratiate themselves with the European Community, Britain would have had launching capability independent of the USA and the USSR and could have operated in Space, commercially, militarily and scientifically, to the extent that was within her means and to her national and international advantage.

In 1973 Lovell wrote in his book *The Origins and International Economics of Space Exploration* (published by the Edinburgh University Press): 'The really disturbing issue is the almost complete failure of any other nation, or group of nations, other than the USA and USSR to engage in these activities.' This was in reference to the extensive operations in Space conducted by the Americans and the Russians to date, covering communications, meteorological forecasting, navigation, study of Earth resources, scientific investigations and military uses.

The UK, and later Europe [he continued] had a wonderful opportunity and has almost completely wasted both the opportunity and extremely large sums of money through lack of vision and leadership. The present European Space bill is two hundred million pounds per annum, as much as the Americans are spending on their Space scientific and applications programmes. It is difficult to be precise about the cumulative amount spent by Europe on Space in the last ten years, but collectively in ELDO and ESRO, and individually as nationals, the bill is about 1.5 billion pounds. Some very good science has been done, but little else, and we are today almost entirely dependent on the US for launching rockets. In the last six years the UK alone has spent at least 168.5 million pounds. It is a deplorable story.

In fact, in 1973 there was still no launching capability in Europe. Indeed, it was not until Christmas Eve 1979 that the first successful test launch of a European three-stage launch vehicle, named *Ariane*, was injected into orbit from the Kourou Space Centre in French Guiana. The second test launch, on 23 May 1980, ended in disaster when the booster rocket exploded shortly after take-off. *Ariane* took seven years to develop, following the Europa failures at the beginning of the 1970s, and its cost to completion, including four qualification test flights, was estimated in 1979 at $758 million at mid-1977 economic conditions, or approximately

£345 million at the December 1979 rate of exchange. The development phase of the project was almost entirely French, with France providing 63.8 per cent of the cost, the remaining 36.2 per cent coming from nine members of ESA (the European Space Agency which had earlier been formed by the amalgamation of ELDO and ESRO): West Germany 20.1 per cent, Belgium 5 per cent UK 2.5 per cent, Spain 2 per cent, Netherlands 2 per cent, Italy 1.7 per cent, Switzerland 1.2 per cent, Sweden 1.1 per cent and Denmark 0.5 per cent. Inevitably the major contracts were in the hands of the French, with Germany coming second. Britain received work only on a few instruments. In the production phase, started at the end of 1979, to meet an order from ESA for eleven *Ariane* launchers for missions between 1981 and 1983 France dominated the entire project. The failure of the second launch was, however, a severe setback to the project, and success was delayed until 1983.

In the 1961 proposal for a global communications system by the British Space Development Company, prepared by its Technical Committee which included members of the De Havilland Aircraft Company, Hawker Siddeley, Rolls-Royce, C. A. Parsons, Decca Radar, Plessey, ATV and Elliott Automation, the launching vehicle, based on Blue Streak, Black Knight and a third stage, was estimated at £64 million. £6 million was allowed for the satellite and £4 million for the ground-station development. This was to complete the initial stages of the plan from 1961 to 1965 with launching-capability being reached by 1965. For the period 1966 to 1968 £5 million per annum was estimated generously 'to cover continued development specifically related to the communication satellite programme, by which time it is considered that the system will have become fully operational'. At that stage, the system would have begun to earn for itself and become self-financing. By 1985 it was conservatively forecast, as had been stated in Chapter 20, that the R&D and capital and operating costs would have been £234.9 million for a revenue of £712.6 million. Of the costs, £89 million would have covered the development and production of the initial launchers, satellites and ground stations, allowing for initial failures and low operational life years of the satellites during the period 1966 to 1968.

Had Britain had the courage in 1961 to proceed on its own, it would not only have had launcher capability fifteen years earlier than the French *Ariane* project but would also have been earning good revenue on its communications system. Other applications could also have been paying for themselves and providing facilities for scientific research as early as the beginning of the 1970s, and launcher design and performance would unquestionably have improved with the on-going progress of research and development which inevitably continues with successful projects.

Commenting on the situation at the beginning of 1980, Lovell said to me: 'Words fail—it is just too disgraceful for contemplation.'

And so, as the seventies were entered and progressed, Lovell and his team at Jodrell Bank concentrated on astronomical research with those instruments that were available to them—the radio telescopes.

The Mk 1A telescope, which was never meant as a substitute for the ill-fated Mk V but as a preservation of Jodrell Bank's ability to remain in the forefront of radio astronomy research by giving new life to the ageing Mk I, finally came into operation in the last weeks of 1971. The Mk I had been out of service since August 1970 when structural changes and modification were initiated after 13 years of continuous use, completing 68,538 hours, as has already been mentioned. Even if the Mk 1A was no substitute for the Mk V, which would have had a 400-foot aperture paraboloid, its performance was still a considerable improvement on the Mk I.

The main purpose of the modifications to the Mk I was to relieve the loading on the cones which carried the bowl or paraboloid in elevation. To do this the engineers had to add several hundreds of tons of weight in steel below the trunnion axis which was the centre of gravity of the elevation motion of the bowl. This had to be counter-balanced by adding weight above the trunnion axis, and this was done by constructing an entirely new shallower bowl of long focal length within the original reflecting membrane. This presented an opportunity to install a reflecting surface which was considerably more accurate than that of the original Mk 1. Whilst the original Mk 1 was not fully efficient in operation on the important hydrogen line wavelength of 21 centimetres, the Mk 1A with the new bowl was, and, in addition, it was accurate down to a wavelength of 6 centimetres. This was not comparable with the Mk V, which would have been accurate down to 3 centimetres and whose other facilities were a substantial advance on the Mk 1A, but the improvement in performance over the Mk 1 was, nonetheless, considerable. Lovell says that he often recalls Rainford's comment, made at the time that the Mk V project began to run into difficulties due to escalating costs, 'that the decision to proceed with the Mk. 1A was probably the wisest we had ever made'.

By the time the Mk 1A became operational, Lovell was no longer being requested to co-operate with the USA and the USSR in their Space activities. Both America and Russia now had their own tracking and control facilities which were fully capable of doing all that Jodrell Bank had done for them in the past. However, co-operation in astronomy with the USA, the USSR, Australia and other countries continued and was soon on an increased scale. Researches were conducted with the Mk 1A on its own, and in interferometric combination with the Mk 11 and Mk

111 at Wardle, or the Defford telescope,[1] for measuring the angular size and structure of various stars. But if he was to be denied the various advantages of the now cancelled Mk V project, Lovell was determined to obtain some compensation for this loss, and early in 1976 the idea of a multi-telescope radio-linked interferometer, to be known as the MTRLI, began its translation into fact. The complete system, which was to consist of five out-station radio telescopes and one telescope at Jodrell Bank, was begun in 1976. The telescopes at Defford in Worcestershire, and Wardle (Jodrell Bank's mobile Mk III telescope) near Nantwich had been used in conjunction with the Mk 1A for interferometry to measure the angular size and structure of stars since 1972, and were to form part of the six-telescope link-up. The control systems and links to Jodrell Bank were by 1979 upgraded to provide better control and phase stability, and by July 1979 the first stage of the MTRLI was nearing completion with one of the new 25-metre (82-foot) aperture telescopes, usable to a wavelength of about one centimetre built at Knockin near Oswestry, linking up to make possible observations using four telescopes. The other two telescopes, one at Darnhall near Winsford, and one at Tabley near Knutsford, were soon to be linked into the system, with the Tabley telescope finished in the late summer of 1979 and the Darnhall telescope due to be completed at the end of the year. When the MTRLI was completed early in 1980, the baselines available with the system ranged from 6.4 kilometres (4 miles) between Wardle and Darnhall to 133.8 kilometres (83 miles) between Defford and Tabley. Bringing this system to fruition was dependent upon the excellent work of Lovell's staff, in particular J. G. Davies, of whom Lovell says: 'I do not think that without his brains behind the computer digital system the MTRLI would ever have worked.'

Phase coherence between the telescope in the MTRLI system is achieved by transmitting pulses at a single frequency in both directions over all the link paths. This is used at an outstation to lock the frequency synthesizer providing the local oscillator, and at Jodrell Bank to measure changes in the effective link path by comparing the phase of the transmitted waveform with that returned from each outstation. Atmospheric variations cause changes of several metres in the link-path length, and by this technique these can be measured with a precision of 1 millimetre. With the distance between Jodrell and Defford at about 130 kilometres (80.8 miles), for example, this is a very remarkable technical achievement. The radio signals received at the outstation are transmitted by microwave

---

[1] This telescope, built by the Royal Radar Establishment on the runway previously used by Lovell's group during the war, was used in collaborative work between RRE personnel and Jodrell from 1965. In 1980 it was purchased by the University of Manchester from the Ministry of Defence, when it became an essential part of the MTRLI network.

link to Jodrell Bank, where they are passed through computer-controlled phase rotators and digital delays to remove the effects of the Earth's rotation and the differences in link-path lengths. They are then correlated in pairs in a 1,024-channel 20-MHZ cross-correlator. Each record of the integrated output of the correlator is passed into the controlling computer for further integration, processing, storage and display. The integrations for a 24-hour period are stored on a disc which is later analysed on a second large computer equipped with displays and graph plotter for the interactive analysis of the data and the production of maps of the sky in various forms.

The strength of the MTRLI system lies in its versatility as regards its wavelength coverage, its sensitivity and its angular diameter coverage. The wide range of angular diameters found in radio sources from Space can be investigated with this instrument. In extra-galactic sources, studies of source structure provide essential data for the understanding of the basic physical processes involved; also many types of source provide unique probes of cosmological models and galaxy evolution. Fundamental galactic studies are possible with the MTRLI including investigations of star-formation using maser sources, pulsar motions and the envelopes around stellar objects. Indeed, this system, which came into operation in 1980, offers the chance to probe the deeper regions of the Universe which were well beyond the capability of the original Mk I telescope. But early in 1980 Lovell was cautious. He told me that the question was 'to what extent the astronomy which we can carry out with the MTRLI in any way compensates for that which could have been done with the Mk V? It is a question which cannot be answered . . . . The fact is that in all these major projects it so often happens that their importance lies not only in the work which they were expected to do, but in the unexpected applications which ensue.' He added: 'Look at the Mk I as a perfect example of this!'

By 1980, with his retirement due in September of the following year, Lovell had taken Jodrell Bank and the new science of radio astronomy a long way from those days of 1945 when he returned to Manchester at the end of World War II. The transformation from two wooden huts in a field in 1946, some Army radar equipment and a team consisting of himself, Dr John Clegg and two friendly gardeners named Alf Dean and Frank Foden, and with the outside assistance of the amateur meteor observer J. P. Manning Prentice, to the Nuffield Radio Astronomy Laboratories at Jodrell Bank in 1980 was nothing short of miraculous. From those small beginnings, due to Lovell's ability, ingenuity and dogged determination, Manchester University had a radio astronomy research centre that was the envy of the world, and Britain held a place in this field of science second to none. At the beginning of 1980 the academic and research staff consisted of Sir Bernard Lovell as Professor and Director, Professors J. G. Davies and R. D. Davies, one Reader, three Senior Lecturers, eleven Lecturers, four Research Fellows, two Fellows, one Research Associate and fifteen students, the majority of whom were working for their PhDs. In support, there was a team of eight working on computer programmes, data-handling developments, Space tracking facilities, computer development, receiver and feed development and radio link systems. In the MSc Teaching School there were ten students, some from overseas, the total number and names varying with completions of the courses and with new entries. The technical staff covering the mechanical workshop, electronics workshop, electronics and digital maintenance, telescope control and engineering consisted of forty-eight senior and junior technicians and engineers. The secretarial, library and administrative staff amounted to nine. Cleaners, gardeners, gatemen and personnel employed in the Concourse Building which was open to the public added a further sixteen individuals. In all, the 1980 team amounted to approximately 131 persons.

In 1979 the academic and research staffs were working in teams to cover a pulsar search programme; interferometric measurements of radio galaxies and quasars; radio studies of flare stars; H-line investigations of the Milky Way and external galaxies, and cosmological studies at high redshift; polarization of discrete radio sources and planetary investigations; surveys and identifications of radio sources; pulsar investigations; and study of hydrogen masers. These examples do not even fully cover the total research activities but they are an indication of the breadth and depth of this internationally respected and famous astronomical research institution of Great Britain. And Jodrell Bank does not work in isolation. Due to Lovell's early and continued liaison with the centres of astronomical research in other countries, notably the Netherlands, Germany, the USA, USSR and Australia, international co-operation with Jodrell Bank in its researches is highly significant, as is the co-operation between Jodrell Bank and other British astronomical research centres. In 1980 the 1979 work continued and increased in all the above fields, and with intensive use of the new MTRLI system since 1980, the work of Jodrell Bank will undoubtedly make even more important contributions to science in the field of astronomical research and investigation.

Great Britain may have failed to take its place in Space via satellites and probes launched by its own rocket-launcher capability, but thanks in large measure to Lovell it has acquired a leading position in astronomical research via its radio telescopes probing the Universe and, whilst moving towards the discovery of the very beginnings of the Universe, revealing more and more of the complexity and immensity of the Cosmos than had ever been known before.

25

Let There Be Light

No book on Bernard Lovell's working life would be complete without a summary of his views on cosmology to which the work at Jodrell Bank has contributed so much vital information. Nor would it be complete without a reflection on his opinions as to whether intelligent life exists elsewhere in the Universe.

As a boy, Lovell had been fascinated by the sky and inquisitive about the secrets it held, and his inquisitiveness was never assuaged. As he grew up, Man's ideas about the Universe were undergoing profound changes as the new telescopes and other tools of research, coming into use with the advances in technology, began to probe ever further into time and Space. For centuries it was believed that the Earth was the centre of the Universe, and that the Sun, the planets and the stars rotated around it. The modern view that the Earth and planets were in motion around the Sun originated with Copernicus—his famous hypothesis was published in 1543, the year of his death. Sixty years later, when Galileo first observed the heavens through a small telescope, he found incontrovertible observational evidence in favour of the Copernican theory. The promulgation of the idea that the Earth could no longer be regarded as fixed at the centre of the Universe was in serious conflict with the teachings of the Church. Galileo faced the Inquisition and in 1633 was made to repudiate his evidence, but he was allowed to live the remaining years of his life under house arrest on his farm near Arcetri.

Early in the twentieth century, although there was then acceptance of the principle that the Earth and the planets moved around the Sun, it was still believed that the Solar System was at the centre of the Universe of fixed stars. Lovell, who was born in 1913, says: 'I was brought up on the idea that the Sun was in the centre of the stellar system of many millions of stars distributed throughout such a volume of space that light [which travels at a speed of 186,000 miles per second] would take 20,000 years to traverse the Universe. Indeed, it was already too large for normal comprehension, and we seemed to be in a highly privileged position in the central regions of this great creation.' But in 1919 the American astronomer Harlow Shapley discovered that the stars in the Milky Way, believed to comprise the entire Universe, were not distributed with spherical symmetry around the Sun. Instead he found that the Milky Way was a system of some 100 billion stars distributed throughout a flattened

disc—and today we understand that within this disc the stars are distributed in spiral arms emerging from a central nucleus. The diameter of the
disc is about 100,000 light years, and the Sun lies in one of the spiral arms,
33,000 light years from the central region. Then in 1926 Hubble, using
the new 100-inch telescope of Mt Wilson, settled the arguments about the
nature of the 'nebulae'. He discovered that some of these nebulae were
great systems like the Milky Way, but remote in Space. At last astronomers were forced to realize that the stars of the Milky Way did not
comprise the totality of the Universe. On the contrary, countless similar
star systems were distributed throughout Space far beyond the confines of
the Milky Way.

These revelations about the nature of the Universe came during
Lovell's student days. Indeed, it was an extraordinary age for a young man
like Lovell to be growing up in. Scientists had penetrated not only far into
time and Space but also, at the other extreme, into the structure of the
atom. He was excited by these great scientific developments but soon
became disturbed by some of the implications. Shortly after his appointment as Assistant Lecturer in Physics at the University of Manchester he
worked on his first book, *Science and Civilization*. Published in 1939, parts
of this book revealed his increasing anxiety about the influence of science
on the world. He wrote: 'Research is the effort to gain knowledge by
application of the scientific method to the Universe, or to parts of it.
Through research man is able to speculate about the structure of the
entire Universe, he has been enabled to harness natural forces to use for
his own desires, to cure disease and find out how to kill hundreds of
human beings in a few minutes. But so far he has not found out a great
deal about himself. . . .' It was the voice of the young idealist who
informed the reader towards the end of the book that as a boy 'his relatives
marched home from the Great War. They said little, but asked him that in
case he ever became a scientist to promise never to help to make any more
bombs and never to discover anything that could be used in war.' Twenty
years later, with a militant Germany, he was to be suspended from his
researches to be employed on doing those very things he abhorred. Yet,
ironically, it was the technological achievements in radio and radar in
World War II, so many of which arose from Lovell's work to enable Royal
Air Force Bomber Command to be effective, that were to provide a new
dimension to man's researches into the Universe when he returned in
1945 to his life work at the University of Manchester. Out of 'Lovell's
radar' was born the new science of radio astronomy.

On Christmas Eve 1953, Lovell gave a BBC broadcast on the subject of
'Man in the Universe'. His idealism is again revealed, but tempered with
maturity after the shock of his wartime experience. But he is beset by a

new problem: the reconciliation of science with religion which un-doubtedly stemmed from the strength of his religious upbringing and which was to have an increasing influence on his thinking. He opened his broadcast with the words: 'How can we reconcile the peace and goodwill message of the Christmas season with the daily news headlines threaten-ing mass destruction?' This was a reference to the development of nuclear weapons. He continued by asking 'How can we, in fact, reconcile religion and science? The tension is between these two. Sometimes it seems to many of us that the benefits of science are a poor recompense for the dangers of the modern world. . . . We have grown to fear science and to despair of religion. We fear science because we feel it might destroy us; and we despair of religion because we feel that it no longer seems able to prepare man to face the contemporary world.' The reason for tension was, he asserted, the failure of our moral and religious teachers to adjust human thought to the ever-increasing knowledge and power of science, and this reason is always changing. At the beginning of the century it was evolution, and in the twenties and thirties it was over the philosophical implications of modern physics and the deeply rooted controversy con-cerning the new astronomical discoveries about the Universe. It was on the subject of the controversy over these astronomical discoveries that he based his talk, believing that it held 'the key to a real and lasting reconcili-ation between science and religion'.

After describing the discoveries of Shapley and Hubble which revealed the location of our Solar System far from the central regions of the Milky Way and provided positive evidence for the existence of other galaxies in the Universe, he referred specifically to Earth. 'Is it still unique?' he asked. 'And are we unique, or is there life elsewhere in the Universe? Now doubts about questions like these make it difficult for established religions to absorb science, and conversely for masses of people to absorb religion.' He elaborated on the different theories about the origin of Earth and the Solar System, including one which protected the uniqueness of man and one which demanded acceptance of the possibility of there being many planets, similar to Earth, supporting life as we know it. 'In this case,' he said, 'the conflict with orthodox religious beliefs is, of course, acute.' But Lovell was careful to point out that all such theories were speculative. 'Only a few years ago,' he said, 'the great telescopes in America seemed to have revealed so complete a picture of Space that there was every reason to believe that we could not expect any more great excitements in obser-vational astronomy . . . but already new types of telescopes which receive radio waves instead of light have revealed a completely unexpected Universe—a Universe whose connection with the common stars and nebulae is at present almost unknown. Again a wall has been removed. . . .' In December 1953 the world facilities for radio astronomy were in their infancy and consisted almost solely of Jodrell Bank's transit telescope, Ryle's interferometer aerials at Cambridge, Hey's Army radar equipment, and the equipment of a radio research group under Pawsey in Australia. The construction of the giant steerable radio telescope at Jodrell Bank had only just begun, but Lovell's vision of its capabilities coloured his hopes for a greater understanding of the Universe.

He concluded his broadcast by saying:

Vast new fields of endeavour have been opened up, and in that aspect alone the enrichment of existence is taking place at this moment in dramatic fashion. This real comprehension of the sublimity and marvellous order of the Universe is in itself an all embracing, cosmic religion, unrestricted by dogma or by the difficulties of an anthropomorphic conception of God. As Einstein once said, 'religious feeling takes the form of rapturous amazement at the harmony of natural law, which reveals an intelligence of such superiority that, compared with it, all the systematic thinking and acting of human beings is an utterly insignificant reflection'. I am convinced that only when this feeling becomes the guiding principle of man's life and work can there be real hope for the world. And we have, surely, the beginnings of such a religion clearly set out for us in the Psalms and the Prophets: 'When I consider thy heavens, the work of thy fingers, the moon and the stars, which thou hast ordained, what is man, that thou art mindful of him?'

Four years later, in 1957, the Mk I radio telescope at Jodrell Bank went into action with a capability of exploring deeper and deeper into the Universe. Lovell now became confident that he and his team would be able to pursue researches of importance to our understanding of the Universe. At that time the various possible cosmological models derived from the general theory of relativity in which the Universe was believed to have evolved from a compact dense state billions of years ago, were in sharp contrast with the steady state or continuous creation theory. As distinct from the evolutionary cosmological models, this theory maintained that the Universe was changeless in time and Space when viewed on the large scale. At that time, in 1957, there was no compelling observational evidence in favour of either an evolutionary or a steady state Universe. In fact Lovell and his group were unconvinced by the radio studies elsewhere which were claimed to give evidence for the evolutionary model. In his 1958 BBC Reith Lectures he maintained a cautious stance about this cosmological problem. He began his lectures by saying that it was with mixed feelings of fear and humility that he undertook the task of talking about the Universe, 'Humility, because we have to deal with the implications of observations which take us back to epochs of time before human beings existed. Fear, because the techniques and tools of our trade are often those which form the basis of military power.' After describing the two theories, he warned that,

When we are dealing with timespans of thousands of millions of years it would be sheer impudence to suggest that the views of the cosmos which have evolved from the techniques developed in our age possess any degree of finality. My present attitude to the scientific aspects of the problem is therefore neutral in the sense that I do not believe that there exist any observational data which are decisively in favour of any particular contemporary cosmology. The optimism with which I believe we are on the verge of producing the necessary observational data is tempered with a deep apprehension, born of bitter experience, that the decisive experiment nearly always extends one's horizons into regions of new doubts and difficulties.

About the possible relation of these theories to theological beliefs, Lovell said:

The probable condition of intense radiation in the primeval atom is entirely consistent with the divine command 'Let there be light'. It would, of course, be wrong of me to suggest that this view of the origin of the Universe demands necessarily the possibility of creation of matter by a divine act. On the contrary, those who reject God adopt a strictly materialistic attitude to the problem of the creation of the primeval atom. They would argue that the creation of the primeval material had no explanation within the framework of contemporary scientific knowledge, but would escape from the dilemma by reserving the possibility that science would, if given the opportunity of studying these initial conditions, find a satisfactory solution. Or they would evade the problem of a beginning altogether by following a further line of thought, due to Gamov, that the primeval atom was not in the beginning, but merely a state of maximum contraction of a Universe which had previously existed for an eternity of time.

Lovell continued his lecture by saying that if the Universe had evolved from a dense initial state, 'the conception that the creation of the primeval material was a divine act can never be attacked by scientific investigation. A set of conditions which existed over twenty thousand million years ago, and which can never return again, is forever beyond investigation.'

In concluding his 1958 lectures, he said: 'On the question of the validity of combining a metaphysical and physical process as a description of creation, this, as I said earlier, is the individual's problem. In my own case I have lived my days as a scientist, but science has never claimed the whole of my existence. Some, at least, of the influence of my upbringing and environment has survived the conflict, so that I find no difficulty in accepting this conclusion.'

By the end of the seventies, the greatly increased knowledge about the Universe derived from observations with the modern radio telescopes and the large optical telescopes appeared to give support to the evolutionary theory.

'In common with the majority of astronomers living today,' Lovell said in 1977,[1]

I accept the observational evidence for the evolution of the Universe from a very hot and extremely condensed state. Opinion differs as to whether the highly condensed condition existed ten billion or fifteen billion years ago or even in a more distant epoch. The time scale is not important for our present consideration, and for simplicity I take the figure as ten billion. The discovery of the microwave background radiation just over 10 years ago revolutionised our insight into the early condition of the Universe and defined to a remarkable extent the range of possible interpretations of the initial state. A radio telescope receiving on a wavelength of a few centimetres directed to any part of the heavens will record radiowaves of an intensity equivalent to a temperature of 2.70 K [K = Temperature in degrees on the absolute scale]. We believe that this radiation enables us to look back 99.99% of the time to the moment when the expansion of the Universe began ten billion years ago.

The great importance of the discovery of the microwave background radiation lies in the fact that, if current interpretation is correct, then these observations relate to a much earlier epoch, about one million years after the beginning of the expansion of the Universe.

'At that stage,' Lovell wrote (in his book *In the Centre of Immensities*, 1978), 'the temperature of the Universe is computed to have been about 5,000°K, the radius about one thousandth of the present value and the mean density a billion times greater than the present value.' At this temperature neutral hydrogen formed without being immediately ionized by the surrounding radiation. This is the earliest moment for which there is observational evidence of the primeval Universe. It was an important phase in the evolutionary state when the Universe was no longer dominated by radiation, and matter evolved as the dominant component. A billion years later this matter had formed into galaxies and other objects which today are observable in the distant regions of the Universe.

The study of the microwave background radiation 'helps to define the state of the Universe when it was about a million years old', Lovell wrote. 'At this early stage perhaps the most remarkable feature is that a feasible physical description can be given. The temperature was no greater than that associated with the surface temperature of an average star; the mean density was still very low compared with densities of our terrestrial experience, and the electrons, protons, hydrogen, helium and photons are

---

[1] In his F.W. Angel Memorial Lecture delivered at the Memorial University of Newfoundland, St John's, Newfoundland on 13 October 1977.

the familiar features of everyday physics.' But he emphasized that the physical conditions in the earlier stages of the first one million years after the beginning of the expansion can only be a matter for conjecture. 'As we approach closer to the beginning, the Universe must have been hotter and denser. Although we have no observational evidence of these early stages, it is important to enquire how much closer to the singularity, that is to time zero, the laws of physics and our knowledge of fundamental particles enables us to speculate.' In retracing time, Lovell posed the question: 'Can we formulate even in a speculative manner a possible sequence of events for the first million years after the beginning of the expansion to the epoch when the temperature had fallen to about 5,000°K and neutral hydrogen was able to exist and the photons measured today as the microwave background were emitted?' He emphasized that in the near vicinity of time zero, the physical theories known to us today fail. 'There is a point when we enter realms where classical concepts and quantum theory no longer suffice to describe the state of the Universe. In our ordinary macrosopic world it is possible to treat the gravitational field without encountering problems which arise from the discontinuities of quantum theory. However, as we consider smaller and smaller dimensions, a stage is reached where this situation is no longer acceptable. As the singularity (time zero) is approached, quantum fluctuations of the gravitational field become so large that the laws of physics can no longer be valid.' The barriers of physical theory are reached where further understanding in any physical sense presents problems of such magnitude that there are 'contemporary thinkers who suggest that the real structure of Space and time may lie completely outside our present concepts, or even that the very foundations of mathematics and its logical axioms are insecure'.

In his F. W. Angel Lecture of October 1977, Lovell stated that observable phenomena are subject to investigation by the tools and methods of science, and given time and technique there was no reason to doubt that knowledge in the language of science can be achieved, although he added: 'but at last in this process of scientific probing we find that the investigations have revealed the existence of phenomena which are neither observable nor deducible from those aspects which can be observed.' Later, he wrote (*In the Centre of Immensities*, 1978) that throughout history one purpose of Man has been to seek solutions to the problem of the 'beginning'. In the first half of the twentieth century the problem became a definitive scientific one. 'We see now,' he said, 'that the observational evidence most widely accepted is that the Universe is expanding, and that there *is* a problem of a beginning—a creation—of matter and of Man's existence in this particular Universe. We have no scientific description of the beginning. It may be that, eventually, a more detailed understanding of the observations will place a different interpretation on the redshift,[1] and thereby we can evade the difficulties of the expansion and of the concentrated beginning. In that case we face the problem of creation at some point in an infinite past time, and again this is not observable nor describable in scientific language.' Under these circumstances, he remarked, it was difficult to see how one could improve on the opinion of Saint Augustine, who in answer to the question of why the world was not created sooner, replied that there was no 'sooner' because time was created when the world was created. 'This, of course, is the essence of general relativity in which neither time nor Space existed before the singularity.'

Lovell's brother-in-law and his oldest friend from student days, the late Professor Deryck Chesterman, spoke to me in 1978 shortly before his death. He knew Bernard Lovell perhaps better than anyone except for his sister, Joyce Lovell. From the time of their meeting at Bristol University as first-year undergraduates, they had remained close friends throughout their lives. Indeed, it was due to Deryck Chesterman that Bernard Lovell met Joyce, as has been related at the beginning of this book. Chesterman's views on Lovell's concern to reconcile science with religion are of interest. He said that Lovell may have thought at one stage that physics could explain totally the mechanism of the Universe, but later he became very interested in the relationship between science and religion. 'It comes out in his Reith Lectures (1958). He discusses these matters in all his lectures and books.' Chesterman went on to say that as knowledge from research and investigation into the beginnings of the Universe increased, Lovell would adjust his views in the light of such new knowledge, but never be satisfied. 'I think his success has been that his experimental skill and determination are enormous, otherwise Jodrell would not have been built—and he has also got this drive to look at what he considers a fundamental problem.' Then, when advances in science make questions that were thought to be fundamental no longer funda-mental, 'he goes on and says right, we will investigate the stage of the Universe umpteen thousand million years ago. So this inspires the development of the telescope and it carries him through mud and steel and sand and everything else, and in the end there is a fine instrument working superbly well and it becomes world famous!' Having penetrated so far into the early history of the Universe, he becomes 'enormously

---

[1] The redshift is a shift of all the spectral lines towards the red or long-wave end of the spectrum. All the galaxies, apart from those in our local group, show redshifts in their spectra. It is generally accepted that these redshifts are a Doppler effect implying that the galaxies are receding and that the Universe is in a state of expansion.

interested in the question of whether in the ten seconds after the beginning of the expansion certain things happened which either would lead to
a Universe as we have it now or would not—and then in the first few
microseconds and so on. Then he interests himself in the conditions
which led to life in the Universe.' Chesterman went on to say that he does
not just look back astronomically but moves into the 'biological world and
the metaphysical world and attempts to assault that as well—which he
does!'

When asked by me what he believed was the motivation, Chesterman
felt that this was a complicated question to answer. He continued by
saying that in his opinion 'he is trying to come to terms with his religious
beliefs and the scientific measure. I don't know why Bernard wants to
merge the religious—no, religious is the wrong word—the ethical, the
metaphysical and the physical in one unity, but it would seem to stem from
his childhood background.' To this comment one must add 'plus his adult
thought and experience'.

Deryck Chesterman's views are interesting and are perhaps close to the
truth. At the end of his book *In the Centre of Immensities* Lovell writes:

> The pursuit of understanding is an essential occupation and purpose of
> modern society, as it has been throughout all the thriving societies of history.
> The prominent fear of the mid-twentieth century that science was all powerful
> and would achieve the ultimate finality in these pursuits is now seen to be
> without foundation. The immense intrinsic values of science and of the
> scientific method to the modern community are well established, and will be
> enhanced by the recognition that they are absolute neither in practical nor
> intellectual pursuits. The rediscovery of the validity of non-scientific modes of
> thought and investigation will establish once more the faith of the people in
> science itself, to the detriment of the pseudosciences which tend to gain
> monopoly in periods of decadence.

These words reveal his search for the synthesis of the ethical, metaphysical and physical aspects of our knowledge. In his last words in this
book he refers to a remark by Marcus Fierz, the Swiss physicist-
philosopher: 'The scientific insights of our age shed such glaring light on
certain aspects of the experience that they leave the rest in even greater
darkness.'

In his F. W. Angel Memorial Lecture, delivered on 13 October 1977,
he said: 'In all the sciences there are hosts of unsolved problems and it is
the essence of the faith of the professional scientist that solutions and
answers can be found by application of the scientific method and technique. In many cases the faith will be justified but it is a strange feature of
our age that in some of the vital investigations concerned with the
fundamental issues of the existence of the Universe and of Man's place

and comprehension of the cosmos we appear to be penetrating to a greater darkness.' Lovell is of the same opinion as Marcus Fierz, whom he quoted.

Lovell's views on the existence of intelligent life elsewhere in the Universe remain cautious. In the twenties, Harlow Shapley of Harvard Observatory estimated that there must be some 10^{20} stars in the Universe with characteristics similar to those of the Sun and that it was reasonable to assume that one in a thousand would have a planetary system and that one in a thousand of these would have a planet at the right distance away to give temperature conditions like those on Earth. Of these planets he estimated that one in a thousand would have the right mass and size to retain an appropriate atmosphere in which life could survive. His final conclusion was that there were a billion stars in the Universe on which conditions could, in principle, favour the emergence of life.

In his book *In the Centre of Immensities* Lovell wrote that the nebular theory of planetary evolution coupled with the modern view that stars are formed from clouds of dust and gas makes it possible to seek a more scientific opinion of the number of stars which may have a planet suitable for the evolution of life. The Milky Way has some hundred billion stars with an enormous range of masses, temperatures and luminosities. The evolutionary history of stars is now fairly well understood. In the condensation of stars from the primeval gas clouds, planetary systems are formed from the particles in the nebula surrounding the contracting star. During contraction the temperature and pressure rise until thermonuclear reactions involving the conversion of hydrogen to helium commence. The contraction then ceases and a state of equilibrium is reached. The eventual lifetime in this stable condition for a star like the Sun is about twelve billion years before the hydrogen supply begins to fail, leading to a catastrophic fate for the star and its planets. 'Clearly,' Lovell writes, 'as far as organic evolution is concerned, any interest must be concentrated on stars with temperatures not too dissimilar from the Sun's and which have been established on the main sequence for several billion years and have a similar future life expectancy.' The 'main sequence' is the term used in astronomy for stars which are in a state of equilibrium. He goes on to say that stars 'with temperatures in the range from about 4,500°K to 7,500°K are the optimum candidates' and that these include about twenty billion stars in the Milky Way alone which may therefore have a planet with Earth-like characteristics. Taking into account the fact that there are some one hundred million galaxies, a large number of which admittedly are known to be undergoing violent evolutionary processes and therefore could not have stars which qualify, 'Shapley's estimate of a billion stars in the Universe with a planet which might favour the emergence of life is seen to be very cautious. The astronomical answer from these theoretical considerations seems inescapable: there are billions of stars even in the observable Universe which could provide a suitable environment for a habitable planet.'

Despite this favourable situation for extra-terrestrial life, Lovell has serious reservations about the probability of its emergence elsewhere than on Earth. One of the weaknesses of the argument that there are stars which could have a planet which is similar to Earth is that no planetary system has ever been observed around even the stars nearest to the Solar System. Due to the poor resolving powers of telescopes on Earth, together with the huge difference in brightness between star and planet obscuring the chance of detecting the planet, this is not surprising. However, Lovell's major doubts rest on the possible uniqueness of the emergence of Earth's habitable atmosphere, and on the critical biological chances of life forming not only elsewhere but even on Earth.

There is a crucial interval in the history of Earth, Lovell says, for which the scientific explanation has to be bridged 'by faith, speculation or guesswork.' This interval is the period of about a billion years after Earth was formed 4.5 billion years ago during which Earth's primeval atmosphere disappeared. Earth, and the planets around any star, would be formed with approximately the same composition as the star itself. 'In the case of the Sun, this means about 2% of heavy elements and the remainder of hydrogen and helium. Indeed, the outer planets (of the Solar System) do have approximately this composition. Earth clearly does not since we should be unable to live in such a hydrogen-helium environment.' Lovell goes on to say that the present atmosphere of Earth is so different from any conceivable primeval atmosphere that one must conclude that at some early stage this early atmosphere was stripped away in a cataclysmic event by forces that cannot be known today; 'our present atmosphere is a secondary event and a widely accepted opinion is that the gases of which it is formed were subsequently exhaled from the solid body of the Earth.' The emergence of the Earth's habitable atmosphere, he believes, involved a series of delicate balances which occurred during the first billion years of its history. He bases this on the fact that micro-structures of single-celled organisms, which are estimated to have existed about 3.2 billion years ago, have recently been discovered in South African rock formations. This would mean that life must have emerged on Earth 3.5 billion years ago, and as Earth formed 4.5 billion years ago, this would imply that Earth lost its primeval atmosphere in the first billion years. To emphasize the unusual conditions of Earth, Lovell compares its atmosphere with Mars and Venus, two neighbouring planets in our Solar System. Venus, for example, is so similar to Earth in mass and size that in the early stages the two planets must have been almost identical, yet the strange processes which provided Earth with a habitable atmosphere did not occur on Venus. 'For the first billion years at least,' he says, 'the two planets must have been almost indistinguishable; they would have generated the same internal heat through radioactive processes and must have suffered the same level of volcanic activity. From the study of the planets Earth, Venus and Mars, it seems that the conditions for the evolution of a habitable atmosphere depend critically on the mass of the planet and its distance from the Sun. We do not know what the limits are, even for our own Solar System.'

Discussion of the possible number of habitable planets in the Universe has, in Lovell's opinion, virtually no scientific basis at the moment. The weakness lies in lack of observational evidence, but he admits that a little knowledge of the conditions in another planetary system 'would be of inestimable significance', and this might come with the advance in design of scientific instruments and techniques, including Space probes. At present, however, it seems that the one planet we know, Earth, 'is unique and narrowly habitable in our own system, and it is habitable because of some unknown and probably cataclysmic event which swept away the atmosphere with which it was formed some time during the first billion years of its existence'.

Even so, life on Earth today is proof that a strange sequence of chance events did take place over 3 billion years ago, but Lovell is of the opinion that the astronomical part of those primeval years is probably forever beyond observation or investigation. 'One might well be justified in feeling that the discussion of life elsewhere in the Universe must remain a fictional matter unless the imaginative leaps required to cover the terrestrial sequences can be resolved within the framework of scientific knowledge.'

Today, however, there are responsible sections of the scientific community who do not question that elsewhere in the Universe there are planetary systems on which intelligent life has developed. Indeed, attempts are being made, particularly in the USA, to establish communication with extra-terrestrial communities. Two American spacecraft, *Pioneer 10* and *11*, which were launched on 3 March 1972 and 6 April 1973, respectively, to examine the planets Jupiter and Saturn, will move out of the Solar System ultimately and travel into interstellar Space. Each carries a 6 × 9 inch gold anodized aluminium plaque engraved with naked figures of a man and a woman and symbols which it is hoped represent in easily understood scientific language some information on the locale, epoch and nature of the builders of the spacecraft. Whilst this is intended to convey a visual message should either of these spacecraft come into contact with intelligent communities on other worlds, it is believed that 'interstellar radio messages can be much richer in information content than this message in a bottle cast into the cosmic ocean,' as Carl Sagan, Professor of Astronomy and Space Science at Cornell University, USA, so aptly put it.

In January 1980 Lovell told me: 'I would not be prepared to deny the possibility that life had evolved elsewhere in the Universe. On the other hand, the recent investigations revealing the hostile conditions of other planets in our own system, and the uniqueness of Earth, leads me to believe that if life has evolved elsewhere in the Universe, then the chances that it has done so are far, far less than has been rather commonly supposed in recent years.'

If there is life elsewhere in the Universe, its discovery may not be for tens or hundreds of years. It seems that such an event is unlikely to occur in Lovell's working life, but if and when it does, it will be an event which has been assisted by the highly significant advances in radio astronomy and Space exploration over the past forty years, advances to which Lovell has been a major contributor.

26

Retirement

On 30 September 1980 Sir Bernard Lovell retired from his appointment as Professor of Radio Astronomy at the University of Manchester. As Emeritus Professor of Radio Astronomy, he remained Director of Jodrell Bank until his successor, Professor Graham Smith, formerly Director of the Royal Greenwich Observatory, took over from him on 1 October 1981, as Professor of Radio Astronomy and Director of Jodrell Bank. Manchester's choice of Graham Smith was particularly welcomed by Lovell; he was a close friend and had been co-Professor with Lovell at Manchester until his appointment to the Royal Greenwich Observatory in 1974.

Inevitably for such an active man as Lovell, retirement was a wrench, even at the age of sixty-eight. But as Lovell says, with administrative duties absorbing more and more of his time in the last few years, he was left with less and less time to devote to research. He was, therefore, in many ways 'thankful to hand over a host of these problems' to his successor. 'Clearly,' he told me, 'the wrench would have been of an entirely different order of magnitude if my departure had coincided with our exciting years of astronomical discovery and Space involvement in the '50s and '60s.'

In fact, Lovell's retirement has not left him idle. He was allowed to retain an office at Jodrell Bank complete with secretarial assistance. The shedding of the administrative load has enabled him to take a greater interest in the on-going researches at Jodrell Bank and in astronomical affairs generally. He is now able to attend more of the scientific meetings of the Royal Society, the Royal Astronomical Society and overseas symposiums on astronomy and Space. He has continued to talk and lecture on a variety of subjects and has been engaged in writing papers, articles and reviews in connection with many aspects of astronomy and Space. But perhaps the most demanding writing task has been his third book on Jodrell Bank entitled *The Jodrell Bank Telescopes* (to be published by the Oxford University Press), which covers the economic and political affairs in respect of attempts to build the Mks 1V, V and VA telescopes, the actual conversion of the Mk 1 telescope to the Mk 1A, and the construction of the multi-telescope system, MTRLI, now known as MERLIN.[1] He hopes he will also be able to clear the remaining archives at Jodrell and publish some of the material of historical interest.

[1] Multiple element radio linked interferometer.

'When I retired,' he told me, 'I had hoped to be able to devote more time to the gardens at The Quinta, to musical activities and to cricket. This hope has been only partially fulfilled; nevertheless, even the extra time I now have for these activities gives me great pleasure. As you know, since 1948 Joyce and I, with the help of the family, have made and developed the gardens at The Quinta which now cover several acres and hold a valuable and rare collection of trees and shrubs.' These gardens are now open to the public and have been described in *The Englishman's Garden* (Penguin, 1982) and elsewhere.

His musical associations continue. He is organist at the local church in Swettenham, president of several musical societies and of the Incorporated Guild of Church Musicians, and serves on the Court of the Worshipful Company of Musicians.

With regard to his love of cricket, whilst this is no longer satisfied by active participation in the game itself, Lovell told me that one of the pleasant events coinciding with his retirement was the invitation to him to become a Vice-President of the Lancashire Cricket Club, an invitation which he accepted with alacrity. 'This enables me,' he said, 'to enjoy excellent facilities there, and I derive very great enjoyment from these contacts. One thing leads to another. I tried to repay their kind gesture by devising an automatic light-recording meter. This is now working at Old Trafford, and perhaps because of the interest which this raised I was asked to help the Test and County Cricket Board on a working party to explore the possibility of developing other electronic means of helping umpires. The application of modern electronic techniques, some of which are now used in astronomical researches, to the solution of the controversial issues in cricket is a fascinating problem.'

When I asked Lovell what was the most exciting event he recalls, on reflection he said:

Undoubtedly our association with the Space programme for which the telescope was not intended! The drama, the tremendous excitement, and the underlying implications of the radar echo from the *Sputnik* carrier rocket on that memorable night of 12 October 1957 remain unforgettable. I still see that wonderful echo and have the vivid memory of the Lab on that Saturday evening and turning to my elder son [Bryan], who was showing more interest in the arts than in science at school, and saying: If the sight of that doesn't turn you into a scientist, nothing ever will! The realization that at Jodrell we had the only instrument in the world capable of detecting and tracking by radar an Intercontinental Ballistic Missile in outer Space was exhilarating beyond words. Equally as memorable, perhaps, was our ability to track *Lunik II* on its epic journey to the Moon in September 1959. It was Jodrell, alone, that was able to provide the irrefutable evidence that *Lunik II* had really made impact on the Moon's surface.

On looking back into the past, however, there were also events which made Lovell despondent—in particular, 'The miserable failure of the UK to follow up the immense Space possibility of the '50s and '60s,' he said. 'I do not mean so much the astronomical research angle—in which we have done quite well—but the commercial and industrial failure. For example, British Telecom and the Government boast about their successes with satellite TV and communications. They only have a 10 to 15 per cent investment in this mammoth communications business and they should be ashamed of this because they could have had the major share—and great riches—if initiative had been shown.' He drew attention to the fact that lack of foresightedness had resulted in Britain losing the lucrative earth-station market to Japan and North America. 'We had all the pioneering, technological and engineering experience in the Mks I and II telescopes—Goonhilly was a copy of the basic structure of the Mk 11—and yet their successors all over the world are made in either Japan, the USA or Canada, when we should have captured this market. It is unbelievable, but nevertheless true, that we had to buy our 80-foot telescopes for MERLIN from the USA and that British Telecom have bought—and are still buying—their earth-station dishes from overseas. Why ever have successive governments allowed this to happen?'

On the wider aspect of Space, Lovell believes Britain should have acted more vigorously in the '60s with Blue Streak and Black Knight and invested heavily in the follow-up. There were plenty of keen and experienced scientists in rocketry and allied Space techniques in Hawker Siddeley, De Havillands, Rolls Royce and the RAE. But they were prevented from taking Britain into Space whilst the politicians were trying to use the country's advanced state in this field of technology to buy their way into the Common Market.

The folly of our action in those years is evidenced by the vital role played by rocketry in the military balance and our consequent dependence on the USA. In the early '60s I was one of the small group of scientific advisers to the Air Staff and we persuaded the Chief of the Air Staff that Britain should go ahead with launching its own military communication satellites. But this was abandoned due to political intervention. Just over ten years later we saw that the UK was beholden to the Americans for launching our own military communication satellites, and for our commercial satellite communications. Then, as you are aware [Lovell continued], the Renwick Pressure Group, of which we were both members, lobbied the then Conservative Government at a high level in an effort to persuade it to embark upon a UK and Commonwealth Space Programme with the emphasis on commercial applications. If we had done this we should have commanded the satellite communication and TV systems instead of the Americans—and with vast rewards.

But the Government, with its obsession for joining the EEC, concentrated on trading its know-how in an effort to establish a joint European approach to Space in exchange for membership of the Common Market. The result was that France, whilst denying Britain entry, went ahead with its own Space programme, and Britain was soon left without its lead in this field of technology. Later she had to beg France for a miserable investment in what was to become the French-dominated Ariane Space programme. By the end of the '70s France had its own rockets for launching satellites into Space.

Like a number of other scientists and engineers, Lovell believes that Britain should still, even at this late stage, get back into the Space field on its own. Such a bold move could give employment to many skilled personnel, make Britain far more independent militarily and commercially, and bring immense financial rewards to this country. On the purely scientific research side, Lovell says:

One thing we ought to do now in Space is to blaze the trail to get a radio telescope either in Space or on the Moon—and later beyond. This would be linked with radio telescopes on Earth to give resolving powers far greater than can be achieved by the terrestrial networks like MERLIN. Some of the most interesting objects far away in the Universe have their central regions (powerhouses) so concentrated that they cannot be resolved until we do this. Also we might be able to measure their distances by parallax. Some months ago I had lunch with the Chairman of SERC [the Science and Engineering Research Council—formerly SRC, the Science Research Council] and some of his staff and they asked me what should be done in Space—astronomically. I replied that if I was a young man I would be making their life a misery until they allowed me to get on with this project. Sadly, their response was simply, 'We wish you were young!'

Who's Who of Persons Mentioned

Allen, James Alfred van. Professor of Physics at the University of Iowa, USA. Responsible for the instrumentation of the early Explorer satellites in the USA's 1957–8 IGY programme. Information on cosmic radiation gathered by these satellites led to the discovery of the van Allen Radiation Belts.

Appleton, Sir Edward, GBE, KCB, FRS, Nobel Laureate. Secretary of the Department of Scientific and Industrial Research (DSIR) 1939–49, and Principal and Vice-Chancellor of the University of Edinburgh until his death in 1965.

Appleyard, E. T. S., BSc, PhD. Senior Lecturer at the University of Bristol. Died in 1939.

Bennett, Air Vice-Marshal D. C. T., CB, DSO, DFC. Air Officer Commanding No. 8 Group (Pathfinders) in Bomber Command 1942–5. In 1945 elected to Parliament in a by-election at Middlesbrough on a Liberal ticket.

Blackett, Patrick Maynard Stuart. Langworthy Professor of Physics at the University of Manchester 1937 to 1953. Nobel Prize for Physics in 1948, Companion of Honour 1965, Order of Merit 1967, President of the Royal Society 1965–70, Life Peer as Baron Blackett 1969. Died 13 July 1974.

Bowen, E. G., CBE, FRS. A Telecommunications Research Establishment scientist during World War II. After the war he became Professor of Electronics at the University of Sydney, NSW, Australia, and Director of CSIRO Radiophysics. Later Australian Attaché (Scientific) in Washington DC, USA.

Bragg, Sir Lawrence, CH, MC, FRS. With his father, Sir William Bragg, he was awarded the Nobel Prize for Physics in 1915. Director of the National Physical Laboratory in 1938, and later succeeded Rutherford as Cavendish Professor of Experimental Physics at Cambridge. Later Fullerton Professor of Chemistry at the Royal Institution.

Brown, R. Hanbury, PhD, FRS. A member of Sir Bernard Lovell's staff at Jodrell Bank 1949–64. 1964–81 Professor of Physics (Astronomy) at the University of Sydney, NSW, Australia. Now Emeritus Professor.

Bullard, Sir Edward, MA, PhD, ScD, FRS. Fellow of Churchill College, Cambridge 1960, Professor of Geophysics, Cambridge 1964–74. 1965 Gold Medal, Royal Astronomical Society.

Burrow, J. H., MSc. Laboratory Technician at the University of Bristol in 1930s and 1940s

Cawley, Sir Charles, CBE. Director of the division at DSIR concerned with University grants after World War II. In 1959 appointed Chief Scientist to the Ministry of Power.

Cherwell, Lord. Formerly Professor Lindemann. Scientific Adviser to the Prime Minister, Sir Winston Churchill, throughout World War II.

Chesterman, W. D., DSc, FInstP, FGS, FRPS. Professor of Physics at the University of Bath after the war. Died in 1978.

Cockburn, Sir Robert, KBE, CB, PhD, MSc, MA. A Telecommunications Research Establishment scientist during World War II. After the war Scientific Adviser to the Air Ministry. In 1954 appointed Controller of Guided Weapons and Electronics at the Ministry of Supply, which post he held until his retirement.

Cockcroft, Sir John Douglas, OM, KCB, FRS. Before the war worked with Rutherford on atomic research at Cambridge. During World War II Superintendent of the Air Defence Establishment. Director of Atomic Energy Research Establishment, Harwell, 1946–59. Master of Churchill College, Cambridge, 1959–67. Nobel Prize for Physics 1951. FRS 1936. Died 1967.

Cook, Sir William, KCB, FRS. In 1962 a member of the UK Atomic Energy Authority.

Cooper, Sir William Mansfield, LLM, LLD., Professor of Industrial Law. Vice-Chancellor of the University of Manchester in 1956–1970.

Davies, J. G., MA, PhD. Left the Royal Aircraft Establishment in January 1947 to join Lovell's team at Manchester. Later appointed Professor of Radio Astronomy at the University of Manchester.

Day, John H., DFC and Bar, DSc, PhD. A Squadron Leader in the Royal Air Force during World War II. After a tour on bomber operations, worked on radar aids to navigation and then completed a second tour despite a lost leg. After the war appointed Professor of Zoology at the University of Cape Town in his home country of South Africa.

Dee, P. I., CBE, PhD, FRS. Head of the group at the Telecommunications Research Establishment during World War II which was responsible for much of RAF Bomber Command's radar aids to navigation and bombing. After the war, appointed Professor and Head of the Department of Natural Philosophy at the University of Glasgow. Died in 1983.

Dinkespiler, M. Director of Planning and Programmes in the European Space Research Organization (ESRO).

Ellyett, C. D., MSc, PhD, FRS. Came from New Zealand to Manchester to take a PhD and worked with Lovell's team. Later appointed Professor of Physics at the University of Newcastle, NSW, Australia.

Fennessy, Sir Edward, CBE, BSc, MIEE. Group Captain in the Royal Air Force in World War II in charge of radar ground stations. Managing Director of Decca Radar Limited after the war. Later Deputy Chairman of the Post Office Corporation.

Finniston, Sir Monty, BSc, PhD, FRS, ARTC, FIM. Chief Metallurgist with the Atomic Energy Authority. Later Chairman of the British Steel Corporation, and then in 1978 Chairman of Sears Engineering and a Director of Sears Holdings Limited.

Flowers, Lord, FRS. As Sir Brian Flowers he became Chairman of the Scientific Research Council (SRC) in 1967.

Greaves, Professor William Michael, MA, FRS. Astronomer Royal for Scotland and Professor of Astronomy in the University of Edinburgh from 1938 until his death in December 1955.

Harris, Marshal of the Royal Air Force Sir Arthur T., Bt., GCB, OBE, AFC, LLD. As Air Chief Marshal he was Commander-in-Chief of Royal Air Force Bomber

Command from February 1942 until the end of World War II in 1945. He died in April 1984.

Hartree, Douglas Rayner, PhD, FRS. Professor of Applied Mathematics at the University of Manchester 1929–37. Professor of Theoretical Physics at the University of Manchester 1937–46. Plummer Professor of Mathematical Physics at the University of Cambridge 1946–58. He died in 1958.

Hawthorne, Sir William, CBE, MA, ScD, FRS. Professor of Applied Thermo-dynamics at the University of Cambridge. Later Master of Churchill College, Cambridge.

Hazard, Cyril, PhD. One of Lovell's team at Jodrell Bank in the 1950s. Later took up the appointment of Lecturer in Physics at the University of Sydney, NSW, Australia. Achieved distinction in 1960 for his discoveries relating to Quasars.

Heitler, Walter, FRS. Originator of the quantum theory of the chemical bond.

Herlofson, Nicolai. A meteorologist in World War II. A Norwegian who worked with Blackett at Manchester for a short while after the war. Later he returned to Norway and was later still appointed to a professorship in the Royal Institute of Technology, Stockholm.

Hey, J. S., MBE, DSc, FRS. During World War II was with the Army Operational Research Group. After the war was put in charge of radio astronomy research at the Royal Radar Establishment, Malvern. Chief Scientific Officer 1966–9.

Hill, Charles, MA, MD, DPH, LLD. Formerly Dr Charles Hill, 'the radio doctor'. Became Postmaster General in the Conservative Government in the 1950s and at the end of 1957 was appointed Chancellor of the Duchy of Lancaster. Now Lord Hill of Luton.

Hilton, W. F., DSc, PhD, DIC, ARCS, FRAeS. One-time head of the Astronautics Division, Advanced Projects Group, Hawker Siddeley Aviation Limited.

Hodgkin, Sir Alan, OM, KCB, MA, DSc, FRS. President of the Royal Society 1970–5. John Humphrey Plummer Professor of Biophysics, Cambridge 1970– . Chancellor of Leicester University 1971– . Nobel Prize for Medicine 1963 (shared). Medical Research Council 1959–63. Master of Trinity College, 1978.

Hoyle, Sir Fred, MA, FRS. Hon. Research Professor, University of Manchester; Professor of Astronomy, Royal Institution of Great Britain since 1969; Visiting Professor of Astrophysics, California Institute of Technology, since 1958; Member of the Science Research Council 1968–72; President of the Royal Astronomical Society 1970–3; Vice-President of the Royal Society 1970–71.

Husband, Sir Charles, CBE, DSc. Senior partner of Husband & Company, Consulting Engineers, Sheffield, London and Colombo. The designer of the radio telescope at Jodrell Bank. Died in 1983.

Jackson, Derek, PhD, FRS. One of the earliest night fighter operators. The only FRS ever to have ridden in the Grand National.

Jackson, Willis, DSc, DPhil, FRS. Later Lord Jackson of Burnley. Now deceased.

Jánossy, L. Professor of Physics at the Eotvos University and at the Central Research Institute of Physics, Budapest. Died 2 March 1978.

Jones, F. E., MBE, BSc, PhD, FRS, FIEE, FRAeS. During World War II he was a research scientist at the Telecommunications Research Establishment and was responsible for the radar bombing device known as OBOE. 1952–6 Deputy Director of the Royal Aircraft Establishment, Farnborough; 1956–62 Technical Director of Mullards Limited; 1962–72 Managing Director of Mullards; 1973 appointed a Director of Philips Electrical Industries.

Jones, R. E. Organist Emeritus of Bath Abbey.

Jones, R. V., CB, CBE, FRS. Professor of Natural Philosophy at the University of Aberdeen since 1946. During World War II he was one of Lord Cherwell's scientific team which advised Churchill on scientific developments. Particularly noted for his work on counter-measures against German radio and radar systems.

Lewis, W. B., CBE, PhD, FRS. During World War II Deputy Chief Superintendent at the Telecommunications Research Establishment. After the war he became Head of the Chalk River Atomic Energy Plant in Canada.

Lighthill, Sir James, FRS. A post-war Director of the Royal Aircraft Establishment and later Lucasian Professor of Mathematics at the University of Cambridge. Provost of University College, London, since 1979.

Lockspeiser, Sir Ben, KCB, FRS. Chief Scientist to the Ministry of Supply 1946–9; Secretary of the Directorate of Scientific and Industrial Research (DSIR) 1949–56. Now retired.

Lovell, J. P. B., BA, BSc, PhD. Lecturer in Geology at the University of Edinburgh. Geologist with BP Exploration since 1981. Son of Sir Bernard Lovell.

Mair, W. A. Formerly Director of the Fluid Motion Laboratory in the University of Manchester, and later Professor of Aeronautical Engineering at the University of Cambridge.

Massevitch, Professor Alla. Professor of Astrophysics at the University of Moscow.

Matheson, Sir Louis. Professor of Engineering in the 1950s at the University of Manchester. In 1959 appointed Vice-Chancellor of the University of Monash, Australia.

Melville, Sir Harry, KCB, FRS. Formerly Professor of Chemistry at the University of Birmingham, he became Secretary of DSIR in 1955. In 1965 he became Chairman of the Science Research Council which replaced DSIR. In 1967 he resigned from the Science Research Council to become Principal of Queen Mary College, University of London.

Mott, Sir Neville, MA, DSc, FRS. Cavendish Professor of Physics at the University of Cambridge 1954–71. Nobel Prize for Physics 1977.

Oliphant, Sir Mark, KBE, FRS. In 1950 became Director of the Research Group of Physical Sciences in the Australian National University, Canberra. 1971–6 Governor General of South Australia.

Pardoe, G. K. C., BSc. Project Manager for Blue Streak at De Havilland Propellers Limited 1957–60; Chief Engineer Weapons and Space Research at Hawker Siddeley Aviation Limited 1960–3; Chief Project Engineer Space Division at Hawker Siddeley Dynamics Limited 1963–73. Now Chairman and Managing Director of General Technology Systems Limited, a high-technology consultancy working for a number of European Governments on Space activities and other related matters.

Powell, C. F., FRS. Nobel Prize winner for his discovery of the pi-meson. Henry

Overton Wills Professor of Physics and Director of the H. H. Wills Physics Laboratory 1964–9. Died in 1969.

Pringle, John William Sutton, MBE, MA, DSc, FRS. Joined the research scientists at the Telecommunications Research Establishment in 1940. After the war he became Linacre Professor of Zoology at the University of Oxford and Fellow of Merton College, Oxford, 1961–79. Died in 1982.

Rabi, Dr I. I. A distinguished American physicist who during the 1930s became noted for his research in theoretical and experimental physics. Later won a Nobel Prize for physics.

Ratcliffe, J. A., CB, CBE, FRS. Served in a senior capacity at the Telecommunications Research Establishment during World War II. After the war he was Reader in Physics and Fellow of Sidney Sussex College, Cambridge. In 1960 he became Director of the Radio Research Station where he remained until his retirement in 1966.

Renwick, Lord Renwick of Coombe, KBE. Formerly Sir Robert Renwick, Bt. Before World War II, Chairman of the London County Electric Supply Company. Brought into the Air Ministry and Ministry of Aircraft Production by Lord Beaverbrook in 1940 as Controller of Communications, Air Ministry, and Controller of Communications Equipment, Ministry of Aircraft Production. Was responsible for co-ordinating radar research and production. After the war he became a senior partner in the stockbroking firm of Greenwell & Company and a well-known financier and industrialist serving on the Boards of numerous companies in the engineering and electronic fields. He died in September 1973.

Rowe, A. P., CBE. Chief Superintendent of the Telecommunications Research Establishment throughout World War II. At the end of the war he was appointed Vice-Chancellor of the University of Adelaide, Australia. He died in 1976.

Rutherford, Ernest. Later Lord Rutherford. 1908 Nobel Prize for Chemistry. Founder of Nuclear Physics. Cavendish Professor of Nuclear Physics at the University of Cambridge 1919–37. President of the Royal Society 1925–30. Died 19 October 1937.

Ryle, Sir Martin, DSc, FRS. Professor of Radio Astronomy at the University of Cambridge since 1959. Worked at the Telecommunications Research Establishment during World War II, 1939–45. Astronomer Royal 1972–   . Nobel Prize for Physics in 1974. Astronomer Royal 1972–82.

Saundby, Air Marshal Sir Robert, KCB, KBE, MC, DFC, AFC, DL. Deputy Commander-in-Chief, Bomber Command 1942–5. Died in November 1971.

Stopford, Lord Stopford of Fallowfield, FRS. An eminent medical scientist. As Sir John Stopford he was Vice-Chancellor of the University of Manchester 1949–56.

Streat, Sir Raymond. Chairman of the Council of the University of Manchester 1956–65.

Sutton, Sir Graham, CBE, FRS. In 1962 Director-General of the Meteorological Office.

Thomson, Sir George Paget, ScD, FRS. Nobel Laureate for Physics, 1937. Chairman of the first British Committee on Atomic Energy; British Delegate to the United Nations Atomic Energy Commission, 1946–7; Master of Corpus Christi College, Cambridge, from 1952 until his death in 1975.

Tizard, Sir Henry, GCB, AFC, FRS. Rector of Imperial College of Science and Technology 1929–42; Chairman of the Aeronautical Research Committee 1933–43; President of Magdalen College, Oxford, 1942–6; President of British Association for 1948; Chairman of the Advisory Council on Scientific Policy and Chairman of the Defence Research Policy Committee 1946–52.

Tyndall, A. M., DSc, LLD, FRS. Professor of Physics at the University of Bristol 1919–46; Acting Vice-Chancellor of the University of Bristol 1946–8. He died in 1961.

Watson Watt, Sir Robert A., CB, FRS. Credited with being 'the Father of Radar'. Director of Communications Development 1938–40; Scientific Adviser on Telecommunications to the Air Ministry and Ministry of Aircraft Production 1940–5; Vice-Controller of Communications Equipment to the Ministry of Aircraft Production 1942–6. He died on 5 December 1973.

Whipple, Professor Fred L. Chairman of the Department of Astronomy, Harvard University 1949–56; Director of the Smithsonian Institution Astrophysical Observatory, Cambridge, Massachusetts, from 1955–73.

Wilson, Charles Thomson Rees, Professor of Natural Philosophy at the University of Cambridge 1925–34. Nobel Prize for Physics in 1927.

Zuckerman, Lord, OM, KCB, MA, MD, DSc, FRS, MRCS, FRCP. Formerly Sir Solly Zuckerman, Chief Scientific Adviser to the Secretary of State for Defence 1960–66, and to H.M. Government 1964–71.

Zulueta, Sir Francis de. Private Secretary to the Prime Ministers Lord Avon, Sir Harold Macmillan and Sir Alec Douglas-Home, 1955–64. Director of bankers Hill Samuel & Company, 1965–73.

Index